Psychological Evaluation of the Developmentally and Physically Disabled

AF895076

Psychological Evaluation of the Developmentally and Physically Disabled

Edited by
VINCENT B. VAN HASSELT
University of California, Irvine
Orange, California
and
MICHEL HERSEN
Western Psychiatric Institute and Clinic
Pittsburgh, Pennsylvania

SPRINGER SCIENCE+BUSINESS MEDIA, LLC

Library of Congress Cataloging in Publication Data

Psychological evaluation of the developmentally and physically disabled.

Includes bibliographies and index.

1. Handicapped children—Psychological testing. 2. Developmentally disabled children—Psychological testing. 3. Physically handicapped children—Psychological testing. I. Van Hasselt, Vincent B. I. Hersen, Michel. [DNLM: 1. Child Development Disorders—psychology. 2. Handicapped—psychology. 3. Mental Retardation—psychology. 4. Psychological Tests—in infancy & childhood. WS 350.6 P974]
RJ507.H35P78 1987 617 87-15275
ISBN 978-1-4899-1997-7

ISBN 978-1-4899-1997-7 ISBN 978-1-4899-1995-3 (eBook)
DOI 10.1007/978-1-4899-1995-3

© Springer Science+Business Media New York 1987
Originally published by Plenum Press, New York in 1987
Softcover reprint of the hardcover 1st edition 1987

All rights reserved

No part of this book may be reproduced, stored in a retrieval system, or transmitted in any form or by any means, electronic, mechanical, photocopying, microfilming, recording, or otherwise, without written permission from the Publisher

To
Betty and Joseph
and
Betty and Leon

Contributors

STEPHEN J. BAGNATO • Children's Hospital, University of Pittsburgh, School of Medicine, Pittsburgh, Pennsylvania

FRANK P. BELCASTRO • Department of Psychology, University of Dubuque, Dubuque, Iowa

MARJORIE H. CHARLOP • Psychology Department, Claremont McKenna College and Claremont Graduate School, Claremont, California

KATHLEEN L. EDWARDS • Western Psychiatric Institute and Clinic, 3811 O'Hara Street, Pittsburgh, Pennsylvania

DOUG GUESS • Special Education Department, University of Kansas, Lawrence, Kansas

ROBERT L. HALE • Division of Counseling and Educational Psychology, Pennsylvania State University, University Park, Pennsylvania

MICHEL HERSEN • Western Psychiatric Institute and Clinic, 3811 O'Hara Street, Pittsburgh, Pennsylvania

STEPHEN P. HINSHAW • Department of Psychology, University of California, Los Angeles, California

ROBERT W. MOTTA • Department of Psychology, Hofstra University, Hempstead, New York

JOHN T. NEISWORTH • Division of Special Education, Pennsylvania State University, University Park, Pennsylvania

LAURA SCHREIBMAN • Department of Psychology, University of California at San Diego, La Jolla, California

ED SCHULTE • Kansas University Affiliated Facility, Lawrence, Kansas

ELLIN SIEGEL-CAUSEY • Special Education Department, University of Kansas, Lawrence, Kansas

LORI A. SISSON • Western Psychiatric Institute and Clinic, 3811 O'Hara Street, Pittsburgh, Pennsylvania

RALPH E. TARTER • Western Psychiatric Institute and Clinic, 3811 O'Hara Street, Pittsburgh, Pennsylvania

JULIA R. VANE • Department of Psychology, Hofstra University, Hempstead, New York

VINCENT B. VAN HASSELT • Department of Psychiatry and Human Behavior, University of California, Irvine, 101 City Drive South, Orange, California

BARBARA C. WILSON • North Shore University Hospital, Cornell University Medical College, Division of Neuropsychology, Department of Neurology, 300 Community Drive, Manhasset, New York

Preface

The past decade has witnessed a considerable upsurge of clinical and research interest in the problems of developmentally and physically disabled persons. Indeed, professionals from the fields of psychology, special education, rehabilitation, psychiatry, and social work have all directed attention to the development and implementation of evaluation and remedial programs. The heightened activity in this area is in part a result of early assessment research with these populations, which provided preliminary evidence of difficulties in social and emotional adjustment in many disabled individuals. In response to these findings, many intervention efforts have been implemented to deal with these issues and improve the life situation of the disabled. Also, there were indications that developmentally and physically disabled children often were deprived of adequate educations. As a result, legal and legislative initiatives have been enacted in recent years to make public education available to all students irrespective of disability.

Central to all therapeutic and psychoeducational endeavors with the disabled is psychological evaluation. Only through careful and comprehensive psychological evaluation can areas of deficit as well as strengths be identified. Once treatment targets and goals have been ascertained, psychological evaluation is needed to determine the efficacy of intervention strategies. However, the field of psychological evaluation, in general, and with disabled persons, in particular, has become highly specialized. This is largely a function of the changing roles of psychological evaluators. These professionals, who traditionally had the sole role of testers, now also interview and observe and test behavior in various settings. Further, they are directly involved in test construction, administration, and interpretation, and have become increasingly involved in policy matters regarding test utilization. With regard to the disabled, the issue of specialization is magnified with the unique issues and problems inherent in working with a particular population. Clearly the examiner must have a thorough knowledge of the materials and literature and an appreciation and understanding of the examinee's specific disabling condition.

The purpose of this book is to organize and integrate material concerning the psychological evaluation of those suffering from developmental and physical disabilities. To accomplish this, we have asked our eminent contributors to present both their clinical and research expertise. Each offers an extensive review of his or her topic and presents relevant strategies and issues in psychological evaluation.

The book is divided into three parts and contains 11 chapters. Part I (Introduction) provides an overview of the area. The second part (General Issues) presents topics of importance that cut across disabilities and describe basic features of psychological evaluation. The final part (Psychological Evaluation of Specific Disorders) discusses in some detail the psychological evaluation approaches that have been employed with disabled persons.

Many individuals have contributed to this volume. We express our gratitude to our contributors for the high quality and comprehensiveness of their efforts. We thank our families for their support during the course of our editorial labors. Finally, but hardly least of all, we express our appreciation to Judith A. Lorenzetty, Mary Newell, Jenifer Brander, and Mary Trefelner for their technical assistance.

VINCENT B. VAN HASSELT
MICHEL HERSEN

Contents

I. INTRODUCTION

1. PHYSICAL AND DEVELOPMENTAL DISABILITIES: AN OVERVIEW

Vincent B. Van Hasselt and Michel Hersen

Introduction ... 3
Purposes of Psychological Assessment with the Handicapped ... 6
Current Issues in Psychological Assessment of the Handicapped ... 8
Summary ... 11
References ... 12

II. GENERAL ISSUES

2. BASIC ISSUES IN PSYCHOLOGICAL EVALUATION

Julia R. Vane and Robert W. Motta

Introduction ... 19
Background Information ... 20
The Psychological Interview ... 20
Psychological Testing ... 24
Characteristics of the Psychologist ... 29
Decision Making ... 32
Summary ... 34
References ... 34

3. EVALUATION OF INTELLIGENCE, ACHIEVEMENT, APTITUDE, AND INTEREST

Robert L. Hale

Introduction 41
Dispensing with the Term *Aptitude* 42
History 43
Current Issues in Assessment 58
Future Directions 62
Summary 63
References 64

4. NEUROPSYCHOLOGICAL ASSESSMENT

Barbara C. Wilson

Introduction 69
History and Development 70
Approaches to Neuropsychological Evaluation 73
Issues in the Assessment of Children 77
A Neuropsychological Assessment Model 79
Future Directions and Summary 83
References 85

III. PSYCHOLOGICAL EVALUATION OF SPECIFIC DISORDERS

5. HEARING IMPAIRMENT

Frank P. Belcastro

Introduction 93
Description 94
History and Development 95
Strategies and Evaluation 96
Strategies for Evaluation 98
Research Findings 103
Case Studies 108
Summary 109
References 110

6. VISUAL IMPAIRMENT

Lori A. Sisson and Vincent B. Van Hasselt

Introduction 115
Description of the Disorder 118
History and Development of Assessment Procedures 119
Strategies for Evaluation 121
Special Considerations and Research Issues 139
Summary 146
References 147

7. AUTISM

Laura Schreibman and Marjorie H. Charlop

Introduction 155
Description 156
History and Development 160
Current Diagnostic Criteria 162
Differential Diagnosis 164
Strategies for Evaluation 166
Behavioral Assessment 170
Case Description 172
Summary 174
References 174

8. DEVELOPMENTAL RETARDATION

John T. Neisworth and Stephen J. Bagnato

Introduction 179
Diagnosis versus Assessment 179
Strategies for Diagnosis of Developmental Retardation 181
Strategies for Evaluation 183
Prominent Measures for Diagnosis and Assessment of Developmental Retardation 185
Norm-Based Assessment: Comparative Evaluation 185
Criterion-Based Assessment: Skill Mastery Evaluation 197
Neuropsychological Assessment: Process Evaluation 199
Case Study 204

Summary 209
References 209

9. HYPERACTIVITY, ATTENTION DEFICIT DISORDERS, AND LEARNING DISABILITIES

Stephen P. Hinshaw

Introduction 213
Description 214
History and Development 221
Strategies for Evaluation 223
Case Description 244
Summary 248
References 249

10. SPEECH AND LANGUAGE DISORDERS

Ellin Siegel-Causey, Ed Schulte, and Doug Guess

Introduction 261
Development and Components of Communication Systems 264
Communication Assessment: Speech and Language 270
Summary 289
References 290
Appendix: Selected Nonlinguistic and Prelinguistic Assessment Tools 294

11. CRANIOCEREBRAL TRAUMA IN CHILDREN

Ralph E. Tarter and Kathleen L. Edwards

Introduction 299
Description 301
Psychological Assessment 315
Case Studies 320
Summary 323
References 324

INDEX 327

I

INTRODUCTION

1

Physical and Developmental Disabilities

An Overview

VINCENT B. VAN HASSELT AND MICHEL HERSEN

INTRODUCTION

Applications of psychological assessment and intervention strategies to the problems of developmentally and physically disabled persons have proliferated in recent years (cf. Golden, 1984; Goldenson, Dunham, & Dunham, 1978; Hersen, Van Hasselt, & Matson, 1983). The heightened activity in this area is attributable, in part, to the burgeoning number of disabled individuals. Indeed, recent surveys reveal that as many as 36 million people, or 15% of the population of the United States, have some form of disability (Bowe, 1980). Of those 65 years or older, nearly 50% report a physical impairment (DeJong & Lifchez, 1983). Further, it has been estimated that 10% of children under age 21 are handicapped (Gliedman & Roth, 1980). Moreover, as a result of improved prenatal care, better nutrition, decreased infant mortality rates due to advances

---

VINCENT B. VAN HASSELT • Department of Psychiatry and Human Behavior, University of California, Irvine, 101 City Drive South, Orange, California 92668. MICHEL HERSEN • Western Psychiatric Institute and Clinic, 3811 O'Hara Street, Pittsburgh, Pennsylvania 15213. Preparation of this chapter was facilitated by Grant G008300135 (National Institute of Handicapped Research) and Grant G008530258 (Special Education Programs) from the U.S. Department of Education. However, the opinions expressed herein do not necessarily reflect the position of the U.S. Department of Education, and no official endorsement by the department should be inferred.

in surgical and medical care, and more effective treatments for infant diseases, the number of disabled persons is expected to rise sharply over the next decade (Anderson, 1969; Dibedenetto, 1976; Mulliken & Buckley, 1983).

Another reason for the increased attention to the disabled is the accumulation of evidence showing various forms of social and emotional dysfunctions in a disproportionate number of these individuals. For example, there is a convergence of data indicating that many disabled children and adults are socially isolated (e.g., Eaglestein, 1975; Van Hasselt, 1983), receive inaccurate feedback regarding their interpersonal behavior from their environment (Richardson, Goodman, Hastorf, & Dornbusch, 1961), and have inadequate socialization experiences due to negative attitudes of nonhandicapped persons toward those with disabilities or deviations in physique (Dion, 1972; Kleck, 1968; Kleck, Richardson, & Ronald, 1974).

Numerous investigative efforts also have shown that many of the disabled evince psychological maladjustment. For example, the literature on the sensorily impaired is replete with discussions of emotional and behavior problems in this population (see reviews by Ammerman, Van Hasselt, & Hersen, 1985; Matson & Helsel, 1986; Van Hasselt, 1983). Psychological assessment research has shown higher levels of psychopathology (e.g., anxiety, depression) in many visually handicapped children and adults relative to nonhandicapped controls or sighted norms (Bauman, 1964; Jan, Freeman, & Scott, 1977; Van Hasselt, Kazdin, & Hersen, 1986). A similar pattern of results has been reported with hearing-impaired persons (Gentile & McCarthy, 1973; Jensema & Trybus, 1975; Vernon, 1969). In their extensive review of work in this area, Matson and Helsel (1986) concluded that "psychiatric problems, especially personality disorders, neurosis and behavior disorders in children and adults are reported to be particularly prevalent in the hearing impaired" (p. 23). The mental health of the mentally retarded also has been the focus of several clinical and investigative endeavors (see Matson & Frame, 1983). These have largely involved evaluation and modification of a wide range of difficulties in these individuals, including depression (Matson, Senatore, Kazdin, & Helsel, 1983); aggression (Repp & Brulle, 1981); social skill deficits (Matson & Zeiss, 1978; Turner, Hersen, & Bellack, 1978; Whitman, Mercurio, & Caponigri, 1970); and self-injury (Griffin, Locke, & Landers, 1975; Matson, Stephens, & Smith, 1978).

A third factor accounting for the upsurge of interest in the disabled is the growing awareness of the pivotal role psychologists may play in improving their life situation. This was perhaps most clearly illustrated by a series of articles in the May 1984 issue of the *American Psychologist*, which was devoted to psychological strategies and issues concerning disabled persons. These articles encompassed a variety of topics, such as laws and legislation enacted for the disabled (Weicker, 1984), interactive effects of disability with other factors (e.g., race, education level, family support) (Asch, 1984a), negative attitudes toward the disabled (Asch, 1984a; Fenderson, 1984; Kahn, 1984), interpersonal adjustment and social discrimination of disabled persons (Asch, 1984a, b), and variables related to vocational adjustment in psychiatrically disabled individuals (Anthony & Jansen, 1984).

In an article entitled "Opportunities for Psychologists in Disability Research," Douglas Fenderson (1984), former director of the National Institute of Handicapped Research, urged greater participation by psychologists in research with the disabled. According to Fenderson,

> the goal of rehabilitation research is to eliminate barriers disabled persons experience in achieving their life goals through the methods and resources of science and technology. Psychologists are among the leading contributors to the removal of barriers so that persons with disabilities may more completely fulfill their roles and responsibilities as citizens. (p. 524)

The need for accelerated activity in this field by psychologists was further underscored in a report by the Task Force on Psychology and the Handicapped (1984). The task force was established in 1979 in response to the widespread social discrimination against the handicapped and other minority groups. In an examination of problems encountered by handicapped individuals, the task force concluded that "psychological occurrences such as discrimination rather than physical impairment *per se*, lead to many of the most severe difficulties for people who have disabilities" (p. 548). The task force pointed out the utility of prioritizing rehabilitation goals to more adequately deal with prejudiced and distorted attitudes and beliefs of the nonhandicapped. The committee also described current approaches for "mainstreaming" handicapped psychologists in conferences and governing functions of the American Psychological Association. Finally, the removal of barriers to academic training and careers in psychology for handicapped students was identified as an area warranting further attention by psychologists.

Legal and legislative initiatives also have had a significant impact on psychological approaches with the disabled. One action of major consequence was the enactment of Public Law (P.L.) 94-142. Passed by Congress in 1975, this act guarantees all handicapped children the right to a free appropriate public education in the "least restrictive environment." Since passage of P.L. 94-142, many handicapped children formerly residing in institutions or residential settings have been "mainstreamed" into public schools for placement in regular or specialized classrooms. As will be discussed shortly, this has resulted in greater involvement of psychological assessors in decisions concerning classification and placement as well as development of subsequent interventions with disabled children and youth. Further, a set of provisions in P.L. 94-142 labeled the Protection in Evaluation Procedures has had a profound effect on the process of psychological assessment. These provisions specify that (a) more than one set of evaluation methods must be utilized to identify children as handicapped; (b) measurement devices must be selected and administered in a racially and culturally nondiscriminatory fashion; and (c) children must be assessed in their native language.

Additional legislation that has directly influenced psychological assessment is the Rehabilitation Act of 1973 (P.L. 93-112). This is a basic civil rights law that prohibits discrimination on the basis of a handicapping condition. Section 504 of this law applies to all handicapped persons regardless of age and is broader in coverage than P.L. 94-142. Consistent with previous federal laws prohibiting discrimination on the basis of race, national origin, and sex, Section 504 states that

> no otherwise qualified handicapped individual shall, solely by reason of his/her handicap, be excluded from participation in, be denied the benefits of, or be subject to discrimination under any program or activity receiving federal financial assistance.

In 1976, the Office of Civil Rights published regulations for Section 504, which recommended the following: (a) placement/denial of placement cannot occur without a comprehensive and individualized assessment of each child's special educational needs; (b) assessment instruments must be properly validated for the specific purpose for which they are to be used; and (c) in addition to formal testing, evaluation of such attributes as physical condition, adaptive skills, and cultural background must be carried out. By legal mandate, failure to adhere to these specifications will result in termination of federal assistance to the offending school, agency, or organization.

It is apparent that assessment has become an integral component of psychological and educational strategies for the disabled. Purposes of psychological assessment with these individuals and some salient issues in this field will be discussed next.

PURPOSES OF PSYCHOLOGICAL ASSESSMENT WITH THE HANDICAPPED

Professionals in psychology, special education, and rehabilitation have outlined several purposes of psychological assessment with disabled individuals (cf. Golden, 1984; Reschley, 1982; Salvia & Ysseldyke,

1985; Ysseldyke & Marston, in press). First, assessment is deemed requisite to accurate diagnosis and classification. For example, assessment might involve tests of intellectual functioning to ascertain possible mental retardation as well as level (mild, moderate, severe, profound). Further, as a result of legislation enacted for the disabled, assessment data are required to specify the nature of a disability and to justify placement decisions (e.g., residential vs. public school, institution vs. community living arrangement). Indeed, accountability for appropriate placement of the disabled has become a paramount issue with administrators, educators, and advocacy groups over the past several years. For adults, diagnosis of disorders and classification of individuals as disabled are needed to ascertain eligibility for various social services, such as welfare, supported housing, medical assistance, and enrollment in vocational training programs. Evaluation in agencies serving handicapped adults also is carried out for career planning.

A second purpose of assessment is to identify psychological disorders or behavior problems that may coexist with a disability. In recent years, there also has been an emphasis on determining the particular strengths of the disabled client. Evaluative procedures under the rubric of *behavioral assessment* have been particularly useful in this regard by providing analyses of *behavioral excesses* and *deficits* (Kanfer & Saslow, 1969). Excesses are behaviors that occur with too great a frequency, intensity, or duration, or that occur when they are not socially sanctioned (e.g., self-injury, self-stimulation, aggression). Deficits are responses that are emitted with insufficient frequency or intensity, or with inadequate form, or fail to occur at appropriate times (e.g., social withdrawal, low activity level, insufficient food consumption). In addition, behavioral assessment has proven useful in identifying concurrent factors that may impact on the client and his or her response to particular treatment approaches. Kanfer and Saslow (1969) and Bellack and Hersen (1977) describe several of these: (a) *behavioral assets*—strengths or skills (e.g., social, adaptive living, and mobility skills) a person has that might be utilized in treatment; (b) *behavioral limitations*—characteristics (e.g., specific physical debility, cognitive impairment) that restrict an individual's activities or ability to adhere to a prescribed training regimen; (c) *environmental supports and restrictions*—physical aspects of the client's environment and significant others that are associated with positive therapeutic outcome (e.g., availability and cooperation of parents or agency personnel); and (d) *motivational analysis*—determination of relevant reinforcers in the environment that might be incorporated in treatment and potential consequences to behavior change that would make the client less likely to change current maladaptive behavior (e.g., a disabled child lacks the social skills to make friends with peers, thereby making school attendance aversive).

Last, but hardly least of all, assessment is needed for selection of treatment targets and for evaluation of intervention efficacy (Kazdin & Straw, 1976; Ross, 1980). Further, the assessment process must be comprehensive, systematic, and carried out on a continuous basis. Whether intervention involves psychotherapy, behavior modification, or educational training, psychological assessment is important for providing accountability, measurement of change, and evaluation of treatment effectiveness.

CURRENT ISSUES IN PSYCHOLOGICAL ASSESSMENT OF THE HANDICAPPED

Recently, a number of concerns regarding current assessment practices have been articulated by professionals working with the disabled. Although an extensive examination of these issues is beyond the scope of this chapter (see Ysseldyke & Shinn, 1981, for a more complete review of the topic), some major points that have received attention include (a) technical adequacy of assessment instruments; (b) qualifications of those administering measures; (c) appropriate uses of tests; and (d) bias in assessment procedures.

TECHNICAL ADEQUACY

A basic assumption in psychological assessment is that measurement devices employed have adequate psychometric properties, namely reliability and validity. *Reliability* refers to the extent to which an evaluation method produces accurate or consistent data. Reliability also indicates the degree to which individual test scores are a function of actual differences in characteristics of interest or are due to error variance (i.e., any condition that is irrelevant to purposes of assessment). In a series of investigations on assessment strategies for special populations, Ysseldyke and his colleagues (Salvia & Ysseldyke, 1985; Ysseldyke, 1978; Ysseldyke, Algozzine, Regan, & Potter, 1980; Ysseldyke & Salvia, 1974) found that many of these instruments have insufficient reliability. For example, a computer simulation study examining the technical adequacy of psychoeducational assessment approaches showed that 59% of the instruments had poor reliability (Ysseldyke *et al.*, 1980). Arter and Jenkins (1979) arrived at a similar conclusion in an overview of perceptual-motor tests with the disabled.

Validity (i.e., the degree to which a test measures what it is supposed to measure) also has been suspect in many assessment devices administered to disabled persons. Because adequate reliability is a prerequisite to test validity, this is not surprising. In their review of evaluation methods, Salvia and Ysseldyke (1985) concluded that many assessment devices currently administered in remedial and special education programs for disabled individuals lack sufficient validity.

A related issue is the failure of test developers to standardize assessment techniques on disabled samples. As Bennett (1983) cogently argued,

> data required for judging technical adequacy . . . must be gathered from applications of these measures to handicapped populations. Unfortunately, text authors and publishers have typically presented evidence for the adequacy of their instruments gathered from *general* rather than handicapped samples. (p. 112)

The importance of appropriate test norms and standardization procedures for the disabled will be discussed further in the next chapter.

QUALIFICATIONS OF PERSONNEL

According to the *Standards for Educational and Psychological Tests* published by the American Psychological Association (1974), assessors should have (a) a fundamental understanding of test and measurement principles, (b) the ability to select, administer, and interpret results of evaluation procedures, and (c) a thorough knowledge of the research literature on all instruments that they are using. When evaluating the disabled, there are the additional requirements of understanding the nature of the disability, awareness of the special needs of these individuals, and the knowledge of the appropriateness of specific instruments to be included in the test battery. However, there are indications that many of those who conduct psychological evaluations with disabled persons do not have such expertise. Indeed, assessment skill has been found to differ considerably between groups of professionals (e.g., special educators, psychologists, counselors, speech therapists) and within occupations serving the handicapped. Ysseldyke and Shinn (1981) stated that this is largely a function of the variability in instruction asessors receive, "which may range from no training or incidental training to quite extensive training" (p. 423).

Several investigations also have revealed that many evaluators select instruments in a routinized manner without considering assessment purposes or technical adequacy of measurement devices (Keogh, Kukic, Becker, McLoughlin, & Kukic, 1975; Thurlow & Ysseldyke, 1979; Ysseldyke *et al.*, 1980). There also is evidence of faulty interpretations of test results in some instances. In the computer simulation study by Algozzine and Ysseldyke (1981) mentioned earlier, evaluation team personnel were presented with case referral information and access to assessment data. Then they were asked to reach a diagnostic decision about the client. Results showed that most team members classified their case as handicapped and eligible for special services even though all assessment data they received actually were in the *normal* range.

INAPPROPRIATE USE OF TESTS

As Ysseldyke and Marston (in press) point out,

> psychologists have been accused of engaging in assessment activities with no suitable purpose. Such practice is evidenced when psychologists engage in the ritualistic practice of routine assessment "because it is the thing to do." Whereas assessment should be a process of collecting data for the purpose of making educational or psychological decisions . . . too often it is the process of collecting data for the purpose of collecting data. (pp. 1–2)

Ysseldyke and Shinn (1981) presented several examples of the inappropriate use of tests with the disabled. One common finding was that many assessors administered the same test battery to all students irrespective of the nature of their disability. Also, intelligence tests (e.g., Wechsler Intelligence Scale for Children) frequently have been utilized to plan remedial or instructional programs and/or to ascertain their efficacy despite the fact that these measures were originally constructed solely for purposes of classification, placement, or eligibility decisions (Ysseldyke & Marston, 1982).

BIAS IN PSYCHOLOGICAL ASSESSMENT

The problem of bias in psychological assessment has been examined for over two decades (e.g., Bayley, 1965; Bloom, 1964; Cattell, 1971; Jensen, 1967, 1971). Most of this research has investigated the fairness of tests and specific test items for disparate racial and cultural groups. More recently, the National Academy of Sciences appointed a Panel on Selection and Placement of Students in Programs for the Mentally Retarded (under the auspices of the Committee on Child Development Research and Public Policy of the National Research Council) to study test bias in the United States (see Heller, Holtzman, & Messick, 1982; Messick, 1984). The panel essentially found that certain characteristics of schools and agencies, home and family environments, and students themselves (e.g., sex, race, socioeconomic status, physical appearance) made nondiscriminatory evaluation practically impossible. Yet the Protection in Evaluation Procedures of P.L. 94-142 clearly state that measurement devices must be selected and administered in a racially and culturally nondiscriminatory fashion. In an attempt to remedy this situation, more recent efforts have included implementation of prereferral interventions, increased academic time for handicapped persons, utilization of direct and continuous measurement strategies for decision making, and attempts to provide more effective instruction to disabled individuals of all races and ethnic groups (Messick, 1984; Ysseldyke, Thurlow, Garden, Wesson, & Deno, 1983).

SUMMARY

Psychological assessment has become an important element of psychological, educational, and rehabilitative approaches with the developmentally and physically disabled. Yet it is apparent that psychological assessment with these populations is at the nascent stage at this time. Indeed, a number of psychometric, conceptual, and ethical issues in this area have yet to be resolved. Nevertheless, progress has been made in development and refinement of assessment methods for many disabled populations. Moreover, these efforts have yielded useful information for both clinical and research objectives.

SCOPE OF THE BOOK

The purpose of the present volume is to provide a comprehensive review of current psychological assessment approaches, with special attention to psychometric properties and appropriateness of specific strategies for developmentally and physically disabled persons. First, however, a number of general issues relevant to assessment of the disabled will be presented. In Chapter 2, Julia R. Vane and Robert W. Motta discuss basic issues in psychological evaluation of handicapped persons. This is followed by Robert L. Hale's description of strategies used to assess intelligence, achievement, aptitude, and interest in disabled individuals. Chapter 4 includes Barbara C. Wilson's discussion of neuropsychological assessment procedures with these populations.

The next section deals with specific developmental and physical disabilities. Hearing impairment is covered in Chapter 5 by Frank P. Belcastro. This is followed by a review of evaluation procedures employed with the visually impaired by Lori A. Sisson and Vincent B. Van Hasselt (Chapter 6). Then, in Chapter 7, Laura Schreibman and Marjorie H.

Charlop discuss psychological assessment approaches with autism. In Chapter 8, John T. Neisworth and Stephen J. Bagnato present psychological assessment methods employed with the mentally retarded. The evaluation of hyperactivity, attention deficit disorders, and learning disabilities is covered in Chapter 9 by Steven P. Hinshaw. In Chapter 10, Ellin Siegel-Causey, Ed Schulte, and Doug Guess review strategies and issues in the evaluation of speech and language disorders. Finally, Ralph E. Tarter and Kathleen L. Edwards discuss neurological impairment due to head trauma in Chapter 11.

Given the exponential increase in studies, journals, and books devoted to various developmental and physical disabilities in recent years, it is clear that this field is expanding rapidly. Indeed, the current philosophical climate, the extended history of care for developmentally and physically disabled persons, and the success achieved with comprehensive approaches to assessment and subsequent intervention all portend that this expansion will continue. This text is dedicated to such growth.

REFERENCES

Algozzine, B., & Ysseldyke, J. (1981). Special education services for normal children: Better safe than sorry? *Exceptional Children, 48,* 238–243.

American Psychological Association. (1974). *Standards for educational and psychological tests.* Washington, DC: Author.

Ammerman, R. T., Van Hasselt, V. B., & Hersen, M. (1985). Social skills training for visually handicapped children: A treatment manual. *Psychological Documents, 15,* 6.

Anderson, R. M. (1969). *Provisions for the education of mentally retarded deaf children in residential schools for the deaf* (U.S. Department of Health, Education, and Welfare, Office of Education Cooperative Research Program). Pittsburgh: University of Pittsburgh.

Anthony, W. A., & Jansen, M. A. (1984). Predicting the vocational capacity of the chronically mentally ill: Research and policy implications. *American Psychologist, 39,* 537–544.

Arter, J. A., & Jenkins, J. R. (1979). Differential diagnosis-prescriptive teaching: A critical appraisal. *Review of Educational Research, 49,* 517–555.

Asch, A. (1984a). The experience of disability: A challenge of psychology. *American Psychologist, 39,* 529–536.

Asch, A. (1984b). Personal reflections. *American Psychologist, 39,* 551–552.

Bauman, M. K. (1964). Group differences disclosed by inventory items. *International Journal for the Education of the Blind, 13,* 101–107.

Bayley, N. (1965). Comparisons of mental and motor test scores for ages 1–15 months by sex, birth order, race, geographical locations, and education of parents. *Child Development, 36,* 379–411.

Bellack, A. S., & Hersen, M. (1977). *Behavior modification: An introductory textbook.* Baltimore: Williams & Wilkins.

Bennett, R. E. (1983). Research and evaluation priorities for special education assessment. *Exceptional Children, 50,* 110–117.

Bloom, B. S. (1964). *Stability and change in human characteristics*. New York: Wiley.

Bowe, F. (1980). *Rehabilitating America*. New York: Harper & Row.

Cattell, R. B. (1971). The structure of intelligence in relation to the nature-nurture controversy. In R. Cancro (Ed.), *Intelligence: Genetic and environmental influences* (pp. 201–238). New York: Grune & Stratton.

DeJong, G., & Lifchez, R. (1983). Physical disability and public policy. *Scientific American, 48*, 240–249.

Dibedenetto, T. A. (1976). Problems of the deaf retarded: A review of the literature. *Education and Training of the Mentally Retarded*, April, 164–170.

Dion, K. K. (1972). Physical attractiveness and evaluation of children's transgressions. *Journal of Personality and Social Psychology, 24*, 207–213.

Eaglestein, A. S. (1975). The social acceptance of blind high school students in an integrated school. *New Outlook for the Blind, 69*, 447–451.

Fenderson, D. A. (1984). Opportunities for psychologists in disability research. *American Psychologist, 39*, 524–528.

Gentile, A., & McCarthy, B. (1973). *Additional handicapping conditions among hearing impaired students, United States, 1971–72*. Washington, DC: Office of Demographic Studies, Gallaudet College.

Gliedman, J., & Roth, W. (1980). *The unexpected minority: Handicapped children in America*. New York: Harcourt, Brace, Jovanovich.

Golden, C. J. (Ed.). (1984). *Current topics in rehabilitation psychology*. New York: Grune & Stratton.

Goldenson, R. M., Dunham, J. R., & Dunham, C. S. (Eds.). (1978). *Disability and rehabilitation handbook*. New York: McGraw-Hill.

Griffin, J. C., Locke, B. J., & Landers, W. (1975). Manipulation of potential punishment parameters in the treatment of self-injury. *Journal of Applied Behavior Analysis, 8*, 458–464.

Heller, K. A., Holtzman, W. H., & Messick, S. (Eds.). (1982). *Placing children in special education: A strategy for equity*. Washington, DC: National Academy Press.

Hersen, M., Van Hasselt, V. B., & Matson, J. L. (Eds.). (1983). *Behavior therapy for the developmentally and physically disabled*. New York: Academic Press.

Jan, J. E., Freeman, R. D., & Scott, E. P. (Eds.). (1977). *Visual impairment in children and adolescents*. New York: Grune & Stratton.

Jensema, C., & Trybus, R. J. (1975). *Reported emotional/behavioral problems among hearing impaired children in special education programs: United States, 1972–73*. Washington, DC: Office of Demographic Studies, Gallaudet College.

Jensen, A. R. (1967). Estimation of the limits of heritability of traits by comparison of monozygotic and dizygotic twins. *Proceedings of the National Academy of Sciences, 58*, 149–156.

Jensen, A. R. (1971). The race × sex × ability interaction. In R. Cancro (Ed.), *Intelligence: Genetic and environmental contributions* (pp. 172–203). New York: Grune & Stratton.

Kahn, A. S. (1984). Psychology in the public forum: Perspectives on persons with disabilities. *American Psychologist, 39*, 516–517.

Kanfer, F. H., & Saslow, G. (1969). Behavioral diagnosis. In C. M. Franks (Ed.), *Behavior therapy: Appraisal and status* (pp. 417–444). New York: McGraw-Hill.

Kazdin, A. E., & Straw, M. L. (1976). Assessment of behavior of the mentally retarded. In M. Hersen & A. S. Bellack (Eds.), *Behavioral assessment: A practical handbook* (pp. 337–368). New York: Pergamon Press.

Keogh, B., Kukic, S., Becker, L., McLoughlin, R., & Kukic, M. (1975). School psychologists' services in special education programs. *Journal of School Psychology, 13*, 142–148.

Kleck, R. E. (1968). Physical stigma and nonverbal cues emitted in face-to-face interaction. *Human Relations, 21,* 19–28.

Kleck, R. E., Richardson, S. A., & Ronald, L. (1974). Physical appearance cues and interpersonal attraction in children. *Child Development, 45,* 305–310.

Matson, J. L., & Frame, C. (1983). Psychopathology. In J. L. Matson & C. Frame (Eds.), *Assessing the mentally retarded* (pp. 115–142). New York: Grune & Stratton.

Matson, J. L., & Helsel, W. J. (1986). Psychopathology of sensory impaired children. In B. B. Lahey & A. E. Kazdin (Eds.), *Advances in clinical child Psychology* (Vol. 9, pp. 377–340). New York: Plenum Press.

Matson, J. L., & Zeiss, R. (1978). Group training of social skills in chronically explosive severely disturbed psychiatric patients. *Behavioral Engineering, 5,* 41–50.

Matson, J. L., Stephens, R. M., & Smith, C. (1978). Treatment of self-injurious behavior with overcorrection. *Journal of Mental Deficiency Research, 22,* 175–178.

Matson, J. L., Senatore, V., Kazdin, A. E., & Helsel, W. J. (1983). Verbal behaviors in depressed and non-depressed mentally retarded persons. *Applied Research in Mental Retardation, 14,* 79–84.

Messick, S. (1984). Assessment in context: Appraising student performance in relation to instructional quality. *Educational Researcher, 13,* 3–8.

Mulliken, R. K., & Buckley, J. J. (1983). *Assessment of multihandicapped and developmentally disabled children.* Rockville, MD: Aspen.

Repp, A. C., & Brulle, A. R. (1981). Reducing aggressive behavior of mentally retarded persons. In J. L. Matson & J. R. McCartney (Eds.), *Handbook of behavior modification with the mentally retarded* (pp. 177–210). New York: Plenum Press.

Reschley, D. J. (1982). Assessing mild mental retardation: The influence of adaptive behavior, sociocultural status, and prospects for nonbiased assessment. In C. R. Reynolds & T. B. Gutkin (Eds.), *The handbook of school psychology* (pp. 205–241). New York: Wiley.

Richardson, A. S., Goodman, N., Hastorf, A. H., & Dornbusch, S. M. (1961). Cultural uniformity in reaction to physical disabilities. *American Sociological Review, 26,* 241–247.

Ross, A. O. (1980). *Psychological disorders of children: A behavioral approach to theory, research and therapy.* New York: McGraw-Hill.

Salvia, J., & Ysseldyke, J. E. (1985). *Assessment in special remedial education.* Boston: Houghton Mifflin.

Task Force on Psychology and the Handicapped. (1984). Final report of the Task Force on Psychology and the Handicapped. *American Psychologist, 39,* 545–550.

Thurlow, M. L., & Ysseldyke, J. E. (1979). Current assessment and decision making practices in model programs for learning disabled students. *Learning Disability Quarterly, 2,* 15–24.

Turner, S. M., Hersen, M., & Bellack, A. S. (1978). Social skills training to teach prosocial behaviors in an organically impaired and retarded patient. *Journal of Behavior Therapy and Experimental Psychiatry, 9,* 253–258.

Van Hasselt, V. B. (1983). Social adaptation in the blind. *Clinical Psychology Review, 3,* 87–102.

Van Hasselt, V. B., Kazdin, A. E., & Hersen, M. (1986). Assessment of problem behavior in visually handicapped adolescents. *Journal of Clinical Child Psychology, 15,* 134–141.

Vernon, P. E. (1969). *Intelligence and cultural environment.* London: Methuen.

Weicker, L. (1984). Defining liberty for handicapped Americans. *American Psychologist, 39,* 518–523.

Whitman, T. L., Mercurio, J. R., & Caponigri, V. (1970). Development of social responses in two severely retarded children. *Journal of Applied Behavior Analysis, 3,* 133–138.

Ysseldyke, J. E. (1978). Implementing the "protection in evaluation procedures" provisions of P.L. 94-142. In *Developing criteria for the evaluation of protection in evaluation procedures provisions* (pp. 15–34). Washington, DC: U.S. Office of Education.

Ysseldyke, J. E., & Marston, D. (1982). Gathering decision-making information through the use of non-test-based methods. *Measurement and Evaluation in Guidance, 15,* 58–59.

Ysseldyke, J. E., & Marston, D. (in press). Issues in psychological evaluation. In V. B. Van Hasselt, P. S. Strain, & M. Hersen (Eds.), *Handbook of developmental and physical disabilities.* New York: Pergamon Press.

Ysseldyke, J. E., & Salvia, J. A. (1974). Diagnostic-prescriptive teaching: Two models. *Exceptional Children, 41,* 181–186.

Ysseldyke, J. E., & Shinn, M. R. (1981). Psychoeducational evaluation. In J. M. Kauffman & D. P. Hallahan (Eds.), *Handbook of special education* (pp. 418–440). Englewood Cliffs, NJ: Prentice-Hall.

Ysseldyke, J. E., Algozzine, B., Regan, R., & Potter, M. (1980). Technical adequacy of tests used by professionals in simulated decision making. *Psychology in the Schools, 17,* 202–209.

Ysseldyke, J. E., Thurlow, M. L., Garden, J., Wesson, C., & Deno, S. L. (1983). Generalization from five years of research on assessment and decision making. *Exceptional Education Quarterly, 4,* 75–94.

II

GENERAL ISSUES

2

Basic Issues in Psychological Evaluation

JULIA R. VANE AND ROBERT W. MOTTA

INTRODUCTION

Psychological evaluation is an attempt to arrive at an understanding of the unique potential of an individual through the use of background information, a psychological interview, observation, and psychological testing. The object of gathering this material is to integrate it so that it will provide an explanation of current behavior, a prediction of future behavior, and the development of plans for the optimal functioning of the individual.

Psychological evaluation is a complex activity in which the psychologist attempts to derive from small samples of present and past behaviors a picture of an individual that includes aspects that may not be fully understood by the individual or those with whom he or she interacts. In attempting to provide an understanding of individuals and to predict their subsequent behavior, the psychologist must utilize the most accurate data possible. Such data will range from indirect to direct. Background information and self-reports are indirect sources in that the relevant behavior and environment are not observed by the psychologist directly but are described by the client or others. Observation by the psychologist of the individual during the interview, during the psychological testing, and the responses to the psychological tests themselves

JULIA R. VANE AND ROBERT W. MOTTA • Department of Psychology, Hofstra University, Hempstead, New York 11550.

are direct sources of information. Determination of the relative importance of this information and its integration into a meaningful whole requires a high level of training and experience on the part of the psychologist who is doing the evaluation.

BACKGROUND INFORMATION

There are several sources of background information that are routinely used as part of the psychological evaluation. One of these is written reports from other professionals with whom the individual may have been involved, such as teachers, physicians, therapists, other psychologists, rehabilitation counselors, social workers, probation officers, and religious leaders. This material tells about aspects of the individual that the psychologist has no other way of verifying except through self-report. Such material is not always readily provided, however. This may often occur when a child is being examined by a school psychologist. The parent may not want the school to have access to previous psychological reports or medical records. This may occur also with self-referred individuals who wish to test the psychologist to see if the present evaluation will produce the same results as a previous one. Frequently, mention of previous therapy is withheld. Often the individual is not aware that this makes it difficult to arrive at an accurate evaluation. Some psychologists reinforce this viewpoint by indicating that they want to reach their own conclusions without being biased by other information. This indicates a lack of knowledge regarding the invalidity of blind diagnosis. The limited samples of behavior upon which the psychologist must rely in order to arrive at an accurate assessment make it imperative to consider all available data.

Medical records and reports of the individual's and family's response to past rehabilitation efforts are important in helping the psychologist arrive at a realistic estimate of the ability of the disabled to function in the general environment. Many individuals who are disabled have extensive medical histories, and psychologists evaluating such individuals must be knowledgeable with regard to many medical terms and syndromes.

THE PSYCHOLOGICAL INTERVIEW

Most psychologists conduct a psychological interview to elicit information regarding the reason for referral, educational background, health, family attitudes and interactions, social relations, work history, and present life status. In order to obtain comprehensive information, most psychologists as well as clinics use interview forms to guide them, but there are no forms that are espoused by all.

Psychologists from different theoretical orientations emphasize different aspects in the psychological interview. Those with a psychodynamic or psychoanalytic background place emphasis on early childhood experiences and interactions of parents and children. Those with a behavioral orientation are interested in the individual's early learning history, present adjustment, environmental factors, and present behavior.

In assessing someone who is developmentally disabled, detailed information is required about the behavioral aspects of the disability itself as well as the individual's emotional responses to and attitudes toward the disability. It is necessary, also, to assess the impact of the disability upon the family. Adjustment of the disabled individual often is related to the degree of self-management and independence encouraged by family members. Much research on disabilities and chronic diseases has tended to focus upon the identified individual, but other studies have shown that adaptation by those with chronic diseases or disabilities is affected by the impact on the individual of family attitudes, expectations, and responses (Bruhn, 1977; Lane & Evans, 1979; Seligman, 1983).

The effect of a disabled individual upon the family has been shown to vary widely. Grossman (1972) studied brothers and sisters of retarded children and found that some seemed little affected, others had strong negative reactions and demonstrated poor adjustment, others responded positively, and some later studied for careers working with the retarded. There can be no doubt that a disabled family member changes the experience of each member of the family. Poznanski (1969), in reviewing the psychiatric difficulties shown by siblings of handicapped children, found that the psychiatrists he interviewed were treating a greater number of siblings of handicapped children than handicapped children themselves. It is clear from the foregoing that there is a need to gather extensive data in this area.

On occasion, one of the difficult aspects of the psychological evaluation is to have the individual respond to the necessary questions. Despite motivation to seek an evaluation, the individual does not always respond with candor and accuracy. In certain situations some material is simply forgotten. In others, the material may be embarrassing, so the individual does not wish to discuss it. Sometimes the individual is not cognitively capable or sophisticated enough to recognize the relevance of the information and so withholds it.

Other reasons also exist. Parents of children who are mildly retarded, hyperactive, or who have learning disabilities often try to avoid accepting the fact that a disability exists. Such parents often believe that the child's failure to exhibit average behavior is due to lack of motivation, failure to work hard enough, or poor handling on the part of educators. Such individuals and parents often react negatively to any suggestion that there is a disability. This is especially true if the psychological evaluation is a first experience. Parents of children with severe and obvious disabilities, such as blindness, deafness, or cerebral palsy, usually have accepted the fact that the problem exists some time before the child is brought in for a psychological evaluation. The severity of the disability makes denial difficult. The parents and the severely handicapped individual may not necessarily have made a good adjustment to the disability, but they do not deny its existence. Almost all parents of the disabled are burdened with guilt and may interpret questions relating to the etiology of the disability as leading to blame for themselves. Observation and awareness of such behavior and emotions are factors to be considered in reaching a psychological evaluation of the individual. With such clients a psychologist must be skillful in order to allay feelings of guilt and to avoid distortion of material. Inaccuracy in reporting, particularly in emotionally charged situations, has been well documented, and the various sources of these inaccuracies has been discussed by Cannell and Kahn (1968), Linehann (1977), and Bellack and Hersen (1977). In the psychological interview, therefore, observation of the individual in order to assess the degree of distortion inherent in the self-report is important.

The Preschool Attainment Record developed by Doll (1966a, b) is a helpful instrument to use for this purpose with children under 7 years of age or with older children who are delayed developmentally. This instrument, which was derived from the Vineland Social Maturity Scale (Doll, 1953), assesses functioning in eight areas: Ambulation, Manipulation, Rapport, Communication, Responsibility, Information, Ideation, and Creativity. It is used in a dual fashion. First, questions regarding the child's functioning such as "can he fasten his shoes?" or "can he get a drink of water by himself?" are asked of the parents. The reliability of the information is double-checked by direct observation of the child. For functions that cannot be observed, the report of the parents must be accepted, but enough can be observed to provide a check upon the parents' style of reporting. Experience with this instrument has shown that most parents tend to report the child as functioning on a somewhat higher level than is usually observed. A large discrepancy between reported and observed behaviors suggests that the parents are not being realistic in their expectations of the child and may be unwilling to accept recommendations based upon realistic assessment. It cannot be expected, however, that parents of a retarded child will readily accept the diagnosis of retardation, particularly if it is the first time the diagnosis has been made. Parents usually need quite some time to adjust to a child's disability. A second and sometimes a third consultation and evaluation often will be necessary before they will be convinced that what is being recommended is best for the child.

In working with the developmentally disabled, educational and occupational history are essential for these are the areas around which future planning takes place. A history of physical development and a medical history are also important. Although a psychologist might assume that problems of health would be uncovered by the family physician, studies by Johnson (1968) and Maguire and Glanville-Grossman (1968) indicated that 60 to 70% of the patients in their studies who were admitted to mental hospitals had physical illnesses, some in addition to psychological problems. A smaller percentage of subjects had illnesses that were causing the psychological problems. A large percentage of these illnesses had been undiagnosed by the family or admitting physician. Hall, Popkin, Devaul, Faillace, and Stickney (1978) reviewed 658 outpatients of a mental health clinic and found that 9% had physical problems that were the probable cause of the mental disturbance and almost half of these had been undetected.

An article by Strickland and Kendall (1983) also highlighted the importance of assessing the health status of the individual. It outlined the many endocrine and nutritional disorders and allergic and drug reactions that have symptoms that are similar to those of psychological disorders. The tables provided in the article giving the symptoms of selected vitamin and mineral deficiencies and the effects of medication and drugs on health should be a part of the knowledge of all clinical psychologists.

One aspect of data collection that is important, not only with the developmentally disabled but with all those who come for a psychological evaluation, is information about the strengths and positive assets of the individual. A fairly typical approach to psychological assessment was indicated by Burisch (1984), when he said that the first question a clinician will try to answer is "what is wrong with this person" (p. 216). Looking for the positive is not something that many psychologists are oriented to do. A study by Stack, Lannon, and Miley (1983) assessed clinicians' expectancies for psychiatric rehospitalization for 280 recently discharged patients. Although clinicians predicted rehospitalization for two thirds of the group, 2 years later less than half actually returned. Wills (1978) found that professional helpers' perceptions of their clients tended to be more negative than positive and that the professionals consistently sampled negative aspects of client behavior. The great majority of questions on inventories used to gather data, whether they are from traditional schools such as the Mental Status Interview or from behavioral schools such as the Behavioral Analysis History Questionnaire (Cautela & Upper, 1976), tend to sample negative aspects of behavior. How reinforcing small bits of such positive information are was examplified by a telephone call from a distant state, received recently from a young man of 25 who had been evaluated previously at our psychology department clinic. Although the report given him had indicated he had a number of problems, he wanted to know more about the fact that the report indicated he had unusually good eye–hand coordination. Would this be useful to him in a new career as a key punch operator?

Even though all the data collected may not be useful at the time of the evaluation, it may have future value. Experience has shown that clients often return at different periods of their lives to discuss other problems that have arisen with a psychologist who knows them and their background. Frequently, data that have been collected earlier are relevant at this time. It is not unusual for a psychologist who has been in practice for some time to have seen a child for several different evaluations and sometimes different members of the child's family for other problems in living. Many private practitioners and those who continue to work in the same mental health setting function more or less as family psychologists who see individuals and their families on a variety of occasions over a period of years. This is particularly true of those who work with the developmentally disabled, many of whom face more crises in living than the average and, therefore, are likely to return to further evaluation and discussions.

PSYCHOLOGICAL TESTING

The results of psychological tests contribute a large part to the overall psychological evaluation. Most of these tests, because they are uniquely within the field of psychology, have been carefully scrutinized and subjected to much research. The major tests have been standardized on large samples of the population. The directions for giving and scoring have been formalized. There is considerable research with respect to the reliability and validity of administration, scoring, and representativeness. There are drawbacks to using these tests with the developmentally disabled, however, because the majority of them have not included disabled populations in the samples upon which the tests are based.

Manuals for psychological tests, such as the Wechsler Intelligence Scale for Children (WISC), the Stanford-Binet Intelligence Scale, the Minnesota Multiphasic Personality Inventory (MMPI), the Thematic Apperception Test, the Rorschach, the Sixteen Personality Factor Questionnaire (PF), and numerous others in regular clinical use give no norms for special populations and make no reference to how the examiner should test an individual who is developmentally disabled.

Most psychologists who are called upon to test the developmentally disabled are faced with an uncomfortable dilemma. On the one hand, there is a desire to adhere to standard test administration, recording, and scoring so that psychometric assumptions derived from the standardization procedures are not violated. On the other hand, there is the reality that by adhering to the procedures certain developmentally disabled groups will be discriminated against because they are unable to respond in the same way as the standardization sample. What typically results from these conflicting issues is a compromise in which the standardization procedures are maintained to the extent that they can be, and modifications are made when necessary so as to do justice to the subject being evaluated.

Test adaptations or modifications that frequently are employed fall into two major categories. Adaptation can be made in the particular order or manner in which the test materials are presented or in terms of which test items are included and which are omitted. Regardless of how these alterations are made, the psychologist who modifies standard procedures is faced with some degree of uncertainty regarding the utility and generalizability of the test data.

A number of testing strategies have been employed for evaluating the disabled. Children who have emotional or hearing problems, for example, are often more receptive to and more likely to respond when nonverbal items are presented first. Although there is some research that would indicate that this level of test adaptation does not markedly affect the validity of certain tests (Frandsen, McCullough & Stone, 1950), for the most part, a substantial body of research in this area is lacking. Other strategies involve reading test items to visually impaired children, allowing the individual who has speech deficits to write responses, using pantomime and demonstration for those who have hearing deficits (Bragman, 1982) and the like.

Other strategies center around the manner in which test items are presented. Baker (1983) noted that with autistic children one must be aware of their unusually complex and varied handicaps and be flexible regarding the use of language, the choice of materials, standardized routines, and length of tests. Assessment procedures necessitating this extreme degree of modification might be useful in planning treatment programs, but their usefulness in comparing the results of the tests to the general population of children remains unanswered.

The process of reinforcing correct responses in order to secure appropriate levels of attention, as is frequently done when evaluating hyperactive and retarded children, has also been used in experimental studies with normal children (Edlund, 1972; Kieffer & Goh, 1981). Ayllon and Kelly (1972), for example, found that the performance of both normal and retarded children was improved by using a simple reinforcement procedure. The authors concluded that "either the performance of the child in a standardized test situation must be maximally enhanced or the resulting test score must not be assumed to be a representative sample of the child's academic performance" (p. 483). It should be kept in mind, however, that when a psychologist conducts an evaluation, what is observed is present functioning. The assumption made in testing is that test performance represents a sample of the child's functioning in varied environmental situations. If examiners reinforce responses of a disabled child in order to compensate for their deficits, there is no way of knowing how such test alteration will affect the ability to predict behavior in the environment where such reinforcement is not present.

The fact that reinforcing test responses and using other strategies in presenting test items will alter test behavior is not surprising in light of the fact that even slight alterations in standardized testing conditions will change performance. Saigh (1981), for example, found that Roman Catholic schoolchildren performed better on the Digit Span test of the Wechsler scales when the examiner wore a crucifix than when he wore a Star of David. If such minor alterations of the test environment can have significant effects, one is left with the question of how useful test results are when significant changes are made as a form of test adaptation.

Using shortened forms of standardized tests, such as only the Verbal section of the WISC with the blind or the Performance section with the deaf or with those with speech problems is common. Reliability data comparable to those of the standardization population have been reported with the visually impaired on the verbal section of the WISC (Hopkins & McGuire, 1966). Validity data are lacking, however, (Tillman, 1973) especially the types of validity studies that relate test performance to non-test situations.

Short forms of intelligence tests such as the Wechsler Scales should, according to Resnick and Entin (1971), fulfill three criteria: (a) The short form should have a significant positive correlation with the standard form IQ; (b) the difference between the average short form and the average standard form IQ should be small; and (c) the proportion of subjects whose short form IQ classification differs from the standard form classification should be small. In a study by Wildman and Wildman (1977), satisfaction of these three criteria was found for a sample of relatively low-IQ adult inpatients using the verbal section of the Wechsler Adult Intelligence Scale (WAIS). Similar, though less precise findings were obtained by Ziegler and Doehrman (1979) in evaluating high-IQ outpatients. In this study, although the differences between Verbal IQ and Full IQ were statistically significant, these differences were relatively small. Hafner, Nelson, Corotto, and Curnutt (1979) examined an abbreviated version of the WAIS on a nonclinical, college student sample using selected subtests. High correlations were obtained between the abbreviated and Full Scale WAIS, but the shortened version underestimated the IQ by about 9 points. These authors recommend using a constant or weight to deal with the problem. If such weights could be developed for the various developmentally disabled groups, this might help in providing valid test measures that are not only useful but psychometrically sound.

The omission of test items as a form of adaptation to the unique needs of the disabled initially appears to be justifiable, but it fails to take into account one of the major reasons for conducting the evaluation (i.e., the assumption that future behavior of the child can be inferred from present test behavior). Despite the fact that high correlations may exist between certain nonverbal measures and overall or total test scores, the hearing- or speech-impaired child who has been tested with visual items will encounter marked difficulty in a classroom where material is presented verbally and there is a general emphasis on verbal skills. Although there is some research in this area (Allen & Collins, 1955; Katz, 1956, 1958), the evaluator is left with little empirical support for major modifications in test procedures as is involved in the omission of items.

Despite the fact that some scales have been adapted for use with the disabled populations, such as various versions of the Binet for the Blind (Tillman, 1973), there are few standardized tests uniquely suited for the disabled. There are certain tests of ability that by the nature of their construction appear to be used more frequently in evaluating the disabled than others. These include the Progressive Matrices (Raven, 1965), which were designed to reflect Spearman's *g* factor of intelligence. This series of tests can be particularly useful for those children who suffer hearing or physical impairments and for certain learning-disabled groups. The response that is required is one of simple selection of a missing form so as to logically match other forms. The response makes no demand on verbal expressive skills and only limited demand on motor skills. Carlson and Dillon (1978) presented the measure as a useful testing instrument especially in situations where feedback to the subject is permitted so as to enhance test performance.

The Leiter International Performance Scale (Leiter, 1969) has a long history of use with the disabled and with cross-cultural populations. This nonverbal assessment device, like the Raven Matrices, has some psychometric weaknesses but can be used for gross screening of intellectual capability. In survey by Levine (1974), the WISC Performance Scales ranked first, and the Leiter Performance Scale was ranked second in frequency of usage with the hearing impaired, despite the fact that both of these were standardized on normal-hearing children, and therefore the norms are not appropriate for use with the hearing impaired. Only the Hiskey-Nebraska Test of Learning Aptitude (Hiskey, 1966) provides norms for the hearing impaired in those tests most frequently used. Gerweck and Ysseldyke (1975) pointed out that the use of instruments that are not standardized with special populations is a clearly questionable practice. If one of the major reasons for conducting evaluations with the developmentally disabled is to predict future behavior and performance, it is reasonable to conclude that many of the current assessment devices are deficient in this respect.

Some psychologists have argued that it would be better to move away from the assessment of constructs such as intelligence and personality as behavioral predictors and to assess the behavior itself (Kazdin & Straw, 1976). Instead of comparing an individual to a standardization sample, behavioral assessment focuses upon general behavioral categories such as behavioral excesses or deficits, socially undesirable behaviors, problems of stimulus control, and others (Bandura, 1968; Ferster, 1965; Gardner, 1971).

In behavioral assessment, frequency of a given behavior, the setting in which the behavior occurs, how long the behavior is maintained, and percentage of specified units of time in which the behavior is observed are measured. If one has carefully assessed the behavior in this way, the issue of validity of measurement does not present a major problem because the behavior is observed within the situation that the individual must perform or in a highly similar situation. Reliability is assessed by examining the extent to which independent observers agree on the frequency, duration, and extent of a given set of behaviors. Kazdin and Straw (1976) reported that meaningful evaluations can be carried out for self-care skills, classroom behavior, language development, social responses, and other behaviors through the use of direct observation, behavioral interviewing, checklists, self-report inventories, and physiological records.

Behavioral observation requires suitable training as does any method of assessment (Wildman, Erickson, & Kent, 1975). Behavioral observers can show change in the way they monitor and record behavior as a function of being observed themselves (Reid, 1970). Observer motivation (Guttman, Spector, Segal, Rakoff, & Epstein, 1971), observer expectations (Skindrud, 1973), and other factors affect accurate observation. Frequently, behavioral assessment requires more than one observer so that reliability of observation can be assessed. This drawback may be the price paid for improving the accuracy of prediction. In using behavioral assessment, problems of standardization are avoided, and fewer assumptions are made. There is some indirect evidence that the predictive accuracy of these tests may be greater than those with traditional approaches (Goldfried & Kent, 1972). The problem of generalizability to situations other than the specific ones sampled and comparison with peers remains a problem. At the present time, neither adaptations of standardized testing or behavioral methods offer the ideal means of evaluating those who are developmentally disabled. More research is required in this area, and it is hoped that it will be forthcoming as psychologists become more aware of the needs of the disabled.

CHARACTERISTICS OF THE PSYCHOLOGIST

The characteristics of the psychologist who conducts the evaluation have been shown to have an impact on the process itself and the outcome. Among the relevant characteristics are appearance, behavior, attitudes, personality, ability, and degree of congruence with the individual who is being evaluated. The impact of these characteristics is not a simple one, however. Their effect is mediated by the characteristics of the individual being evaluated, who comes with a variety of attitudes, motives, and stereotypes, which are triggered by the characteristics of the psychologist. Thus an interaction occurs that varies from evaluation to evaluation because even if the psychologist behaved in the same manner in each instance, the individuals being evaluated differ and thus evoke different responses from the psychologist.

This interaction effect undoubtedly has contributed to the contradictory research results sometimes found when the effectiveness of certain characteristics of professional interviewers and mental health professionals are investigated. As Pope (1979) stated in discussing psychotherapy:

> Professional psychotherapists tend to attribute success in treatment to the technical or procedural aspects of their work. Patients, on the other hand, tend more frequently to attribute whatever gains they make in treatment to the personal qualities of the therapist or the relationship that develops. (p. 332)

Research frequently has shown that attitudes, prejudices, and expectations of the interviewer are reflected in the kinds of data obtained during the interview (Cleary, Mechanic, & Weiss, 1981; Ferber & Wales, 1952; Hanson & Marks, 1958; Rosenthal, 1969; Sudman, Bradburn, Blair, & Stocking, 1977). Other studies have demonstrated that congruence in race (Banks, 1972; Banks, Berenson, & Carkhuff, 1967; Carkhuff & Pierce, 1967; Gardner, 1971; Williams, 1964), religion (Robinson & Rhode, 1947), social class (Lorion, 1973, 1974), and age (Erlich & Riesman, 1961) may facilitate the interview. In some programs for drug addicts and in Alcoholics Anonymous, congruence or actual experience with the problem behavior on the part of the professional is considered crucial. Status and level of perceived expertise of the professional have been shown to have an effect on the interview outcome as well (Pope, 1979; Ross, 1973; Wasserman & Kassinove, 1974, 1976; Zamostny, Corrigan, & Eggert, 1981). There have been conflicting results from studies attempting to determine the extent to which the sex of the interviewer or therapist is an important variable in the interaction between client and professional (Casas, Brady, & Ponterotto, 1983; Geer & Hurst, 1976; Hill, 1975; Rice, Gurman, & Gasin, 1974; Tanney & Birk, 1976). Some findings show that same-sex interviewers obtained better results.

The qualities of warmth, genuineness, and empathy on the part of the interviewer have been considered essential to a good relationship not only by adherents of client-centered counseling (e.g., Rogers, 1957; Rogers, Gendlin, Kiesler, & Truax, 1967; Truax & Mitchell, 1971), but by many others. Although studies have demonstrated the effectiveness of therapists possessing these qualities, other studies have yielded conflicting results (Chinsky & Rappaport, 1970; Garfield & Bergin, 1971; Rachman, 1973). Articles by behavior therapists tend to emphasize technique and strategies for behavior change, and for this reason behaviorists are assumed to be uninterested in therapist qualities. Although this might be a logical conclusion in view of the limited space allotted to this topic in articles and texts such as those of Hersen and Bellack (1976) and Rimm and Masters (1979), the latter do state:

> Another obvious goal of the initial interview is to establish rapport. . . . The therapist's way of relating to his client, while not necessarily communicating "unconditional positive regard," nevertheless should be marked by warmth and a concern for the client's welfare. (p. 27)

Some studies have been directed to determining the interaction effect of professional on client and client on professional. Bandura, Lipsher, and Miller (1960), Russell and Snyder (1963), and Heller *et al.* (1963) found that hostility on the part of the client affected interviewers in different ways depending upon the therapist's own hostility and dependency needs. A series of studies by Van der Veen (1965), Houts, MacIntosh, and Moos (1969), and Moos and MacIntosh (1970) showed that both patients and therapists were more strongly influenced by the patients than patients by therapists. Conger (1971) found that reinforcement by clients of certain therapist responses had mixed effects across therapists. Betz and Whitehorn (1956) and Whitehorn and Betz (1954, 1960) found that therapists with a certain constellation of personality attributes, as measured by the Strong Vocational Interest Blank, were more successful with certain clients. Type A therapists were found to be more successful with schizophrenic patients, whereas Type B therapists had better outcomes with neurotic patients. Again, the results from subsequent research have produced conflicting results, probably because the interaction of client and professional is never a static one.

As may be seen by the foregoing, so many elements enter into the interaction between professional and client that no studies are likely to demonstrate just what combination of characteristics are ideal for the most effective evaluation. One thing we do know is that the relationship or the establishment of rapport between the interviewer and client is of great significance. From a behavioral viewpoint, rapport is established when the interviewer or the interview itself becomes reinforcing for the client. Experienced professionals are adept in rapidly determining what characteristics are most likely to be reinforcing for a client and in utilizing them in the interview. It is not possible, however, for one professional to have all characteristics that would appeal to all clients because one cannot be both a man and a woman, several different ages or races, or have expertise in all areas.

Experience in training doctoral students to work with clients has shown that certain students do well with certain clients and not with others, but we have not been able to predict this in advance. We have noted, however, that students find success reinforcing, and if they associate this success with certain types of clients, they frequently ask for that kind of client again. The tendency is to assign such a client to such a student and to avoid asigning them to the kind of clients with whom they have not been successful. The reinforcing factor of success with certain clients often leads students to choose to specialize in work with this kind of client. It is this selective specialization process that frequently makes it difficult to compare the effectiveness of professionals with different kinds of clients because some who are successful with one group may not be with another. It also explains one of the reasons research has not been able to identify one, or even two, particular types of individuals who would make a good psychologist or therapist.

In working with the developmentally disabled, are there any particular characteristics of the psychologist that are essential for success? Actually the developmentally disabled vary so widely that interactions with the psychologist will vary widely as well. Some disabled may wish to work with those who have similar disabilities; others will not. Experience with this population seems important for beginning professionals, however, so that they may discover whether or not they find working with the disabled rewarding. Those who do not find it rewarding should be urged to work with other groups, for it is to the best interest of any group of clients to be able to work with those who find working with them reinforcing.

DECISION MAKING

Combining and integrating the material obtained during the interview and through observation and testing so that it may be communicated to the individual is the most complex aspect of the psychological evaluation. Usually this is done in an intuitive manner based on past experience and clinical judgment. There are no generally accepted guidelines to assist in determining which factors should receive the most weight in the final evaluation.

Research with regard to decision making by professionals has shown that decisions are often reached on the basis of limited data, even when a fairly substantial amount of data is available (Clavelle & Turner, 1980; Lanyon, 1972). Other studies have shown that professional decisions often are made rapidly and based on material presented in the early minutes of the interview (Gauron & Dickinson, 1966; Kendell, 1973; Sandifer, Hordern, & Green, 1979). Still other studies have shown that one way clinicians simplify the data obtained is to categorize and label them. This is an essential aspect of the psychological evaluation, for today a label often is required for admission to certain programs and for insurance purposes. Considerable research has gone into determining the reliability of psychiatric labeling (Matarazzo, 1983) and into training individuals so that they may arrive at accurate diagnostic labels, which has not proven to be an easy task (Langer & Abelson, 1974).

Interest in clinical decision making has remained high since Meehl's original work was published in 1954. Several articles such as those by Haase, Strohmer, Biggs, and Keller (1983), Strohmer, Biggs, Haase, and Keller (1983), Strohmer, Haase, Biggs, and Keller (1982), and Wiggins (1981) have outlined models of clinical decision making. Although these models are explanatory, none of them is presented in a form that would be useful to the average psychologist. The statement by Strohmer *et al.* (1982) that "a reasonable description of the clinical judgment process should recognize the role of mediating inferences and also take into account the limitations of the counselor as an information processor" (p. 605) suggests the need for further exploration into ways of processing, categorizing, and weighing information to aid with clinical assessment. With the use of computers, this is something we might expect in the future.

One way psychologists reach the final evaluation is to form a series of hypotheses leading to conclusions that will be presented to the individual who has been evaluated. Aspects considered are the individual's intellectual and physical capabilities, the level of functioning in terms of these capabilities, the use of capabilities to further the goals for which the individual sought evaluation, the environmental supports that can be utilized to realize these goals (i.e., educational or training programs, therapy or treatment programs, significant individuals), and the individual's motivation and ability to implement any change that may be necessary to achieve the goals.

One of the significant aspects of the evaluation is the reaction of individuals when the conclusions are reported to them. Conclusions may be received with satisfaction, displeasure, rejection, or silence. Beginning psychologists often are disturbed when their findings are disputed and press on with further details to prove the results are correct. The experienced psychologist explores these disagreements, knowing that what emerges at this stage will give further clues regarding the individual's willingness to accept recommendations. Some disagreements are based upon misunderstandings on the part of the client. Intelligence test results are often misunderstood. Other disagreements occur because of previously unrevealed information, such as "I did go for treatment for that, and it didn't help me." It is disturbing to have such information brought up at this time, for it may require a revision of conclusions. The experienced psychologist will accept this behavior as another example of the way in which the client is likely to function in life, and as additional data upon which to base hypotheses and recommendations. It is hoped that the final assessment will center around positive, constructive approaches, capitalize upon the strengths of the individual, and consider as many different realistic ways as possible to enhance the individual's ability to cope with life. If the psychological evaluation serves this function, it will make a major contribution and be well worth the time and involvement of all concerned.

SUMMARY

Much research has focused upon the process of psychological evaluation and the different aspects that contribute to arriving at conclusions and recommendations regarding the individual evaluated. Results of this research suggest that each step in the assessment process, namely gathering background information, interviewing, selection, and administration of tests, and combining the results obtained into a decision regarding the individual are subject to many influences. For example, all the aspects of this process are influenced by the training, experience, and personality characteristics of the psychologist who conducts the evaluation. Although designers and administrators of tests, trainers of psychologists, and the psychologists themselves have exerted great efforts to make the process of psychological evaluation as objective as possible, it is clear that no psychological evaluation can be completely objective. If this were so, there would be no need for the individual psychologist to be involved at all. On the surface, this might seem desirable. It is not desirable, however, for what is needed for a good psychological evaluation is a psychologist with sufficient training, experience, intelligence, and flexibility to be able to look at the results objectively and then translate them into something that is meaningful for the individual. More research is needed in this area, but it is difficult to carry out because it involves a complex interaction of two individuals as well as the use of the material developed through the evaluation and consideration of the situation that brought the individual to request the evaluation. The more knowledge obtained regarding the influence of interacting factors involved in the psychological evaluation, the more effective psychological evaluations will be.

REFERENCES

Allen, R. M., & Collins, M. G. (1955). Suggestions for the adaptive administration of intelligence tests for those with cerebral palsy. *Cerebral Palsy Review, 16*, 11–14.

Ayllon, T., & Kelly, K. (1972). Effects of reinforcement on standardized test performance. *Journal of Applied Behavioral Analysis*, 477–484.

Baker, A. F. (1983). Psychological assessment of autistic children. *Clinical Psychology Review, 3,* 41–59.

Bandura, A. (1968). A social learning interpretation of psychological dysfunction. In P. London & D. Rosenhan (Eds.), *Foundations of abnormal psychology*. New York: Holt, Rinehart & Winston.

Bandura, A., Lipsher, D., & Miller, P. (1960). Psychotherapists' approach avoidance reactions to patients' expression of hostility. *Journal of Consulting Psychology, 24,* 1–8.

Banks, W. M. (1972). The differential effects of race and social class in helping. *Journal of Clinical Psychology, 29,* 90–92.

Banks, G., Berenson, B. G., & Carkhuff, R. R. (1967). The effects of counsellor race and training upon counseling process with Negro clients in initial interviews. *Journal of Clinical Psychology, 23,* 70–72.

Bellack, A. S., & Hersen, M. (1977). Self-report inventories in behavioral assessment. In J. D. Cone & R. P. Hawkins (Eds.), *Behavioral assessment: New directions in clinical psychology* (pp. 52–78). New York: Brunner/Mazel.

Betz, B. J., & Whitehorn, J. C. (1956). The relationship of a therapist to the outcome of therapy in schizophrenia. *Psychiatric Research Reports, 5,* 89–140.

Bragman, R. (1982). Review of research on test instructions for deaf children. *American Annals of the Deaf, 127,* 337–346.

Bruhn, J. G. (1977). Effects of chronic illness on the family. *Journal of Family Practice, 4,* 1057–1060.

Burisch, M. (1984). Approaches to personality inventory construction. *American Psychologist, 39,* 214–227.

Cannell, C. F., & Kahn, R. L. (1968). Interviewing. In G. Lindzey & E. Aronson (Eds.), *The handbook of social psychology* (Vol. 2, 2nd ed.). Reading, MA: Addison-Wesley.

Carkhuff, R. R., & Pierce, R. (1967). Differential effects of therapist race and social class upon patient depth of self-exploration in the initial clinical interview. *Journal of Consulting Psychology, 31,* 632–634.

Carlson, J. S., & Dillon, R. (1978). Measuring intellectual capabilities of hearing-impaired children: Effects of testing the limits procedures. *The Volta Review, 80,* 216–224.

Casas, J. M., Brady, S., & Ponterotto, J. G. (1983). Sexual preference biases in counseling: An information processing approach. *Journal of Counseling Psychology, 30,* 139–145.

Cautela, J. R., & Upper, D. (1976). The Behavioral Inventory Battery: The use of self-report measures in behavioral analysis and therapy. In M. Hersen and A. S. Bellack (Eds.), *Behavioral assessment: A practical handbook* (pp. 77–110). Elmsford, NY: Pergamon.

Chinsky, J. M., & Rappaport, J. (1970). Brief critique of meaning and reliability of "accurate empathy" ratings. *Psychological Bulletin, 73,* 379–382.

Clavelle, P. R., & Turner, A. D. (1980). Clinical decision-making among professionals and paraprofessionals. *Journal of Clinical Psychology, 36* (3), 833–838.

Cleary, P. D., Mechanic, D., & Weiss, R. R. (1981). The effect of interviewer characteristics on responses to a mental health interview. *Journal of Health & Social Behavior, 22,* 183–193.

Conger, J. C. (1971). The modification of interview behavior by client use of social reinforcement. *Behavior Therapy, 2,* 52–61.

Doll, E. A. (1953). *Measurement of social competence: A manual for the Vineland Social Maturity Scale.* Circle Pines, MN: American Guidance Service.

Doll, E. A. (1966a). *Preschool attainment record: Manual.* Circle Pines, MN: American Guidance Service.

Doll, E. A. (1966b). An attainment scale for appraising young children with expressive handicaps. *The Cerebral Palsy Journal, 27,* 3–5.

Edlund, C. V. (1972). The effects on the behavior of children, as reflected in the IQ scores, when reinforced after each correct response. *Journal of Applied Behavior Analysis, 5,* 317–319.

Erlich, J., & Riesman, D. (1961). Age and authority in the interview. *Public Opinion Quarterly, 25,* 39–56.

Ferber, R., & Wales, H. (1952). Detection and correction of interviewer bias. *Public Opinion Quarterly, 16,* 107–127.

Ferster, C. B. (1965). Classification of behavioral pathology. In L. Krasner & L. P. Ullmann (Eds.), *Research in behavioral modification* (pp. 121–147). New York: Holt, Rinehart & Winston.

Frandsen, A. N., McCullough, B. R., & Stone, D. R. (1950). Serial versus consecutive order administration of the Stanford-Binet Intelligence Scale. *Journal of Consulting Psychology, 14,* 316–346.

Gardner, L. M. (1971). The therapeutic relationship under varying conditions of race. *Psychotherapy: Theory, Research and Practice, 8,* 78–87.

Gardner, W. I. (1971). *Behavioral modification in mental retardation.* Chicago: Aldine.

Garfield, S. L., & Bergin, A. E. (1971). Therapeutic conditions and outcome. *Journal of Abnormal Psychology, 77,* 108–114.

Gauron, E. F., & Dickinson, J. K. (1966). Diagnostic decision making in psychiatry: Information usage. *Archives of General Psychiatry, 14,* 225–232.

Geer, C. A., & Hurst, J. C. (1976). Counselor-subject sex variables in systematic desensitization. *Journal of Counseling Psychology, 23,* 296–301.

Gerweck, S., & Ysseldyke, J. E. (1975). Limitations of current psychological practices for the intellectual assessment of the hearing impaired: A response to the Levine study. *The Volta Review,* April, 243–248.

Goldfried, M. R., & Kent, R. N. (1972). Traditional versus behavioral personality assessment: A comparison of methodological and theoretical assumption. *Psychological Bulletin, 77,* 409–420.

Grossman, F. K. (1972). *Brothers and sisters of retarded children.* Syracuse: Syracuse University Press.

Guttman, H. A., Spector, R. M., Segal, J. J., Rakoff, V., & Epstein, W. B. (1971). Reliability of coding affective communications in family therapy sessions: Problems of measurement and interpretation. *Journal of Consulting and Clinical Psychology, 37,* 397–402.

Haase, R. F., Strohmer, D. C., Biggs, D. A., & Keller, K. E. (1983). Mediational inferences in the process of counselor judgment. *Journal of Counseling Psychology, 30,* 275–278.

Hafner, J. L., Nelson, D. A., Corotto, L. V., & Curnutt, R. H. (1979). The validity of the WAIS short form with a non-clinical population. *Journal of Clinical Psychology, 35,* 820–821.

Hall, R. C. W., Popkin, M. D., Devaul, R. A., Faillace, L. A., & Stickney, S. K. (1978). Physical illness presenting as psychiatric disease. *Archives of General Psychiatry, 35,* 1315–1320.

Hanson, R. H., & Marks, E. S. (1958). Influence of the interviewers on the accuracy of survey results. *Journal of the American Statistical Association, 53,* 635–655.

Heller, K., Myers, R. A., & Kline, L. V. (1963). Interview behavior as a function of standardized client roles. *Journal of Consulting Psychology, 27,* 117–122.

Hersen, M., & Bellack, A. S. (Eds.). (1976). *Behavioral assessment: A practical handbook.* Elmsford, NY: Pergamon.

Hill, C. E. (1975). Sex of client and sex and experience level of counselor. *Journal of Counseling Psychology, 22,* 6–11.

Hiskey, M. S. (1966). *Hiskey-Nebraska Test of Learning Aptitude*. Lincoln: Union College Press.

Hopkins, P. J., & McGuire, L. (1966). The validity of the Wechsler Intelligence Scale for Children. *The International Journal for the Education of the Blind, 15*, 65–73.

Houts, P. S., MacIntosh, S., & Moos, R. H. (1969). Patient-therapist interdependence: Cognitive and behavioral. *Journal of Consulting & Clinical Psychology, 33*, 40–45.

Johnson, D. A. W. (1968). The evaluation of routine physical examination in 250 psychiatric cases. *Practitioner, 200*, 686–691.

Katz, E. (1956). A method of selecting Stanford-Binet Intelligence Scale test items for evaluating the mental abilities of children severely handicapped by cerebral palsy. *Cerebral Palsy Review, 1*, 13–17.

Katz, E. (1958). The "Pointing Modification" of the revised Stanford-Binet Intelligence Scale, Forms L and M, years II through VI: A report of research in progress. *American Journal of Mental Deficiency, 62*, 698–707.

Kazdin, A. E., & Straw, M. K. (1976). Assessment of the behavior of the mentally retarded. In M. Hersen & A. S. Bellack (Eds.), *Behavioral assessment: A practical handbook* (pp. 337–368). Elmsford, NY: Pergamon Press.

Kendell, R. E. (1973). Psychiatric diagnoses: A study of how they are made. *British Journal of Psychiatry, 122*, 437–445.

Kieffer, D. A., & Goh, D. S. (1981). The effects of individually contracted incentives on intelligence test performance of middle and low SES children *Journal of Clinical Psychology, 37* (1), 175–179.

Lane, D. S., & Evans, D. (1979). Measures and methods in evaluating patient education programs for chronic illness. *Medical Care, 17*, 30–42.

Langer, E. J., & Abelson, R. P. (1974). A patient by any other name . . . Clinician group difference in labeling bias. *Journal of Consulting and Clinical Psychology, 42*, 4–9.

Lanyon, R. E. (1972). Technological approach to the improvement of decision making in mental health services. *Journal of Consulting and Clinical Psychology, 39*, 43–48.

Leiter, R. G. (1969). *Leiter International Performance Scale*. Chicago: Stoelting.

Levine, E. (1974). Psychological tests and practices with the deaf. A survey of the state of the art. *The Volta Review, 76*, 298–319.

Linehann, M. M. (1977). Issues in behavioral interviewing. In J. D. Cone & R. P. Hawkins (Eds.), *Behavioral assessment: New directions in clinical psychology* (pp. 30–51). New York: Brunner/Mazel.

Lorion, R. P. (1973). Socioeconomic status and traditional treatment approaches reconsidered. *Psychological Bulletin, 79*, 263–70.

Lorion, R. P. (1974). Patient and therapist variables in the treatment of low-income patients. *Psychological Bulletin, 81*, 344–354.

Maguire, G. P., & Granville-Grossman, K. L. (1968). Physical illness in psychiatric patients. *British Journal of Psychiatry, 115*, 1365–1369.

Matarazzo, J. D. (1983). The reliability of psychiatric and psychological diagnosis. *Clinical Psychology Review, 3*, 103–145.

Meehl, P. E. (1954). *Clinical versus statistical prediction: A theoretical analysis and review of the evidence*. Minneapolis: University of Minnesota Press.

Moos, R. H., & MacIntosh, G. (1970). Multivariate study of the patient-therapist system: A replication and extension. *Journal of Consulting and Clinical Psychology, 35*, 298–307.

Pope, B. (1979). *The mental health interview*. New York: Pergamon Press.

Poznanski, E. (1969). Psychiatric difficulties in siblings of handicapped children. *Pediatrics, 8*, 232–234.

Rachman, S. J. (1973). The effects of psychological treatment. In H. Eysenck (Ed.), *Handbook of abnormal psychology* (pp. 329–371). New York: Basic Books.

Raven, J. C. (1965). *Progressive matrices.* New York: The Psychological Corporation.

Reid, J. B. (1970). Reliability assessment of observation data: A possible methodological problem. *Child Development, 41,* 1143–1150.

Resnick, R. J., & Entin, A. D. (1971). Is an abbreviated form of the WISC valid for Afro-American children? *Journal of Consulting and Clinical Psychology, 36,* 97–99.

Rice, D. G., Gurman, A. S., & Gasin, A. M. (1974). Therapist sex, style and theoretical orientation. *Journal of Nervous and Mental Disease, 159,* 413–421.

Rimm, D. C., & Masters, J. C. (1979). *Behavior therapy.* New York: Academic Press.

Robinson, D., & Rhode, S. (1947). Two experiments with an anti-Semitism poll. *Journal of Abnormal and Social Psychology, 41,* 136–144.

Rogers, C. R. (1957). The necessary and sufficient conditions of therapeutic personality change. *Journal of Consulting Psychology, 21,* 95–103.

Rogers, C. R., Gendlin, E. T., Kiesler, D. V., & Truax, C. B. (1967). *The therapeutic relationship and its impact: A study of psychotherapy with schizophrenics.* Madison: University of Wisconsin Press.

Rosenthal, R. (1969). Interpersonal expectations: Effects of the experimenter's hypothesis. In R. Rosenthal & R. L. Rosnow (Eds.), *Artifact in behavior research.* New York: Academic Press.

Ross, J. A. (1973). Influence of expert and peer upon Negro mothers of low socioeconomic status. *Journal of Social Psychology, 89,* 79–84.

Russell, P. D., & Snyder, W. U. (1963). Counselor anxiety in relation to amount of clinical experience and quality of affect demonstrated by clients. *Journal of Consulting Psychology, 27,* 358–363.

Saigh, P. A. (1981). The validity of the WISC-R examiner verbal praise procedure as a concurrent predictor of academic achievement of intellectually superior students. *Journal of Clinical Psychology, 37,* 647–649.

Sandifer, M. G., Hordern, A., & Green, I. M. (1970). The psychiatric interview: The impact of the first three minutes. *American Journal of Psychiatry, 126,* 938–973.

Seligman, M. (1983). Sources of psychological disturbance among siblings of handicapped children. *Personnel and Guidance Journal, 61,* 529–531.

Skindrud, K. (1973). Field evaluation of observer bias under overt and covert monitoring. In L. A. Hamerlynck, L. C. Handy, & E. J. Mash (Eds.), *Behavioral change: Methodology, concepts, and practice* (pp. 97–145). Champaign, IL: Research Press.

Stack, L. C., Lannon, P. B., & Miley, A. D. (1983). Accuracy of clinicians' expectancies for psychiatric rehospitalization. *American Journal of Community Psychology, 11,* 99–113.

Strickland, B. R., & Kendall, K. E. (1983). Psychological symptoms: The importance of assessing health status. *Clinical Psychology Review, 3,* 179–199.

Strohmer, D. C., Haase, R. F., Biggs, D. A., & Keller, K. E. (1982). Process models of counselor judgment. *Journal of Counseling Psychology, 29,* 597–606.

Strohmer, D. C., Biggs, D. A., Haase, R. F., & Keller, K. E. (1983). Hypothesis formation and testing in clinical judgment. *Journal of Counseling Psychology, 30,* 607–610.

Sudman, S., Bradburn, N. M., Blair, E., & Stocking, C. (1977). Modest expectations: The effects of interviewers prior expectations on responses. *Sociological Methods & Research, 6,* 171–83.

Tanney, M. F., & Birk, J. M. (1976). Women counselors for women clients? A review of the research. *The Counseling Psychologist, 6,* 28–31.

Tillman, M. H. (1973). Intelligence scales for the blind: A review with complications for research. *Journal of School Psychology, 11* (1), 80–87.

Truax, C. B., & Mitchell, K. M. (1971). Research on certain therapist interpersonal skills in relation to process and outcome. In A. E. Bergin & S. L. Garfield (Eds.), *Handbook of psychotherapy and behavior change: An empirical analysis* (pp. 121–157). New York: Wiley.

Van der Veen, F. (1965). Effects of the therapist and the patient on each other's therapeutic behavior. *Journal of Consulting Psychology, 29*, 19–26.

Wasserman, T., & Kassinove, H. (1974). Effects of type of recommendation, attire and perceived expertise and sex on teacher compliance. *Journal of Social Psychology, 93*, 187–92.

Wasserman, T., & Kassinove, H. (1976). Effects of type of recommendation, attire, and perceived expertise on parental compliance. *Journal of Social Psychology, 99*, 43–50.

Whitehorn, J. C., & Betz, B. J. (1954). A study of psychotherapeutic relationships between physicians and schizophrenic patients. *American Journal of Psychiatry, 111*, 32–331.

Whitehorn, J. C., & Betz, B. J. (1960). Further studies of the doctor as a crucial variable in the outcome of treatment with schizophrenic patients. *American Journal of Psychiatry, 117*, 214–223.

Wiggins, J. S. (1981). Clinical and statistical prediction: Where are we and where do we go from here? *Clinical Psychology Review, 1*, 3–18.

Wildman, B. G., Erickson, M. T., & Kent, R. N. (1975). The effect of two training procedures on observer agreement and variability of behavior ratings. *Child Development, 46*, 520–524.

Wildman, R. W., & Wildman, R. W., II. (1977). Validity of Verbal IQ as a short form of the Wechsler Adult Intelligence Scale. *Journal of Consulting and Clinical Psychology, 45*, 171–172.

Williams, J. A. (1964). Interviewer-respondent interaction: A study of bias in the information interview. *Sociometry, 27*, 338–352.

Wills, T. A. (1978). Perceptions of clients by professional helpers. *Psychological Bulletin, 84*, 968–1000.

Zamostny, K. P., Corrigan, J. D., & Eggert, M. A. (1981). Replication and extension of social influence processes in counseling: A field study. *Journal of Counseling Psychology, 28*, 481–489.

Ziegler, M. E., & Doehrman, S. (1979). The generalizability of Verbal IQ as an estimate of Full Scale IQ on the Wechsler Adult Intelligence Scale. *Journal of Clinical Psychology, 35*, 805–807.

3

Evaluation of Intelligence, Achievement, Aptitude, and Interest

ROBERT L. HALE

INTRODUCTION

There are numerous tests and assessment methods covering the areas of ability, aptitude, achievement, and interest. The commonly accepted definitions of these terms are as follows. *Ability* is a person's current power to perform a task. *Aptitude,* on the other hand, is defined as one's potential to perform a task given maximum training and opportunity. Both of these concepts are intertwined with *achievement,* which is interpreted as the level that individuals demonstrate their current or past performance. As a concept, *interest* stands somewhat apart from the other terms. *Interest* is defined very closely to the word *like*. For example, a person may like (have an interest) in a sport but have no aptitude or ability in his or her interest. The measurements used in ability and aptitude tests have concentrated on academic or cognitive tasks, whereas interest surveys have typically concentrated on the world or work. One

Portions of this chapter from "Intellectual Assessment" by Robert L. Hale, 1983. In M. Hersen, A. E. Kazdin, & A. S. Bellack (Eds.), *The Clinical Psychology Handbook* (pp. 345–376). New York: Pergamon Press. Adapted with permission.

ROBERT L. HALE • Division of Counseling and Educational Psychology, Pennsylvania State University, University Park, Pennsylvania 16802.

can then contrast these cognitive tests with interest tests. The most highly developed measurement devices in the cognitive domain are the intelligence tests. Because the history of the testing movement, contemporary issues, and debates concerning the future of the testing movement are most dramatically illustrated in relation to the assessment of intelligence, a major portion of this chapter will be devoted to the discussion of the assessment of intelligence, its historical development, current status, and future direction. Interlaced with this primary discussion, parallel issues concerned with the assessment of achievement and interest will be discussed. Later, selected issues concerning the assessment of achievement and interest that are difficult to discuss in relation to intelligence testing will be addressed.

DISPENSING WITH THE TERM *APTITUDE*

As stated before, evaluating a person's *aptitude* involves measuring his or her *potential.* In the physical sciences, if one is measuring the potential of an object, the object is put under increasing stress until the breaking point. Measurement is a continuous process under these conditions until a failure point is reached. In the social sciences, we speak of potential, but because of ethical standards and practical considerations in testing, subjects are rarely subjected to stress to the point of breaking. Most of the aptitude tests in the social sciences cannot be differentiated from achievement tests through analysis of the items used in the test. The only reason these tests are thought of as measuring potential is that they have been shown to have predictive validity. The concept of predictive validity will be taken up later in great detail. However, the reader should be aware that the predictive validities of most tests simply allow us to predict how well persons will do on certain criterion measures if all conditions remain as they are. For example, performance on the Meier Art Judgment Test, an instrument measuring artistic aptitude, is extremely sensitive to art training. The degree to which scores differ because of previous training instead of aptitude cannot be determined from available data (Anastasi, 1982). Because of the difficulties inherent in using terms like *potential* this chapter will no longer differentiate between aptitude tests and other tests that have the ability to predict criterion scores. The saying that the best predictor of future performance is past performance in the same area is, in general, still quite true.

HISTORY

THE DEVELOPMENT OF INTELLIGENCE TESTS

European Influences. It is impossible to tease apart the history of the testing movement in the United States from the political history of the time. Like many early social issues, the roots of the testing movement in America began in Europe. The more important of those European influences were the establishment of Galton's anthropometric laboratory at the International Health Exhibition in 1884, the development of the statistical techniques of correlation by Karl Pearson and Charles Spearman, the concern with precise measurement of various types of perceptual, memory, reading, and conceptual differences in the laboratories in Germany, and the focus on higher mental functions in France. These influences culminated in the development of the Binet-Simon Scale in 1905. This intelligence test was given its impetus for construction by the Minister of Public Instruction in Paris in 1904. The minister appointed a committee, of which Binet was a member, to find a way to separate mentally retarded from normal children in the schools (Sattler, 1982). Originally, mental test results were to be used to determine how well children should achieve in school.

Early Developments in the United States. As Marks (1976–1977) clearly points out, the decision to investigate individual differences or similarities is clearly arbitrary. One has to ask, "Why did it become so important to differentiate between people?" (Marks, 1976–1977, p. 3). One answer to this question is that in the United States the assessment of mental ability provided a way of organizing a society that by all accounts was very chaotic at the beginning of the 20th century. This was the beginning of the age of social reform, and mental testing was seen as a way to organize the provision of services that would be primarily dispensed through education.

No longer was America going to tolerate the notion of robber barons building fortunes on the backs of children and immigrant labor. In 1901, Theodore Roosevelt succeeded William McKinley as president and greatly influenced the social reform movement. Roosevelt and the country took on two broad social aims. First, people were to be set free from the daily grind of work and poverty. Second, the immigrant was to be set free from the liabilities of his or her native tongue.

> Roosevelt's bravest mission was to try and see through social legislation and the new resources of education, that the immigrants should no longer be looked on as nationally identifiable pools of cheap labor. The country must

> stop talking about German-Americans and Italian-Americans and Polish-Americans: [As Roosevelt stated] "We have room but for one language here, and that is the English language, for we intend to see that the crucible turns our people out as Americans." There must be no more "hyphenated Americans." (Cooke, 1974, p. 299)

Marks (1976–1977) and Fass (1980) discuss 10 factors that were part of the American experience and directly influenced the testing movement. The 10 factors are (1) massive immigration with ethnic and racial diversity, (2) urbanization, (3) the growing influence of science, (4) the progressive educational movement, (5) World War I, (6) the supposed utility of the army tests, (7) the putative empirical relation between race and IQ, (8) stricter school attendence laws, (9) the development of child labor legislation, and (10) the belief in a competitive meritocratic society. All of these factors literally forced upon the schools a mandate to educate a population that was very heterogeneous. The impact of each of these 10 factors on the social fabric of America was enormous. Although we cannot discuss each factor in detail, as an example,

> between 1901 and 1910 alone, nearly nine million people migrated to this country—more than the combined populations of the states of New York, Maryland, and New Hampshire in 1900. (Kownslar & Frizzle, 1967, pp. 600–601)

Other evidence supporting the social reform nature of the age can be noted in the passing of the Keating–Owen child labor act in 1916 and the fact that the last state to enact laws requiring child school attendance was Mississippi in 1918. This combination of political-social attitude, child labor laws, and compulsory attendance laws assured that most youngsters would be in school. The task of turning these children into competent Americans then fell on the schools. To educate the diverse mass that characterized American society, the detection of individual differences was thought to be necessary. Because the early development of the mental test by Binet clearly stemmed from an expressed need to differentiate between those French children who could be successful in traditional educational programs in France, a ready-made instrument was available. Goddard first translated Binet's scales into English in 1910 and used the test to distinguish among the "feebleminded" children attending the Vineland Training School in New Jersey. Terman later incorporated the concept of the intelligence quotient developed by Stern in 1912 and later described in his book (Stern, 1914) into this mental test. This became the Stanford revision in 1916 and was used to identify "feebleminded" children in California.

School Organization. The primary organizational structure in the public schools has traditionally been chronological age and not mental age. The complete separation of children into "graded" classrooms, each with its own teacher was reportedly accomplished first by John Philbrick, who reorganized the Quincy, Massachusetts, grammar school in 1847 (Potter, 1967). The Ohio state commissioner of education reported that between 1854 and 1855, nearly 150 towns had converted to age-graded schools. Mental tests appeared to have potential in helping organize school systems within the age categories already adopted. With the additional structure offered by mental measures, the schools might better cope with their educational task. After all, mental tests were designed for exactly that purpose. They were used in World War I when over 1.7 million men were evaluated with the army alpha and beta tests. The publicly assumed success (see Gould, 1981) of these intelligence tests in the face of a national emergency helped contribute to their increased use in assessment areas outside of the military. The persons who worked directly on the army tests (i.e., Robert Yerkes, Lewis Terman, Edward Thorndike, Henry Goddard, and Arthur Sinton Otis, etc.) were responsible for the developments that led to the first group assessment techniques incorporated in the schools. The Otis Group Intelligence Scale and the National Intelligence Tests were introduced by the World Book Company in 1918.

Before proceeding, a review of what the measures of intellectual functioning had been able to demonstrate is in order. First, on a limited basis, the tests were successful in demonstrating that they could differentiate between children who could be successful in schoolwork and those who could not (they could predict academic success). This is not to say that they could predict standardized achievement test results. The first standardized achievement battery to evaluate the academic areas of reading, spelling, sentence meaning, and vocabulary appeared in the first volume of the *Journal of Educational Research* (Pressey, 1920). However, the Stanford-Binet had been able to differentiate between pupils judged by their teachers to be adequately and inadequately achieving (Sattler, 1974). Second, the public believed that the tests had demonstrated on a very large scale that they could differentiate leadership ability in army inductees. Third, and perhaps regretfully most important, the army report (Yerkes, 1921) brought to the public's attention the alleged differences in mental ability among blacks and whites as well as inductees from Eastern Europe. Although these racial differences were based on inadequate statistical procedures and analyses (see Gould, 1981), the racial interpretations given to the data ultimately captured the public's attention and increased their use not only as a method of organizing schools but as a method of catagorizing persons in society at large.

One of the most unfortunate linkages in the history of intellectual assessment and the testing movement is the well-documented prejudicial attitudes of Terman and Goddard. It is really unnecessary to reiterate the racial slurs in their writings. Through the influence of these men and others, the original intent of Binet (to identify and assist children who were in need of special educational services) was frequently changed to one of rank-ordering children. Children who frequently scored exceeding low on measures of intellectual development were often denied any opportunity for an educational experience. This denial of service only ended recently with the *P.A.R.C. v. Commonwealth of Pennsylvania* decision in 1972. This legal decision established the right of all children to an appropriate education. Because mentally retarded children could not be denied educational programs, the decision put an end to one of the major misuses of the IQ.

The Development of Interest Measures

Although the previous discussion has, as promised, concentrated on the cognitive measures, research on interests proceeded during the same time period. Concern was expressed in finding out the interests of both adults and older youngsters so that they could be provided service in making career choices. These efforts were capped in 1927 with the publication of the Strong Vocational Interest Blank.

Item Development

Intelligence Tests. One of the startling facts that quickly emerges when one explores the actual test questions over the history of development of intelligence tests is that the actual items have changed very little. In *The Measurement of Intelligence,* Terman (1916) lists the tests as arranged by Binet in 1911 shortly before his death. Examples include the following: (a) at age 3 a child is supposed to point to nose, eyes, and mouth; (b) at age 6, distinguish between pictures of pretty and ugly faces; (c) at age 9, answer easy comprehension questions; (d) at age 12 compose one sentence given three words; and (e) at the adult level, given differences between pairs of abstract terms. These items as well as many others listed by Terman should be quite familiar to current users of the Stanford-Binet. Likewise, the interested observer can find many similarities in the present Wechsler intelligence scales and the 1939 Wechsler Bellevue. Both authors and reviewers of the Stanford-Binet and Wechsler intelligence scales have pointed out that the test items are distinct from items typically found in academic achievement tests. For example, Sattler (1982) states, "In the last revision, the 1911 scale (Binet, 1911), further refinements were made, particularly in selecting tests that would measure intelligence rather than academic knowledge" (p. 99). However, both Wechsler and Binet employed empirical methods to find questions that differentiated between children who were successful and those who were unsuccessful in the public schools.

> Binet's tests were given to mentally retarded children at the Salpêtrière and to mentally retarded and normal children in the primary schools of Paris. (Sattler, 1982, p. 99)

Tests that differentiated between these groups of children were included in the scale. Most of the original item tryouts that were incorporated in the 1949 Wechsler Intelligence Scale for Children were tried out by Ventura Smith, a school psychologist working in the Westport, Connecticut, school systems. Again, items were chosen that differentiated between successful and unsuccessful children in academic environs.

Achievement Tests. Of course, the development of items for academic achievement tests depends upon the area of content the test is intending to measure. Arithmetic tests ask persons to solve mathematical calculations. Reading tests typically asks persons to read words, sentences, and explain to the examiner what the examinee has just read. Thus academic achievement tests depend upon supporting their item selection through reliance on content validity. Authors of achievement tests typically support the content validity of their tests by showing that their tests have been constructed using logical test construction methods and that the items in the exam adequately cover the material that is being tested.

Interest Inventories. Items for the interest inventories were developed along empirical lines similar to those used to develop intelligence tests. As noted earlier, the first formal interest inventory was the Strong Vocational Interest Blank (SVIB).

> The general approach followed in its construction was first formulated by E. K. Strong, Jr., while attending a 1919–1920 graduate seminar on interest measurement at the Carnegie Institute of Technology. The SVIB introduced two principal procedures in the measurement of occupational interests. First, the items deal with the respondent's liking or dislike for a wide variety of specific activities, objects, or types of persons that he or she commonly encountered in daily living. Second the responses were empirically keyed for different occupations. These interest inventories were thus among the first tests to employ criterion keying of items, subsequently followed in the development of such personality measures as the Minnesota Multiphasic Personality Inventory and the California Psychological Inventory. (Anastasi, 1982, p. 536)

The SVIB uses very strong criterion-related validity procedures in the item selection for the specific occupational scales. If an item were able to differentiate between two different occupations, then it was used in the occupational scale. Items thus were chosen for the different occupational scales based on empirical decisions.

USES OF INTELLIGENCE TESTS

Several uses of IQs that are currently in vogue in education will be discussed in turn. Because intelligence test items lack specific subject content, the tests themselves have been used for many purposes. Only the more important current uses will be discussed.

Measuring Intelligence. If one asks psychologists why they give intelligence tests, the first response one is likely to get is that intelligence tests are administered in order to measure the client's intelligence. Of course, this begs the question of exactly what intelligence is. The psychologist is responding that he or she is using the tests to measure the construct of *intelligence.* It follows the user should be able to adequately define the construct and support the use of the test by citing construct validity evidence.

Methods of establishing the construct validity of a test are not nearly as precisely worked out as establishing predictive validity. However, Nunnally (1978) lists the following three aspects of construct validation:

> (1) specifying the domain of observables related to the construct; (2) from empirical research and statistical analyses, determining the extent to which the observables measure the same thing, several different things, or many different things; and (3) subsequently performing studies of individual differences and/or controlled experiments to determine the extent to which supposed measures of the construct produce results which are predictable from highly accepted theoretical hypotheses concerning the construct. (p. 98)

Although it is well beyond the scope of this chapter to discuss construct validation in any detail, a brief comment concerning each of these aspects with respect to the major individual intelligence tests is in order. First, under the aspect of specifying the domain of observable behaviors related to intelligence, there is still much debate. Wechsler believed that performance items were part of adult intellectual functioning and introduced them into his scales. He continued to attempt to introduce what he termed *nonintellective* measures into his intelligence tests. He believed that other personality variables were important in the assessment of intelligence but were not evaluated by present intelligence tests (Wechsler, 1950). Logically, Wechsler would have argued that present tests do not adequately cover the domain of observables that are related to intelligence. As noted earlier, present intelligence tests, like the original versions, are narrowly composed of items that differentiate between persons adequately achieving in academic environs and persons who are failing in those same environs.

The second aspect discussed by Nunnally—seeing whether the tests measure one or many things—is often approached through both reliability and factor analytic investigations. High internal consistency reliability estimates indicate that the scales are measuring a unitary construct. The factor analytic investigations across the Stanford-Binet and the Wechslers yield strikingly similar results from investigation to investigation. The number of factors present on the Stanford-Binet depends upon the age of the subjects included in the sample. At older ages, the Binet yields a single factor that is titled Verbal Fluency. The factor structure at younger ages is considerably more complex. However, as Sattler (1982) has pointed out, a single "general" factor appears to carry most of the variance on the Stanford-Binet.

The Wechsler Intelligence Scales are primarily two factor instruments. Exploratory factor analytic studies (Blaha & Vance, 1979; Carlson & Reynolds, 1981; Kaufman, 1975; Peterson & Hart, 1979; Reschly, 1978; Schooler, Beebe, & Koepke, 1978; Silverstein, 1969; Wallbrown, Blaha, & Wherry, 1974) indicate that either a two- or three-factor solution can be found depending upon the population under investigation. The two-factor structure, of course, accounts for the most variance and is robust from study to study. Confirmatory factor analytic studies (Ramanaiah & Adams, 1979; Ramanaiah, O'Donnell, & Ribich, 1976) indicate that these intelligence tests have a structure composed of two factors. These two factors have been named Verbal Comprehension and Perceptual Organization. Although a third factor named Freedom from Distractability has been found in some exploratory studies, the factor does not appear to be stable from sample to sample. The third factor is also difficult to interpret—some authors stating that it is measuring a subject's ability to concentrate on the material presented, others arguing that it is measuring numerical fluency. Furthermore, Gutkin (1978) has shown that the reliability estimates for the factor do not meet the .90 criteria for use in individual decision making. Thus, even if it existed, the third factor would be of little use to clinicians who wished to use it for differentiating between individual subjects.

Factor analysis (see Gould, 1981) has been a primary tool used by social scientists in identifying the number of unique entities their tests measure. Spearman, an English psychologist, initially developed principal components analysis because he noted that many tests of mental ability correlated highly with one another. He wondered whether their could be some simple explanation for what these instruments were measuring. Thurstone developed factor analytic techniques where factors were rotated. Thurstone believed that his techniques would uncover the *simple structure* beneath measures of intelligence. Mathematically, factor analyses both without rotations and with rotations are equivalent. Philosophically, however, there are large differences. Depending upon which mathematical model one adopts, the results of factor analytic studies on intelligence tests typically indicate that one factor (General Intelligence) or several may account for mental abilities tests. Readers should note that the results given by factor analytic studies are quite controversial. Gould (1981) summarizes the current consensus in factor analytic inquiry quite well: "The very fact that estimates for the number of primary abilities have ranged from Thurstone's seven or so to Guilford's 120 or more indicates that vectors of the mind may be figments of the mind" (p. 309).

In summary, if one is using an intelligence test to measure the construct of intelligence, definitions of that construct should be offered. Present intelligence tests appear to measure only one or two factors adequately. These factors appear to be Verbal (Reasoning, Fluency, and/or Comprehension) and Perceptual Organization. It should be remembered that these factors may only be true in a mathematical sense and may not correspond to any psychological or physiological truth. The factors these tests measure are important, however, because of their relationship with the skills necessary for the successful performance of an individual in a modern academically oriented society.

Measuring Strengths and Weaknesses. Subtest analysis of intelligence tests has been mainly confined to the Wechsler series for the obvious reasons that the physical structure of the Wechslers simply lends itself to this type of analysis. Psychologists often reply that by analyzing the patterns, an individual shows on the Wechsler test that specific aptitudes (strengths and weaknesses) can be evaluated. If the reader simply conducts a cursory review of the research literature, the results appear to be quite controversial. However, a more intensive investigation will lead the observer to the realization that the literature is quite consistent. From a practical point of view, the literature can be broken down into two types of studies. First are those investigations that start with previously defined groups of children (e.g., reading disabled, conduct disordered, etc.) and ask if significant subtest differences can be found between these groups or between a group and the standardization sample data.

This is termed a *classical validity* study. The second set of investigations starts with the subtest results and asks if knowledge of these subtest results can aid in the prediction or differentiation of a socially significant criterion. This criterion might be a child's academic achievement or handicapping condition. These studies are termed *clinical utility* studies. Wiggins (1973) provides an in-depth discussion of the distinctions between classical validity and clinical utility. Miller (1980) contends that the inconsistency that is thought to exist in this body of research exists because, although investigators have found statistically significant Wechsler profiles to be characteristic of certain handicapped groups, there has been a failure to demonstrate that these profiles are distinctive enough to allow practitioners to differentiate between handicapped and normal children. In other words, he argues that significant patterns have been found using the classical validity research strategy, but the clinical research does not support the use of these results. Our review of the literature supports this contention. In those studies starting with intact groups (Ackerman, Peters, & Dykman, 1971; Dean, 1977; Rugel, 1974; Smith, Coleman, Dokecki, & Davis, 1977; Vance, Wallbrown, & Blaha, 1978), significant subtest differences have been found between children classified as handicapped and those classified as normal. In those investigations that started with subtest results and attempted to classify children into diagnostic categories (Hale, 1979; Hale & Landino, 1981; Hale & Raymond, 1981) or those studies where reclassification could take place (Tabachnick, 1979, Thompson, 1980) high degrees of diagnostic error were encountered. In one investigation (Hale, 1979), a 100% error rate was found when classifying reading underachievers using a significant discriminant function identified in the same group of children. In another related investigation, Hale and Landino (1981) found, using significant Wechsler Intelligence Scale for Children—Revised (WISC-R) subtest differences to reclassify behaviorally disordered and normal boys, that the results obtained were no better than chance. Other investigations have found that patterns of subtest strengths and weaknesses on the WISC-R derived by Kaufman (1975) or sophisticated profile cluster schemes (Skinner & Lei, 1980) do not aid in the prediction of a child's academic achievement level (Hale & Raymond, 1981; Hale & Saxe, 1983).

In summary, these results suggest that knowledge of a child's subtest profile does not appreciably help the clinician in predicting either academic achievement levels or behavioral difficulties. There is increasing evidence that subtest analysis of the Wechsler scales lacks utility for making special education placement decisions (Hale, 1979; Hale & Landino, 1981; Thompson, 1980; Vance, Singer, & Egin, 1980). If one uses subtest analytic procedures, they should only be used to support a hypothesis. These hypotheses should be tested with other instrumentation with adequate technical standards before the differences are thought of as being verified.

Predicting Academic Achievement. The primary usage of intelligence tests (or other instruments that use the term *aptitude*) is to predict some criterion of interest. Thus when considering intelligence tests, their major use today is the same as when Binet developed the test—to allow predictions concerning academic achievement. Under this usage, the definition of IQ might be: An IQ allows one to predict a person's academic achievement in a typical academic environment if the person is left to his or her own devices and all things remain equal. The term *typical academic environment* would exclude those academic environs where emphasis was not placed on traditional educational curricular materials. The phrase *left to his or her own devices* would exclude persons from the prediction model if they were given support services (i.e., special education). Finally, *all things remain equal* would exclude persons when traumatic events, like the death of a loved one, might be expected to affect their test scores. The assumptions included in this model include the fact that IQ is a changeable entity and that when predicting academic achievement, one is predicting a culturally bound criterion. Intelligence in any practically meaningful sense of the word can be increased by education and exposure to the mainstream culture; it is not a fixed inborn quantity. The reports by Sowell (1981), where the intelligence quotients of certain immigrant groups have risen by 24 points, and the findings that the army test scores were highly correlated with years of residence in America (Yerkes, 1921) both corroborate allegations that intellectual scores improve with exposure to the American middle-class culture. The assumptions currently made that the cultural standards for the criterion (middle-class academic achievement) are the most appropriate standards on which to measure and train individuals remains open to debate. However, the use of intelligence tests in this manner assumes that they can demonstrate adequate predictive validity.

The Primary Predictive Model. The following discussion on the predictive model in psychology includes all tests that are frequently referred to as aptitude tests (see the earlier discussion of aptitude). Each instrument alleging that it is an aptitude test needs to establish high levels of predictive validity whether the test is an individual intelligence test or a special ability test like the Seashore Measures of Musical Talents. Although the predictive model can utilize any predictor test and any criterion of interest, the following discussion will focus on intelligence measures as the predictor tests and academic achievement as the criterion of interest.

The correlation coefficient between a selected test of intelligence and a selected measure of academic achievement is a direct method of evaluating IQs in relation to the academic prediction model. If one were to attempt to predict a person's academic achievement level with absolutely no prior knowledge about the person (the descriptive statistics model), one would predict that the person would obtain mean (or average) scores on the criterion. Predictions with 68% confidence intervals would include the mean ± one standard deviation. Predictions with 95% confidence intervals would include the mean ± two standard deviations. If, on the other hand, one knows something about the person and that knowledge has some relationship to the criterion of interest, better predictions can be made. A problem will illustrate the value of predictive validity coefficients. If we were trying to predict Wide Range Achievement Scores (WRAT) or standard scores (Jastak & Jastak, 1976) for a youngster where the mean score equals 100 and the standard deviation for the test is equal to 15, then knowing nothing about the youngster and using 95% confidence intervals, one would predict that every youngster would score between 70 and 130. If through research, one found that the correlation between IQ and WRAT standard scores was equal to .60, then one's predictive ability is improved. Differential predictability is possible for individual children. First, one could construct a regression equation using the descriptive statistics from both the IQ measure and the criterion measure using the following equation:

$$Y' = \left\{ \left(r_{xy} \frac{(S_y)}{(S_x)} (X - \overline{X}) \right) + \overline{Y} \right\}$$

where Y' is the expected criterion score, r_{xy} is the correlation, S_y is the standard deviation of the criterion, S_x is the standard deviation of the predictor score (intelligence), X is the child's predictor score (IQ), and $\overline{X}$ and $\overline{Y}$ are the means of the predictor and criterion scores, respectively. If one were trying to predict the expected academic achievement score for a child with an IQ = 80, the preceding prediction (regression) equation could be used. Substituting known values into that equation, we would have the following:

$$Y' = \left\{ \left(.60 \frac{15}{15} (80 - 100) \right) + 100 \right\} = 88$$

This point estimation makes more sense than simply guessing the average score. Our child was below average on the intellectual measure;

therefore a better prediction of academic achievement would also be below average. If one wishes to place confidence intervals around predicted scores, the standard error of estimate is used instead of the standard deviation. The formula for the standard error of estimate is:

$$SE_e = S_y\sqrt{1 - r_{xy}^2}$$

Substituting our known values into this equation we have:

$$SE_e = 15\sqrt{1 - .36} = 12$$

Thus originally, for 95% confidence intervals, one added and subtracted two standard deviations from the mean—giving an interval estimation of 60 points. For the same level of confidence, we now expect the child to perform at the predicted level and add and subtract two standard errors of estimate—giving an interval estimation of 48 points. Our new predictions using the prediction model are more accurate than the predictions made under the descriptive statistics model.

In summary, one should evaluate "aptitude" tests through use of the predictive model. Of course, the higher the correlation found between the predictor and criterion variables the more accurate the predictions will be and the more valuable the instrument for predictive purposes.

Uses of Achievement Tests

Criterion- versus Norm-Referenced Tests. The major purposes that achievement tests serve are to (a) measure the amount of knowledge a person (or group) has acquired in a specified area in relation to the amount acquired by typical persons (or groups) of the subject's age; (b) to measure whether a person (or group) knows or does not know specific information in relation to a well-defined achievement objective. These two purposes are characterized by the two major types of achievement tests—norm referenced and criterion referenced. The current state of affairs within achievement testing is summarized quite well by Hambleton (1982):

> The 10-year battle for supremacy in the testing world is nearly over. There is no winner and two facts are clear: (1) both criterion-referenced tests and norm-referenced tests have important roles to play in providing data for decision-making; (2) what differences exist are significant but the two kinds of tests have much in common. On the latter point, it would be a rare individual indeed who could sort tests from a review of the test items only. (p. 354)

Although a full chapter might be written on the differences and concerns engendered in discussions regarding criterion- and norm-referenced testing, several major points of difference and statistical techniques should be highlighted. As Hambleton (1982) clearly points out, norm-referenced tests are developed in a manner where substantial test score variability is assured. A heterogeneous distribution of test scores is necessary if comparisons between individuals or groups are going to be meaningful. Criterion-referenced test developers use item statistics like difficulty and discrimination indexes mainly to detect flawed items that need to be corrected. Norm-referenced tests take as their anchor point the average score. Criterion-referenced tests use the 0% and 100% correct points as anchors. For mastery or nonmastery decisions using criterion-referenced tests, some other percentage correct number is typically chosen (i.e., 80%). Because of these differences and the different purposes to which norm- and criterion-referenced tests are put, different statistical methods are needed to assess the adequacy of the tests.

Criterion Test Statistics. It is assumed that the reader is familiar with the technical standards used to evaluate the adequacy of norm-referenced tests. The literature in this area is plentiful. However, methods of evaluating the worth of criterion-referenced tests are of recent origin. Hambleton (1982) presents a detailed account of different methods that may be used to evaluate the adequacy of criterion-referenced tests. Only two of the methods he describes will be discussed. The interested reader is referred to his work. Two decisions that can be made using criterion-referenced tests can be evaluated mathematically.

Criterion-referenced tests are typically scored in such a manner that the proportion-correct scores are reported. For example, if the domain of interest was two-digit addition and 10 items were included in this domain, and a subject correctly answered 5 of the items, the reported score would be 0.50. Knowing that all tests include error, one might wish to estimate the proportion of items in the item domain that the subject could answer correctly. Confidence intervals can be set up around this observed score by calculating a standard error of estimation derived from the binominal test model. The formula is:

$$\text{standard error of estimate} = \sqrt{\hat{\pi}\,(1 - \hat{\pi})/n}$$

where n = number of items measuring an objective and $\hat{\pi}$ is the proportion-correct score. If 10 items were used in the test to measure the domain and the subject obtained a proportion-correct score of 0.50, then the standard error of estimate would equal 0.1581. Therefore, there would be approximately a 95% chance that the subject's domain score would be between 0.50 ± 2(0.1581) or 0.1838 to 0.8162.

A second score often reported for examinees on criterion-referenced instrumentation is whether or not they have mastered the information. Mastery or nonmastery scores are reported, given that the subject score has exceeded some arbitrary cutoff. One needs a measure of the decision consistency using mastery/nonmastery scores. If two test administrations are given, kappa (k) (Cohen, 1960) can be used. This statistic has an added advantage that the decision consistency is corrected for the agreement due to chance alone. The formula for k is:

$$k = (p_o - p_c)/(1 - p_c)$$

Where p_o is the sum of the proportion of identical decisions made on the two administrations of the test and p_c is the expected value for correct decision making, p_c is typically determined by multiplying the marginals to find the expected values just like when working chi-square problems. For example, if the examiner received the following from two administrations of the exam:

Administration 1	*Administration 2*		*Marginal*
	Nonmaster	Master	
Nonmaster	.30	.10	.40
Master	.20	.40	.60
Marginal	.50	.50	

p_o would equal .30 + .40 = .70, the proportion of subjects correctly placed back in their original cells. p_c would equal (.40 × .50) + (.60 × .50) = .50. Kappa would then equal (.7 − .5)/(1 − .5) = .4. The k coefficient can be thought of as a measure of decision accuracy over and above that provided by chance. For determining whether this decision accuracy is statistically significant, the interested reader is referred to Cohen (1960, 1968) and Fleiss, Cohen, and Everitt (1969).

Another practical consideration in criterion-referenced testing that can be dealt with mathematically is the issue of test length. As Hambleton (1982) has pointed out, when the primary use of the test scores is descriptive, the formula for the standard error of estimate can be solved for n. By specifying the typical value for $\hat{\pi}$ in a group of subjects and the standard error of estimate, the approximate test length can be estimated. Hambleton states that when in doubt, a typical value of $\hat{\pi}$ can be set at 0.50. This will give the user a conservative test length (usually longer than needed). The following formula would be used for these calculations:

$$n = \frac{\hat{\pi}\,(1 - \hat{\pi})}{(\text{standard error of estimate})^2}$$

where n = number of items measuring an objective and $\hat{\pi}$ is the proportion-correct score.

For example, if we use 0.50 as our typical proportion-correct estimate and wish to create a test with a standard error of estimate of .2, then the n needed for our objective will be (0.50)(1 − 0.5)/.04 = 6.25. Seven items will need to be developed for our criterion-referenced test to measure this domain with the desired precision.

MEASURING INTERESTS

The development of interest inventories has had its imputus through career and educational counseling and occupational classification. Generally, it is thought that performance is determined through the interaction of a person's ability and interest. Without a certain level of ability, even an individual with high interest will be unable to perform adequately. Given ability, but little interest, the performance levels of the person will again be low. However, in combination, ability and interest interact to produce higher performance than either one in isolation. This interactive effect is so strong that several scholars have proposed that the task of predicting occupational classification or work and educational success can only be adequately approximated if both interest and ability measures are combined (Anastasi, 1982; Lohnes 1978). This predictive model could be mathematically evaluated through the statistical techniques of multiple regression or discriminant analysis.

Two theoretical models currently are in vogue within interest inventory research. First, Holland (1973) has developed what he calls a hexagonal model of general occupational themes. This model proposes that six themes can account for general occupational choices in persons. These broad themes are (1) realistic, (2) investigative, (3) artistic, (4) social, (5) enterprising, and (6) conventional. The Strong-Campbell Interest Inventory is built around the Holland hexagon.

The second model is derived from the work conducted on the Project TALENT data. Project TALENT was created when, in 1959, the U.S. Office of Education agreed to support a massive census of the abilities and personality characteristics of American high-school youth. The primary purpose of this study was to survey the talents of youth in order to estimate the numbers of persons qualified for training in science, engineering, and other professional fields. Over 440,000 youths in over 1,300 high schools were evaluated in the project. According to Paul Lohnes (1978) empirical evidence suggests that four areas of interest describe the Project TALENT interest data. These areas are (1) technical-manual, (2) social-cultural, (3) business, and (4) science.

It is currently left up to the individual counselor or psychologist to determine which of the many interest inventories will best serve the purpose of the assessment. This decision should, of course, be made on the technical merits of the instrument, whether the occupational interests surveyed are appropriate for the client and whether the interest inventory is age appropriate. If the counselor uses the ability and interest data in a model that combines them, it would be expected that better decisions or suggestions could be made concerning the client. However, if clients express a vocational interest, the benefits accrued from administering an interest inventory are minimal. Lohnes (1978) in a review of the Career Assessment Inventory, succinctly summarized the benefit of mass administrations of interest inventories.

> Research continues to show that an expressed vocational goal, when the goal is firmly expressed, remains the best predictor of the field in which vocational placement is eventually achieved. . . . One of the silliest things that can happen in a school guidance program is the mass administration of an interest inventory. (p. 993)

CURRENT ISSUES IN ASSESSMENT

INTELLIGENCE TESTS

The major issues concerning intelligence scales described by Hale (1983) include (a) the heritability of IQs, (2) bias in intelligence testing, (c) stability of IQs, and (d) the equivalence of scores across different intelligence tests. Each of these issues will be briefly discussed.

Heritability of IQs. A measure of the heritability of a trait is given by the correlation between the genetic constitutions of a group of individuals and the trait in which one is interested. Heritability estimates for intelligence are given by correlating IQs with different degrees of kinship within groups of people, such as monozygotic or dizygotic twins. Sattler (1982) reports that "studies of European and North American Caucasian populations suggest that the heritability of intelligence varies from .40 to .80" (p. 49). The coefficient of determination (r_{xy}^2) would therefore indicate that somewhere between 16% and 64% of the variance in IQ is accounted for by genetics. This range of numbers in and of itself does not conflict with statements that the environment is important in the expression of intelligence or that supplementary environmental or educational programs can increase intelligence. As noted earlier, academic or social success is more often the real criterion of interest for psychologists using intelligence tests. Noting that correlations between IQ and achievement are around .60, even if intelligence scores were 100% determined by genetics, it would not necessarily follow that achievement would also be perfectly determined. Much of the confusion begins when the words *inherited* and *inevitable* are thought of as being synonymous. For example, diabetes mellitus is inherited, but certainly its debilitating effects are mitigated by the environmental manipulation of insulin.

Gould (1981) and MacKenzie (1980) both point out a serious flaw in our statistical thinking about heritability. Both authors note that studies of heritability of IQ are of the "within-group" type. That is, the investigations permit an estimate of heritability *within* a single, coherent population (white Americans, for example). The extension of this percentage figure derived from the *within-group* study to explain differences *between* groups is simply unfounded. Gould (1981) gives the following example.

> Human height has a higher heritability than any value ever proposed for IQ. Take two separate groups of males. The first, with an average height of 5 feet 10 inches, live in a prosperous American town. The second, with an average height of 5 feet 6 inches, are starving in a third-world village. Heritability is 95 percent or so in each place—meaning that relatively tall fathers tend to have tall sons and relatively short fathers short sons. This high within-group heritability argues neither for nor against the possibility that better nutrition in the next generation might raise the average height of third-world villagers above that of prosperous Americans. Likewise, IQ could be highly heritable within groups, and the average difference between whites and blacks in America might still only record the environmental disadvantages of blacks. (pp. 156–157)

If we take a practitioner's point of view, the exact heritability index is not of great importance. Even extremely high heritability of IQ should not prevent the provision of environmental and educational support to those persons whose functioning may be enhanced by those social support services.

Bias in Intellectual Assessment. The detection of bias in assessment devices is a complex issue. Because tests are employed for different purposes they have different types of validity. Therefore, a test can never be said to be valid—only valid for the purpose that it is being used. Neither can a test be said to be biased, only biased for a purpose that it is being used. Both Jensen (1980) and Reynolds (1982) present methods of bias investigation in detail. However, their consideration of bias focuses on its relation to content, construct, and content validity. Their excellent literature reviews indicate that empirical data support the position that intelligence and achievement measures are *not* biased against minority members using technical definitions of bias. These authors do not focus attention on definitions of bias using the same constructs that lay persons assume. Although, in my opinion, those assumptions are in error, it is necessary to focus on them, as these misassumptions lie at the heart of the argument. The major misassumption of the lay person is that the IQ is a measure of potential; this issue was discussed earlier. The second major misassumption is that IQs are immutable. Nonprofessionals believe that IQs are quite stable.

STABILITY OF IQs

IQs and other measures of "aptitude" are not immutable measures of individuals. Just how much they may be expected to change is a complex interaction between many factors such as (a) the person's familiarization with mainstream cultural standards, (b) the age at which the initial test was administered, (c) the time interval between testing, (d) intervening environmental changes such as special education, (e) whether the person is handicapped and others. In general, however, the following rules of thumb may be advanced. First, if a person is not familiar with the culture, his or her IQ would be expected to change with increasing familiarization. No current intelligence test is "culture free." The data provided by Thomas Sowell (1981) supports this contention. Jews, who initially scored low as a group on intelligence tests and who have faced centuries of anti-Semitism, presently have the highest family incomes in the United States,and their IQs rose above the national average by the 1920s. And according to Sowell,

> Polish IQs which averaged eight-five in earlier studies—the same as that of blacks today—had risen to 109 by the 1970s. This twenty-four point rise is greater than the current black–white difference (fifteen points). (1981, p. 9)

Thus, the current black–white differences noted on IQs could be accounted for by cultural unfamiliarity and the former academic mistreatment of blacks. Second, infant intelligence tests measure perceptual skills to a greater degree than intelligence tests given to older children and adults. Because more growth may be evidenced by younger children and the material being measured by intelligence tests actually changes over certain ages, IQs are more stable if the scores are obtained after 5 years of age (Sattler, 1982). Third, the longer the time interval between testing, the less stable the measurements tend to be. Fourth, environmental changes, such as special education, may be expected to change IQs (Morris & Clarizio, 1977). Fifth, retarded children tend to have more stable IQs than children with higher IQs. In summary, it should be stressed that intelligence tests are measures of *current* levels of functioning and may be expected to change over the life on an individual. As an example of the changes that may be typical, a longitudinal study by Hindley and Owen (1978) indicated that 50% of the British children between 6 months and 17 years of age had IQ changes of 10 points or more.

Equivalence of Scores across Different Intelligence Tests. Another misconception concerning intelligence tests is that they all measure the same thing and their scores are equivalent. Definitions of handicapping conditions, like mental retardation, often require the measurement of intelligence (frequently the reporting of the IQ is required). Although state departments of education may formally circulate lists of approved tests (Lambert, 1981), for the most part, psychologists are free to choose among the tests available in order to measure intelligence. This freedom is necessary for professional flexibility, but the examiner should be aware that not all IQs are equal. As Sattler (1982) reports:

> An evaluation of the IQs provided by the WISC-R and other tests indicates that for group purposes, IQs on the Stanford-Binet and WISC-R are generally similar. The Slosson Intelligence Test, on the average, yields IQs that are about 5 points higher than those of the WISC-R. The McCarthy Scales of Children's Abilities, on the average, yields GCI's (General Cognitive Indexes) that are lower by about 6 points. (p. 149)

Interest Inventories and Sexual Fairness. One of the technical difficulties with interest inventories (largely eliminated after 1974) was their inherent sexism. Items on the Strong Vocational Interest Blank were grouped into separate forms for men and women. In the 1970s, David Campbell, who was in charge of the research on this instrument, conducted the revision producing the Strong-Campbell Interest Inventory that combined the earlier forms, eliminated the sex-oriented items, and eliminated the Masculinity–Femininity scale. Concern about sexual biases inherent in interest inventories was so pronounced that The National Institute Of Education funded a project that was published under the title *Sex-Fair Interest Measurement: Research and Implications,* which was edited by Tittle and Zytowski (1978). This report, among other things, presents guidelines for the assessment of sexual fairness in interest inventories. As Anastasi (1982) points out, there are still difficulties with sexual fairness in the interest inventories because of the

> large discrepancies in the proportion of men and women in some occupations, such as engineering or nursing, these differences would tend, in one

way or another, to influence the interpretation of results obtained by males and females on interest inventories. (p. 536)

FUTURE DIRECTIONS

Much of *Intelligence* (1979, Vol. 3) was devoted to predictions about the form and purposes of intelligence tests in the year 2000. Horn (1979) and Resnick (1979) suggest that realistically, tests very similar to the present ones will be needed. Brown and French (1979) stress that the tests' major function will continue to be prediction. Thus these cognitive tests will continue to serve as our primary "aptitude" instruments. The near future assures that the traditional tests will be present. The Stanford-Binet is currently being revised, and the Wechsler Adult Intelligence Scale was revised in 1981.

INCORPORATING NEUROPSYCHOLOGY

There is increasing awareness among evaluation specialists that the measurement of neuropsychological functioning may lead to better understanding and prediction of academic- and job-related skills and deficits (Gaddes, 1975; Hynd & Obrzut, 1981; Rourke, 1975). Several instruments have now been developed and standardized that show promise in their ability to measure ability in areas other than the traditional verbal and performance areas of intelligence tests (i.e., Kaufman Assessment Battery [Kaufman & Kaufman, 1983]; Luria-Nebraska Neuropsychological Battery [Golden, Hammeke, & Purisch, 1980]). The evidence supporting these new instruments and their linkage to academic remediation programs is currently quite weak, however (Bracken, 1985). One only needs to be reminded of other promising ability measurement–treatment programs that when finally evaluated have simply had no value. Included in those failed efforts are neurological organization programs (Ayres, 1972; Delacato, 1966), perceptual training programs (Frostig, 1967; Getman, 1965), perceptual-motor training programs (Barsch, 1967; Kephart, 1971), and psycholinguistic training programs (Kirk & Kirk, 1971). Caution should certainly be exercised in jumping on the bandwagon of current neuropsychological assessment strategies.

COMPUTER TECHNOLOGY

In my opinion, the largest future influence on assessment will take place because of new computer technology. In the area of assessment, new measurement technologies are being developed, and with the computing power available, new strategies for combining the results of different instrumentation to make psychological decisions are emerging (McDermott, 1984). Many microcomputer applications have been directed toward handicapped persons. Job opportunities that were closed to people with certain handicapping conditions are now open with assistance from computers. For example, with voice-assisted word processors, the blind can efficiently perform many office duties including the typing of manuscripts. Even the complicated act of walking is being performed by persons with spinal cord injuries that would have previously only allowed them locomotion in wheelchairs. With inhanced and new abilities supported by computer technology, interests and therefore interest inventories will need to be revised along with ability and achievement tests.

SUMMARY

This chapter has shown that historically, cognitive "aptitude" measures developed out of a concern for identifying children who were unable to learn in school. In the United States, because of the sociopolitical climate in the early twentieth century, intelligence tests were not only used to differentiate between children experiencing academic problems but as a yardstick with which to organize an entire society. The development of achievement and interest surveys was accomplished during the same time period but with far less fanfare. One of the startling facts pointed out is that the items have actually changed very little since the early 1900s.

The major uses of intelligence, achievement, and interest tests have been outlined. Particular emphasis was placed on the assessment of an intelligence score to predict other criteria of interest. Some of the newer methods of evaluating criterion-referenced tests were introduced along with a discussion of two prominent theories of interest measurement.

The prominent current interests surrounding these constructs included bias in intellectual assessment, the stability of IQs, equivalence of scores from different intelligence tests, and the sexual fairness of interest inventories. In general, the aptitude measures were not found to be biased. However, scores from cognitive measures were not necessarily as stable as laypersons believe, and scores from different cognitive measures are certainly not equivalent. Finally, it was pointed out that the current interest inventories were probably not sexually fair even though an effort has been made by persons responsible for the construction of the inventories.

The future directions for the measurement in these areas will probably be influenced by new advances both in neuropsychology and computer technology. The latter influence is perceived by the author to have the most potential for causing change in our measurement techniques. With the impact of computer technology on handicapped populations and the job market in general, persons' interests will certainly change. These changes will necessitate changes both in aptitude and interest measurement devices.

REFERENCES

Ackerman, P. T., Peters, J. E., & Dykman, R. A. (1971). Children with specific learning disabilities; WISC profiles. *Journal of Learning Disabilities, 4,* 33–49.

Anastasi, A. (1982). *Psychological testing* (5th ed.). New York: Macmillan.

Ayres, A. (1972). Improving academic scores through sensory integration. *Journal of Learning Disabilities, 6,* 338–343.

Barsch, R. (1967). *Achieving perceptual motor efficiency* (Vol. 1). Seattle: Special Child Publications.

Binet, A. (1911). Nouvelles recherches sur la mésure du nieveau intéllectuel chez les enfants d'école. *L'Annèe Psychologigue, 17,* 145–210.

Blaha, J., & Vance, H. B. (1979). The hierarchical factor structure of the WISC-R for learning disabled children. *Learning Disability Quarterly, 2,* 71–75.

Bracken, B. A. (1985). A critical review of the Kaufman Assessment Battery for Children (K-ABC). *School Psychology Review, 14,* 21–36.

Brown, A. L., & French, L. (1979). The zone of potential development: Implications for intelligence testing in the year 2000. *Intelligence, 3,* 255–273.

Carlson, L., & Reynolds, C. R. (1981). Factor structure and specific variance of the WPPSI subtests at six age levels. *Psychology in the Schools, 18,* 48–54.

Cohen, J. (1960). A coefficient of agreement for nominal scales. *Educational and Psychological Measurement, 20,* 37–46.

Cohen, J. (1968). Weighted kappa: Nominal scale agreement with provision for scaled disagreement of partial credit. *Psychological Bulletin, 70,* 213–220.

Cooke, A. (1974). *Alistair Cooke's America.* New York: Knopf.

Dean, R. S. (1977). Patterns of emotional disturbance on the WISC-R. *Journal of Clinical Psychology, 33,* 486–490.

Delacato, C. (1966). *Neurological organization and reading.* Springfield, IL: Charles C. Thomas.

Fass, P. S. (1980). The IQ: A cultural and historical framework. *American Journal of Education, 88,* 431–458.

Fleiss, J. L., Cohen, J., & Everitt, B. S. (1969). Large sample standard errors of kappa and weighted kappa. *Psychological Bulletin, 72,* 323–327.

Frostig, M. (1967). Testing as a basis for educational therapy. *Journal of Special Education, 2,* 15–34.

Gaddes, W. H. (1975). Neurological implications for learning. In W. M. Cruikshank & D. P. Hallahan (Eds.), *Perceptual and learning disabilities in children: Vol. 1. Psychological practices* (pp. 148–194). Syracuse, NY: University Press.

Golden, C. J., Hammeke, T. A., & Purisch, A. D. (1980). *The Luria-Nebraska Neuropsychological Battery.* Los Angeles: Western Psychological Services.

Gould, S. J. (1981). *The mismeasure of man*. New York: Norton.

Gutkin, T. B. (1978). Some useful statistics for the interpretation of the WISC-R. *Journal of Consulting and Clinical Psychology, 46*, 1561–1563.

Hale, R. L. (1979). The utility of WISC-R subtest scores in discriminating among adequate and underachieving children. *Multivariate Behavioral Research, 14*, 245–253.

Hale, R. L., & Landino, S. A. (1981). The utility of WISC-R subtest analysis in discriminating among groups of conduct problem, withdrawn, mixed and nonproblem boys. *Journal of Consulting and Clinical Psychology, 49*, 91–95.

Hale, R. L., & Raymond, M. R. (1981). Wechsler Intelligence Scale for Children—Revised (WISC-R) patterns of strengths and weaknesses as predictors of the intelligence-achievement relationship. *Diagnostiqué, 6*, 35–42.

Hale, R. L., & Saxe, J. E. (1983). Profile analysis of the Wechsler Intelligence Scale for Children—Revised. *Journal of Psychoeducational Assessment, 1*, 155–161.

Hambleton, R. K. (1982). Advances in criterion-referenced testing technology. In C. R. Reynolds & T. B. Gutkin (Eds.), *The handbook of school psychology* (pp. 351–379). New York: Wiley.

Hindley, C. B., & Owen, C. F. (1978). The extent of individual changes in IQ for ages between 6 months and 17 years in a British longitudinal sample. *Journal of Child Psychology and Psychiatry and Allied Disciplines, 19*, 329–350.

Holland, J. L. (1973). *Making vocational choices: A theory of careers*. Englewood Cliffs, NJ: Prentice-Hall.

Horn, J. L. (1979). Trends in the measurement of intelligence. *Intelligence, 3*, 229–239.

Hynd, G. W., & Obrzut, J. E. (1981). School neuropsychology. *Journal of School Psychology, 19*, 45–49.

Jastak, J. F., & Jastak, S. R. (1976). *Manual, the Wide Range Achievement Test* (rev. ed.). Wilmington: Guidance Associates of Delaware.

Jensen, A. R. (1980). *Bias in mental testing*. New York: Free Press.

Kaufman, A. S. (1975). Factor structure of the WISC-R at 11 age levels between 6½ and 16½ years. *Journal of Consulting and Clinical Psychology, 43*, 133–147.

Kaufman, A., & Kaufman, N. (1983). *Kaufman assessment battery for children, interpretative manual*. Circle Pines, MN: American Guidance Service.

Kirk, S., & Kirk, W. (1971). *Psycholinguistic learning disabilities: Diagnosis and remediation*. Urbana: University of Illinois Press.

Kownslar, A. O., & Frizzle, D. B. (1967). *Discovering American history*. New York: Holt, Rinehart & Winston.

Lambert, N. M. (1981). Psychological evidence in Larry P. versus Wilson Riles. *American Psychologist, 36*, 937–952.

Lohnes, P. R. (1978). Review of the Career Assessment Inventory. In O. K. Buros (Ed.), *The eighth mental measurements yearbook* (pp. 1549–1550). Highland Park, NJ: Gryphon.

MacKenzie, B. (1980). Hypothesized genetic racial differences in IQ; A criticism of three lines of evidence. *Behavior Genetics, 10*, 225–234.

Marks, R. (1976–1977). Providing for individual differences: A history of the intelligence testing movement in North America. *Interchange, 1*, 3–16.

Miller, M. M. (1980). On the attempt to find WISC-R profiles for learning and reading disabilities (A response to Vance, Wallbrown, and Blaha). *Journal of Learning Disabilities, 13*, 338–340.

Morris, J. J., & Clarizio, S. (1977). Improvement in IQ of high risk, disadvantaged preschool children enrolled in a developmental program. *Psychological Reports, 41*, 1111–1114.

Nunnally, J. C. (1978). *Psychometric theory* (2nd ed.). New York: McGraw-Hill.

Peterson, C. R., & Hart, D. H. (1979). Factor structure of the WISC-R for a clinic referred population and specific subgroups. *Journal of Consulting and Clinical Psychology, 47,* 643–645.

Potter, R. E. (1967). *The stream of American education.* New York: Van Nostrand Reinhold.

Pressey, S. L. (1920). Scale of attainment No. 1: An examination of achievement in the second grade. *Journal of Educational Research, 1,* 572–581.

Ramanaiah, N. V., & Adams, M. L. (1979). Confirmatory analysis of the WAIS and the WPPSI. *Psychological Reports, 45,* 351–355.

Ramanaiah, N. V., O'Donnell, J., & Ribich, F. (1976). Multiple group factor analysis of the Wechsler Intelligence Scale for Children. *Journal of Clinical Psychology, 32,* 329–830.

Reschly, D. J. (1978). WISC-R factor structures among Anglos, blacks, Chicanos, and Native-American Papagos. *Journal of Consulting and Clinical Psychology, 46,* 417–422.

Resnick, L. B. (1979). The future of IQ testing in education. *Intelligence, 3,* 241–253.

Reynolds, C. R. (1982). The problem of bias in psychological assessment. In C. R. Reynolds & T. B. Gutkin (Eds.), *A handbook for school psychology* (pp. 178–208). New York: Wiley.

Rourke, B. P. (1975). Brain-behavior relationships in children with learning disabilities: A research program. *American Psychologist, 30,* 911–920.

Rugel, R. P. (1974). WISC subtest scores of disabled readers: A review with respect to Bannatyne's recategorization. *Journal of Learning Disabilities, 7,* 57–63.

Sattler, J. M. (1974). *Assessment of children's intelligence* (rev. reprint). Philadelphia: W. B. Saunders.

Sattler, J. M. (1982). *Assessment of children's intelligence and special abilities.* Boston: Allyn & Bacon.

Schooler, D. L., Beebe, M. C., & Koepke, T. (1978). Factor analysis of WISC-R scores for children identified as learning disabled, educable mentally impaired, and emotionally impaired. *Psychology in the Schools, 15,* 478–485.

Silverstein, A. B. (1969). An alternative factor analytic solution for Wechsler's intelligence scales. *Educational and Psychological Measurement, 29,* 763–767.

Skinner, H. A., & Lei, H. (1980). Modal profile analysis: A computer program for classification research. *Educational and Psychological Measurement, 40,* 769–772.

Smith, M. D., Coleman, J. M., Dokecki, P. R., & Davis, E. E. (1977). Recategorized WISC-R scores of learning disabled children. *Journal of Learning Disabilities, 10,* 437–443.

Sowell, T. (1981). *Ethnic America.* New York: Basic Books.

Stern, W. (1914). *The psychological methods of testing intelligence.* Baltimore: Warwick & York.

Tabachnick, B. G. (1979). Test scatter on the WISC-R. *Journal of Learning Disabilities, 12,* 626–628.

Terman, L. M. (1916). *The measurement of intelligence.* Boston: Houghton-Mifflin.

Thompson, R. J., Jr. (1980). The diagnostic utility of the WISC-R measures with children referred to a developmental evaluation center. *Journal of Consulting and Clinical Psychology, 48,* 440–447.

Tittle, C. K., & Zytowski, D. G. (Eds.). (1978). *Sex-fair interest measurement: Research and implications.* Washington, DC: National Institute of Education.

Vance, H. B., Wallbrown, F. H., & Blaha, J. (1978). Determining WISC-R profiles for reading disabled children. *Journal of Learning Disabilities, 11,* 656–661.

Vance, H. B., Singer, M. C., & Engin, A. W. (1980). WISC-R subtest differences for males and female LD children and youth. *Journal of Clinical Psychology, 36,* 953–957.

Wallbrown, F. H., Blaha, J., & Wherry, R. J. (1974). The hierarchical factor structure of the Wechsler Adult Intelligence Scale. *British Journal of Educational Psychology, 44,* 47–56.

Wechsler, D. (1950). Cognitive, conative, and non-intellective intelligence. *American Psychologist, 30,* 78–83.

Wiggins, J. S. (1973). *Personality and prediction: Principles of personality assessment*. Menlo Park, CA: Addison-Wesley.

Yerkes, R. M. (Ed.). (1921). Psychological examining in the United States Army. In R. M. Yerkes (Ed.), *Memoirs of the National Academy of Sciences* (Vol. 15). Washington, DC: U.S. Government Printing Office.

4

Neuropsychological Assessment

BARBARA C. WILSON

INTRODUCTION

This chapter provides a summary of major landmarks in the development of neuropsychology, and a discussion of contemporary issues and future directions as they apply to the neuropsychological assessment of the developmentally and physically disabled.

Neuropsychological assessment can play an important role in the evaluation of a patient with known or suspected central nervous system dysfunction. An appropriate neuropsychological evaluation is able to provide information as to the integrity of the central nervous system with respect to level of cognitive function, language, memory, sensory, and perceptual functions in the various modalities, aspects of motor function, and affect. It can provide data that will enable the delineation of patterns of cognitive function and dysfunction, and thus it can be useful in the development of data-based recommendations for intervention. As an area of research, neuropsychology focuses on the clarification of the relationships between brain function and behavior. The significant degree of interaction between these two broad dimensions, application and research, is a reflection of the clinician–researcher model, still very much in evidence in neuropsychology. The roots of this current-day practice lie in the history and development of the field in which the practicing clinician, usually the neurologist, made observations of patients'

BARBARA C. WILSON • North Shore University Hospital, Cornell University Medical College, Division of Neuropsychology, Department of Neurology, 300 Community Drive, Manhasset, New York 11005.

behavior following insult to the central nervous system and then asked questions about what he or she had seen. Interest in brain function predates contemporary medicine, and a brief review of the historical antecedents seems in order.

HISTORY AND DEVELOPMENT

The first known reference to the brain, in fact the first known written representation of the word, and the first references to localization of function are to be found in the *Edwin Smith Surgical Papyrus*, thought to date between 2500 and 3000 B.C. Translation and commentaries provide us with descriptions of the posttraumatic behavior and modes of treatment, and they constitute the first treatise on cortical localization of function (Breasted, 1930). The Hippocratic writings of the fourth and fifth centuries B.C. are thought to be the work of a group of physicians who, in addition to writing about other aspects of medicine, provided early insights into brain–behavior relationships. Hippocrates was clearly aware of the contralateral control of some behavioral functions and "warned against prodding blindly at a wound of the temporal area of the skull lest paralysis of the contralateral side should ensure" (Gibson, 1962). *On the Sacred Disease*, a Hippocratic discussion of epileptic patients, provides important and, according to McHenry (1969), the soundest of antiquity's discussions of the brain. Much of what followed in studies of brain–behavior relationships was concerned with issues of localization of function. The ideas of Aristotle and Galen contributed to early theoretical formulations of brain function; the ventricular or cell doctrine, the prevailing theory for a long time, held that the loci of mental processes were the ventricles of the brain. Galen, the "prince of practitioners," integrated his thinking with what was known of the anatomy of the brain at that time and developed the concept of "psychic pneuma." Although he was, himself, an observer who produced careful behavioral descriptions and who saw the need for continued study of the anatomy of the brain, his formulations became doctrine and held sway for centuries.

It was not until the sixteenth century with Vesalius, an amiable critic of Galen's, that the scientific method was brought to bear on research in the area. His contribution, beyond those he made to structural neuroanatomy, lay in his use of the observational method and his willingness to subject cherished dogmas to the test of direct observation.

Over the next decades, knowledge of the anatomy of the brain increased at an accelerated rate, and although the tradition of direct observation continued, speculation about brain function rather than research in the area prevailed. For the next century and a half, notions about the seat of the mind or soul and of the location in the brain of *the* cerebral organ were of paramount concern. These notions were not based on data but on "reasoning." The most influential of these formulations was presented by the philosopher Descartes, who located the seat of the soul in the pineal gland. This line of conjecture ultimately gave way, and the belief that there was a single seat of mental activity was abandoned.

In the late 1700s, there was an onrush of research that was generated as a result of the interaction between "faculty psychology" and the search for the neural substrates that subserved the ever-increasing list of mental faculties. As in earlier days, localization of function was again the prominent line of theorizing and of research. The foremost proponent of the mental faculties position was Gall, who postulated that each of the separate innate mental faculties was subserved by a distinct cerebral organ, all of which were to be found in the cerebral cortex. Spurzheim, who joined Gall in Vienna at the end of the eighteenth century, coined the term *phrenology* and added a dimension to the work of Gall that was as without foundation as were Gall's original formulations. Spurzheim developed a phrenological map that identified the mental faculties in relation to specific areas that were represented on the surface of the cranium (Miller & Buckout, 1973). Spurzheim took the position that an experienced phrenologist could determine the nature of an individual by palpating the prominences on his or her cranium, produced as a result of the development of the cerebral organs. The ideas of Gall and Spurzheim were influential for a long time, and although their work was largely without scientific foundation, it provided the stimulus for much productive research.

Flourens, working in the same period as Gall and Spurzheim, refuted the localization position and argued for a more holistic view of brain function (1842). He is the spiritual godfather of Pierre Marie (1906), Ivory Shepard Franz (1902, 1912), and Karl Lashley (1929, 1938) and of the contemporary if not currently held theories of mass action and equipotentiality of the brain. Lashley's theoretical contributions stimulated an intense period of research activity. Although the interpretations of some of his findings have not been lasting, his experimental rigor and use of statistical methods in the analysis of data ushered neuropsychology into the realm of science.

Modern neurology and the beginnings of neuropsychology can be dated from the lesion studies of the nineteenth century. Bouillaud, in 1825, and Dax, in a paper presented in 1836 and published in 1865, noted the association between the loss of vocal language and lesions of the anterior or frontal lobes. Broca, in 1861, indicated the probability of frontal lobe involvement in expressive language, but it was not until 1885 that he believed he had sufficient data to state that "*Nous parlons avec l'hemisphere gauche*" (see Benton, 1965, and Joynt, 1964, for further discussion). Wernicke's contributions during this period were of great importance, not only for his identification of receptive aphasia but because he "was one of the first to see clearly the importance of the connections between different parts of the brain in the building up of complex activities," (Geschwind, 1965a, p. 144). (See Benton, 1965, 1976; Boring, 1950; Clarke & Dewhurst, 1972; Clarke & O'Malley, 1968; Geschwind, 1965b, c; Gibson, 1962, 1969; Magoun, 1958; and Walsh, 1978, for more extended discussions.) Later developments were again related to current thinking in psychology; in this instance, the associationist postulates in psychology and the globalist position were utilized by those studying the function of the nervous system, as exemplified by the work of Pavlov (1949). He conceptualized the central nervous system as a network of analyzers in reciprocal interaction and was directly concerned with the relationship between observed behavior and the interaction between neural systems.

Since World War II there has been a tremendous increase in knowledge and sophistication in all of the neural sciences; new technology and techniques have emerged that have permitted heretofore impossible studies of the structure and function of the nervous system. In this period, the methods of experimental psychology were brought to bear on the study of brain–behavior relationships. Teuber (1959), a student of Lashley's, encouraged psychologists to study brain–behavior relationships and was instrumental, along with Benton (1965; Benton, deS. Hamsher, Varney, & Spreen, 1983) and others (e.g., Elithorn, 1965; Halstead, 1947; Smith, 1962, 1966), in the development of methods and procedures that have been used in the pursuit of neuropsychological research. These same methods and procedures, and the resultant data, have provided the base for systematic clinical neuropsychological investigation. As studies in neuroanatomy and neurophysiology progressed and as the field of psychology continued to develop, the increased interactions among these disciplines paved the way for the formalization of neuropsychology as an entity. It began to be recognized as a distinct discipline in the late 1940s and early 1950s (see Hebb, 1949; Teuber, 1948), and although it continues its close research and clinical ties to the basic neurosciences, neurology and psychology, neuropsychology has continued to develop its own knowledge base, methods, and measures. Continued research in neuropsychology and related areas has led to an expanding body of data that has relegated many of the older theories and interpretations of central nervous system function to history.

A major position in the field today holds that emphasis on the functional rather than the structural organization of the nervous system is the productive route to knowledge of neurological and neuropsychological phenomena. The organization of the central nervous system is seen as a dynamic combination of multiple and multiply connected complex systems and of areas of the brain that are specific and those that are nonspecific mediators of given behaviors. Studies of brain–behavior relationships are being conducted today that are capable of answering questions impossible to pose even a decade ago as a result of the development of radio-imaging techniques, including the computerized axial tomography (CAT) and positron-emission tomography (PET) scans and the newer MRI techniques. These and other techniques and areas of neuroscience have, in a relatively short span of time, provided new insights and a bounty of new information to be integrated with what came before. (See Filskov & Boll, 1981, 1986; Gaddes, 1985; Hecaen & Albert, 1978; Heilman & Valenstein, 1985, for further discussion of recent developments and directions.)

Clinical neuropsychological assessment, with its early emphasis on localization and lateralization of lesions, continued to develop as the information about specific brain lesions and their behavioral concomitants became available. Much of this clinicopathologic data resulted from careful studies of brain-injured war veterans (e.g., Teuber, 1959, 1966, 1968) and from studies of a range of patient populations with identifiable lesions of the brain (e.g., Luria, 1966; Reitan, 1955, 1964; Smith, 1975, 1981). There was a shift in emphasis from identifying the presence or absence of "brain damage," to the identification of change or loss in specific neuropsychological functions, to a somewhat revised view of assessment, the seeking of "syndromes" rather than "symptoms," which was in greater harmony with current views of the nervous system as a dynamic set of interrelated systems.

Although neuropsychologists continue to be productive in both applied and basic research, the thrust of this book, and therefore of this chapter, has to do with the psychological evaluation of the developmentally and physically handicapped. The remainder of the chapter, therefore, will deal primarily with issues of neuropsychological assessment, although relevant research contributions will be cited.

APPROACHES TO NEUROPSYCHOLOGICAL EVALUATION

A major issue in clinical neuropsychology has to do with the various approaches to neuropsychological assessment that are in evidence today. This is not to say that there is necessarily a single approach that will satisfy the requirements of every assessment. This is to bring into question the dichotomy, hopefully more apparent than real, between the actuarial and clinical-observational points of view. Just as the purely qualitative assessment, relying only minimally on standardized assessment procedures, is inadequate to answer the questions posed in a given evaluation, so is the purely actuarial approach inadequate to address questions peculiar to the individual patient. The issue is not a new one, and aspects of the problem were addressed back in the 1950s in a seminal book by Paul Meehl (1954). The quantitative point of view, as applied to individual assessments, may be exemplified by practitioners who rely on a standardized battery of tests and take a strict actuarial approach to the interpretation of the assessment data. In the extreme of this position, there is no review of historical information so that the clinician will not be influenced by anything beyond the quantitative data in arriving at a diagnostic formulation. Test administration within this assessment paradigm is frequently delegated to a psychology technician in order to provide further objectivity. As Davison (1974) points out:

> Utilization of a standardized battery, particularly when it is administered by someone other than the neuropsychologist who will interpret it, presents great advantages for research in that the objective data can be evaluated without contaminating influences, and all subjects secure scores on the same variables. However, the method presents great liabilities for *some* clinical diagnostic problems, among them the adequate specification of an individual's characteristics for the purpose of predicting behavior in his ambient existence. For this purpose the data collector must have a clear idea of the practical problem to which he is predicting and the freedom, knowledge, and ingenuity to add tests to the battery for individual cases and to *improvise* an individualized assessment when necessary. The clinician must recognize his responsibility not simply for addressing the referral problem, but toward the patient as a whole. (p. 354)

The Halstead-Reitan Neuropsychological Test Battery (Reitan & Davison, 1974), which has undergone additions and deletions over the years, is probably the earliest battery of standardized tests devised for the study of brain-damaged patients. Diagnostic statements are based on the evaluation of performance and cutting scores reflecting group data. Studies have indicated problems in the diagnostic efficiency and reliability of the battery (Davison, 1974; Dodrill & Troupin, 1975; Matarazzo, Wiens, Matarazzo, & Goldstein, 1974; Russell, 1980). It does appear to reliably discriminate brain-damaged patients from normals, although that question has limited relevance in the clinical setting. It does not appear to do as well in discriminating neurologically impaired from psychiatric patients (Heaton, Baade, & Johnson, 1978; Lacks, Harrow, Colbert, & Levine, 1970). Evaluation of the battery in terms of its ability to localize lesions has suggested that only with the later addition of the sensory examination have efforts at localization, using multivariate statistical analyses of the data, proved sound (Adams, Rennick, & Rosenbaum, 1975; Wedding, 1979). Goldstein and Shelly (1973) found that evidence of sensory suppression, elicited by performance on sensory tests in the battery, was the single most powerful variable that distinguished between right and left hemisphere lesion groups. Lezak (1983) points out that

> this battery's greatest diagnostic strengths come from several brief examination techniques on which neurologists have relied for decades to make the same diagnostic distinctions. (p. 565)

A more recently developed test battery, the Luria-Nebraska Neuropsychological Battery, has been devised by Golden (1980b) and his colleagues (Golden, 1981; Golden, Hammeke, & Purisch, 1980). It was, indeed, developed in Nebraska, but it has little to do with Luria. This battery of tests is taken from Christensen's work (1979) in which she organized Luria's examination techniques and provided materials and a manual to aid in the clinical assessment of the patient. Golden's addition was a standardization of some of the tasks and their inclusion in a battery. (See Lezak, 1983, pp. 569–572, and Spiers, 1981, for further discussion of the contents and issues related to test construction.) This should not be construed as an evaluation instrument within Luria's framework. In fact, the very standardization of the tasks and the addition of quantitative scoring flies in the face of Luria's approach to assessment; Luria worked within an hypothesis-testing framework, in that his examination was flexible and fluid and followed where the patient's behavior led. Apart from the misnomer, there are problems of test construction that may contribute to the unreliability of results that have been noted. Although Golden and his colleagues claim that their battery is a reliable and valid diagnostic instrument (e.g., Golden, 1980a; Golden, *et al.*, 1978; Hammeke, Golden, & Purisch, 1978; Purisch, Golden, & Hammeke, 1978), others have concluded to the contrary (Adams & Brown, 1980; Crosson & Warren, 1982; Delis & Kaplan, 1982).

There are other concerns about the use of fixed batteries, of which the Halstead-Reitan and Luria-Nebraska are the two most frequently used in clinical practice. Even if either or both of them, interpreting data within a strictly actuarial framework, could reliably separate brain-damaged from normal or psychotic individuals and could localize and lateralize brain lesions, one must ask if these are answers to the questions most neuropsychologists are asked to address (see Wilson & Davidovicz [1987] for further discussion of this issue). The same question must be put to the clinician who eschews standardized measures and relies on clinical judgment in formulating not only a diagnostic statement but a delineation of function and dysfunction and appropriate remedial planning. No longer is the question of diagnosis the major issue for neuropsychology. With increased frequency, the referral issues involve the delineation of patterns of cognitive function and dysfunction for the purposes of prediction of later outcome, the development of recommendations relative to therapeutic intervention, modifications in expectations of patient and family, baseline measures prior to and for the subsequent evaluation of intervention—surgical, pharmacological, psychotherapeutic, cognitive. These are certainly among the salient issues in the assessment of the developmentally and physically handicapped, and they cannot be answered by actuarial statements as to the probability of the presence of brain damage or of right or left hemisphere lesion. What is needed is an approach to assessment that utilizes the strengths of standardized procedures and normative data together with historical and observational data. It is a given that the same quantitative scores may be achieved in different ways by different patients. How the score is achieved is at least as important as the score itself. As Elithorn (1965, p. 663) has pointed out,

> the flexibility of cerebral mechanisms is such that the solution of most test items can be reached by many devious routes. The method the subject used in tackling a problem will in general provide more information as to the character of a skill or of a psychological deficit than will the knowledge as to the subject's success or failure.

There are behaviors that are critical to the understanding of the functioning capacities of the patient that cannot be captured by test scores. They must be evaluated in other ways. Although it may be more objective to have a standardized test battery administered by a technician, have it scored by computer, and deliver a series of actuarial statements, it does not necessarily provide all the information that may be available for use in the definition of the patient's problem nor in the development of appropriate recommendations or intervention strategies. The need for the inclusion of clinical observations is very important if a holistic view of the patient is to be obtained. It would, of course, be useful, particularly for research purposes, if clinical observations in designated domains could be quantified. There is work in progress in this area, for example, in the development of a clinical-observational scale of spontaneous language in preschool children (Murray & Tortolani, 1985; Tortolani, Murray, Risucci, & Wilson, 1986), which serves to enhance the interpretation of language-loaded psychometric data. The Conners Behavioral Checklist (Conners, 1969) is an attempt at the notation of observed behavior to aid in the diagnosis of hyperactivity, although it would be a grievous error if this were the sole criterion on which such a diagnosis were to be based. There are few, if any, single measures, methods, or procedures that provide sufficient data for the statement of a meaningful diagnosis.

An additional concern with reference to the administration of standardized batteries has to do with the limitations that are imposed by the requirement of standardized stimulus presentation and response modes if the norms are to be utilized in strictly quantitative fashion. This is of particular concern when the subject of the assessment is physically and/or developmentally disabled and is unable to deal with the standardized administration procedures or response formats. One's position here is dictated by what is seen as the end point of the evaluation. If the individual's performance on a series of tests relative to the performance of the normative sample(s) is the issue of concern, then administration of a test battery in a standardized fashion, scored by computer and interpreted by a psychologist who has not seen the patient, is probably cost-efficient and appropriate. If the questions to be addressed by the evaluation concern themselves with obtaining the maximum performance the patient has available, his or her style of problem solving, suggestions as to methods that would facilitate performance, with aspects of adaptation, of prediction of patient performance in other than test situations, and with the development of remedial and therapeutic programs, then the clinician must be directly involved and must be able to vary test procedures and patient response modes as the progress of the evaluation dictates. Wilson and Davidovicz (1987) discuss the effect of physical and sensory defects in the evaluation of children, and the position is readily generalized to adults:

> It is more useful to say that this three and a half year old physically handicapped child was able to complete a formboard at roughly the three year level when in a side lying position with the individual shapes handed to him than to say "could not do" when standard administration procedures were used.

Both bits of data are necessary, that the task could not be performed under standard conditions and that the perceptual abilities tapped by the formboard appeared to be mildly impaired, once the motor demands were minimized.

ISSUES IN THE ASSESSMENT OF CHILDREN

Until now, we have addressed assessment issues that are germane to both adults and children. As Hecaen and Albert (1978) suggest, adult neuropsychology is the study of established patterns of behavior, whereas child neuropsychology is the study of disturbances in the acquisition of cognitive functions regardless of the pathological origin. Child neuropsychology, unlike its adult counterpart, has not benefited from a long history of systematic research into the relationships between brain function and behavior. The clinical data base is more limited as well because child neuropsychology is a relatively new enterprise. These concerns are magnified when the content of developmental child neuropsychology is taken into account; issues of plasticity and recovery of function (e.g., Basser, 1962; Dennis, 1980; Dennis, Lovett, & Wiegel-Crump, 1981; Rudel, 1978; Smith, 1974; Smith, Flick, Ferriss, & Sellerman, 1972; Woods & Teuber, 1973); neural maturation (e.g., Conel, 1939–1967; Dodgson, 1962; Trevarthen, 1974); developmental lag (e.g., Kinsbourne, 1973; Satz, 1976); the impact of environment on cognition (e.g., Hanson *et al.*, 1976; McCall, Appelbaum, & Hogarty, 1973; Wolf, 1966); and the effects of prenatal (e.g., Keller, 1981; Werner & Smith, 1977; Werner, Berman, & French, 1971) and perinatal events (e.g., Burg, Hart, Quinn, & Rapoport, 1978; Burg, Rapoport, Bartley, Quinn, & Timmins, 1980) are among a longer list of potentially relevant variables. (See Spreen, Tupper, Risser, Tuokko, & Edgell, 1984, for detailed discussions of issues in developmental neuropsychology.) There are unanswered questions as to the contributions of these interactive factors to the behaviors observed and inferred during the course of a neuropsychological assessment. We cannot address each of the variables in turn because there is a vast literature related to each of them. To offer some indication of the complexity involved, citation of Rudel's (1978) findings on the effects of brain damage sustained during childhood (i.e., plasticity and recovery of function) suggest that sequelae may appear either shortly after the insult and disappear rapidly or may appear shortly after the insult and be permanent or, yet again, may show themselves only after a period of time. Neurophysiological, environmental, and developmental variables, each unique to the individual in their interactions, are among those that must be considered contributory to the end result.

Unlike the adult patient population, a large proportion of the children brought to neuropsychological evaluation are not suffering the effects of acquired lesions. Their behavioral deficits are not the result of a closed head injury, stroke, or tumor. Most children seen for assessment present with developmental deficits that have no documentable origin, or they are children who have suffered brain damage secondary to pre- or perinatal events. The referral questions most frequently posed include those of differential diagnosis between global retardation, language disorders, and autism in the younger child. The school-aged child is frequently referred because of learning problems, and the referral questions revolve around issues of specification of the deficit patterns and the primacy of emotional and/or neuropsychological contributions to the observed problems. These evaluations require an understanding of the neuropsychological presentations of each of the clinical entities. The differential diagnosis or the specification of cognitive patterns is frequently the least of the problems. Offering appropriate recommendations becomes more the issue, and a difficult one it is. The assessment of children with other developmental disorders, such as cerebral palsy or genetically determined patterns of cognitive dysfunction, demands that the neuropsychologist have an appreciation of the disorders and of their possible ramifications for the future.

There are, of course, children who are referred with acquired lesions secondary to such things as trauma and infection. Again, clinical data are not as abundant for children as for adults, and the developmental considerations have already been suggested. In such situations, clinicians frequently resort to extrapolation from adult lesion data in an attempt to understand and to predict. This is not always useful because there is controversy within the adult literature, but what is more important, not enough is known about the developmental changes in terms of the possibly changing neural substrates that subserve given behaviors. Wilson (1986, p. 123) points out, with reference to a study involving preschool children, that

> imputing mediation of the Peabody Picture Vocabulary Test to the left parietal lobe (Hartlage, Telzrow, DeFillippes, Shaw, and Noonan, 1983) is as gratuitous as any inferential localization of function in the young child.

To sum up, it is our position that the clinician should be directly involved in the assessment of the patient, that a hypothesis-testing model affords the best opportunity for discovery, and that the most appropriate assessment paradigm is that that addresses the questions posed by the individual patient. We also believe that the most appropriate remediation or rehabilitation strategies flow from good diagnostic data; the more immediate the evaluation is to the patient's needs, the better the opportunity for well-directed intervention.

A NEUROPSYCHOLOGICAL ASSESSMENT MODEL

The content of the neuropsychological assessment should include a detailed history, regardless of the age of the patient. Inappropriate questions and uninformed diagnoses are often the result of inadequate histories; a case in point includes the referral of an 18-year-old drug abuser with the question as to the possibility that drugs had produced the presence of defective reading and spelling. When the neuropsychologist asked about early developmental history and prior school performance, the referring professional looked surprised and noted that such information had not been collected. It was as though the patient were born the day he walked into the treatment facility. As historical information was gathered, the patient turned out to have been significantly delayed in the acquisition of speech and language, and although later was shown to have high average intelligence, had been identified as learning disabled in the third grade, with a history of behavioral disturbance dating back almost that far. Historical information can save us from errors. It can also point us in the right direction by providing information that leads to the development of hypotheses about the presence or absence of deficits in neuropsychological processes.

A process-oriented model of assessment is one that concerns itself with the delineation of those aspects of neuropsychological function that are intact as well as those that appear to be compromised, utilizing historical, observational, and quantitative test data. One may take the position that "deficits" need not be demonstrated in order to hypothesize the presence of neuropsychological dysfunction. A pattern of "relative efficiencies," inter- and/or intramodal, may provide information that is relevant to the delineation of patterns of function and dysfunction in the absence of actual deficit scores. A child with a developmental learning disability may show a pattern of test scores, all within the normal range, with clear differences in levels of efficiency between, for example, lower auditory-receptive skills as compared to visually mediated skills. No deficit scores are in evidence, but there is a strong probability of a pattern of relative inefficiency in language-related areas. This, as a hypothesis, can be further studied within the branching model subscribed to here. The application of this model minimizes the importance of the medical-diagnostic label and focuses on the development of a profile of skills that may vary on a continuum from intact to deficient, or even absent. Such an approach requires that the question be, "What behaviors need to be assessed?", rather than "What test shall I use?" If the behaviors in question can be specified, then appropriate measures can be identified, either standardized or improvised. There are few unidimensional tests, so that a careful task analysis needs to be done to ensure that there is maximal understanding of the possible confounds in each of the test measures. Smith (1975, p. 89), making a similar point, has used the Wechsler Digit Symbol subtest to point out that "the responses are the end product of the integration of visual perceptual, oculomotor, fine manual motor and mental functions." If the score is deficient, wherein lies the deficit? An understanding of the demands of the subtest will enable or at least facilitate the pursuit of answers, relying on the hypothesis-testing approach to direct the way.

There are a variety of ways in which to describe or characterize the content of the quantitative aspects of a neuropsychological assessment. One way is to think of the data in terms of neuropsychological constructs such as auditory comprehension, short-term auditory memory, visual spatial ability, and so on. The constructs we use are defined by their measures and have proved useful in the organization of test data and in the development of functional profiles. One of the features of this model is the fact that, if the behaviors in question and the measures selected to assess them are clearly understood, the examiner can select the tests of his or her choice (Risucci, 1983) and can still be dealing with the constructs in question. The constructs that are shown in Figures 1 and 2 represent some of the major cognitive functions with which we are concerned and include aspects of short-term auditory and verbal memory (AM1, AM2, VM1, VM2, VM3), levels of auditory-cognitive function (AC1, AC2, VC1, VC2, VC3), and visual discrimination and visual spatial functions (VS, VSP1, VSP2). Others not included in the profiles presented here include fine and graphomotor function, various aspects of word retrieval, auditory discrimination, and additional levels of auditory-cognitive skills. This list is not exhaustive but includes the most commonly assessed functions. Further details concerning the constructs, the measures used to assess them, and the conversion of all measures to a common metric for readier communication and for graphic representation can be found in Wilson (1986), Wilson and Davidovicz (1987), and Wilson and Wilson (1978). The fact that the assessment data can be expressed graphically is a decided advantage when one is working within an interdisciplinary setting, which is frequently the case when assessments are provided to physically or developmentally handicapped people. The meaning of test scores in their many guises is not always available to nonpsychologists, but percentiles are.

Figure 1 presents major aspects of the profile of a 10-year, 11-month-old girl with cerebral palsy who was referred because of difficulty in the acquisition of academic skills. The pattern clearly demonstrates good verbal cognitive and memory skills and compromised visual perceptual functions. The difference between the Verbal IQ and the Performance IQ is highly significant. The neuropsychological pattern is consonant with school performance and provides specific information that may be of use in the development of intervention strategies.

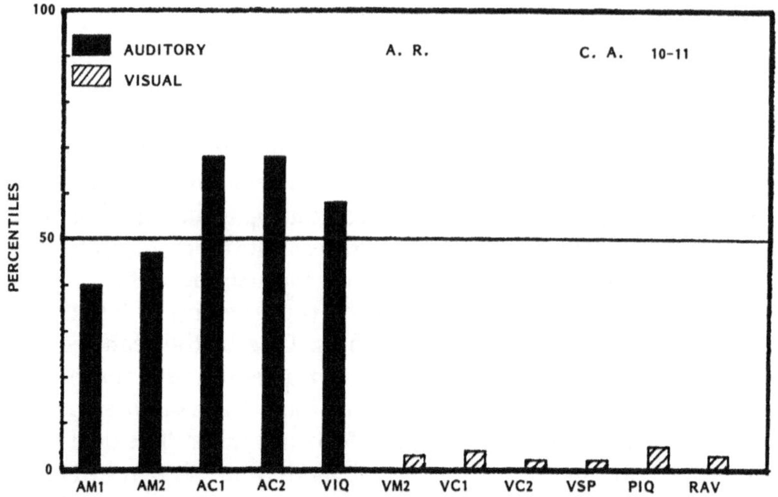

FIGURE 1. The neuropsychological profile of a cerebral palsied child, A. R., 10 years, 11 months of age. The profile indicates the presence of average auditory-verbal skills and significantly deficient visually mediated behaviors.

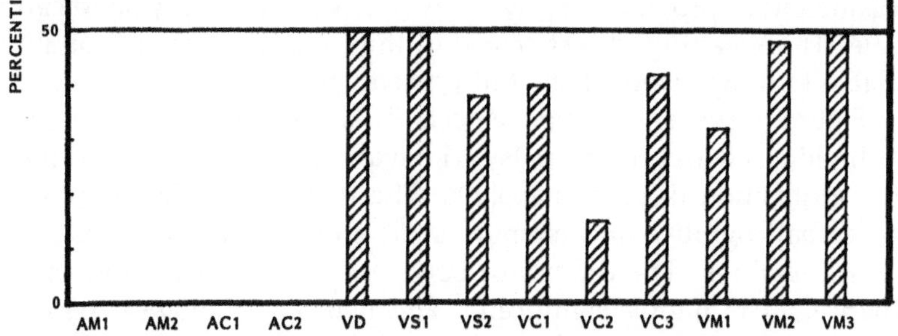

FIGURE 2. The neuropsychological profile of G. G., 3 years, 3 months of age, with auditory-verbal agnosia. She was unable to process any of the auditory-verbal material but demonstrated average performance in visually mediated areas.

Figure 2 presents the most relevant aspects of the profile of a 3-year, 3-month-old girl with auditory verbal agnosia, a profound developmental language disorder. The area in which no scores appear is an indication that she was unable to demonstrate any level of competence in terms of the auditory-verbal constructs represented. On the other hand, she was able to perform within the average range on visually mediated measures that had little or no language loading, such as those represented by the construct Visual Cognitive 1, involving simple match-to-sample tasks. The profiles represented in Figures 1 and 2 present systematic patterns of function and dysfunction and were, to their teachers and parents, recognizable descriptions of the children.

FUTURE DIRECTIONS AND SUMMARY

Neuropsychology is developing in a variety of ways and is taking new directions in the basic neurosciences, in methods and techniques of assessment, in the development of classification systems, and in members of the subgroups; only empirical data are considered. This approach is akin to the actuarial approach to assessment and is exemplified by the work of Petrauskas and Rourke (1979) and Satz and Morris (1981). As a description of the characteristics of a group, within a research framework, such an approach may be useful; it is less useful in providing descriptors for a member of the group. Wilson, Iacoviello, and Risucci (1981) utilized a *Q*-factor analysis to determine whether or not a statistically coherent and clinically useful typology of learning disabilities could result. The results, based on over 200 sets of assessment data, were indeed, statistically coherent. From the clinical point of view, the members of the individual subtypes were not particularly similar, certainly not similar enough to warrant the development of subtype-specific remedial paradigms. A sophisticated measure of central tendency is, after all, a measure of central tendency. The approach we have taken since then involves the clinician in the initial identification of subtype placement of preschool-language-disordered children, using quantitative data as described previously. Interpretation of these data is tempered by clinical-observational information related to the relevant language variables. This clinically derived typology was then subjected to empirical validation. The initial study, without the inclusion of observational data, yielded good agreement between the clinically and empirically derived subtypes (Wilson & Risucci, 1986). The lack of concordance occurred in those subtypes for which the observational data are required to make the necessary distinctions. The Scales for the Assessment of

Language Samples (SALS) (Tortolani *et al.*, 1986; Murray & Tortolani, 1985) were developed as the clinical instrument to provide the observational data that were to be utilized in conjunction with the quantitative data. The data thus far lead us to believe that it is possible to develop a classification system that includes psychometric and observational data and that can be empirically validated. Such a typology is potentially useful in the furtherance of research and certainly in the development of remedial strategies designed for the individual subtypes. This is not to suggest that recipes will become available for cognitive habilitation of learning disabilities or language disorders. It is to suggest that subtype-specific paradigms can be developed and then modified for the individual child or adult.

In its development, clinical neuropsychology has moved from concerns related to localization of lesions to the delineation of syndromes. It has become involved in predicting outcomes for individual patients and in the development of recommendations and strategies for the remediation or compensation of neurologically based cognitive deficits. Neuropsychology has been asked to go beyond diagnosis and prescription and to become directly involved in the cognitive habilitation or rehabilitation process. There have been neuropsychologists, neurologists, and others working in the area of rehabilitation who have led the way in the development of methods of cognitive retraining and biofeedback techniques for use with patients who, in the main, have had acquired lesions (see Diller & Gordon, 1981, and Cleeland, 1981, for overviews). We take the position that reasonable approaches to the further development and implementation of cognitive habilitation strategies in relation to the developmentally disabled can be provided by the neuropsychologist. Special education techniques have been the mainstay for this population until now, and although they have clearly offered much to the recipients, an infusion of the neuropsychological approach may serve to stimulate thinking in new and diverse directions. An integration of what we as neuropsychologists know about brain and behavior, translated into terms of neuropsychological assessment, clinically oriented subtypes, and data-based intervention strategies could provide the basis for cognitive training programs. The objective data need to be translated into remedial terms and taken in conjunction with the patient's individuality so that an individualized and flexible program, with ongoing evaluation an integral part, may be developed. Issues of emotional status, social factors, and cognitive and social style are relevant and subject to change. Approaching cognitive training as an integral part of an assessment is the next logical step for the field as a whole to take. Some have already led the way. It is difficult to think about the neuropsychological assessment of the physically and developmentally handicapped without asking the next question: "What can we do to help?"

REFERENCES

Adams, K. M., & Brown, S. J. (1980, September). *Standardized behavioral neurology: Useful concept, mixed metaphor, or commercial enterprise.* Paper presented at the American Psychological Association Convention, Montreal.

Adams, K. M., Rennick, P., & Rosenbaum, G. (1975, February). *Automated clinical interpretation of the neuropsychological battery: An ability-based approach.* Paper presented at the third annual meeting of the International Neuropsychological Society, Tampa, Florida.

Basser, L. S. (1962). Hemiplegia of early onset and the faculty of speech with special reference to the effects of hemispherectomy. *Brain, 85,* 427.

Benton, A. L. (1965). The problem of cerebral dominance. *Canadian Psychologist, 6,* 332–348.

Benton, A. L. (1976). Problems in test construction in the field of aphasia. *Cortex, 3,* 32–58.

Benton, A. L., deS. Hamsher, K., Varney, N. R., & Spreen, O. (1983). *Contributions to neuropsychological assessment. A clinical manual.* New York: Oxford University Press.

Boring, E. G. (1950). *A History of experimental psychology* (2nd ed.). New York: Appleton-Century-Crofts.

Bouillaud, J. (1825). Recherches cliniques propres a de monter que la perte de la parole correspond a la lesion des lobules anterieurs du cerveau et a confirmer l'opinion de M. Gall sur le siege de l'organe du langage articule. *Archives Generales de Médecine, 8,* 25–45.

Breasted, J. H. (1930). *The Edwin Smith Surgical Papyrus.* Chicago University of Chicago Press.

Broca, P. (1861). Perte de la parole. Ramollissement chronique et destruction partielle du lobe antérieur gauche du cerveau. *Bulletin Société Anthropologique,* Paris, 2, 219.

Burg, C., Hart, D., Quinn, P., & Rapoport, J. (1978). Newborn minor physical anomalies and prediction of infant behavior. *Journal of Autism and Childhood Schizophrenia, 8,* 427–439.

Burg, C., Rapoport, J. I., Bartley, L. S., Quinn, D. O., & Timmins, P. (1980). Newborn minor physical anomalies and problem behavior at age 3. *American Journal of Psychiatry, 137,* 791.

Christensen, A. L. (1979). *Luria's neuropsychological investigation text* (2nd ed.). Copenhagen: Munksgaard.

Clarke, E., & Dewhurst, K. (1972). *An illustrated history of brain function* Oxford: Sandford.

Clarke, E., & O'Malley, C. D. (1968). *The human brain and spinal cord* Berkeley: University of California Press.

Cleeland, C. S. (1981). Biofeedback as a clinical tool: Its use with the neurologically impaired patient. In S. S. Filskov & T. J. Boll (Eds.), *Handbook of clinical neuropsychology* (pp. 734–753). New York: Wiley.

Conel, C. K. (1939–1967). *The postnatal development of the human cerebral cortex* (Vols. 1–8). Cambridge, MA: Harvard University Press.

Conners, C. K. (1969). A teacher rating scale for use in drug studies with children. *American Journal of Psychiatry, 126*, 884–888.
Crosson, B., & Warren, R. L. (1982). Use of the Luria-Nebraska Neuropsychological Battery in aphasia: A conceptual critique. *Journal of Consulting and Clinical Psychology, 50*, 22–31.
Davison, L. A. (1974). Current status of clinical neuropsychology. In R. M. Reitan & L. A. Davison (Eds.), *Clinical neuropsychology: Current status and applications* (pp. 1–18). New York: Wiley.
Dax, M. (1865). Lesions de al moitie gauche de l'encephale coincidant avec trouble des signes de al pensee. (lu a Montpellier en 1836). *Gazette Hebdomadaire Médical Série, 2*, 259–262.
Delis, D., & Kaplan, E. F. (1982). The assessment of aphasia with the Luria-Nebraska Neuropsychological Battery: A case critique. *Journal of Consulting and Clinical Psychology, 50*, 32–39.
Dennis, M. (1980). Capacity and strategy for syntactic comprehension after left or right hemidecortication. *Brain and Language*, 10, 287–317.
Dennis, M., Lovett, M., & Weigel-Crump, C. A. (1981). Written language acquisition after left or right hemidecortication in infancy. *Brain and Language, 12*, 54–91.
Diller, L., & Gordon, W. A. (1981). Rehabilitation and clinical neuropsychology. In S. B. Filskov & T. J. Boll (Eds.), *Handbook of clinical neuropsychology* (pp.). New York: Wiley.
Dodgson, M. C. H. (1962). *The growing brain: An essay in developmental neurology*, Bristol, England: Wright.
Dodrill, C. B., & Troupin, A. S. (1975). Effects of repeated administrations of a comprehensive neuropsychological battery among chronic epileptics. *Journal of Nervous and Mental Disease, 161*, 185–190.
Elithorn, A. (1965). Psychological tests. An objective approach to the problem of task difficulty. *Acta Neurologica Scandinavica, (Suppl. 13*, Part 2), 661–667.
Filskov, S. B., & Boll, T. J. (Eds.). (1981). *Handbook of clinical neuropsychology* (Vol. 1). New York: Wiley.
Filskov, S. B., & Boll, T. J. (Eds.). (1986). *Handbook of clinical neuropsychology* (Vol. 2). New York: Wiley.
Flourens, P. (1842). *Examen de phrenologie*. Hachette: Paris.
Franz, I. S. (1902). On the functions of the cerebrum: The frontal lobes in relation to the production and retention of simple sensory-motor habits. *American Journal of Physiology, 8*, 1–22.
Franz, I. S. (1912). New phrenology. *Science, 35*, 321–328.
Gaddes, W. H. (1985). *Learning disabilities and brain function, A neuropsychological approach*. (2nd ed.) New York: Springer-Verlag.
Geschwind, N. (1965a). Alexia and color-naming disturbance. In G. Ettlinger (Ed.), *Functions of the corpus callosum*. London: Churchill.
Geschwind, N. (1965b). Disconnection syndromes in animals and man. Part I. *Brain, 88*, 237–294.
Geschwind, N. (1965c). Disconnection syndromes in animals and man. Part II. *Brain, 88*, 585–644.
Gibson, W. C. (1962). Pioneers of localization of function in the brain. *Journal of the American Medical Association, 80*, 944–951.
Gibson, W. C. (1969). The early history of localization in the nervous system. In P. Vinhen & G. E. Bruyn (Eds.), *Handbook of clinical neurology* (Vol. 2). Amsterdam: North-Holland.

Golden, C. J. (1980a). In reply to Adams': "In search of Luria's battery: A false start." *Journal of Consulting and Clinical Psychology, 48,* 517–521.

Golden, C. J. (1980b). *Manual for the Luria-Nebraska Neuropsychological Test Battery.* Los Angeles: Western Psychological Services.

Golden, C. J. (1981). A standardized version of Luria's neuropsychological tests. In S. B. Filskov & T. J. Boll (Eds.), *Handbook of clinical neuropsychology* (pp. 608–644). New York: Wiley, 1981.

Golden, C. J., Hammeke, T. A., & Purisch, A. D. (1980). Diagnostic validity of a standardized neuropsychological battery derived from Luria's neuropsychological tests. *Journal of Consulting and Clinical Psychology, 46,* 1258–1265.

Goldstein, G., & Shelly, C. H. (1973). Univariate vs. multivariate analysis in neuropsychological test assessment of lateralizaed brain damage. *Cortex, 9,* 204–216.

Halstead, W. C. (1947). *Brain and Intelligence: A quantitative study of the frontal lobes.* Chicago: University of Chicago Press.

Hammeke, T. A., Golden, C. J., & Purisch, A. D. (1978). A standardized, short and comprehensive neuropsychological test battery based on the Luria neuropsychological evaluation. *International Journal of Neuroscience, 8,* 135–141.

Hanson, J. W., Jones, K. L., & Smith, D. W. (1976). Fetal alcohol syndrome: Experience with 41 patients. *Journal of the American Medical Association, 235,* 1458.

Hartlage, L. C., Telzrow, C.F., DeFillipes, N. A., Shaw, J. B., & Noonan, M. (1983). Personality correlates of functional asymmetry in preschool children. *Clinical Neuropsychology,* 14–15.

Heaton, R. K., Baade, L. E., & Johnson, K. L. (1978). Neuropsychological test results associated with psychiatric disorders in adults. *Psychological Bulletin, 85,* 141–162.

Hebb, D. O. (1949). *The organization of behavior.* New York: Wiley.

Hecaen, H., & Albert, M. L. (1978). *Human neuropsychology.* New York: Wiley.

Heilman, K. M., & Valenstein, E. (1985). *Clinical neuropsychology* (2nd ed.). New York: Oxford University Press.

Joynt, R. (1964). Paul Pierre Broca: His contribution to the knowledge of aphasia. *Cortex, 1,* 206–213.

Keller, C. A. (1981). Epidemiological characteristics of preterm births. In S. I. Friedman & M. Sigman (Eds.), *Preterm birth and psychological development.* New York: Academic Press.

Kinsbourne, M. (1973). Minimal brain dysfunction as a neurodevelopmental lag. In F. de la Cruz, B. H. Fox, & R. H. Roberts (Eds.), *Minimal brain dysfunction. Annals of the New York Academy of Science,* 2005.

Lacks, P. B., Harrow, M., Colbert, J., & Levine, J. (1970). Further evidence concerning the diagnostic accuracy of the Halstead organic test battery. *Journal of Clinical Psychology, 26,* 480–481.

Lashley, K. S. (1929). *Brain mechanisms and intelligence: A quantitative study of injuries to the brain.* Chicago: University of Chicago Press.

Lashley, K. S. (1938). Factors limiting recovery after central nervous system lesions. *Journal of Nervous and Mental Disease, 88,* 733–755.

Lezak, M. (1983). *Neuropsychological assessment* (2nd ed.). New York: Oxford University Press.

Luria, A. R. (1966). *Higher cortical functions in man* (2nd ed.). New York: Basic Books.

Magoun, H. W. (1958). Early development of ideas relating the mind with the brain. In G. E. W. Wolstenholm & C. M. O'Connor (Eds.), *The neurological basis of behavior.* London: Churchill.

Marie, P. (1906). Révision de la question de l'aphasie. *Semaine Med.,* 241–247, 493–500, 565–571.

Matarazzo, J. D., Wiens, A. N., Matarazzo, R. G., & Goldstein, S. G. (1974). Psychometric and clinical test-retest reliability of the Halstead impairment Index in a sample of healthy, young, normal men. *Journal of Nervous and Mental Disease, 158*, 37–49.

McCall, R. B., Appelbaum, M. I., & Hogarty, P. S. (1973). Developmental changes in mental performance. *Monographs of the Society for Research in Child Development, 38*, 1–83.

McHenry, L. C. (1969). *Garrison's history of neurology*. Springfield, IL: Charles C. Thomas.

Meehl, P. E. (1954). *Clinical versus statistical prediction*. Minneapolis: University of Minnesota Press.

Miller, G. A., & Buckout, R. (1973). *The science of mental life*. New York: Harper & Row.

Murray, S., & Tortolani, B. (1985, August). *Development of clinical-observational language scales for use in classification research*. Paper presented at the American Psychological Association Conference, Los Angeles.

Pavlov, I. P. (1949). *Complete collected works* (Vols. 1–6). Moscow and Leningrad: Izd. Akad. Nank. SSSR.

Petrauskas, R. J., & Rourke, B. P. (1979). Identification of subtypes of retarded readers: A neuropsychological multivariate approach. *Journal of Clinical Neuropsychology, 1*, 17–37.

Purisch, A. D., Golden, C. J., & Hammeke, T. A. (1978). Discrimination of schizophrenia and brain injured patients by a standardized version of Luria's neuropsychological tests. *Journal of Consulting and Clinical Psychology, 46*, 1266–1273.

Reitan, R. M. (1955). Certain differential effects of left and right cerebral lesions in human adults. *Journal of Comparative and Physiological Psychology, 48*, 474–477.

Reitan, R. M. (1964). Psychological deficits resulting from cerebral lesions in man. In J. M. Warren & K. A. Akert (Eds.), *The frontal granular cortex and behavior*. New York: McGraw-Hill.

Reitan, R. M., & Davison, L. A. (Eds.), *Clinical neuropsychology: Current status and applications*. New York: Wiley.

Risucci, D. A. (1983). *Experimental validation of a typology of language-impaired preschool children*, Unpublished doctoral dissertation, Hofstra University, Hempstead, NY.

Rudel, R. G. (1978). Neuroplasticity: Implications for development and education. In J. S. Chall & A. F. Mirsky (Eds.), *Education and the brain* (Part II). Chicago: University of Chicago Press.

Russell, E. W. (1980, September). *Theoretical basis of Luria-Nebraska and Halstead-Reitan batteries*. Paper presented at the American Psychological Association Convention, Montreal, Canada.

Satz, P. (1976). Cerebral dominance and reading disability: An old problem revisited. In R. M. Knights & D. J. Bakker (Eds.), *The neuropsychology of learning disorders*. Baltimore: University Park Press.

Satz, P., & Morris, R. (1981). Learning disability subtypes: A review. In F. Pirrozollo & J. Wittrock (Eds.), *Neuropsychological and cognitive processes in reading*. New York: Academic Press.

Smith, A. (1962). Psychodiagnosis of patients with brain tumors. *Journal of Nervous and Mental Disease, 135*, 513–533.

Smith, A. (1966). Intellectual functions in patients with lateralized frontal tumors. *Journal of Neurology, Neurosurgery, and Psychiatry, 29*, 52–59.

Smith, A. (1974). Diaschisis and neuropsychology. *The Bulletin of the International Neuropsychological Society*, April, pp. 2–3.

Smith, A. (1975). Neuropsychological testing in neurological disorders. In W. J. Friedlander (Ed.), *Advances in neurology* (Vol. 7, pp. 49–110). New York: Raven Press.

Smith, A. (1981). Principles underlying human brain functions in neuropsychological sequelae of different neuropathological processes. In S. B. Filskov & T. J. Boll (Eds.), *Handbook of clinical neuropsychology* (Vol. 1, pp. 175–226). New York: Wiley.

Smith, A., Flick, G. L., Ferriss, G. S., & Sellerman, A. H. (1972). Prediction of developmental outcome at seven years from prenatal, perinatal and postnatal events. *Child Development, 43,* 495.

Spiers, P. A. (1981). Have they come to praise Luria or to bury him? The Luria-Nebraska Battery controversy. *Journal of Consulting and Clinical Psychology, 49,* 331–341.

Spreen, O., Tupper, D., Risser, A., Tuokko, H., & Edgell, D. (1984). *Human developmental neuropsychology.* New York: Oxford University Press.

Teuber, H.-L. (1948). Neuropsychology. In M. R. Harrower (Ed.) *Recent advances in diagnostic psychological testing.* Springfield, IL: Charles C Thomas.

Teuber, H.-L. (1959). Some alterations in behavior after cerebral lesions in man. In A. P. Bass (Ed.), *Evolution of nervous control* (pp. 157–170). Washington, DC: American Association for the Advancement of Science.

Teuber, H.-L. (1966). Effects of occipital lobe lesions in pattern vision. *Supplement 8th International Congress of Neurology, 3,* 79–192.

Teuber, H.-L. (1968). Disorders of memory following penetrating missile wounds of the brain. *Neurology, 18,* 287–288.

Tortolani, B., Murray, S., Risucci, D. A., & Wilson, B. C. (1985). *Scales for the assessment of language samples* (SALS). Paper presented at the meeting of the American Psychological Association, Los Angeles.

Trevarthen, C. B. (1974). Cerebral embryology and the split brain. In M. Kinsbourne & W. L. Smith (Eds.), *Hemispheric disconnection and cerebral function.* Springfield, IL: Charles C Thomas.

Walsh, K. W. (1978). *Neuropsychology. A clinical approach.* New York: Churchill Livingston.

Wedding, D. A. (1979). *A Comparison of statistical, actuarial, and clinical models used in predicting presence, lateralization and type of brain damage in humans.* Unpublished doctoral dissertation, University of Hawaii.

Werner, E., & Smith, R. (1977). *Kauai's children come of age* Honolulu: University of Hawaii Press.

Werner, E., Berman, J., & French, F. (1971). *The children of Kauai: A longitudinal study from the prenatal period to age 10.* Honolulu: University of Hawaii Press.

Wilson, B. C. (1986). Neuropsychological assessment of the preschool child with developmental deficits. In S. Filskov & T. J. Boll (Eds.), *Handbook of clinical neuropsychology* (Vol. 2, pp. 121–171). New York: Wiley.

Wilson, B. C., & Davidovicz, H. M. (1987). The neuropsychological assessment of the child with cerebral palsy. *Seminars in Speech and Language, 8,* 1–18.

Wilson, B. C., & Risucci, D. A. (1986). A model for clinical-quantitative classification. Generation 1: Application to language disordered preschool children. *Brain and Language, 27,* 281–309.

Wilson, B. C., & Wilson, J. J. (1978). Language disordered children: A neurolopsychological view. In C. Banks & B. Feingold (Eds.), *Developmental disabilities of early childhood* (pp. 148–171). Springfield, IL: Charles C. Thomas.

Wilson, B. C., Iacoviello, J. M., & Risucci, D. A. (1981). Unpublished data.

Wolf, R. (1966). A measurement of environments. In A. Anastasi (Ed.), *Testing problems in perspective.* Washington, DC: American Council on Education.

Woods, B. T., & Teuber, H.-L. (1973). Early onset of complementary specialization of cerebral hemispheres in man. *Transactions of the American Neurological Association, 98,* 113–117.

III

PSYCHOLOGICAL EVALUATION OF SPECIFIC DISORDERS

5

Hearing Impairment

FRANK P. BELCASTRO

INTRODUCTION

The process by which people communicate with each other involves the sending and receiving of messages from one person to another. Although people use different modalities to communicate, the senses of vision and hearing permit us to contact our environment without being near to it. Reception of auditory messages occurs continually, whether listening or responding to both verbal and nonverbal sounds. The auditory channel assists in developing appropriate speech skills by serving as a monitor of one's own speech; it also is essential for comprehension and learning.

The primary objective of educators of the hearing impaired is successful intervention to meet the receptive and expressive language deficits that limit the participation of this population in normal communication (Council for Exceptional Children, 1966). Additional handicaps borne by the hearing impaired are concomitant speech deficits. The previously mentioned deficiencies constitute a cycle in which the existing impaired human environment leads to an impaired psychological environment that results in disturbed human behavior. The cycle is completed by the creation of a more impaired human environment (Ehrlich, Ehrlich, & Holdren, 1972).

Because of Public Law 94-142, the field of hearing impairedness, along with other areas of special education, is in a period of rapid change

FRANK P. BELCASTRO • Department of Psychology, University of Dubuque, Dubuque, Iowa 52001.

with a focus on expanding services to the hearing impaired while they remain in their neighborhood schools or own homes. This has presented a challenge to regular teachers, school principals, school psychologists, and other specialists who now must participate more fully in programs for these special persons. Thus knowledge about behavioral aspects of the hearing impaired and of psychological evaluation with this population is greatly needed.

DESCRIPTION

The hearing impaired are required to process information totally or partially through sensory channels other than hearing. They accomplish this in a manner that is different from those whose hearing is intact. The way they process information and the extent to which this occurs depend on a variety of factors: (a) extent and type of hearing loss, (b) age of onset of hearing loss, (c) age when corrective instruction was initiated, (d) degree of intelligence, and (e) quality of instruction. These factors are the basis for classification of the hearing impaired.

Although a variety of terms have been used to describe this population, most of these have been used to differentiate among hearing-impaired persons. The *deaf* are those who have nonfunctional hearing for everyday purposes of life. The *hard-of-hearing* have hearing that is defective, yet still functional (Committee on Nomenclature, 1938). The deaf are composed of two distinct groups: the *congenitally deaf,* who were born deaf, and the *adventitiously deaf,* who were born with normal hearing but who later became deaf as a result of illness, accident, or trauma.

From an educational perspective, the development of language is a critical consideration and, thus, definitions differ. The *prelingually deaf* are those persons who were deaf before speech and language developed; the *postlingually deaf* are those who became deaf after speech and language development (Mandell & Fiscus, 1981).

Although many surveys have been conducted, determining the prevalence of hearing-impaired persons is an arduous task. Although the number most often quoted is 5% (Hull, Mielke, Willeford, & Timmons, 1976), estimates ranging from 1% to 3% and up to 10% are reported in the literature (Illinois Commission on Children, 1968; United States Dept. of Health, Education, and Welfare, 1975).

A comparative analysis of these and other studies indicates that this variability is due to a number of considerations, including types of samples surveyed, testing methods, unilateral and bilateral loss inclusion, the community surveyed, longevity of the population, degree of socialized medicine, occurrence of epidemics or other disasters, and most significantly, lack of a consistent definition for hearing impairment.

Almost 25% of the American hearing-impaired school-aged population is identified as either Hispanic (9%) or black (15%) (Gentile & McCarthy, 1973; Moores & Oden, 1977). Yet, there are relatively few Hispanic and black educators of the hearing impaired. Further, attention has been directed to the phonemic and grammatical distinctions between English and the different black and Hispanic dialects. The implications for educating these neglected hearing-impaired children generally have been ignored (Smith, Neisworth, & Hunt, 1983).

HISTORY AND DEVELOPMENT

From early history until late Middle Ages, the deaf were stereotyped as idiots, fools, and uneducable, and they often were killed (Hodgson, 1954). The deaf were social outcasts in ancient Greece. As a reflection of their unenviable position, the Mosaic law asked that they not be cursed. It was the success of Spanish educators of the seventeenth century at teaching the hearing impaired that first cast doubt on negative stereotypes and led to the establishment of schools for the hearing impaired in France and Germany. Americans studied at these schools and subsequently established the first institutions for the hearing impaired in the United States in the nineteenth century (Moores, 1978).

Because psychology was still in its nascent stage, educators of the hearing impaired in the late nineteenth century conducted primitive psychological investigations of their own. One pervasive educational problem at the time was the estimation of intelligence in hearing-impaired applicants for school admission. In response to the need for work in this area, Greenberger (1899) developed procedures for testing the intelligence of hearing-impaired children—a momentous and singular achievement.

Over the next 25 years, there was a considerable increase in psychological investigations of the hearing impaired. These involved examinations of personality achievement and other attributes in these individuals. The major focus, however, was on the testing of intelligence through paper-and-pencil nonlanguage group tests, and performance scales (Pintner, Eisenson, & Stanton, 1941).

Due to the conflicting estimates of the intelligence of the hearing impaired, efforts were made to design new measurement devices. These endeavors focused on construction of intelligence tests designed for and standardized specifically on the hearing impaired and on the establishment of the concurrent validity of the instruments. However, these efforts failed to yield an adequate measure of intellectual functioning (Levine, 1976). Additional research attempted to determine information-processing patterns of the hearing impaired using Piagetian-type tasks. Furth (1964, 1966) concluded that no basic malfunctions in the cognitive capacities of the deaf existed and that any observed decrements could be attributed to communication, experiential, and linguistic deficits.

The post–World War II decades brought a compelling need for rehabilitation services. As a result of legislation in this area, psychologists began directing services toward the hearing impaired (Office of Vocational Rehabilitation, 1956). Indeed, during the 1960s, the number of psychologists entering the field of hearing impairment increased considerably. Many of these professionals were hearing impaired themselves. One of the major activities carried out by these psychologists was that of evaluation (Levine, 1981).

Finally, at the 1974 National Conference of The Preparation of Psychological Service Providers to the Deaf, preliminary action was undertaken to establish psychological practice for the hearing impaired as a professional speciality in its own right (Levine, 1977).

STRATEGIES AND EVALUATION

There is an increasing mandate from recent federal legislation as well as practitioners and consumer agencies to provide psychological evaluations of hearing-impaired persons. These assessments are a prerequisite to planning an appropriate educational program and to achieving a better understanding of the hearing-impaired individual. Ongoing assessment also is necessary to determine whether the recommended program is successful (Brackett, 1981).

BASIC CONSIDERATIONS

Certain considerations are fundamental to the psychological evaluation of the hearing impaired. These are listed next.

1. The most frequent recommendation is that the person conducting the assessment of hearing-impaired children is a psychologist who is not only experienced with them but also trained in hearing-impaired education and psychology (Boyle, 1977; Levine, 1981; Myklebust, 1960; Sullivan & Vernon, 1979; Vernon, 1976). The specialized training, experience, and knowledge are crucial in order to (a) avoid

gross psychodiagnostic errors and (b) reduce problems caused by the hearing handicap that result in a sensory impairment as well as serious linguistic deprivation problems in the acquisition and use of receptive and expressive language skills. Unfortunately, a survey of psychologists working with the hearing impaired revealed that there was little in their professional backgrounds that would qualify them to provide adequate psychological services to the hearing impaired (Levine, 1974).

2. Nonverbal performance instruments must be employed to evaluate the hearing impaired. However, nonverbal instruments that require verbal directions are inappropriate.

3. Verbal measurements are appropriate only with those hearing impaired who have sufficient verbal language to respond. Results can reveal verbal ability and areas of strength. Further, they can be used to aid in mainstreaming placement by comparing language skills of the hearing with those of the hearing impaired. For those with insufficient verbal language, verbal tests inevitably measure the hearing-impaired subject's language deficits rather than the attributes named by the tests. Psychologists must not confuse difficulty in communication with lack of intelligence.

4. Use of oral/auditory communication during the psychological examination requires that the examiner gain the subject's attention, look expectantly at the subject, maintain eye contact, eliminate obstructions that block the subject's view, speak in short and simple sentences, insist that the subject wear his or her hearing aid, and maintain an optimal distance of 2 to 3 feet from the subject.

5. Evaluation of the hearing impaired requires more time than is needed with hearing subjects. Often several test sessions are necessary. The typical reaction of the hearing impaired to timed tests is to emphasize quick completion over correctness of answers. In general, nontimed tests are more valid than those with time limitations (Hiskey, 1956).

6. Because multiple measures and comparisons are the most useful in the assessment of the hearing impaired, it follows that two or more performance scales should be administered (Vernon & Brown, 1964). With this approach, test validity is increased, and intertest result confirmation is obtained.

7. The value of interpreters is questionable because their use may result in loss of rapport between examiner and subject. Also, low standards of validity are found in such evaluations (Vernon, 1967).

8. The cooperative efforts of a multidisciplinary team best meet the evaluative needs of the hearing impaired through the use of primary and secondary teams. The ideal primary team includes an audiologist, speech/language pathologist, otologist, aural rehabilitation specialist,

psychologist, and learning disability specialist. Employed on a consulting basis, the secondary team includes a geneticist, pediatrician, occupational therapist, ophthalmologist, physical therapist, neurologist, and an audiologist who specializes in electrophysiological measurements (Matkin, Hook, & Hixson, 1979).

9. Except for use as a rough screening device, group testing of the hearing impaired is a questionable strategy and is not recommended (Sachs, 1977). Only in a one-to-one situation can an examiner (a) establish and maintain rapport, (b) apply procedures for the use of oral/aural communication, (c) ascertain the extent to which the subject depends on visual clues, (d) determine the degree to which the subject is able to utilize auditory stimuli, (e) ensure that the subject understands instructions, and (f) assess receptive and expressive language skills.

10. The maintenance of rapport should be a primary goal of the examiner because many hearing-impaired persons are difficult to assess due to social and interpersonal problems.

11. Wherever possible, instructions and verbal test items should be provided in written as well as oral form. This approach reduces the obstacles presented by oral communication.

12. A general rule for examiners conducting psychological evaluations of the hearing impaired is to begin with the least threatening procedure. Specifically, those aspects of the evaluation involving nonverbal communication should be administered initially. Then verbal elements of the evaluation should be presented.

13. The psychological evaluation is an assessment not only of the hearing-impaired individual but also of the environment that shapes that person. This viewpoint broadens the frame of reference of examiners so that they recognize their own influences on the assessment process, the importance of the client's case history, and the value of observations that evaluate the shaping influence of the environment. The focus of psychological evaluation is thus shifted from rehabilitation of the hearing-impaired person *only*, to rehabilitation of both the individual and his or her environment.

STRATEGIES FOR EVALUATION

Before recommendations for treatment can be made or educational programs formulated, the psychologist collects relevant data via the following methods: (a) tests of intelligence, academic achievement, communication, personality, and work performance or potential; (b) case history; (c) medical examination; (d) observation; and (e) interview. The advantage of using all of the previously mentioned strategies is that each provides a different type of information. Further, these data are obtained from disparate sources. This presents a broader scope than would be possible from any single strategy alone.

The amount of data needed for comprehensive evaluation of a particular individual varies. In some cases, a full evaluation is necessary. In others, only selected data are required. The information needed depends on the subject, the situation, and the perceptions and judgment of the examiner.

TESTS

Psychological tests provide objective information about an individual's present status with regard to relevant behaviors and abilities. The appeal of psychological tests lies in their ability to cover a wider and more diverse range of attributes in less time and with fewer errors than any other psychological technique (Levine, 1981).

Several criteria should be used in evaluating the performance of the hearing impaired. A subject's performance should be compared in the following ways: (a) in relation to himself or herself (i.e., how does present performance differ from the last evaluation); (b) with the performance of other hearing-impaired subjects; and (c) to his or her normally hearing peers in order to determine if lower standards have been set for these hearing-impaired subjects and to ascertain if mainstreaming is necessary or appropriate. Several reviews and analyses of psychological tests with necessary adaptations for the hearing impaired are available (see Boyle, 1977; Levine, 1981; Mittler, 1970; Sullivan & Vernon, 1979; Vernon, 1976; Zieziula, 1982).

Intelligence Tests. The determination of intellectual ability is considered the most important aspect of the psychological evaluation of the hearing impaired. Speech and language problems of these individuals and their inability to understand what is said often result in psychosocial problems and academic retardation. These handicaps frequently are misinterpreted by teachers and others as a lack of intelligence. A valid measure of intellectual capacity can be of great value in correcting these misinterpretations.

The intelligence tests most frequently used with the hearing impaired are the Wechsler and Leiter tests (Levine, 1974). Only the Performance Scales of the Wechsler Intelligence Scales for Children—Revised (WISC-R) (Wechsler, 1974) and the Wechsler Adult Intelligence Scale—Revised (WAIS-R) (Wechsler, 1981) are used. The Performance Scales are comprised of five subtests: Picture Completion, Picture Arrangement, Block

Design, Object Assembly, Coding (WISC-R only), and Digit Symbol (WAIS-R only). These individually administered tests are excellent for use with the hearing impaired. Ray (1979) has developed special administrative procedures for the WISC-R Performance Scales specifically for use with this population. Because verbal intelligence is not measured, these tests should be supplemented by other performance tests. The other commonly employed instrument with the hearing impaired is the Leiter International Performance Scale—Arthur Adaptation (Arthur, 1950). This culture-free, nonverbal, individually administered measure consists of a series of short subtests that require a person to match wooden blocks with pictures, ranging from simple to complex. It has an age level of 2 to 8 years. Still in the developmental stage, this test has questionable validity, reliability, and standardization and is not recommended for use with hearing-impaired children.

Academic Achievement Tests. To determine levels of current functioning in specific subject areas and to carry out adequate academic planning for hearing-impaired persons, some estimation of their academic achievement is necessary. Two achievement tests are most frequently used for this purpose. The Wide Range Achievement Test (WRAT) (Jastak & Jastak, 1978) consists of three subtests: Reading, Spelling, and Arithmetic. It consists of Levels I (5–12) and Level II (12 years and older). Because most subtests are administered orally and because the examiner must be fluent in total communications in order to administer the Reading and Spelling subtests, the WRAT is of questionable utility for the hearing impaired. In addition, its administrative procedures and psychometric properties are deficient.

The Stanford Achievement Test, Special Edition for Hearing Impaired Students (SAT-HI) (Madden, Gardner, Rudman, Karlsen, & Merwin, 1984) is a multiple-skill, individually or small-group administered test with four core subjects on six different levels: vocabulary, reading comprehension, mathematics computation, and mathematics concepts. It has an age level of 8 to 21 years. Further, the SAT-HI has excellent reliability, validity, and normative data. This instrument was designed specifically for the hearing impaired and is highly recommended for measuring academic achievement. Grade-equivalent scores are provided for comparison with both hearing and hearing-impaired subjects.

When achievement test results are interpreted, comparisons between hearing and hearing-impaired subjects require knowledge not only of the average achievement levels for the normal hearing subjects but also the same levels for the hearing-impaired subjects. Of the graduates from day and residential schools, about 4% attain a 10th-grade level in educational achievement; 41% attain a 7th- or 8th-grade level;

27% attain a 5th- or 6th-grade level; and about 29% attain a 4th-grade level or below (Vernon, 1971).

Communication Tests. Tests in this category concentrate on means of communication utilized for daily interaction. No standardized tests are available in this area. A variety of self-developed rating scales of communication functioning currently are employed in the field. Unfortunately, these have not demonstrated adequate psychometric properties. One of these is the Denver Scale of Communication Function (Alpiner, Chevrette, Glascoe, Metz, & Olsen, 1978). This individually administered test consists of 25 questions. Responses are judged as belonging to one of four categories: family, social-vocational, self, and general communication experience. Although the test was designed for those hearing-impaired adults with acquired hearing loss, the poor validity and reliability data make its use questionable. It should be used only as a supplementary test because its interpretation relies heavily on the audiologist's skill and experience.

The Illinois Test of Psycholinguistic Abilities (ITPA) (Kirk, McCarthy, & Kirk, 1968) is an individually administered measure consisting of 10 subtests: Auditory Reception, Visual Reception, Auditory Association, Visual Association, Verbal Expression, Manual Expression, Grammatic Closure, Visual Closure, Auditory Sequential Memory, and Visual Sequential Memory. It has an age level of 2 to 10 years.

The Visual subtests appear to be appropriate for hearing-impaired children (Weiss, Goodwin, & Moores, 1975). Nevertheless, its sophisticated English-language component along with its questionable validity do not recommend it for use with the hearing impaired.

Personality Tests. Personality tests have yielded little useful data concerning hearing-impaired adults. They have been of even less value with hearing-impaired children whose personalities have less structure than adults and who are inexperienced self-reporters (McCoy, 1972). With the hearing impaired, personality evaluation is far more complex than intelligence testing. This area of assessment depends on extensive verbal interchange or reading skills, both of which are usually deficient in these individuals. Further, personality assessment also demands a rapport that is difficult to establish because the subject often does not fully understand what is being verbalized or written. For these reasons, psychologists use family and school history, teacher reports and ratings, and their own observations of drawings, play, social responses, and family and classroom interaction in order to understand the personality of a hearing-impaired person.

The two personality tests most frequently used with the hearing impaired are the Bender Visual-Motor Gestalt Test (1963 ed.) (Bender, 1938) and the Draw-A-Person Test (Machover, 1971). The first test is individually administered and requires respondents (5–10 years of age) to copy each of nine figures on a separate piece of blank paper. Although the purpose of this instrument is to detect disturbances associated with brain defects, retardation, and regression-associated personality defects, its employment as a personality test is questionable. Little if any free personality projection is permitted because the task is one of copying. Its popularity is largely due to its ease and speed of administration. It shares with other projective tests a lack of reliability and validity. For these reasons, it is not recommended for use with the hearing impaired.

The Draw-A-Person Test is individually administered and requires the respondent to draw a male and a female figure. It is geared to children 5 years of age and above. This test should not be used as the primary tool for personality assessment. Because it is deficient with regard to normative, reliability, and validity data, it is not recommended.

WORK EVALUATION

Work evaluation is a relatively new area in programming and rehabilitive services for the hearing impaired. Aptitude tests are being replaced with hands-on experimentation in simulated work settings. Also, work samples are being developed, revised, and adapted for this population.

One work evaluation test is the Singer Vocational Evaluation System (Singer, Inc., 1971). This instrument requires the examinee to select which of 25 work samples to complete. Each work sample simulates an actual job and is presented in a work station as a self-contained unit. Individually administered to adults, the work samples range from drafting, plumbing, electrical wiring, cooking and baking, and soil testing to welding, filing, shipping and receiving, medical services, and cosmetology. The Singer has been adapted and normed for the hearing impaired and is a highly appropriate, recommended tool.

The Valpar Component Work Sample Series (Valpar Corp., 1974) consists of 16 work samples that range from numerical sorting, problem solving, and eye-hand-foot coordination to soldering, money handling, drafting, clerical comprehension, and aptitude. Administrative instructions for the hearing-impaired adults are available, and 12 of the 16 work samples are normed on a hearing-impaired sample. This series is recommended for assessing vocational skills.

CASE HISTORY

The case history provides a narration of the experiences and events that have shaped the individual. It is obtained from a variety of sources (e.g., parents, spouse, teachers) and spans the chronological range. The case history attempts to identify etiological factors and possible interventions for extant difficulties.

MEDICAL EXAMINATIONS

The medical examination and audiological and neuropsychological assessments are necessary for clarifying the hearing-impaired client's health status. They also are useful in determining the extent of deficits and their effect on the functioning of hearing-impaired persons.

OBSERVATION

Direct observation enables the examiner to evaluate the individual in a variety of interpersonal and social contexts with peers, teachers, instructional methods, curricula, and the like. In addition, a person's level of communication skill can be ascertained through parental observation, description of the subject's expressive abilities, and determination of his or her awareness of environmental sounds and voices. Hearing impairment affects the ease with which communication occurs. In turn, communication forms the basis for social interaction. The best estimate of the quality of social performance and emotional reactions is obtained from careful and systematic observations.

INTERVIEW

The interview provides information directly from the individual and enables the examiner to obtain a view of the subjects' perceptions of the world in which they live, their place in it, and their hopes, problems, and coping mechanisms. The examiner gets a glimpse of the world through the eyes of the subject while offering the individual considerable latitude for self-expression.

RESEARCH FINDINGS

The following is a review of research involving psychological evaluation of the hearing impaired. This work is divided into six sections: (a) intelligence, (b) academic achievement, (c) social and personal adjustment, (d) personality, (e) occupational adjustment, and (f) communication approaches.

INTELLIGENCE

Inasmuch as the progress of hearing-impaired children is partly dependent on intelligence and conceptual abilities, it is not surprising that the largest number of research studies are in this area. Psychological tests that rely on the use of verbal language to measure intelligence (or personality and other attributes) are inappropriate because they measure language deficiencies rather than intelligence (Myklebust, 1954; Vernon, 1976). Rather, nonverbal performance tests yield the most valid measures of intelligence with this population (Vernon & Brown, 1964).

Research data indicate that (a) the distribution of intelligence in the hearing impaired is the same as that of the hearing population when nonverbal IQ scales are used (McConnell, 1973, Vernon, 1967), (b) very few IQs substantially below the 90s have been found in the hearing impaired (Pronovost, Bates, Clasby, Miller, & Thompson, 1976), and (c) they develop intellectually in their thinking processes and in concrete ways of thinking in a manner similar to hearing peers (Altshuler, 1974; Furth & Youniss, 1971; Moores, 1978; Youniss, 1974).

The hearing impaired are inferior to hearing subjects on some intellectual tasks but equal or superior on others. For example, they are deficient on digit span, picture span, memory, and memory for movement (Myklebust, 1960), poorer with digits but equal with nonsense forms of visual memory span tests (Olsson & Furth, 1966), lower in verbal language intelligence but equal on logic and deduction intelligence (Furth, 1973), poorer on picture arrangement and coding subtests of the WISC-R but similar on the other four subtests of the Performance Scale (Sisco & Anderson, 1978).

In a review of 50 years of research on intelligence in the hearing impaired, Vernon (1968) reported the lack of a clear relationship between type of deafness and IQ, degree of hearing loss and IQ, or age of onset of deafness and IQ. Birch, Stuckless, and Birth (1963) examined the association between scores on the Leiter International Performance Scale and subsequent school achievement and found a significant, positive relationship between the two. Brill (1962) studied the same association albeit with different tests and showed that the distribution for the hearing impaired was similar to that of hearing subjects.

Using two different approaches, Furth (1966) and Darbyshire (1965) tested hearing-impaired persons on Piagetian tasks. Results from both investigations demonstrated that the hearing impaired were not inferior to hearing subjects, given sufficient time to complete tasks.

Stewart (1978) administered the WISC and WAIS to hearing-impaired subjects to determine the correspondence between eight observable social behaviors and performance scales. The findings suggested that there is some relationship between these two variables. In another study (Hirshoren, 1979), the Performance Scale of the WISC-R was given to hearing-impaired students to ascertain the reliability and validity of the scale. Results indicated that the reliability coefficients for the four unspeeded tests and for the performance IQ compared favorably with those found by Wechsler's standardization sample. Further, concurrent and predictive validities were adequate (Hirshoren, 1979).

Brooks and Riggs (1980) administered the WISC and WISC-R Performance Scales to hearing impaired students attending public schools. They reported significant correlations between the two scales for each similar subtest, confirming the validity of the WISC-R. However, correlations between the WISC-R Performance subtests and reading achievement were nonsignificant.

ACADEMIC ACHIEVEMENT

The major impact of hearing impairment is on language and related achievements (e.g., reading). Studies of academic achievement in the hearing impaired have failed to show substantial improvement over the years. Achievement tends to be lowest in areas that rely on knowledge of English, such as reading, social studies, and science and higher in spelling and arithmetic computation (Moores, 1978).

On the average, deaf students are at least 3 to 4 years below grade level, whereas partially hearing students are from ½ to 2 years behind (Kodman, 1963; Ling, 1972; McConnell, 1973). Trybus and Karchmer (1977) reported that one half of the students in classes for the deaf read below the mid-fourth-grade level and that only 10% of the 18-year-olds read at the eighth-grade level or above. More than 25% of all mainstreamed hearing-impaired students could not be integrated into any academic subject (Libbey & Pronovost, 1980). Jensema (1975) found that the less severe the hearing loss, the greater the academic achievement.

Pugh (1946) administered reading tests to deaf students and found that they became increasingly retarded in reading as the language requirements for understanding increased in complexity. Almost 30 years later, an investigation by Gentile (1973) showed a similar pattern of results. Research by Craig and Craig (1977) revealed that approximately 25% of students enrolled in classes for the deaf are multihandicapped. Further, Jensema (1975) reported that these students tended to score lower in reading achievement than students who were hearing impaired only.

Rudner (1978) used standard achievement tests to determine items that were biased against hearing-impaired examinees. Twenty-six such items, which fell into the categories of conditionals, inferentials, comparatives, negation, and lengthy passages, were identified.

The academic achievements of hearing-impaired students of hearing parents have been compared to the academic achievement of hearing-impaired students of hearing-impaired parents (Messerly & Aram, 1980). This work showed that hearing-impaired students of hearing parents either equaled or surpassed the achievement of the other group. Results were the reverse with samples of deaf students (Meadow, 1981; Stuckless & Birch, 1966; Vernon & Koh, 1970).

Social and Personal Adjustment

The inability to hear or understand verbal and nonverbal nuances of language affects interpersonal relations and adjustment. In a survey of 43,946 hearing-impaired students, Jensema and Trybus (1975) reported that only 8% had significant emotional and behavioral problems. Also, rates were higher among males and those with additional handicapping conditions.

Meadow (1975) reviewed investigations of social and psychological adjustments in deaf children. This examination revealed that deaf children (a) scored lower than hearing children in social maturity, (b) of deaf parents scored higher in social maturity than deaf children of hearing parents, (c) had fewer social interactions than did hearing children, (d) had inflated ideas about their capabilities and about what others think of them, and (e) had more adjustment problems. In addition, the incidence of severe emotional disturbance and behavioral disorders appeared to be the same for both deaf and hearing populations.

Baroff (1969) studied the adjustment of deaf adults. Seventy-five percent of those interviewed claimed they had close friends. A higher percentage reported being with others on a social basis at least once a week. Finally, nearly half of the sample stated that they had both hearing and deaf friends.

Personality

Data in this area are viewed with skepticism by professionals in the field because of the questionable validity of personality tests with this population (Davis, 1981). This is due to the communication problems inherent in hearing loss, the extensive verbal interchange or reading skills on which these tests depend, and the presupposition of rapport and confidence on the part of respondents who often do not fully understand what is being said or written (Levine, 1960; Moores, 1978; Rosen, 1967). Also the literature is replete with examples of the hearing impaired erroneously being labeled *emotionally disturbed* on the basis of assessment instruments that are primarily verbal (Donoghue, 1968; Moores, 1978; Vernon, 1976).

OCCUPATIONAL ADJUSTMENT

Research confirms that despite their handicap, hearing-impaired adults adjust to virtually any kind of job that does not require the ability to hear well (Kirk & Gallagher, 1979). In a survey of occupational functioning, Schein and Delk (1974) found fewer deaf individuals in professional fields, managerial positions, and clerical and sales positions in comparison to persons with hearing. They state that this was due to the necessity of communication in such positions. In addition, greater numbers of deaf individuals served as skilled and semiskilled workers, and machine operators in similar jobs.

COMMUNICATION APPROACHES

The methodology for teaching communication skills is based on one of three philosophies: oral, manual, or total communication. Although there appears to be a modicum of difference in intelligence between children taught orally and those trained through total communication (see Wooden, 1963), Furth (1973) contends that oral instruction is not very effective for deaf children. Lipreading is a difficult task, and only 33% of English speech sounds are visible (Hardy, 1970). Moreover, even the most proficient lipreaders process only 25% of what is said. Estimates for processing by deaf children are much lower (approximately 5%) (Vernon & Koh, 1970). Children exposed to manual communication are superior in academic achievement and other areas relative to children deprived of such exposure (Meadow, 1968; Stuckless & Birch, 1966; Vernon, 1970).

The superiority of total communication as a teaching methodology is supported by results of several investigations (Meadow, 1968; Moores, Weiss, & Goodwin, 1978; Stuckless & Birch, 1966; Vernon & Koh, 1970). It also is more effective as an administration mode on the WISC-R Performance Scale (Sullivan, 1982) in comparison to pantomime (Graham & Shapiro, 1953; Murphy, 1957) and visual aids (Neuhaus, 1967; Reed, 1970).

CASE STUDIES

To demonstrate the differing development among children with disparate degrees of hearing loss, case studies are presented involving a hard-of-hearing child (Sarah), a deafened child (Joan), and a deaf child (Frank). Figure 1 profiles these differences that were taken from their psychological evaluations. All three subjects are 10 years old and are average in height and weight for their ages.

Sarah's 40-decibel hearing loss is classified as mild. The only differences between her and an average student are in vocabulary, reading comprehension, speech development, and language development. Even these

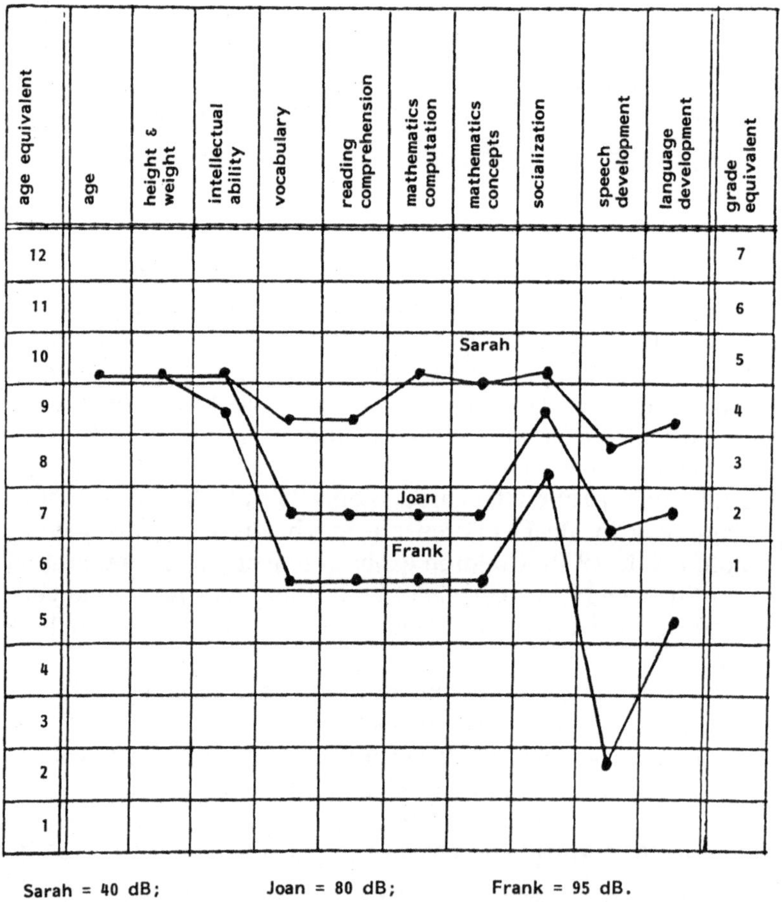

FIGURE 1. Profiles of three hearing-impaired children with different degrees of hearing loss.

differences are minimal. Sarah is slightly retarded in speech development, having articulatory defects of substitution, omission, and distortion. She has been fitted with a hearing aid and is receiving speech remediation and speech-reading lessons. Otherwise, she is functioning well in a regular classroom.

Joan's 80-decibel loss is classified as severe even after being fitted with a hearing aid. Although she was born with normal hearing, she suffered a serious hearing loss at Age 5 and is classified as postlingually deaf. However, she is still able to learn through the auditory channel with the help of a hearing aid because she had learned to talk normally and had developed much language ability prior to her hearing loss. Because she has not developed in language normally since Age 5, retardation in language has resulted. Her language development, along with her academic development, presently is at the second-grade level. Although she is normal in intelligence, her educational progress has been slowed by her hearing loss. She is progressing satisfactorily in a mainstreamed classroom because of speech remediation, speech-reading lessons, auditory training, and other specialized techniques.

Frank's 90-decibel hearing loss is classified as extreme. He has never heard the spoken word because he was born deaf. Despite instruction, he presently talks only as well as a child of two, and his language development is at the 5-year-old level. His socialization has suffered due to his very restricted ability to communicate and to learn. Academically, he is at the beginning first-grade level. Educationally, he is retarded about four years and has been placed in a class for the deaf even though he is slightly below normal intellectually.

SUMMARY

The hearing impaired were described and the history and development of the psychological evaluation of this population were presented. Decision making is a fundamental aspect of applied psychology. To arrive at decisions, basic principles must be considered, and strategies for evaluation must be followed in order to produce meaningful data. Although several efficacious efforts have been made in this regard, most present assessment measures must be replaced. This is primarily due to problems of inaccuracy and poor predictive power. The need to develop new techniques and strategies for assessing the hearing impaired has been recognized and is only now beginning to receive the attention it deserves. Research findings confirm this need and also yield issues to be addressed. The most critical of these is the effect of language and communication on the psychological evaluation process.

REFERENCES

Alpiner, J., Chevrette, W., Glascoe, G., Metz, M., & Olsen, B. (1978). Denver Scale of Communication Function. In J. G. Alpiner (Ed.), *The handbook of adult rehabilitative audiology* (pp. 127–132). Baltimore: Williams & Wilkins.

Arthur, G. (1950). *The Arthur Adaptation of the Leiter International Performance Scale*. Chicago: Stoelting.

Altshuler, K. Z. (1974). The social and psychological development of the deaf child: Problems, treatment, and prevention. *American Annals of the Deaf, 119*, 365–376.

Baroff, G. S. (1969). Patterns of socialization and community integration. In J. D. Ranier, K. Z. Altshuler, & F. J. Kallman (Eds.), *Family and mental health problems in a deaf population* (pp. 66–91). Springfield, IL: Charles C Thomas.

Bender, L. (1938). *A visual motor gestalt test and its clinical use* (Research Monograph No. 3). New York: American Orthopsychiatric Association.

Birch, J. R., Stuckless, E. R., & Birch, J. W. (1963). An eleven-year study of predicting school achievement in young deaf children. *American Annals of the Deaf, 108*, 236–240.

Boyle, P. (1977). Psychology. In B. F. Jaffe (Ed.), *Hearing loss in children* (pp. 26–55). Baltimore: University Park Press.

Brackett, D. (1981). Assessment: Adaptations, interpretations, and implications. In M. Ross & L. Nober (Eds.), *Educating hard of hearing children* (pp. 47–66). Washington, DC: The Alexander Graham Bell Association for the Deaf.

Brill, R. G. (1962). The relationship of Wechsler IQ's to academic achievement among deaf students. *Exceptional Children, 28*, 315–321.

Brooks, C. R., & Riggs, S. T. (1980). WISC-R, WISC, and reading achievement relationships among hearing-impaired children attending public schools. *Volta Review, 82*, 96–102.

Committee on Nomenclature (1938). Conference of executives of american schools for the deaf. *American Annals of the Deaf, 83*

Council for Exceptional Children (1966). *Professional standards for personnel in the education of exceptional children*. Washington, DC: National Education Association.

Craig, W. N., & Craig, H. (Eds.), (1977). *American Annals of the Deaf, 122*, 2.

Darbyshire, J. (1965). *The development of reasoning in the deaf, along with an experimental study in the use of adaptations of some of Piaget's tests with groups of deaf and hearing children*. Unpublished doctoral dissertation, Queens University, Belfast, Northern Ireland.

Davis, J. (1981). Psychosocial considerations and evaluation. In M. Ross & L. W. Nober (Eds.), *Educating hard of hearing children* (pp. 67–76). Washington, DC: Alexander Graham Bell Association for the Deaf.

Donoghue, R. J. (1968). The deaf personality, a study in contrasts. *Journal of Rehabilitation of the Deaf, 2*, 37–51.

Ehrlich, P. R., Ehrlich, A. H., & Holdren, J. P. (1972). *Human Ecology*. San Francisco: Freeman.

Furth, H. G. (1964). Research with the deaf: Implications for language and cognition. *Psychological Bulletin, 62*, 145–164.

Furth, H. G. (1966). *Thinking without language*. New York: Free Press.

Furth, H. G. (1973). *Deafness and learning: A psychological approach*. Belmont, CA: Wadsworth.

Furth, H. G., & Youniss, J. (1971). Formal operations and language: A comparison of deaf and hearing adolescents. *International Journal of Psychology, 6*, 49–64.

Gentile, A. (1973). Further studies in achievement testing, hearing impaired students: 1971. *Annual Survey of Hearing Impaired Children and Youth* (Series D, No. 13). Washington, DC: Gallaudet College Office of Demographic Studies.

Gentile, A., & McCarthy, B. (1973). Additional handicapping conditions among hearing impaired students, United States, 1971–1972. *Annual Survey of Hearing Impaired Children and Youth* (Series D, No. 14). Washington, DC: Gallaudet College Office of Demographic Studies.

Graham, E. E., & Shapiro, E. (1953). Use of the Performance scale of the WISC and the deaf child. *Journal of Consulting Psychology, 17,* 396–398.

Greenberger, D. (1899). Doubtful cases. *American Annals of the Deaf, 34,* 93–99.

Hardy, M. P. (1970). Speechreading. In H. Davis & A. S. Silverman (Eds.), *Hearing and deafness* (pp. 73–90). New York: Holt, Rinehart & Winston.

Hirshoren, A. (1979). Psychometric characteristics of the WISC-R Performance scale with deaf children. *Journal of Speech and Hearing Disorders, 44,* 73–79.

Hiskey, M. S. (1956). A study of the intelligence of deaf and hearing children. *American Annals of the Deaf, 101,* 329–339.

Hodgson, K. W. (1954). *The deaf and their problems.* New York: Philosophical Library.

Hull, F., Mielke, P., Willeford, J., & Timmons, R. (1976). *National Speech and Hearing Survey* (Project No. 50978). Washington, DC: Bureau of Education for the Handicapped.

Illinois Commission on Children (1968). *A comprehensive plan for hearing impaired children in Illinois.* Springfield, IL: Author.

Jastak, J. F., & Jastak, S. R. (1978). *The Wide Range Achievement Test.* Wilmington, DE: Jastak Associates.

Jensema, C. (1975). *The relationship between academic achievement and the demographic characteristics of hearing impaired children and youth.* Washington, DC: Gallaudet College Office of Demographic Studies.

Jensema, C., & Trybus, R. (1975). *Reported emotional/behavioral problems among hearing impaired children in special education programs: United States 1972–73* (Series R, No. 1). Washington, DC: Gallaudet College Office of Demographic Studies.

Kirk, S., McCarthy, J., & Kirk, W. (1968). *The Illinois Test of Psycholinguistic Abilities* (rev. ed.). Urbana: University of Illinois Press.

Kirk, S. A., & Gallagher, J. J. (1979). *Educating exceptional children.* Boston, MA: Houghton Mifflin.

Kodman, F. (1963). Educational status of hard of hearing children in the classroom. *Journal of Speech and Hearing Disorders, 28,* 297–299.

Levine, E. S. (1960). *Psychology of Deafness.* New York: Columbia University Press.

Levine, E. S. (1974). Psychological tests and practices with the deaf: A survey of the state of the art. *Volta Review, 76,* 298–319.

Levine, E. S. (1976). Psychological contributions. In R. Frisina (Ed.), *A bicentennial monograph on hearing impaired* (pp. 17–39). Washington, DC: Alexander Graham Bell Association for the Deaf.

Levine, E. S. (Ed.). (1977). *The preparation of psychological service providers to the deaf* (PRWAD monograph no. 4). Silver Springs, MD: Professional Rehabilitation Workers with the Deaf.

Levine, E. S. (1981). *The ecology of early deafness.* New York: Columbia University Press.

Libbey, S. S., & Pronovost, W. (1980). Communication practices of mainstreamed hearing-impaired adolescents. *Volta Review, 82,* 197–213.

Ling, D. (1972). Rehabilitation of cases with deafness secondary to otitis media. In A. Glorig & K. S. Gerwin (Eds.), *Otitis media* (pp. 137–157). Springfield, IL: Charles C Thomas.

Machover, K. (1971). *Personality projection in the drawing of the human figure* (8th ed.). Springfield, IL: Charles C Thomas.

Madden, R., Gardner, E. F., Rudman, H. C., Karlsen, B., & Merwin, J. C. (1984). *Stanford Achievement Test, Special Edition for Hearing Impaired Students.* Washington, DC: Gallaudet College Center for Assessment and Demographic Studies.

Mandell, C. J., & Fiscus, E. (1981). *Understanding Exceptional People*. St. Paul: West.
Matkin, N. D., Hook, P. E., & Hixson, P. K. (1979). A multidisciplinary approach to the evaluation of hearing impaired children. *Audiology: An Audio Journal for Continuing Education*. New York: Grune & Stratton.
McConnell, F. (1973). Children with hearing disabilities. In L. M. Dunn (Ed.), *Exceptional children in the schools: Special education in transition* (2nd ed., pp. 191–219). New York: Holt, Rinehart & Winston.
McCoy, G. F. (1972). *Diagnostic evaluation and educational programming for hearing impaired children*. Springfield: Illinois State Office of Superintendent of Public Instruction.
Meadow, K. P. (1968). Early communication in relation to the deaf child's intellectual, social, and communicative functioning. *American Annals of the Deaf, 113*, 29–41.
Meadow, K. P. (1975). The development of deaf children. In E. Hetherington (Ed.), *Review of child development research* (pp. 441–507). Chicago: University of Chicago Press.
Meadow, K. P. (1981). Burnout in professionals working with deaf children. *American Annals of the Deaf, 126*(1), 13–22.
Messerly, C. L., & Aram, D. M. (1980). Academic achievement of hearing-impaired students of hearing parents and of hearing-impaired parents: Another look. *Volta Review, 82*, 25–32.
Mittler, P. (1970). *The psychological assessment of mental and physical handicaps*. London: Methuen.
Moores, D. F. (1978). *Educating the deaf: Psychology, principles and practices*. Boston: Houghton Mifflin.
Moores, D. F., & Oden, C. (1977). Educational needs of black deaf children. *American Annals of the Deaf, 122*, 313–318.
Moores, D. F., Weiss, K. L., & Goodwin, M. W. (1978). Early education programs for hearing-impaired children: Major findings. *American Annals of the Deaf, 123*, 925–936.
Murphy, K. P. (1957). Tests of ability and attainments. In A. W. G. Ewing (Ed.), *Educational guidance and the deaf child* (pp. 117–135). Manchester: Manchester University Press.
Myklebust, H. R. (1954). *Auditory disorders in children. A manual for differential diagnosis*. New York: Grune & Stratton.
Myklebust, H. R. (1960). *The psychology of deafness*. New York: Grune & Stratton.
Neuhaus, M. (1967). Modifications in the administration of the WISC performance subtests for children with profound hearing losses. *Exceptional Children, 33*, 573–574.
Office of Vocational Rehabilitation. (1956). *New hope for the disabled: Public Law 565*. Washington, DC: U.S. Government Printing Office.
Olsson, J. E., & Furth, H. G. (1966). Visual memory-span of the deaf. *American Journal of Psychology, 79*, 480–484.
Pintner, R., Eisenson, J., & Stanton, M. (1941). *The psychology of the physically handicapped*. New York: Crofts.
Pronovost, W., Bates, J., Clasby, E., Miller, N. J., & Thompson, R. (1976). Hearing impaired children with associated disabilities. *Exceptional Children, 42*, 439–443.
Pugh, G. (1946). Summaries from appraisal of the silent reading abilities of acoustically handicapped children. *American Annals of the Deaf, 91*, 331–349.
Ray, S. (1979). *An adaptation of the Wechsler Intelligence Scale for Children—Revised for the Deaf*. Natchitoches: Northwestern State University of Louisiana.
Reed, M. (1970). Deaf and partially hearing children. In P. Mittler (Ed.), *The psychological assessment of mental and physical handicaps* (pp. 207–242). London: Methuen.
Rosen, A. (1967). Limitations of personality inventories for assessment of deaf children and adults as illustrated by research with the MMPI. *Journal of Rehabilitation of the Deaf, 1*, 47–52.

Rudner, L. M. (1978). Using standard tests with the hearing impaired: The problem of item bias. *Volta Review, 80*, 31–40.

Sachs, B. B. (1977). Psychological assessment of the deaf person. *Mental Health in Deafness, 1*, 93–95.

Schein, J. D., & Delk, M. T. (1974). *The deaf population of the United States*. Silver Springs, MD: National Association of the Deaf.

Singer Incorporated. (1971). *Singer Vocational Evaluation System*. Rochester: Author.

Sisco, F. H., & Anderson, R. J. (1978). Current findings regarding the performance of deaf children on the WISC-R. *American Annals of the Deaf, 123*, 115–121.

Smith, R. M., Neisworth, J. T., & Hunt, F. M. (1983). *The exceptional child* (2nd ed.). New York: McGraw-Hill.

Stewart, J. H. (1978). Performance IQ scores and social behaviors of deaf students. *Dissertation Abstracts International, 38*, 4432B.

Stuckless, E., & Birch, J. (1966). The influence of early manual communication on the linguistic development of deaf children. *American Annals of the Deaf, 111*, 499–504.

Sullivan, P. M. (1982). Administration modifications on the WISC-R Performance Scale with different categories of deaf children. *American Annals of the Deaf, 127*, 780–788.

Sullivan, P. M., & Vernon, M. (1979). Psychological assessment of hearing impaired children. *School Psychology Digest, 8*, 271–290.

Trybus, R. J., & Karchmer, M. A. (1977). School achievement scores of hearing impaired children: National data on achievement status and growth patterns. *American Annals of the Deaf, 122*, 62–69.

United States Department of Health, Education, and Welfare (1975). *National health survey: Prevalence of selected impairments*. Rockville, MD: Author.

Valpar Corporation. (1974). *Valpar Component Work Sample Series*. Tucson: Author.

Vernon, M. (1967). Relationship of language to the thinking process. *Archives of General Psychiatry, 16*, 325–333.

Vernon, M. (1968). Fifty years of research on the intelligence of deaf and hard-of-hearing children: A review of literature and discussion of implications. *Journal of Rehabilitation of the Deaf, 2*, 1–12.

Vernon, M. C. (1970). Psychological evaluation and interviewing of the hearing impaired. *Rehabilitation Research and Practical Review, 1*, 45–52.

Vernon, M. (1971). Myths in the education of deaf children. *Hearing and Speech News, 39*, 13, 16–17.

Vernon, M. (1976). Psychological evaluation of hearing-impaired children. In L. Lloyd (Ed.), *Communication assessment and intervention strategies* (pp. 37–65). Baltimore: University Park Press.

Vernon, M., & Brown, D. W. (1964). A guide to psychological tests and testing procedures in the evaluation of deaf and hard-of-hearing children. *Journal of Speech and Hearing Disorders, 29*, 414–423.

Vernon, M., & Koh, S. (1970). Effects of manual communication on deaf children's educational achievement, linguistic competence, oral skills, and psychological development. *American Annals of the Deaf, 115*, 527–536.

Wechsler, D. (1974). *Wechsler Intelligence Scale for Children—Revised*. New York: Psychological Corporation.

Wechsler, D. (1981). *Wechsler Adult Intelligence Scale—Revised*. New York: Psychological Corporation.

Weiss, K., Goodwin, M., & Moores, D. (1975). *Evaluation of programs for hearing-impaired children: 1969–1974*. (Research Report No. 91). Minneapolis: University of Minnesota, Development and Demonstration Center in Education of Handicapped Children.

Wooden, H. Z. (1963). Deaf and hard-of-hearing children. In L. M. Dunn (Ed.), *Exceptional children in the schools* (pp. 20–37). New York: Holt, Rinehart & Winston.

Youniss, J. (1974). Operational development in deaf Costa Rican subjects. *Child Development, 45,* 212–216.

Zieziula, F. R. (Ed.). (1982). *Assessment of hearing-impaired people.* Washington, DC: Gallaudet College Press.

6

Visual Impairment

LORI A. SISSON AND VINCENT B. VAN HASSELT

INTRODUCTION

A review of historical aspects of blindness, as well as societal perspectives toward and treatment of the blind, reveals an erratic course over the ages (see Kirtley 1975; Lowenfeld, 1976). In prehistoric societies, the blind and other disabled individuals were considered liabilities. This was largely due to limitations imposed by such disorders in carrying out activities (e.g., hunting, building shelter) requisite to survival. Later, in Greek and Roman civilizations, laws permitted killing of blind infants because they were considered a burden to the state. Although many famous blind scholars, philosophers, and poets (e.g, Homer) lived during this period, most had acquired the handicap later in life.

The Middle Ages generally was a time of great hardship for the blind, although some inroads toward improving their existence were made. Many had to rely on begging in order to survive or were confined to asylums. Blinding of criminals was commonly practiced as an extreme form of punishment. Some monasteries, however, provided food, shelter, and medical care to blind individuals. Also, charitable organizations

---

LORI A. SISSON • Western Psychiatric Institute and Clinic, 3811 O'Hara Street, Pittsburgh, Pennsylvania 15213. VINCENT B. VAN HASSELT • Department of Psychiatry and Human Behavior, University of California, Irvine, 101 City Drive South, Orange, California 92668.
Preparation of this chapter was facilitated by grant G008300135 (National Institute of Handicapped Research) and contract 300-82-0368 (Early Childhood Research Institute) from the Department of Education. However, the opinions expressed herein do not necessarily reflect the position or policy of the U.S. Department of Education and no official endorsement by the department should be inferred.

were formed to provide assistance. Most notably, King Louis IX of France created the Congregation of the Three Hundred in 1254 to care for blinded crusaders.

A number of gains also were made in non-Western societies. In Japan, blind individuals were encouraged to pursue careers in the fields of music, art, acupuncture, and religion. Many achieved considerable notoriety for their contributions in these areas. In Egypt, welfare programs were initiated for the disabled, which included training and provision of employment for the blind. Charity toward the disabled also was considered a religious duty by Egyptian priests. In addition, the first educational program for the blind was established at Egypt's University of Al-Ashar in A.D. 970.

The history of the education of the blind is a relatively brief one. The first school program specifically developed to provide education for blind students was established in Paris by Valentin Hauy in 1784. Shortly afterward, schools for the blind were founded in Milan, Berlin, Amsterdam, and other European cities. In particular, the Viennese school started by Johann Wilhelm Klein in 1804 has received much historical attention. Klein firmly believed that employment was a critical goal for the blind and that vocational training should be provided as part of the total educational process. To provide this needed instruction, he established the Institute for the Care and Employment of the Blind in 1826. In the early 1830s, schools for the blind opened in several cities (Boston, Philadelphia, New York) in the United States. Since that period and up until the mid-twentieth century, most blind children were educated in these schools. However, considerable controversy arose concerning the segregation of the blind from the rest of society as a result of their placement in these settings. Of perhaps greatest concern was the lack of opportunity for adequate socialization.

A major change in the education of the blind occurred with the passage of Public Law (P.L.) 94-142, the Education for All Handicapped Children Act, in 1975. Under the provisions of this law, all handicapped students have the right to a free and appropriate public education in the "least restrictive environment." Enactment of P.L. 94-142 resulted in a substantial shift in educational and treatment practices, most importantly, deinstitutionalization of many severely handicapped children into community residential and educational settings. Further, it underscored the importance of technically adequate and comprehensive evaluation to decisions regarding educational placement and programming. Consequently, considerable attention has been directed to the psychoeducational assessment of visually handicapped children in recent years (Ysseldyke & Shinn, 1981).

It was not until the return of blinded veterans from World War I that extensive rehabilitative services were instituted for blind adults. Almost concurrently, the American Foundation for the Blind began to implement research programs and technical assistance for visually handicapped persons. During the 1950s and 1960s, rehabilitation centers for blind adults were established to provide education and training in a wide variety of areas. Some of these included daily living skills (e.g, use of telephone and public transportation, money exchange and identification), mobility, and communication (e.g, braille, typing, use of talking book machines). At present, there are more than 800 organizations spending over $470 million annually to provide training, services, and education to blind adults and their families (Koestler, 1976). Further, in response to calls for adequate assessment of strengths and weaknesses across a wide range of skills (Van Hasselt & Sisson, in press; Ysseyldyke & Shinn, 1981), psychological evaluation has assumed a prominant role in decisions concerning career planning, access to vocational training programs, agency placement, and eligibility for social services.

The purpose of this chapter is to review assessment methods used with the visually handicapped. The need for examination and understanding of these approaches with this population is threefold: (a) information pertaining to psychometric properties of assessment techniques is necessary for interpreting results of research, (b) psychological assessment data are being increasingly utilized to make decisions about the lives of blind individuals, and (c) assessment is a major factor in determinations of heuristic psychological, educational, habilitative, or rehabilitative intervention for visually handicapped persons. We will first provide a description of visual disorders. This will be followed by a presentation of the history and development of assessment procedures for the visually handicapped. Then specific strategies for evaluation will be covered. This will include assessment methods tapping intellectual functioning, educational/vocational skills, social competency and adaptive living skills, and personality and behavior disorders. Often instruments and procedures devised for normally developing sighted persons are employed with visually handicapped persons. Thus interviewing, standardized testing, and behavioral assessment are used, although modifications and adaptations in administration may be necessitated by the visual deficit. Next, special considerations relevant to assessment of visually handicapped persons will be discussed. Finally, issues pertaining to research with this population will be elaborated, and suggestions for future assessment endeavors will be offered.

DESCRIPTION OF THE DISORDER

Although there is no universally accepted definition of blindness, the one adopted for most legal and economic decisions was originally part of the Social Security Act of 1935. This act was formulated mainly for identification of aged individuals requiring increased benefits. According to this legislation, legal blindness is defined as

> visual acuity for distant vision of 20/200 or less in the better eye, with best correction; or visual acuity of more than 20/200 if the widest diameter of field of vision subtends an angle no greater than 20 degrees. (National Society for the Prevention of Blindness, 1966, p. 10)

More simply stated, a person is considered legally blind if he or she can see no more at a distance of 20 feet than someone with normal sight can see at a distance of 200 feet or if there is severe restriction of the visual field.

Recent national health surveys (National Society to Prevent Blindness, 1980) indicate that nearly 11.5 million persons in the United States have some form of visual impairment. Approximately 500,000 of these individuals are legally blind. Although it is estimated that almost 37,000 children and youth in this country have this diagnosis, blindness is largely associated with the aging process, and about half of the legally blind population is over 65 years of age (Vaughan & Asbury, 1977).

According to the National Society to Prevent Blindness (1980), there are four major causes of blindness. The first is *glaucoma*, a slowly progressive disorder involving a substantial increase in intraocular pressure. This pressure reduces the supply of blood to the retina and causes nerve cells to be destroyed. The second principal cause of blindness is *macular degeneration*, which is characterized by damaged blood vessels in the macular area of the retina. This part of the eye is responsible for clear and sharp vision. *Cataracts* is a lens opacity that clouds and ultimately obstructs vision if not treated. This problem most commonly occurs in older individuals, although it may be found in young children as a result of maternal rubella during the first trimester of gestation, genetic inheritance, or trauma. The fourth leading cause of blindness is *optic nerve atrophy*, a problem most frequently found in youth and middle age. It involves a diminution of the optic nerve that may occur for a variety of reasons, most notably, degenerative diseases.

In addition to being a physical condition, the effects of a serious vision loss "may extend far beyond the visual system itself to affect every area of development, both perceptual and nonperceptual" (Warren, 1981, p. 195). For perceptual functioning, a severe visual handicap results in a discontinuous and inaccurate information source concerning people and objects. Auditory input alone is insufficient for providing information commensurate with input available through the visual channel. With regard to conceptual development, vision plays a major role in (a) identification of objects and events, (b) acquisition of concepts pertaining to structure of physical space and spatial relationships, and (c) consolidation of disparate perceptual characteristics into more integrated concepts (see Warren, 1977).

Numerous investigations also have examined the effects of visual impairment on socialization. This literature shows that a disproportionately large number of visually handicapped children and adults exhibit problems in social functioning (see review by Van Hasselt, 1983). Factors implicated in their poor social adjustment include difficulties acquiring nonverbal interpersonal skill components, such as physical gestures and facial expressions (Van Hasselt, Hersen, & Kazdin, 1985); deficits in assertion skills (Van Hasselt, Hersen, Kazdin, Simon, & Mastantuono, 1983); inability to acquire social skills by modeling via utilization of visual cues (Farkas, Sherick, Matson, & Loebig, 1981); inaccurate feedback concerning interpersonal effectiveness from the environment (Kleck, Ono, & Hastorf, 1966; Scott, 1969); and negative reactions from family members, peers, and others in the visually handicapped person's social environment (Barry & Marshall, 1953; Sommers, 1944).

There also is a convergence of evidence to suggest behavioral and emotional problems in many visually handicapped children and adults (e.g., Blank, 1959; Cruickshank, 1964; Jan, Freeman, & Scott, 1977; Van Hasselt, Kazdin, & Hersen, 1986). For example, Jan *et al.* (1977) assessed psychopathology in 86 children who were either blind or had partial vision. They found that "developmental" disorder (i.e., peculiar and persistent deviations in specific [usually multiple] areas that were judged as having negative impacts on the child's total adaptation) was present in 41% of the blind but in only 8% of a sample of sighted controls. Similarly, evidence of psychopathology as reflected by Minnesota Multiphasic Personality Inventory (MMPI) profiles of blind adults has been reported (Klimasinski, 1972).

HISTORY AND DEVELOPMENT OF ASSESSMENT PROCEDURES

Although the number of visually handicapped persons in the United States is relatively small and the problems inherent in developing tests for them are considerable (see "Special Considerations and Research Issues"), efforts to adapt evaluation methods and procedures for use with this population were initiated early in the history of psychological testing. There are several trends that are readily apparent in the history of assessing the visually handicapped. First, although early psychologists (Hayes, 1929; Irwin & Goddard, 1914) focused upon assessment of intelligence and academic achievement of blind but otherwise normally developing schoolchildren, a shift in emphasis has extended target populations to adults, younger children, and multihandicapped persons. The popularity of vocational guidance in the 1930s and 1940s coupled with the considerable interest in rehabilitation of the handicapped in the 1940s and 1950s provided the impetus for testing adults in addition to handicapped children and youth (Bauman & Kropf, 1979; Goldman, 1970). More recently, increased concern for the education and care of the preschool child and the burgeoning number of multihandicapped blind has extended testing efforts to include these groups as well (Bauman & Kropf, 1979; Langley, 1979). Along with this shift, the abilities assessed have been broadened. Measures of interest, personality, dexterity, and other aptitudes have supplemented intellectual and achievement tests (Bauman & Kropf, 1979). Developmental and other special batteries have been devised to assist in evaluation of young, and/or multihandicapped persons (Ellis, 1978; Langley, 1979).

Second, initial assessment activities were completely verbal in form (Goldman, 1970). Early intellectual assessment was typically conducted via adaptations of the Stanford-Binet Intelligence Scale, which included only those items of purely verbal content, omitting performance tasks altogether (Hayes, 1929; Irwin & Goddard, 1914). Verbal sections of the Wechsler scales were also commonly used. Performance sections were excluded because they required some vision. Many psychologists working with the visually handicapped lamented the latency in development of instruments that paralleled performance tests for the sighted. This concern was heightened because of the belief that verbal measurement might be less truly representative of functioning for visually handicapped than for normally seeing individuals. According to Cutsforth (1932), many visually handicapped persons develop a pseudoverbal skill that can inflate verbal mental measurements. They often show a prowess with words that covers very bare and limited concepts. Alternatively, many visually handicapped persons have deficient educational experiences. Consequently, verbal measurement of intellectual ability in this group is likely to be lowered and true ability underestimated (Bauman, 1971b, 1973a; Dauterman, Shapiro, & Suinn, 1967; Goldman, 1970). Bauman initiated nonverbal testing of the visually handicapped in the 1940s with her Non-Language Learning Test (Bauman, 1971b, 1973a; Goldman,

1970). This instrument was comprised of formboards. However, other nonverbal intelligence tests using adapted mazes and blocks followed (Rich & Anderson, 1965; Suinn, Dauterman, & Shapiro, 1966).

The third trend in the history of assessing the visually handicapped was a move away from assessment by a small group of specifically trained psychologists associated with residential schools and special agencies for the blind to assessment by a more diverse group of examiners associated with public schools and other community establishments. Social and political forces have served as a major impetus for this change. Mainstreaming of visually handicapped children into regular classrooms, which culminated in the passage of P.L. 94-142, placed increased responsibility on classroom teachers and school psychologists to attend to the special needs of this population (Bauman & Kropf, 1979; Parker, 1969; Porter & Holzberg, 1979; Spungin & Swallow, 1975). Further, the trend toward deinstitutionalization forced community agencies to evaluate and treat visually handicapped children and adults, some of whom are also mentally retarded, behaviorally disordered, or have multiple physical disabilities in addition to blindness (Bauman & Kropf, 1979; Langley, 1979). Finally, the requirement for affirmative action in hiring has encouraged employers to think in terms of abilities, rather than disabilities, of handicapped job applicants and to use results of psychological testing in assignment of tasks to handicapped employees (Bauman & Kropf, 1979).

STRATEGIES FOR EVALUATION

INTELLECTUAL ASSESSMENT

Interviewing. The importance of interviewing to the assessment of intellectual functioning in visually handicapped individuals is fourfold. First, the examiner must determine the course of development of the individual, especially the attainment of developmental milestones and self-care, mobility, and other daily living skills (Langley, 1979; Van Hasselt & Sisson, in press). This information is particularly valuable in the evaluation of children because it provides a context within which to interpret results of standardized tests and behavioral assessment. For example, until the individual can respond to sound cues, tactually explore the environment, travel independently, and so forth, he or she is severely restricted in opportunities for acquiring information tapped by most intelligence tests.

Second, input from parents and/or significant others (e.g., family members, friends, co-workers, employers) pertaining to their own reactions, feelings, knowledge, and behavior toward the visually handicapped is seriously needed to ascertain the quality of the environment and exposure to normal learning experiences (Bauman, 1972; Boyd & Otos, 1981). The examiner must assess what significant others know, or falsely believe, about blindness as a physical and/or psychological disability. What do they see as the limits to the individual's ability to function in a seeing world? Are they unrealistically demanding or, as is more frequently the case, are they overprotective of the visually handicapped individual? When there are two or more caretakers, the attitudes and behaviors of all should be evaluated. Inconsistent training and disputes concerning issues of care resulting from disparate beliefs about the visually handicapped individual's abilities and needs may be detrimental to his or her development and independent functioning (Boyd & Otos, 1981).

Third, the availability of adequate resources for learning, including opportunities similar to those of sighted peers, and adapted learning materials that parallel those used by sighted individuals must be ascertained (Bauman, 1972). Because utilization of such resources may affect performance on tests of cognitive ability, this information is essential to appropriate interpretation of assessment data. In addition, this information may be necessary to the development of relevant interventions in cases in which inadequate or inappropriate learning situations prevail.

A fourth topic deserving attention in the interview is determination of the reason for referral as well as hopes and expectations for outcome (Van Hasselt & Sisson, in press). Is the referring party seeking confirmation of opinions already formulated? Or, are they likely to be open to and accepting of evaluation results and recommendations for the future? Too often, advocates for handicapped individuals have developed strong opinions and plans of action. They may have scheduled intellectual assessment only at the insistance of the school district or other training agency or to arm themselves with another tool to help achieve their own placement goals. Assessment of motivation for psychological evaluation will help ensure that results are used in the best interests of the client.

Unfortunately, we are unaware of any structured interview or questionnaire procedure that taps the above-mentioned issues. Thus it is recommended that the examiner be flexible when interviewing the visually impaired client and significant others. Although obtaining such information might seem to be straightforward, we caution that reporting facts of development and educational opportunities by others in the client's environment may be distorted by inaccurate recall or attitudes about the blind that have resulted in overprotection or inappropriate performance expectations. Therefore, detailed descriptions of situations and behaviors and corroborative data from other sources may be helpful in accurate determination of necessary information.

Standardized Testing. The usual method of obtaining information about intellectual functioning is via standardized tests. These involve presentation of numerous tasks to the subject in order to evaluate performance across several areas. Early employment of standardized tests with visually handicapped school-aged children involved a number of adaptations of the Binet intelligence scales. First, Irwin and Goddard (1914) omitted those items requiring vision from the Binet-Simon when assessing children with visual impairments. This adaptation is frequently referred to as the Irwin-Binet. Later, Hayes (1929) proceeded in a similar fashion with Terman's revision of the Binet to evaluate blind children. This procedure, referred to as the Hayes-Binet, was updated in 1943 (Hayes, 1943) and resulted in the Interim Hayes-Binet Intelligence Tests. Hayes (1950) reported a test–retest reliability coefficient of .90 and a correlation of .83 with the Wechsler-Bellevue Verbal Scale. The Interim Hayes-Binet was widely utilized despite certain deficiencies: dependence on normative data derived from sighted subjects only (Morse, 1971), absence of nonverbal materials (Morse, 1971), and failure to be updated over extended time periods (Boyd & Otos, 1981).

The Perkins-Binet (Davis, 1980) is the most recent Binet revision. Although the Perkins-Binet consists primarily of items selected and adapted from earlier forms, it was specifically developed to overcome deficits of the previous versions. For example, it provides separate forms and norms for children with usable vision (Form U) and no usable vision (Form N). Approximately 25% of the items in Form U and over 30% of the items in Form N are performance-type items (i.e., items perceived through tactual versus auditory modes). Preliminary investigations of psychometric properties of the Perkins-Binet have shown acceptable split-half reliability coefficients using a prepublication research version (Coveny, 1972). Also, high correlations with verbal scales of the Wechsler Intelligence Scale for Children—Revised have been found (Teare & Thompson, 1982). Although the Perkins-Binet appears to be an important addition to the armamentarium of tests for the visually handicapped, several problems in administration and scoring remain (Ward & Genshaft, 1982, 1983). Further determination of the psychometric characteristics of this instrument also is necessary (Teare & Thompson, 1982).

The Wechsler scales for children and adults have been available since the 1950s. They are generally accepted as useful for both visually handicapped and sighted individuals because they provide separate verbal and performance subtests and corresponding IQs. Indeed, a study by Bauman and Kropf (1979) indicated that the test most frequently administered to visually handicapped clients of all ages in the United States and Canada was some form of the Wechsler test. Typically, only the Verbal Scale is administered. However, many psychologists also employ the Performance Scale when the client has useful vision. The Wechsler Intelligence Scale for Children (WISC) (Wechsler, 1949), the Wechsler Adult Intelligence Scale (WAIS) (Wechsler, 1955), and their respective revisions (Wechsler, 1974, 1981) are more adaptable for use with the visually handicapped than the more recently developed Wechsler Preschool and Primary Scale of Intelligence (WPPSI) (Wechsler, 1967), which has an unusually large number of items requiring vision. Further, the WPPSI intersperses verbal and performance subtests. The effects of failing to follow this format on verbal and performance IQ scores are unknown (Bauman, 1973a; Bauman & Kropf, 1979).

Although verbal subtests of the Wechsler Scales require minimal modification, Bauman (1973a) has suggested that some items may be rephrased when they appear unsuitable for the blind individual. For example, the item, "What should you do if you see a train approaching a broken track?", may be restated as, "What should a person do if he sees a train approaching a broken track?". However, even if such items are not rephrased, few visually handicapped persons have difficulty with them because most are aware that the question is hypothetical (Bauman, 1973a). Also, visual bias may not be easily discernible. Researchers have found visually handicapped children to give better answers on the train-track item than sighted children although providing inadequate answers to "How many pennies in a nickel?" and "How many things in a dozen?" (Jan *et al.*, 1977).

The WISC and WAIS Verbal Scales consist of six subtests: Information, Similarities, Arithmetic, Vocabulary, Comprehension, and Digit Span. The performance of normal sighted individuals is typically consistent across all subtests. Large discrepancies are often interpreted as reflecting learning disabilities, neurological impairment, emotional problems, environmental deprivation, and the like. In contrast, research and clinical experience have indicated that variability in subtest scores is the rule rather than the exception in the case of the visually handicapped (Bauman, 1972; Tillman, 1967a, b; Tillman & Osborne, 1969). Although scores on Digit Span may be high, suggesting well-developed rote-memory capacities, it is not uncommon to find lower scores on Similarities and Comprehension. These reflect less adequate conceptual thinking abilities and social judgment. Due to greater scatter for this population, subtest pattern analysis may have limited value (Hopkins & McGuire, 1966), although this has been debated (Spungin & Swallow, 1975). Depending on the purpose of assessment, the Verbal Scale IQ may not provide as adequate a measure as some of the individual subtest scores (Bauman, 1972; Sattler, 1982).

Given their widespread application, there is a surprising paucity of literature concerning reliability and validity of the Wechsler scales for visually handicapped children and adults. Apparently, the acceptable psychometric properties of these tests when used with sighted individuals have been assumed for the visually handicapped as well. Investigations of the Wechsler verbal scales have shown satisfactory reliability (Tillman, 1973). However, much less is known about their validity. The WISC Verbal Scale and the Hayes-Binet have been compared in various samples of visually handicapped children. Although the two scales have been found to be highly correlated (Hopkins & McGuire, 1966, 1967), there are inconsistent findings regarding their comparability. Some researchers report equivalent IQ scores (Gilbert & Rubin, 1965; Lewis, 1957), whereas others show WISC IQs to be lower than Binet IQs (Hopkins & McGuire, 1966, 1967). Both the WISC and Binet tests have shown moderate correlations with academic achievement as measured by teacher ratings (Denton, 1954), grades (Lewis, 1957), and achievement test scores (Hecht & Newland, 1965). The WAIS Verbal Scale has been found to be moderately correlated with more recently developed nonverbal measures of intelligence (Shurrager & Shurrager, 1964; Streitfeld & Avery, 1968) but has predicted grades in school equally well (Streitfeld & Avery, 1968). Dauterman, Shapiro, and Suinn (1967) have also alluded to the utility of certain WAIS Verbal subtests in the prediction of vocational performance.

Major limitations of the Wechsler scales as they are typically used with the visually handicapped are the absence of any performance items and the lack of normative data on visually handicapped individuals.

A number of other verbal tests of intellectual functioning have been developed or adapted for use with the visually handicapped with varying degrees of success. These include both individual (e.g., the Slosson Intelligence Test for Children and Adults [Hammill, Crandell, & Colarusso, 1970]) and group (e.g., Otis Classification Test, Part II [Sargent, 1931]) tests. Although a complete review of this literature is beyond the scope of this chapter, the reader is referred to Bauman and Kropf (1979), Bullard and Barraga (1971), Langley (1979), and Swallow (1981) for a listing of these instruments. In addition, Scholl and Schnur (1976) provide bibliographies of research related to their application.

Fewer nonverbal tests of intellectual functioning are available. It has already been mentioned that such tests are important to the intellectual assessment of blind persons who may use a visual vocabulary without understanding concepts or who may have suffered from inadequate educational experiences. In addition, performance testing with concrete materials measures abilities not tapped through words, even in persons with normal visual and verbal skills (Dauterman *et al.*, 1967; Goldman, 1970; Sattler, 1982). Bauman was the first to attempt to fill this void for the visually handicapped with her development of the Non-Language Learning Test (Bauman & Hayes, 1951). This instrument consists of a small formboard and blocks shaped such that they will fit into recesses in the formboard only when placed in certain combinations. Problem solving and learning are observed while patterns are copied by the examinee. Bauman considers this test to be a clinical instrument and has stressed qualitative rather than quantitative observations (Bauman, 1971b, 1973a; Goldman, 1970). Acceptable correlations between this test and the Wechsler-Bellevue Verbal IQ and a clear differentiation between successfully employed and unemployed blind groups have been reported (Dauterman *et al.*, 1967; Goldman, 1970).

The next major stride in performance test development with the visually handicapped occurred with an attempt to adapt the Wechsler Performance Scale for use with this population. The Performance Scale for the Adult Blind (PSAB) was developed in the mid-1950s by Shurrager, Shurrager, and Wattron (Wattron, 1956) and led to the present form called the Haptic Intelligence Scale for the Adult Blind (HIS) (Shurrager, 1961; Shurrager & Shurrager, 1964). The HIS is composed of six subtests, four of which resemble the Digit Symbol, Block Design, Object Assembly, and Picture Completion tests of the WAIS Performance Scale. Additional subtests include the Pattern Board and Bead Arithmetic, the latter involving the use of an abacus. The HIS was normed on a sample of 700 totally blind adults selected to follow closely the proportion of various ages, sexes, and geographic patterns found in the WAIS normative group. The reliability of the scale as a whole is high, and correlation with the WAIS Verbal Scale is .65 (Shurrager & Shurrager, 1964). Factor analyses of the WAIS Verbal Scale and HIS combination have yielded two strong factors, Nonverbal Ability and Verbal Intelligence (Eber, 1967; Miller, 1977). Eber (1967) has also reported an Immediate Memory factor. Although the HIS was constructed to be used in conjunction with the WAIS Verbal Scale (much as the WAIS Performance Scale is used with sighted individuals), it has been found to add little to the prediction of academic achievement over WAIS Verbal IQ scores (Streitfeld & Avery, 1968). Further, it is cumbersome and time-consuming to administer. An abbreviated form of the HIS (Avery & Streitfeld, 1969) may hold promise for clinical and research use.

Other nonverbal tests are tactual adaptations of the Kohs Block Design Test (also called the Ohwaki-Kohs or Stanford-Kohs [Suinn, Dauterman, & Shapiro, 1966]) and Raven's Progressive Matrices (known as the Tactual Progressive Matrices [Rich & Anderson, 1965]). Newland (1979) has also constructed a test of nonverbal intelligence. The Blind Learning Aptitude Test uses molded-plastic three-dimensional sheets and requires the examinee to identify the next element in a pattern of differences, similarities, progressions, and so forth. Unfortunately, of the above-mentioned performance measures, only the Tactual Progressive Matrices and the Blind Learning Aptitude Test provide norms for children under 16 years of age. Moreover, use of these tests is complicated by cumbersome materials, lack of sufficient numbers of easy or hard items, the inordinate amount of time required for administration, and nonavailability of norms for persons with usable versus no usable vision (Bauman, 1971a; Dauterman *et al.*, 1967; Morse, 1971). Further, moderate correlations of test scores with verbal tests and educational levels raise questions about what they measure (Dauterman *et al.*, 1967).

Behavioral Assessment. The value of intellectual assessment through standardized tests was seriously challenged in the late 1960s and early 1970s. These instruments were criticized as being inadequate, inefficient, detrimental, and otherwise inappropriate (Anastasi, 1982; Bersoff, 1973). Behavior therapists, in particular, pointed to the situational specificity of test results. This led to poor prediction of performance in the classroom or on the job, inability to provide data relevant to development of instructional or remediational strategies, and limited usefulness in monitoring behavior change (Bersoff, 1973). Although direct behavioral observation of "intelligent behavior" was advocated as an alternative to standardized testing, few reports of the successful use of this strategy are available. This is true both for normal and handicapped populations.

However, professionals who work with visually handicapped individuals are aware of the limitations of available assessment devices in the evaluation of their clients (Bauman, 1971a, b, 1972, 1973a; see also "Special Considerations and Research Issues"). This understanding has led them to advocate caution when interpreting test results. In addition, Bauman (1972) and Hansen, Young, and Ulrey (1982) have argued that it may be more important to focus on functional skills the examinee has acquired and how he or she solves problems than on performance on tasks designed to measure abilities of sighted individuals. Others have argued that a comprehensive intellectual evaluation should include information specific to the behavioral demands of the residential, classroom or employment setting in which the visually handicapped individual currently functions or will be placed subsequently (Bateman, 1965; Bauman, 1973a; Van Hasselt & Sisson, in press). Although such recommendations are no doubt followed in clinical situations, no reports of use of such procedures are available.

EDUCATIONAL/VOCATIONAL ASSESSMENT

Interviewing. It was noted that much information necessary for comprehensive intellectual assessment was efficiently obtained through interviewing the client and/or significant others. Similarly, educational and vocational assessment procedures usually include an interview. Because common developmental and environmental factors influence results of both intellectual and educational/vocational evaluations, topics covered in the interviews are likely to be quite similar. For example, results of educational achievement tests depend on exposure to normal learning experiences at home and in the classroom (Bauman, 1972). Performance on manual-dexterity tests is tied to familiarity with materials employed and ability to discriminate and meet task demands (Bauman, 1973a). Further, items endorsed on interest inventories reflect prior opportunities to participate in a variety of academic (e.g., laboratory, industrial arts, physical education courses) and extracurricular (e.g., field trips, sports, clubs) activities (Bauman, 1971a). Thus the examiner must determine the extent to which the visually handicapped individual's environment has provided adequate training, realistic expectations for performance across a number of tasks, and varied socialization experiences.

In addition, several paper-and-pencil self-report instruments, designed to assess vocational interests in the sighted, have been modified for administration to the visually handicapped in an interview format. These instruments will be discussed next.

Standardized Testing. Educational achievement was one of the earliest areas of concern in the evaluation of visually handicapped children. Initial use of achievement tests with this population dates back to 1918 when such materials as the Gray Oral Reading Check Tests, the Metropolitan Achievement Tests, the Myers-Ruch High School Progress Test, and several editions of the Stanford Achievement Tests were adapted for the visually handicapped, usually by translation into braille (Bauman, 1971a, 1973a). Other achievement tests include the Sequential Tests of Educational Progress, the Cooperative School and College Ability Tests, the Diagnostic Reading Tests, the Wide Range Achievement Test, and the Iowa Tests of Basic Skills (Scholl & Schnur, 1976). Considerable effort has been expended in developing braille and large print adaptations of the Stanford Achievement Tests (Nolan & Ashcroft, 1959) and the Sequential Tests of Educational Progress (Trismen, 1967). Consequently, these instruments can be used with some confidence. However, the choice of an achievement test for mainstreamed visually handicapped children is affected by tests being used with sighted peers (Bauman & Kropf, 1979). Further, time required for administration of adapted achievement tests is far greater than for regular print versions employed with sighted children. Finally, the equivalence of content and procedures of administration for adapted and nonadapted forms of the tests are usually assumed, not empirically demonstrated. (See Nolan, 1962, for an excellent discussion of problems in adapting educational achievement tests for use with visually handicapped children.)

Arrangements can also be made for administration of the Scholastic Aptitude Test, Graduate Record Examination, and other tests required for admission to graduate-level programs to visually handicapped high-school and college students (Bauman, 1971a, b, 1973a). The College Entrance Examination Board and the Educational Testing Service administer and score these tests under the same strict control applied to sighted students. Generally, extended time periods are allowed to provide the visually handicapped respondent ample time to complete the test. Studies of the effect of this modification on predictive value have yet to be conducted. Nevertheless, results are treated as the equivalent of scores obtained by sighted students on the regular print version of the test (Bauman, 1973a).

Assessment of vocational aptitude has traditionally involved administration of dexterity tests. The most popular of these are the Crawford Small Parts Dexterity Test, the Minnesota Rate of Manipulation Test, and the Pennsylvania Bi-Manual Worksample (Bauman & Kropf, 1979). Norms are available on these measures for both the totally blind and partially sighted. Essentially, these instruments evaluate manipulative skills, such as placing pegs in pegboards, twisting nuts and bolts together, using a tweezer to pick up small objects, and using a screwdriver with small screws. Because a wide range of jobs currently is open to visually handicapped persons, assessment of manipulative skills *per se* may not be as important as it was previously. However, dexterity tests can provide more information than the mere measure of manual speed. These tasks permit the examiner to observe the client in action and to assess learning, orientation, attention, and motivation in the work space.

Vocational assessment must include determination of the individual's interests in addition to what he or she does well. Thus a wide variety of interest inventories are used with the visually handicapped, usually by oral presentation. The Strong-Campbell Vocational Interest Blank and the Kuder Preference Record frequently are employed (Bauman & Kropf, 1979). These tests are most applicable to high-school graduates considering professional or semiprofessional goals, although some scales may be relevant at lower levels. Unfortunately, both the Kuder and the Strong interest inventories contain some items that pertain to positions not readily held by the blind. Further, both present some difficulties in administration. As a result, Bauman (1973b) has developed an interest inventory that (a) refers only to activities that could be carried out independently by persons who are legally blind, (b) involves no comparison or selection of responses that might be confusing and lead to errors, and (c) is easily administered via tape recording or mechanical answer system. It is surprising that little mention of the use of Bauman's interest inventory appears in the vision literature.

Behavioral Assessment. Silberman (1981) has listed the following as important characteristics of evaluation procedures with visually handicapped students: (a) measures should be taken directly on the task or objective being taught; (b) the measurement scale should be sensitive to small changes in the target behavior; (c) assessment should be conducted often, preferably on a daily basis; (d) measurement results should be valid and reliable; and (e) the instrument should be efficient and economical. Silberman (1981) contends that attention to these criteria will ensure meaningful assessment of students' strengths and weaknesses, early detection and modification of inadequate instructional procedures, and efficient use of classroom personnel. Clearly, use of traditional standardized tests fails to meet Silberman's requirements. Such tests measure too broad a range of learning skills to be useful and are not designed for frequent administration. Instead, many educators have advocated the use of behavioral assessment procedures to evaluate educational needs and progress (Langley, 1979; Silberman, 1981; Spungin & Swallow, 1975).

The first step in the behavioral assessment of educational progress is to define the target behavior in units that will reflect small increments of change. A task-analysis approach is helpful in this process. In addition, a number of detailed checklists and developmental scales exist to assist in evaluation and programming for the young and multihandicapped blind child. For example, the Project Vision-Up Curriculum (1979) contains detailed programming in six major areas, including conceptual development, motor skills, communication, daily living skills, socialization, and functional vision. One can repeatly assess a child and record functioning levels on a Vision-Up profile. Based on assessment outcome, the teacher can select curriculum cards suggesting specific activities to be performed to help achieve instructional objectives in the various skill areas. By using these materials, a teacher can continuously assess, teach, and reevaluate a child's progress. Other assessment tools are available to assess cognitive, motor, and language development, as well as self-help skills and social adaptation. A complete listing of these instruments is beyond the scope of this chapter. The reader is referred to Langley (1979) and Silberman (1981) for information concerning these devices.

Behavioral assessment of educational progress also requires determination of the types of data to be collected (e.g., frequency, duration, accuracy, trials to criterion) and the most useful direct observation procedures (event recording, duration recording, or time sampling). Finally, empirical documentation of efficacious training procedures may involve the use of single-subject research methodology (see "Special Considerations and Research Issues" section). Gelfand and Hartmann (1985), Silberman (1981), and Van Hasselt and Hersen (1981) have discussed the utility and techniques of a behavioral approach for assessment of behavior change in the classroom setting.

Although no reports of behavioral assessment of vocational aptitude in visually handicapped individuals are available, it is clear that such a strategy may yield interesting and meaningful results. Further development and refinement of behavioral assessment methods for use in the work setting clearly is needed.

SOCIAL COMPETENCY AND ADAPTIVE LIVING SKILLS ASSESSMENT

Interviewing. The importance of the interview to the assessment of social competency and adaptive living skills lies in determing the extent to which the visually handicappd individual has been encouraged to be independent and has been provided appropriate feedback regarding social performance. Further, the most widely used social competency assessment scales for the blind, the Maxfield-Buchholz (Maxfield & Buchholz, 1958) and Overbrook scales (Bauman, 1972, 1973a), require that detailed information across a number of adaptive and social skills areas be obtained from an informant, usually by interview.

Standardized Testing. Several social competency scales have been developed to assess level of social functioning in the visually handicapped. One of these is the Maxfield-Buchholz Scale of Social Maturity for Pre-School Blind Children (Maxfield & Buchholz, 1958). This instrument is an adaptation of the Vineland Social Maturity Scale (Doll, 1947, 1965) and is used for developmental screening in visually handicapped children in the 0- to 72-month age range. The Maxfield-Buchholz scale evaluates children in such areas as dressing, feeding, locomotion, motor development, communication, and socialization. Items at the 0- to 1-year age level tap physical development (e.g., rolling over, balancing the head, reaching for objects, grasping with thumb and finger). Items at higher age levels evaluate such skills as self-care, play, and adjustment to group situations. Use of this scale allows comparison of a blind child with other blind children of the same age, as well as with sighted children via the original Vineland scale (Ellis, 1978).

The Overbrook Social Competency Scale (Bauman, 1972, 1973a) is an upward extension of the Maxfield-Buchholz scale. It begins at age 6 (where the latter measure ends) and continues through the high school and young-adult period. Although present norms are tentative, the Overbrook scale can be used to provide supplementary information on those aspects of individual development that are related to independence in daily living, interpersonal skills, mobility, and many aspects of group activity.

The Maxfield-Buchholz and Overbrook scales share several characteristics. First, they are typically completed by an informant (e.g, parent, teacher, counselor) who has had considerable contact with the individual. Second, they are most applicable to children, with most research centering on individuals in the 3-to-21 age range. Third, most scales of this type, particularly variants of the original Vineland, yield a summative score referred to as a social quotient (SQ). The SQ presumably reflects social competence relative to normative data on maturity level. Several investigators have utilized these measures to compare visually handicapped children to sighted norms (e.g., McGuinness, 1970; McKay, 1936). Samples of totally blind and partially sighted children also have been compared (Maxfield & Fjeld, 1942). Results of these studies essentially show that visually handicapped children display deficits in social competence relative to sighted norms and that totally blind children receive lower social maturity scores than partially sighted counterparts (see review by Van Hasselt, 1983).

Ammerman, Van Hasselt, and Hersen (1985) have pointed out several problems inherent in use of these global social competency scales. First, variants of the Vineland for the visually handicapped have questionable validity. For example, the relationship between SQ and specific aspects of social functioning, such as interaction with peers, has yet to be demonstrated empirically. Second, questions have been raised concerning normative samples used for Vineland derivatives. Reynell and Zinkin (1975) explain that the Maxfield-Buchholz scale was standardized on children with retrolental fibroplasia and thus involved a high proportion of premature births. This impairs its claim to be a "normal" sample. Third, most investigations utilizing these measures have included heterogeneous subject populations. Groups of visually handicapped children have varied considerably with respect to extent of vision loss, etiology of the disorder, age range, and environmental setting. Fourth, the finding that social maturity differs as a function of setting or environment (McGuinness, 1970) precludes drawing definitive conclusions about visually handicapped children as a whole. Finally, use of global summative scores does not permit identification of specific interpersonal or other skills deficits. Such information, which is requisite to subsequent formulation of efficacious interventions, requires a more fine-grained analysis of social functioning (Van Hasselt, 1983, 1987).

Behavioral Assessment. Behavior therapists have contributed more to the assessment of social competency, particularly social interaction skills, than to any other area of evaluation of the visually handicapped. Behavioral strategies used with this group fall into the categories of self-report, analogue observations, and direct observations of behavior.

A commendable effort toward adaptation of a self-report device for assessing social skills in visually handicapped children is reported by Matson, Heinze, Helsel, Kapperman, and Rotatori (in press). These researchers examined the psychometric properties of the Matson Evaluation of Social Skills with Youngsters (MESSY) with this population. The MESSY is a social skills assessment scale in Likert format, developed originally for sighted children hospitalized for behavior disturbances. It includes both a self-report and a teacher-report version that consist of 62 and 64 items, respectively (Matson, Rotatori, & Helsel, 1983). Examples of self-report items include: "I make other people laugh," "I feel good if I help someone," and "I like to be alone." The instrument was adapted for administration to the visually handicapped by providing information in large print and on audio cassettes. In their study, Matson *et al.* (in press) evaluated 75 visually handicapped subjects (9 to 22 years of age) on the MESSY self-report and teacher-report scales. Results showed internal reliability on Gottman Split-Half and Spearman-Brown to be .78 or higher on both forms.

In response to the need for more fine-grained analysis of social functioning in visually handicapped children, Van Hasselt, Kazdin, Hersen, Simon, and Mastantuono (1985) constructed a role-play test that (a) had adequate psychometric properties; (b) included items relevant to the visually handicapped child's social environment; and (c) permitted a more molecular analysis of social behavior than previously employed instruments. This test, constructed by the behavior-analytic model (Goldfried & D'Zurilla, 1969), consists of 39 items that tap conversational and negative assertion skills. Conversational role-play scenes were designed to evaluate interactions necessary for initiating a conversation and making friends. An example of a conversational skill scenario is provided next:

NARRATOR: You are walking toward a classroom. The door is partially open, and a small group of people is gathered in front of the door. You are new in class and don't know anyone. You would really like to get to know them. You hear/notice one of them walking over to you. (Subject's response)

To assess level of negative assertion skill, scenes similar to the following are utilized:

NARRATOR: A classmate is playing his or her radio during class time. You find this distracting and are unable to work effectively. He or she says:

PROMPT 1: Listen to this song, it's a new one on the radio. (Subject's response 1)

PROMPT 2: It will only last a few minutes. (Subject's response 2)

In this procedure, a participant's responses to both types of role-play scenarios are videotaped and rated retrospectively on a number of behavioral components implicated as requisite to interpersonal effectiveness in the social skills and vision literatures (e.g., Bonfanti, 1979; Eisler, Hersen, Miller, & Blanchard, 1975; Reardon, Hersen, Bellack, & Foley, 1979; Sanders & Goldberg, 1977). Some of these include speech disturbances, response latency, requests for new behavior, open-ended questions, smiles, posture, direction of gaze (eye contact), and stereotypic behaviors. Van Hasselt *et al.* (1985) found that the role-play test discriminated between samples of visually handicapped and sighted adolescents on several of these components. Also, Van Hasselt *et al.* (1983) used a subset of these items as a vehicle for assessment and training to improve assertive skills in four visually handicapped adolescents.

Self-report and analogue procedures are not appropriate for very young or multihandicapped children. Thus, Sisson, Van Hasselt, Hersen, and Strain (1985) employed direct observations of social behavior to assess progress of four multihandicapped blind children in a peer-mediated social skills intervention program. Three general classes of social behavior (initiations, responses, continued interactions), along with three topographical features (positive, inappropriate, and negative social behavior), were defined. Trained observers recorded instances of these behaviors during intervention and nonintervention sessions. Results showed that the observation code was sensitive to changes in social behaviors that occurred as a function of increased social initiations from nonhandicapped confederate peers.

ASSESSMENT OF EMOTIONAL ADJUSTMENT AND BEHAVIOR DISORDERS

Interviewing. An examination of the vision literature reveals little use of interview procedures in evaluations of emotional and behavioral adjustment in the visually handicapped. This is surprising in light of the fact that many visually handicapped persons are able to clearly articulate their feelings and concerns. One exception is a study by Van Hasselt *et al.* (1986), which involved administration of the Youth Self-Report Form (YSRF) of the Child Behavior Checklist (Achenbach & Edelbrock, 1983) to visually handicapped adolescents in an interview format. Interviewers read aloud all YSRF questions and response alternatives and recorded subjects' answers. Results showed that visually handicapped subjects in a residential placement evinced greater dysfunction than mainstreamed visually handicapped subjects or sighted controls.

We have previously elaborated the importance of parental and caretaker interviews to the comprehensive assessment of visually handicapped children (Van Hasselt & Sisson, in press). Others, also, emphasized the role of the parental interview in evaluating children and youth (Boyd & Otos, 1981; Hepfinger, 1962). Presumably, the focus of such interviews in assessing emotional adjustment and behavior disorders would be upon child-rearing practices, previous treatment including counseling and medication, and expectations for behavior across situations. Unfortunately, the one report of such an approach (Jan *et al.*, 1977) lacks sufficient detail regarding the interview procedures.

Standardized Testing. Several devices have been used to examine personality traits or characteristics in the visually handicapped. These are generally adaptations of measures originally designed for and standardized on the sighted. For example, an early study involved administration of the Bernreuter Personality Inventory (BPI) to visually handicapped residential students (Petrucci, 1953). The BPI consists of 125 items and provides scores on the following subscales: Self-sufficiency, Self-confidence, Sociability, Neurotic Tendencies, Dominance-Submission, and Introversion-Extroversion. A comparison with sighted norms revealed that visually handicapped subjects were more introverted, submissive, neurotic, and less self-sufficient and confident than sighted norms.

The California Psychological Inventory (CPI) and the Minnesota

Multiphasic Personality Inventory (MMPI) also have been used with visually handicapped samples. The first measure consists of 480 true-false items and yields 18 scale scores. Some of these scales are Sociability, Self-control, Sense of Well-being, Dominance, and Flexibility. Bast (1971) adapted the CPI for the visually handicapped by presenting items in a tape-recorded format. The MMPI is the most widely used psychopathology assessment device. It includes 500 affirmative statements requiring responses of either "true," "false," or "cannot say." The MMPI provides scores on 10 clinical scales (e.g., Hypochondriasis, Depression, Paranoia, Schizophrenia) as well as three validity scales. A braille version of this instrument was developed by Cross (1947).

As with most personality measures, neither the CPI nor the MMPI have been standardized on the visually handicapped. Further, existing research on the use of the MMPI with this population has been based on small, nonrepresentative samples and has been generally limited in scope (Cross, 1947; Dean, 1957). In an important study, Adrian, Miller, and DeL'aune (1982) attempted to ascertain the adequacy the CPI and MMPI with visually handicapped persons. These measures were administered to 128 men and women (18 to 55 years), who were totally blind or partially sighted from a young age. A number of differences (consistently in a negative direction) were exhibited by visually handicapped subjects when compared to sighted norms for both instruments. Although the authors concluded that results reflected the sensitivity of both inventories to adjustment patterns of the visually handicapped, they also argued that more deviant scores in the visually handicapped may not necessarily mean greater psychopathology. Instead, deviant scores

> may be indicative of the unique adaptive processes used by individuals who have experienced blindness or severe visual impairment from birth, infancy or early childhood. Interpretations of test scores for a congenitally blind or early visually impaired person based on deviations from normative scores of a sighted group . . . could be totally irrelevant and result in inappropriate clinical judgments. (p. 178)

These investigators highlight the need to obtain sufficient normative data on visually handicapped individuals for relevant and meaningful interpretations of test results.

One of the few instruments developed specifically for the visually handicapped is the Anxiety Scale for the Blind (ASB) (Hardy, 1968). The 78 items on this true-false inventory were screened by clinical experts and standardized on a sample of 122 visually handicapped adolescents and young adults (13 to 22 years of age). The association between ASB scores and teacher ratings and Taylor Manifest Anxiety Scale (TMAS) scores was examined. Although correlations were low with teacher ratings (r = .20 to .30), they were acceptable with the TMAS (r = .60 to .79) across subject subgroups.

Bauman also has constructed the Emotional Factors Inventory (EFI) and the Adolescent Emotional Factors Inventory (AEFI) (Bauman, 1971a, 1973a) for use with visually handicapped adolescents and young adults. Items for these scales were derived directly from experiences related by visually handicapped persons. Both the EFI and AEFI are comprised of a series of subscales that tap sensitivity, depression, attitudes of distrust, social competency, somatic symptoms, and attitudes regarding blindness. The AFI also includes a measure of adjustment specific to school, family, and heterosocial relationships. Normative data for visually handicapped individuals are available for both measures. Bauman (1973a) has stated that these tests are most appropriate for youth over age 13. Further, it is recommended that they be administered via audiotape or large print to ensure privacy in making responses.

Some efforts have been made to adapt projective personality tests for the visually handicapped. One of these, the Thematic Apperception Test (TAT) in standard form, presents cards containing vague pictures in black and white. The examinee is asked to make up a story to fit each picture. He or she also is asked to describe what led to the event in the picture, to tell what is happening at present, to express what the characters in the picture are feeling, and to give the outcome. In some cases, this measure has been administered to visually handicapped persons by the examiner's verbally describing TAT pictures in plain terms and asking the client to make up a story (Lebo, 1960; Lebo & Bruce, 1960).

The Auditory Projective Test (Malikin & Freedman, 1970) provides scenes that parallel TAT pictures in tape-recorded form. This test consists of three parts. In the first, scenes are spoken unemotionally in an artificial language between various role-playing characters (e.g., an older woman and a boy, a man and a woman). After listening to the interaction, the examinee is asked to develop a story based on the stimulus presented. In the second part of the test, English is used instead of the artificial language. Finally, sound effects (e.g., running footsteps and gunshots, a stormy background with footsteps entering a house) are presented.

The Rotter Incomplete Sentences Blank (Rotter & Williamson, 1947) also has been used with visually handicapped persons. This instrument consists of 40 phrases that the client is asked to complete in a manner that expresses his or her true feelings. Responses are interpreted with regard to such factors as style, content, expressed attitudes, and conflicts. The Teare Sentence Completion Test (Teare, 1966) is a similar projective test composed of 43 unfinished sentences. Each presents situations commonly encountered in everyday life. Also, many items specifically relate to difficulties associated with a visual handicap. Some areas tapped by this device include authority, peer relationships, and family situations.

Harris (1947, 1948) attempted to develop a projective technique that would parallel the Rorschach test, which requires the sighted examinee to interpret a series of inkblots reproduced on cards. The Bas-Relief Test consists of 22 fiber and wood plates with raised designs. Responses to these ambiguous raised-form stimuli are interpreted in a manner similar to Rorschach percepts. However, little attention has been directed to further application of this technique.

For several years, there has been considerable debate in psychology over the validity of personality and projective techniques. Empirical support for the technical adequacy of these measures with the visually handicapped is particularly scarce. Consequently, results of evaluations of these individuals with projective methods must be interpreted with considerable caution.

Behavioral Assessment. Direct behavioral observations, the hallmark of behavioral assessment (Bellack & Hersen, 1977), frequently have been used to evaluate a wide range of problem behaviors in the visually handicapped. Most of these efforts have involved assessment of maladaptive patterns of responding in multihandicapped blind children. Some of these include self-stimulation (e.g, rocking, head rolling, finger flicking), self-injury (e.g., eye poking, head banging), and aggression. (An extensive review of behavioral assessment and treatment approaches with the visually handicapped is provided by Van Hasselt, 1987.) Investigators utilizing direct observation procedures generally have employed some variant of time sampling to ascertain frequency of occurrence of targeted behaviors. For example, direct observations conducted by Harris and Romanczyk (1976) indicated two categories of self-injury (head and chin banging) in an 8-year-old mentally retarded male with severe visual and hearing impairments. Data concerning frequency of these responses were collected throughout the day at school and home by staff and parents respectively. Self-injurious behaviors decreased dramatically in both settings as a function of treatment (overcorrection).

In another report, Conley and Wolery (1980) observed rate of eye gouging in a 7-year-old mentally retarded, visually handicapped female. Fifteen-minute observation sessions were conducted during the school day by classroom aides who recorded occurrence of the targeted response over successive 10-second intervals. Observational data revealed a sharp drop in rate of eye gouging with implementation of positive practice overcorrection.

SPECIAL CONSIDERATIONS AND RESEARCH ISSUES

THE EXAMINER

One of the first considerations in assessing visually handicapped individuals is the qualifications of the examiner. Expertise in assessment procedures includes familiarity with available instruments designed specifically for the visually handicapped and common adaptations of instruments developed for nonhandicapped individuals. Further, the examiner must have an understanding of the nature and the needs of persons with visual handicaps (Bauman, 1971a, b; Vander Kolk, 1977). He or she should know how to guide and explain visual material to visually handicapped individuals. If the examiner cannot accomplish this comfortably, the assessment process and results obtained may be adversely affected (Bauman, 1971b).

Also, the professional must examine his or her own attitudes toward and expectations of the visually impaired (Bateman, 1965). Today, many sighted persons view visually handicapped individuals as equals with regard to their ability to benefit from education and vocational training and to compete for employment. However, vestiges of earlier negative attitudes toward this population still remain. Attitudes about the visually handicapped person's role in society and extreme positions of either denying the real limitations of blindness or of imposing unreal and unnecessary restrictions can bias the interpretation of a client's behavior.

THE REFERRAL QUESTION

The psychologist, in conjunction with family members, school or agency personnel, and other professionals, must formulate clear and specific questions to be addressed by assessment (Bateman, 1965; Bauman, 1973a). For example, rather than evaluating a young child for the purpose of making an "educational prognosis," a series of specific diagnostic questions might be posed: Are the child's self-help skills in toileting, dressing, and feeding sufficient to handle age-appropriate demands? Is the child able to sit, attend, and follow instructions to the degree necessary in the classroom? Is tactual discrimination adequate for beginning braille? Does the child demonstrate conceptual understanding congruent with potential classmates? Of course such questions can only be answered with respect to the requirements and characteristics of relevant school or classroom settings.

AMOUNT OF VISION

Most legally blind individuals have some degree of vision. It is incumbent upon the examiner to determine what materials can and cannot be seen and used functionally (Bauman, 1973a). This might be accomplished by questioning the referring party as well as the individual. For tests available in braille, large print, and regular print forms, it is recommended that the examinee indicate which is the preferred mode. When oral administration is an option, such as with certain personality or interest inventories, the individual might select orally over visually presented materials. It is sometimes necessary to offer a trial with the various materials to ascertain the most appropriate assessment approach (Bateman, 1965).

DEVELOPMENTAL CONSIDERATIONS

Knowledge of the impact of a visual disorder across major areas of development is a prerequisite to appropriate interpretation of test results, especially in the case of young children. An extensive review of these effects is beyond the scope of this chapter. However, a brief overview of the effects of severe visual disorder on several developmental areas is provided next. The interested reader is also referred to Fraiberg (1977), Langley (1979), and Warren (1977).

Motor Development. Although their hands must eventually become a major perceptual organ, many visually handicapped children demonstrate more significant delays in functional hand usage (e.g., fingering, grasping, transferring objects) than in any other developmental area. Not until 10 to 12 months does the visually handicapped infant begin to reach for objects based on auditory cues alone (Fraiberg, 1977). Until this occurs, the child is severely limited in learning about the environment. Crawling in the visually handicapped infant is usually achieved by 13 months followed by independent walking at 19 months (Adelson & Fraiberg, 1974). In comparison, most nonhandicapped children attain these milestones by 7 and 11 months, respectively.

Tactual exploration and independent mobility skills must also be developed in the individual who becomes blind later in life. A comprehensive psychological evaluation must assess the extent to which the adventitiously blinded older child or adult has made advances in these skill areas. Alternatively, the reasons for his or her delay in making this important adjustment to visual impairment must be determined. Proficiency in these areas is a prerequisite to further learning and to reassuming a productive role within the family, school, and work settings (Bauman, 1971a).

Language Development. Although visually handicapped children may babble and imitate words sooner than sighted children, they often show delays when combining words to make wants known (Fraiberg, 1977). It is not uncommon for young blind children to obtain higher expressive than receptive language scores on language scales. Echolalic tendencies and strengths in retrieving stored facts contribute to the inflated expressive scores. Although they can recall digit series and complete familiar analogies, visually handicapped children have difficulty following two- and three-stage commands, understanding concepts of space, number and plurality, and in discriminating objects described with two variables (e.g., big, square) (Langley, 1979).

"Verbalisms" frequently are noted in the language of visually handicapped individuals of all ages. The term *verbalism* was coined by Cutsforth (1932) to describe the use of a visual vocabulary by the visually impaired. These individuals may accurately use words and describe concepts without the requisite visual experience to understand concrete, functional meanings. Thus the examiner must be careful and flexible when assessing the visually handicapped, taking time to explore fully the meaning of each verbal response.

Social Development. A number of deficits and delays in this area are common in visually handicapped infants and toddlers. For example, smiling is less frequent and more muted in visually handicapped than sighted infants. Moreover, smiles may diminish with time, possibly as a result of lack of visual reinforcement or imitation of the mother's smile (Freedman, 1964). This is significant because the smile is one of the first signs of parent–child attachment, and normal attachment has been associated with adequate socialization in later years (Matas, Arend, & Stroufe, 1978). In addition, because they may remain quiet and still when others approach, visually handicapped children may appear to lack affect (Langley, 1979). Other difficulties in social development include (a) prolonged separation anxiety resulting in passivity, decreased environmental exploration, and fear of changes in daily routine; (b) failure to engage in representative play; and (c) delays in acquisition of self-care (e.g., feeding, dressing, toileting) skills.

Problems in social behavior may persist into adulthood. It has been noted previously (Van Hasselt, 1983) that this may be due to lack of social experiences, inability to learn interpersonal behaviors by direct visual observation, and inaccurate feedback concerning social performance. Given the pervasiveness of social skills deficits among visually handicapped individuals (Van Hasselt, 1983) and the fact that social behaviors are often the first behaviors observed by others (Bauman, 1971a, 1973a), social competency assessment is an integral part of evaluation of the visually handicapped client.

TEST ADMINISTRATION

General Considerations. Hansen *et al.* (1982) list six general principles to be considered when assessing a visually handicapped child. These principles are equally applicable to the assessment of adults. First, they recommend that the evaluation be carried out over a period of several weeks rather than in only one session. This strategy permits observation of a wide variety of behaviors. Second, the examinee should be provided sufficient time to explore and adapt to the testing environment. The visually handicapped person may take longer than a sighted peer to adjust to new sounds, smells, temperatures, and interactions with a stranger. Third, the individual should be given adequate time to become familiar with each test object before a standardization response is expected. This usually is accomplished through tactile manipulation, which may be less efficient than visual inspection by a nonhandicapped examinee. Fourth, the examiner must note the normal and dysfunctional behaviors exhibited by the visually handicapped client. In particular, stereotyped responses (e.g., hand flapping, rocking, and eye pressing or poking) may interfere with test administration and affect reliability of obtained data. Fifth, the examiner must be flexible in evaluating the individual. It was mentioned earlier that focusing on functional skills and problem-solving strategies may yield more important information than performance scores on tasks designed to measure abilities of the sighted. Finally, the sixth general principle concerns supplemental use of systematic, direct, behavioral observations, both within the assessment setting and in the individual's natural environment. These are considered essential in obtaining a complete picture of strengths and weaknesses in all areas of functioning, as well as in subsequent development of appropriate intervention and instructional strategies.

Selection of Instruments. The selection of standardized instruments for assessment of visually handicapped persons presents special problems. Many available aptitude, achievement, and personality tests require that the examinee have the visual capability to read written materials, perceive and/or manipulate small or colored objects, and respond on written record forms. A few tests have been developed specifically for use with the visually handicapped. Others have been adapted for use with this population through translation into braille or large print. However, the most common procedure is for the examiner to select appropriate subtests, informally modify test materials and content, and alter response requirements when testing visually handicapped persons. Several authors (Bauman & Kropf, 1979; Bullard & Barraga, 1971; Langley, 1979; Scholl & Schnur, 1976; Swallow, 1981) have compiled lists of tests and subtests, along with appropriate modifications or adaptations that are frequently used with visually handicapped individuals.

One commonly employed adaptation of assessment instruments for use with the visually handicapped is reading items aloud, either in person or through an audiotape recording (Bauman, 1971b, 1973a). This can be accomplished efficiently when items require an open-ended or a true-false response. In multiple-choice tests or certain tests of judgment, however, the person's score is likely to be reduced by difficulties inherent in remembering accurately each of several alternative answers. If such measures are frequently used, possible responses should be put into braille or large print so that repeated references to them can be made (Bauman, 1971b).

A drawback of presenting test items orally is the lack of privacy this procedure affords the visually handicapped individual relative to the sighted person, who reads the test and responds in written form. This disadvantage may be circumvented by having the examinee type or braille answers or place specially prepared tickets (one for each response) in different piles (Bauman, 1973a; Cundick, Crandell, & Hendrix 1974). Of course, time required for oral presentation of test items, brailling answers, or sorting tickets will be considerable.

As mentioned before, several more commonly used tests appear in braille and large-print formats. However, only a small number of visually handicapped individuals read braille, and even fewer read it well. The slowness of reading braille, even by the most proficient reader, requires an adjustment in the standard time limits. At present, the somewhat arbitrary ratios of 2.5 to 1 (Nolan, 1962) or 2 to 1 (Bauman & Kropf, 1979; Swallow, 1981) are recommended adjustment factors. Large-print users also will require significantly more reading time than the standard for sighted persons using regular printed tests (Swallow, 1981).

A further limitation of braille, large print, and oral forms of presentation is their failure to overcome the problem of showing pictures or other diagrams. Such nonverbal content is difficult to adapt into a tactual format, and even simple representations may lose all meaning when embossed (Bauman & Kropf, 1979). Pictorial or graphical details also may be lost for the large-print reader (Swallow, 1981).

Other adaptations of assessment materials and procedures include adding a sound element to materials, substituting two- or three-dimensional objects for pictures, creating raised-line figures, supplying supplemental oral directions, and manually guiding the individual in the exploration of stimulus items or manipulating him or her through task demands (Langley, 1979).

Interpretation of Test Results. Interpretation of psychological test results is generally based on normative data indicating performance of age-mates on the tasks utilized. At least two assumptions are made when an individual's performance on a test or other protocol is compared to that of the normative group. First, it is assumed that he or she has been exposed to testing conditions that are similar in all important aspects to the conditions in effect for the normative sample. This is accomplished by standardization of test administration. Changes in standard testing conditions necessitated by the visual handicap will influence the meaning of results. However, there is a paucity of research concerning the interpretation of individual test scores obtained under these altered conditions (Nolan, 1962; Swallow, 1981). Data indicating, for example, whether a braille version of a test measures the same constructs or predicts to the same criteria as the original version have not been secured for many popular adaptations (Bennett, 1983).

A second assumption made when an individual's performance is compared to a normative group is that the latter includes individuals who are similar across a number of relevant characteristics (e.g., age, sex, race, family socioeconomic status). Similarity in these characteristics is presumed to suggest similar life experiences. However, visually handicapped persons are not included in these normative groups. Their life experiences have been affected by the visual disorder and a host of other factors as well. What is important is that visually handicapped persons may not have had the same opportunity to learn as their sighted peers. Even when adequate educational resources have been available, it is important to remember that obtaining information through braille or audiotape is a slower study procedure than print reading by sighted persons. Thus only highly motivated visually handicapped individuals will have had exposure to educational material at a level commensurate with that of nonhandicapped peers (Bauman, 1971a). It has been noted that others are often overprotective of the visually handicapped, resulting in restricted activities and failure to become independent in daily living skills. This, coupled with lessened performance demands relative to sighted individuals, may be reflected in results of tests of specific knowledge, aptitudes, interests, and personality (Bauman, 1973a).

One approach to more meaningful interpretation of assessment results might be the development of population-specific norms for the more commonly used measures (see discussions by Bateman, 1965; Bauman & Kropf, 1979; Nolan, 1962). This is quite a burdensome task, however. The establishment of norms for visually handicapped individuals is extremely time consuming and costly because the potential population base is small, scattered, heterogeneous, and difficult to identify and define (Bauman & Kropf, 1979; Vander Kolk, 1977). Besides failing to meet the criterion of cost-efficiency, establishing separate test norms for visually handicapped individuals has yet another shortcoming. Many times an examiner's purpose in assessment is to evaluate the potential of the individual in relation to demands of a seeing world. Thus interpretation of assessment data must be approached with caution and guided by a thorough understanding of the many factors that may contribute to a visually handicapped individual's performance in the assessment context as well as in the natural setting.

RESEARCH ISSUES

As mentioned throughout this chapter, many frequently employed assessment measures have not been standardized on visually handicapped persons. Also, few efforts have been made to ascertain the technical adequacy (i.e., reliability and validity) of these instruments with the visually impaired. We have already outlined the problem in evaluating this population with tools developed for sighted: the influence of confounding variables associated with the handicapping condition, including sensory deprivation, overprotection, decreased social exposure, and inadequate opportunities for learning and adaptive skill acquisition relative to sighted peers. Ammerman *et al.* (1985) also have argued that assessment devices must be both parametrically adequate and meaningful for visually handicapped individuals. Further, they have discussed the usefulness of fine-grained functional skill analyses over more traditional standardized testing to determine strengths and deficits in the visually handicapped. In functional skills assessment, the emphasis would be placed on specific abilities requisite to adequate life adjustment. According to this approach, adequate mobility and use of mobility aides, social skills, grooming and self-care skills, fluency in braille or other communication methods, and the like are considered more relevant to the overall functioning of the visually handicapped person than an IQ score based on sighted norms. This is not unlike the position of

Silberman (1981), described earlier. Functional skills assessment also frequently is employed in the assessment of other handicapped individuals, in particular, the mentally retarded (Beck, 1983). It is clear that additional research relating to the development of adequate assessment measures for the visually handicapped is needed.

A more general concern has been expressed regarding the lack of empirically based assessment and design strategies for evaluating the efficacy of various interventions for the visually handicapped (Bauman, 1973a; Bonfanti, 1979; Van Hasselt & Hersen, 1981; Van Hasselt & Sisson, in press). Of those empirical studies that have been conducted, a disproportionate number suffer from serious methodological shortcomings (Belcastro, 1978). Most notably, the lack of experimental control makes it difficult to interpret results. Van Hasselt and Hersen (1981) have discussed several possible reasons for this situation. First, traditional research designs involving experimental groups, control groups, and statistical analyses may not lend themselves readily to investigations with the visually handicapped. Indeed, perfectly matched samples, prerequisites to testing in group designs, are often difficult to obtain in the field of visual impairment (Bonfanti, 1979). Further, group-comparison strategies are extremely costly, time consuming, and require a high degree of statistical sophistication.

As an alternative to group-comparison designs, Van Hasselt and Hersen (1981) have suggested the potential utility of single-case experimental designs in vision research. This approach circumvents many of the problems inherent in the use of group-comparison methods (see Barlow & Hersen, 1973; Barlow & Hersen, 1984). First, there is a focus on intensive study of the individual, with each subject serving as his or her own control. This eliminates the difficulties in obtaining large numbers of visually handicapped persons needed for group comparisons. Second, the subject's behavior is measured repeatedly over time, all target behaviors are clearly specified, and measurement procedures are precisely defined. Third, in contrast to statistical analyses in group-comparison research, the results of single-case designs are portrayed graphically and analyzed visually. Because this procedure makes it easier to form clinical judgments about the magnitude of behavioral change, it is easier to determine the clinical significance of results.

SUMMARY

In this chapter we have described approaches and issues pertaining to the psychological evaluation of the visually handicapped. Comprehensive assessment may be increasingly important in light of changing attitudes toward the handicapped that allow for their placement into less restrictive residential, educational, and employment settings. Such assessment, including interviews, standardized tests, and behavioral assessment, is necessary to identify and address the special needs of visually handicapped individuals who may show deficits in cognitive, social, and emotional/behavioral functioning concomitant with visual impairment.

The unique limitations inherent in the visual deficit present difficulties in conducting psychological evaluation. Typically, the instruments and strategies devised for nonhandicapped persons are employed with the visually handicapped. However, modifications and adaptations of traditional assessment techniques are often necessary. Some of these include screening the content of items for visual material, presenting test items in braille or large print, careful interpretation of test results (especially with those instruments lacking normative data or well-documented psychometric properties), and the like. Unfortunately, the available literature in this field does not provide adequate information regarding how modifications of traditional procedures affect the results obtained and their predictive value. Also, few assessment devices have been designed specifically for visually handicapped individuals. Moreover, there is a paucity of data attesting to adequate parametric properties of most instruments used with this population. It is clear that empirical research is needed to target these important issues. Until such investigations are conducted, psychologists must be cautious in their selection of suitable measures for assessment. Further, they must be careful to administer assessment techniques in a way that is relevant to the needs of their visually handicapped client. In addition, it is encumbent upon the examiner to interpret any results obtained in light of current knowledge about the impact of severe vision loss on development and the effect of the handicapped individual's environment on acquisition of academic and adaptive skills.

REFERENCES

Achenbach, T. M., & Edelbrock, C. (Eds.). (1983). *Manual for the child behavior profile*. New York: Queen City Printers.

Adelson, E., & Fraiberg, S. (1974). Gross motor development in infants blind from birth. *Child Development, 45*, 114–126.

Adrian, R. J., Miller, L. R., & DeL'aune, W. R. (1982). Personality assessment of early visually impaired persons using the CPI and the MMPI. *Journal of Visual Impairment and Blindness, 76*, 172–178.

Ammerman, R. T., Van Hasselt, V. B., & Hersen, M. (1985). Social skills training for visually handicapped children: A treatment manual. *Psychological Documents, 15*, 6.

Anastasi, A. (1982). *Psychological testing* (5th ed.). New York: Macmillan.

Avery, C. D., & Streitfeld, J. W. (1969). An abbreviation of the Haptic Intelligence Scale for clinical use. *Education of the Visually Handicapped, 1,* 37–40.

Barlow, D. H., & Hersen, M. (1973). Single-case experimental designs: Uses in applied clinical research. *Archives of General Psychiatry, 29,* 319–325.

Barlow, D. H., & Hersen, M. (1984). *Single-case experimental designs: Strategies for studying behavior change.* New York: Pergamon Press.

Barry, H., Jr., & Marshall, F. E. (1953). Maladjustment and maternal rejection in retrolental fibroplasia. *Mental Hygiene, 37,* 570–580.

Bast, B. (1971). A predictive study of employability among the visually impaired with the California Psychological Inventory. *Dissertation Abstracts International, 32,* 1717B–1818B.

Bateman, B. (1965). Psychological evaluation of blind children. *The New Outlook for the Blind, 59,* 193–197.

Bauman, M. K. (1971a). Special considerations for assessment of the blind client. In G. D. Carnes, C. E. Hansen, & R. M. Parker (Eds.), *Readings in rehabilitation of the blind client* (pp. 33–38). Austin, TX: Editors.

Bauman, M. K. (1971b). Tests and their interpretation. In G. D. Carnes, C. E. Hansen, & R. M. Parker (Eds.), *Readings in rehabilitation of the blind client* (pp. 39–52). Austin, TX: Editors.

Bauman, M. K. (1972). Special problems in the psychological evaluation of blind persons. In R. D. Hardy & J. G. Cull (Eds.), *Social and rehabilitation services for the blind* (pp. 218–225). Springfield, IL: Charles C Thomas.

Bauman, M. K. (1973a). Psychological and educational assessment. In B. Lowenfeld (Ed.), *The visually handicapped child in school* (pp. 93–115). New York: John Day.

Bauman, M. K. (1973b). An interest inventory for the visually handicapped. *Education of the Visually Handicapped, 5,* 78–83.

Bauman, M. K., & Hayes, S. P. (1951). *A manual for the psychological examination of the adult blind.* New York: The Psychological Corporation.

Bauman, M. K., & Kropf, C. A. (1979). Psychological tests used with blind and visually handicapped persons. *School Psychology Digest, 8,* 257–270.

Beck, S. (1983). Overview of methods. In J. L. Matson & S. E. Breuning (Eds.), *Assessing the mentally retarded* (pp. 3–26). New York: Grune & Stratton.

Belcastro, F. P. (1978). Use of behavior modification with visually handicapped subjects: A review of the research. *Education of the Visually Handicapped, 9,* 114–118.

Bellack, A. S., & Hersen, M. (1977). *Behavior modification: An introductory textbook.* Baltimore: Williams & Wilkins.

Bennett, R. E. (1983). Research and evaluation priorities for special education assessment. *Exceptional Children, 50,* 110–117.

Bersoff, D. N. (1973). Silk purse's into sow's ears: The decline of psychological testing and a suggestion for its redemption. *American Psychologist, 25,* 892–899.

Blank, H. R. (1959). Psychiatric problems associated with congenital blindness due to retrolental fibroplasia. *The New Outlook for the Blind, 53,* 237–244.

Bonfanti, B. H. (1979). Effects of training on nonverbal and verbal behaviors of congenitally blind adults. *Journal of Visual Impairment Blindness, 73,* 1–9.

Boyd, R. D., & Otos, M. (1981). Visual handicaps. In J. E. Lindemann (Ed.), *Psychological and behavioral aspects of physical disability* (pp. 335–374). New York: Plenum Press.

Bullard, B., & Barraga, N. C. (1971). Subtests of evaluative instruments applicable for use with pre-school visually handicapped children. *Education of the Visually Handicapped, 3,* 116–122.

Conley, O. S., & Wolery, M. R. (1980). Treatment by overcorrection of self-injurious eye gouging in preschool blind children. *Journal of Behavior Therapy & Experimental Psychiatry, 11*, 121–125.

Coveny, T. E. (1972). A new test for the visually handicapped: Preliminary analysis of reliability and validity of the Perkins-Binet. *Education of the Handicapped, 4*, 97–101.

Cross, O. H. (1947). Braille edition of the Minnesota Multiphasic Personality Inventory for use with the blind. *Journal of Applied Psychology, 31*, 189–198.

Cutsforth, T. D. (1932). The unreality of words to the blind. *Teachers Forum, 4*, 86–89.

Cundick, B. P., Crandell, J. M., & Hendrix, L. (1974). A new method for the group testing of blind persons. *The New Outlook for the Blind, 68*, 398–403.

Dauterman, W. L., Shapiro, B., & Suinn, R. M. (1967). Performance tests of intelligence for the blind reviewed. *International Journal for the Education of the Blind, 17*, 8–16.

Davis, C. (1980). *Perkins-Binet Tests of Intelligence for the Blind*. Watertown, MA: Perkins School for the Blind.

Dean, S. I. (1957). Adjustment testing and personality factors of the blind. *Journal of Consulting Psychology, 21*, 171–177.

Denton, L. R. (1954). Intelligence test performance and personality differences in a group of visually handicapped children. *Bulletin of Maritime Psychological Association*, December, 47–50.

Doll, E. A. (1947). *Social Maturity Scale*. Circle Pines, MN: American Guidance Service.

Doll, E. A. (1965). *Social Maturity Scale*. Circle Pines, MN: American Guidance Service.

Eber, H. W. (1967). The factor structure of the WAIS-Verbal and HIS-Test combination. *The Journal of Educational Research, 61*, 27–28.

Eisler, R. M., Hersen, M., Miller, P. M., & Blanchard, E. B. (1975). Situational determinants of assertive behaviors. *Journal of Consulting and Clinical Psychology, 43*, 330–340.

Ellis, D. (1978). Methods of assessment for use with the visually handicapped and mentally handicapped: A selective review. *Child: Care, Health and Development, 4*, 397–410.

Farkas, G. M., Sherick, R. B., Matson, J. L., & Loebig, M. (1981). Social skills training of a blind child through differential reinforcement. *The Behavior Therapist, 4*, 24–26.

Fraiberg, S. (1977). *Insights from the blind: Comparative studies of blind and sighted infants*. New York: Basic Books.

Freedman, D. G. (1964). Smiling in blind infants and the issue of innate vs. acquired. *Journal of Child Psychology and Psychiatry, 5*, 171–184.

Gelfand, D. M., & Hartmann, D. P. (1985). *Child behavior analysis and therapy* (2nd ed.). New York: Pergamon Press.

Gilbert, J. G., & Rubin, E. J. (1965). Evaluating the intellect of blind children. *The New Outlook for the Blind, 59*, 238–240.

Goldfried, M. R., & D'Zurilla, T. A. (1969). A behavior-analytic model for assessing competence. In C. D. Spielberger (Ed.), *Current topics in clinical and community psychology* (Vol. 1, pp. 151–196). New York: Academic Press.

Goldman, H. (1970). Psychological testing of blind children. *American Foundation for the Blind Research Bulletin, 21*, 77–90.

Hammill, D. D., Crandell, J. M., & Colarusso, R. (1970). The Slosson Intelligence Test adapted for visually limited children. *Exceptional Children, 36*, 535–536.

Hansen, R., Young, J., & Ulrey, G. (1982). Assessment considerations with the visually handicapped child. In G. Ulrey & S. Rogers (Eds.), *Psychological assessment of handicapped infants and young children* (pp. 108–114). New York: Thieme-Stratton.

Hardy, R. D. (1968). A study of manifest anxiety among blind residential school students. *New Outlook for the Blind, 62*, 173–180.

Harris, S. L., & Romanczyk, R. G. (1976). Treating self-injurious behavior of a retarded child by overcorrection. *Behavior Therapy, 7,* 235–239.
Harris, W. W. (1947). Notes on initial experiments with bas-relief projective material for blind subjects. *Rorschah Research Exchange, 11,* 80–81.
Harris, W. W. (1948). A bas-relief projective technique. *Journal of Psychology, 26,* 3–17.
Hayes, S. P. (1929). The new revision of the Binet Intelligence Tests for the Blind. *Teachers Forum, 2,* 2–4.
Hayes, S. P. (1943). A second scale for the mental measurement of the visually handicapped. *New Outlook for the Blind, 37,* 37–41.
Hayes, S. P. (1950). The visually handicapped. *American Psychologist, 5,* 339–340.
Hecht, P. J., & Newland, T. E. (1965). Learning potential and learning achievement of educationally blind third–eight graders in a residential school. *International Journal for the Education of the Blind, 15,* 1–6.
Hepfinger, L. M. (1962). Psychological evaluation of young blind children. *New Outlook for the Blind, 56,* 309–315.
Hopkins, K. D., & McGuire, L. (1966). Mental measurement of the blind: The validity of the Wechsler Intelligence Scale for Children. *International Journal for the Education of the Blind, 15,* 65–73.
Hopkins, K. D., & McGuire, L. (1967). IQ constancy and the blind child. *International Journal for the Education of the Blind, 16,* 113–114.
Irwin, R. B., & Goddard, H. H. (1914). *Adaptation of the Binet-Simon tests.* Vineland, NJ: Authors.
Jan, J. E., Freeman, R. D., & Scott, E. P. (Eds.). (1977). *Visual impairment in children and adolescents.* New York: Grune & Stratton.
Kirtley, D. D. (1975). *The psychology of blindness.* Chicago: Nelson-Hall.
Kleck, R. E., Ono, H., & Hastorf, A. H. (1966). The effect of physical deviance upon face-to-face interaction. *Human Relations, 19,* 425–436.
Klimasinski, K. (1972). An attempt to test the personality of the blind using the MMPI. *American Foundation for the Blind: Research Bulletin, 24,* 65–74.
Koestler, F. A. (1976). *The unseen minority: A social history of blindness in the United States.* New York: David McKay.
Langley, M. B. (1979). Psychoeducational assessment of the multiply handicapped blind child: Issues and methods. *Education of the Visually Handicapped, 10,* 97–114.
Lebo, D. (1960). The development and employment of VTATs or pictureless TATs. *Journal of Psychology, 50,* 197–204.
Lebo, D., & Bruce, R. S. (1960). Projective methods recommended for use with the blind. *The Journal of Psychology, 50,* 15–38.
Lewis, L. L. (1957). The relation of measured mental ability to school marks and academic survival in the Texas School for the Blind. *International Journal of Education of the Blind, 66,* 56–60.
Lowenfeld, B. (1975). *The changing status of the blind: From separation to integration.* Springfield, IL: Charles C Thomas.
Malikin, D., & Freedman, S. (1970). Test construction or adaptation for use with blind adults. In L. L. Clark & Z. Z. Jastrzembska (Eds.), *Proceedings of the conference on new approaches to the evaluation of blind persons* (pp. 73–97). New York: American Foundation for the Blind.
Matas, L., Arend, R. A., & Stroufe, L. A. (1978). Continuity of adaptation in the second year: The relationship between quality of attachment and later competence. *Child Development, 49,* 547–556.

Matson, J. L., Rotatori, A. F., & Helsel, W. J. (1983). Development of a rating scale to measure social skills in children: The Matson Evaluation of Social Skills with Youngsters (MESSY). *Behaviour Research and Therapy, 21,* 335–340.

Matson, J. L., Heinze, A., Helsel, W. J., Kapperman, G., & Rotatori, A. F. (in press). Assessing social behaviors in the visually handicapped: The Matson Evaluation of Social Skills with Youngsters (MESSY). *Journal of Clinical Child Psychology.*

Maxfield, K. E., & Bucholz, S. (1958). *The Maxfield Scale of Social Maturity for use with preschool blind children.* New York: American Foundation for the Blind.

Maxfield, K. E., & Fjeld, H. A. (1942). The social maturity of the visually handicapped preschool child. *Child Development, 13,* 1–27.

McGuinness, R. M. (1970). A descriptive study of blind children educated in the itinerant teacher resource room, and special school setting. *Research Bulletin, American Foundation for the Blind, 20,* 1–56.

McKay, B. E. (1936). Social maturity of the preschool blind child. *Training School Bulletin, 33,* 146–155.

Miller, L. R. (1977). Abilities structure of congenitally blind persons: A factor analysis. *Journal of Visual Impairment and Blindness, 71,* 145–153.

Morse, J. (1971). The adaptation of a nonverbal abstract reasoning test for use with the blind: Review of related research and bibliography. *Research Bulletin, American Foundation for the Blind, 23,* 30–26.

National Society for the Prevention of Blindness. (1966). *N.S.P.B. fact book: Estimated statistics on blindness and visual problems.* New York: Author.

National Society to Prevent Blindness. (1980). *Vision problems in the U.S.: Facts and figures.* New York: Author.

Newland, T. E. (1979). The blind learning aptitude test. *Journal of Visual Impairment and Blindness, 73,* 134–139.

Nolan, C. Y. (1962). Evaluating the scholastic achievement of visually handicapped children. *Exceptional Children, 28,* 493–496.

Nolan, C. Y., & Ashcroft, S. C. (1959). The Stanford Achievement Arithmetic Computation Tests: A study of an experimental adaptation for braille administration. *International Journal of Education of the Blind, 8,* 92–98.

Parker, J. (1969). Adapting school psychological evaluation to the blind child. *The New Outlook for the Blind, 63,* 305–311.

Petrucci, D. (1953). The blind child and his adjustment. *The New Outlook for the Blind, 47,* 240–246.

Porter, J., & Holzberg, B. C. (1979). The changing role of the school psychologist in the age of PL 94-142: From conducting testing to enhancing instruction. *Education of the Visually Handicapped, 10,* 71–74.

Project Vision-Up Curriculum. (1979). Boise, ID: Educational Products and Training Foundation.

Reardon, R. C., Hersen, M., Bellack, A. S., & Foley, J. M. (1979). Measuring social skills in grade school boys. *Journal of Behavioral Assessment, 1,* 87–105.

Reynell, J., & Zinkin, P. (1975). New procedures for the development assessment of young children with severe visual handicaps. *Child: Care, Health and Development, 1,* 61–69.

Rich, C. C., & Anderson, R. P. (1965). A tactile form of the progressive matrics for use with blind children. *Personnel and Guidance Journal, 43,* 912–919.

Rotter, J. B., & Williamson, B. (1947). The Incomplete Sentence Test. *Journal of Consulting Psychology, 11,* 43–48.

Sanders, R. M., & Goldberg, S. G. (1977). Eye contacts: Increasing their rate in social interactions. *Journal of Visual Impairment and Blindness, 71*, 265–267.

Sargent, R. F. (1931). The Otis Classification Test, Form A, Part II, adapted for use with classes of blind children. *Teachers Forum, 4*, 30–33.

Sattler, J. M. (1982). *Assessment of children's intelligence and special abilities* (2nd ed.). Boston: Allyn & Bacon.

Scholl, G., & Schnur, R. (1976). *Measure of psychological, vocational, and educational functioning in the blind and visually handicapped*. New York: American Foundation for the Blind.

Scott, R. A. (1969). The socialization of blind children. In D. Goslin (Ed.), *Handbook of socialization theory and research* (pp. 1025–1045). Chicago: Rand McNally.

Shurrager, H. C. (1961). *A Haptic Intelligence Scale for Adult Blind*. Chicago: Illinois Institute of Technology.

Shurrager, H. C., & Shurrager, P. S. (1964). *Manual for the Haptic Intelligence Scale for the Blind*. Chicago: Psychological Research Technology Center, Illinois Institute of Technology.

Silberman, R. K. (1981). Assessment and evaluation of visually handicapped students. *Journal of Visual Impairment and Blindness, 75*, 109–114.

Sisson, L. A., Van Hasselt, V. B., Hersen, M., & Strain, P. S. (1985). Peer interventions: Increasing social behaviors in multihandicapped children. *Behavior Modification, 9*, 293–321.

Sommers, V. S. (1944). *The influence of parental attitudes and social environment on the personality development of the adolescent blind*. New York: American Foundation for the Blind.

Spungin, S. J., & Swallow, R. M. (1975). Psychoeducational assessment: Role of the psychologist to teacher of the visually handicapped. *Education of the Visually Handicapped, 1*, 67–76.

Streitfeld, J. W., & Avery, C. D. (1968). The WAIS and HIS tests as predictors of academic achievement in a residential school for the blind. *International Journal of Education of the Blind, 18*, 73–77.

Suinn, R. M., Dauterman, W. L., & Shapiro, B. (1966). The Stanford-Ohwaki-Kohs tactile block design intelligence test for the blind. *The New Outlook for the Blind, 60*, 77.

Swallow, R. M. (1981). Fifty assessment instruments commonly used with blind and partially seeing individuals. *Journal of Visual Impairment and Blindness, 75*, 65–72.

Teare, R. J. (1966). *The Sentence Completion Test (SC) manual*. McLean, VA: Champion Press.

Teare, J. F., & Thompson, R. W. (1982). Concurrent validity of the Perkins-Binet tests of intelligence for the blind. *Journal of Visual Impairment and Blindness, 76*, 279–280.

Tillman, H. M. (1967a). The performance of blind and sighted children on the Wechsler Intelligence Scale for Children: Study I. *The International Journal for the Education of the Blind, 16*, 106–112.

Tillman, H. M. (1967b). The performances of blind and sighted children on the Wechsler Intelligence Scale for Children: Study II. *International Journal for the Education of the Blind, 16*, 65–74.

Tillman, H. M. (1973). Intelligence scales for the blind: A review with implications for research. *Journal of School Psychology, 11*, 80–87.

Tillman, H. M., & Osborne, R. T. (1969). The performance of blind and sighted children on the Wechsler Intelligence Scale for Children: Interaction effects. *Education of the Visually Handicapped, 1*, 1–4.

Trismen, D. A. (1967). Equating braille forms of the sequential tests of educational progress. *Exceptional Children, 66*, 419–424.

Vander Kolk, C. J. (1977). Intelligence testing for visually impaired persons. *Journal of Visual Impairment and Blindness, 71*, 158–163.

Van Hasselt, V. B. (1983). Social adaptation in the blind. *Clinical Psychology Review, 3,* 87–102.

Van Hasselt, V. B. (1987). Behavior therapy for visually handicapped persons. In M. Hersen, P. Miller, & R. M. Eisler (Eds.), *Progress in behavior modification: Vol. 21* (pp. 13–44). New York: Sage.

Van Hasselt, V. B., & Hersen, M. (1981). Applications of single-case designs to research with visually impaired individuals. *Journal of Visual Impairment and Blindness, 75,* 359–360.

Van Hasselt, V. B., & Sisson, L. A. (in press). Assessing exceptional populations: Visual handicaps. In C. L. Frame & J. L. Matson (Eds.), *Handbook of assessment in child psychopathology: Applied issues in differential diagnosis and treatment evaluation.* New York: Plenum Press.

Van Hasselt, V. B., Hersen, M., Kazdin, A. E., Simon, J., & Mastantuono, A. K. (1983). Training blind adolescents in social skills. *Journal of Visual Impairment and Blindness, 77,* 199–203.

Van Hasselt, V. B., Kazdin, A. E., Hersen, M., Simon, J., & Mastantuono, A. K. (1985). A behavioral-analytic model for assessing social skills in blind adolescents. *Behaviour Research and Therapy, 23,* 395–405.

Van Hasselt, V. B., Kazdin, A. E., & Hersen, M. (1986). Assessment of problem behavior in visually handicapped adolescents. *Journal of Clinical Child Psychology, 15,* 134–141.

Vaughan, D., & Asbury, T. (1977). *General ophthalmology.* Los Altos, CA.: Lange Medical Publications.

Ward, M. E., & Genshaft, J. (1982). A review of the Perkins-Binet tests of intelligence for the blind with suggestions for administration. *School Psychology Review, 11,* 338–341.

Ward, M. E., & Genshaft, J. (1983). The Perkins-Binet tests: A critique and recommendations for administration. *Exceptional Children, 49,* 450–452.

Warren, D. H. (1977). *Blindness and early childhood development.* New York: American Foundation for the Blind.

Warren, D. H. (1981). Visual impairments. In J. M. Kauffman & D. P. Hallahan (Eds.), *Handbook of special education* (pp. 195–221). Englewood Cliffs, NJ: Prentice-Hall.

Wattron, J. B. (1956). A suggested performance test of intelligence. *The New Outlook for the Blind, 50,* 115–121.

Wechsler, D. (1949). *Manual for the Wechsler Intelligence Scale for Children.* New York: Psychological Corporation.

Wechsler, D. (1955). *Manual for the Wechsler Adult Intelligence Scale.* New York: Psychological Corporation.

Wechsler, D. (1967). *Manual for the Wechsler Preschool and Primary Scale of Intelligence.* New York: Psychological Corporation.

Wechsler, D. (1974). *Manual for the Wechsler Intelligence Scale for Children—Revised.* New York: Psychological Corporation.

Wechsler, D. (1981). *Manual for the Wechsler Adult Intelligence Scale—Revised.* New York: Psychological Corporation.

Ysseldyke, J. E., & Shinn, M. R. (1981). Psychoeducational evaluation. In J. M. Kauffman & D. P. Hallahan (Eds.), *Handbook of special education* (pp. 418–440). Englewood Cliffs, NJ: Prentice-Hall.

7

Autism

LAURA SCHREIBMAN AND MARJORIE H. CHARLOP

INTRODUCTION

Traditional psychological evaluation of childhood disorders has typically included a battery of tests geared toward assessing the child's functioning in a variety of areas. Some of these areas are social maturation, intellectual ability, communication (expressive and receptive language), physical development and developmental milestones, family interactions and parental adjustment, and emotional functioning. Tests used in such batteries include IQ scales (e.g., Weschler tests, Stanford-Binet, Bayley scales), language assessments (e.g., Peabody Picture Vocabulary Test), and assessments of emotional adjustment (Children's Apperception Test, Rorschach, Draw-A-Person). These tests often are inappropriate for assessment of severe pathology due to a variety of factors. Lack of motivation, noncompliance, absence of speech, hyperactivity, attentional deficits, and withdrawal from environmental stimulation are commonly seen in handicapped individuals and usually interfere with obtaining accurate test scores or with the interpretation of these scores. Thus the utility of using these tests with severe forms of child psychopathology is questionable.

LAURA SCHREIBMAN • Department of Psychology, University of California at San Diego, La Jolla, California 92093. MARJORIE H. CHARLOP • Psychology Department, Claremont McKenna College and Claremont Graduate School, Claremont, California 91711. Preparation of this chapter was supported by U.S.P.H.S. Research Grants MH 28231, MH 39434, and MH 28210 from the National Institute of Mental Health and by NIH Biomedical Research Support Grant NIH 2507RR07019-18.

For severe forms of pathology, such as autism and childhood psychoses, assessment and diagnosis involve determining the presence of symptoms or characteristics that comprise the disorder. Thus the use of diagnostic criteria (presence or absence of symptomatology) and later, the use of behavioral checklists, has become the major mode of psychological assessment of severe forms of child psychopathology (Newsom & Rincover, 1982). They can be used to provide a diagnosis as well as an evaluation of later improvement. In addition, another form of evaluation, typically behavioral in nature, has been employed to assess the presence or absence of specific behaviors in a given child. This type of assessment is used in the design of appropriate treatment strategies rather than for diagnostic purposes.

The assessment of autism, a syndrome that was only first identified in 1943, possesses quite an extensive history. This chapter will provide a description of the syndrome, a summary tracing the history of its assessment and diagnosis, and a presentation of several assessment tools.

DESCRIPTION

Autism is a severe developmental disability characterized by an extreme impairment in adaptive functioning accompanied by the presence of bizarre behaviors. It is estimated to occur in about 1 out of every 2,500 children and is usually not diagnosed until the child is between 2 and 5 years of age (Schreibman, Koegel, Charlop, & Egel, 1982). Although there are many theories regarding the etiology of the disorder, there are no consistent findings in support of any one of them (Egel, Koegel, & Schreibman, 1980). Today, it is generally accepted that autism is caused by organic factors and that it is probably present (although not usually observed) from birth (Schreibman, Charlop, & Britten, 1983). The severity of the syndrome and the nature of its characteristics make it resistant to many forms of treatment. Behavioral approaches to treatment have been most successful in that they (a) treat the disorder symptomatically, (b) do not depend heavily upon the child's verbal skills, which are usually severely impaired, and (c) do not require knowledge of the etiology in order to treat the disorder. Although certain factors are conducive to more successful treatment outcome (e.g., speech by the age of 5 years, IQ above 50, and early intervention), the prognosis for an autistic child generally remains poor.

To understand the focus of evaluation of autism, a clear description of the behavioral characteristics of the syndrome is warranted. The following list of features is drawn from a composite of diagnostic criteria widely used (and described in subsequent portions of this chapter). It is important to stress that not all autistic children display all of these behaviors.

SOCIAL BEHAVIOR

Failure to develop normal social relationships is a hallmark feature of autism (Rimland, 1964; Rutter, 1978; Wing, 1978). These children typically do not bond with their parents, do not seek affection, prefer to be alone, and may avoid eye contact with others. It is frequently reported that when autistic children do interact with people they usually treat them as objects or as a means of getting what they want (Schreibman & Koegel, 1982). For example, an autistic child may hug his or her mother as the only way of reaching a cookie behind her. Autistic children are typically unaffectionate and resist attempts at holding and cuddling.

As infants, autistic children generally lack attachment behavior and do not mold to their parent's body when held, as do normal infants. Rather, they either remain stiff or rigid or "go limp" when picked up. When older, autistic children seldom seek out their parents for attention or comfort (Rutter, 1978). They also do not interact appropriately with peers and often will avoid contact with other children. Their interaction with toys is minimal and frequently mechanistic and inappropriate when it occurs. Thus contact with the social environment (including toy play) is seriously impaired in autistic children.

SPEECH AND LANGUAGE

One of the most striking characteristics of autistic children is their failure to acquire appropriate speech (Ornitz & Ritvo, 1976b; Wing, 1976). Approximately 50% of autistic children are functionally nonverbal, occasionally emitting a few sounds (Rimland, 1964). Other children may acquire speech, but it is typically pathological and noncommunicative in nature. The most common speech anomaly in verbal autistic children is echolalia. There are two major types of echolalia generally seen in autistic children. Autistic children displaying immediate echolalia repeat or "echo" what was just said by another (Carr, Schreibman, & Lovaas, 1975). For example, if the child was asked, "What's your name," he or she would respond with "What's your name." The other major type of echolalia, delayed echolalia, is present when the child repeats words he or she has heard sometime in the past. For example, a delayed echolalic response may be something the child's teacher had said days earlier ("Do your ABCs") or something the child's mother had said a few hours earlier ("Eat your beef stew"). Delayed echolalia usually occurs more frequently in a fearful or punishing situation (Charlop & Cugliari, 1984; Miller, 1969). The verbalizations are generally out of context, and the children do not appear to know the meaning of what they say. These speech anomalies are problematic in that they may seriously interfere with appropriate communication and learning.

Some autistic children may learn to use speech to communicate. However, this speech is often characterized by several abnormalities. First, pronominal reversal is often present (Kanner, 1943; Rutter, 1978). For example, the child may say, "You want a peanut," although meaning, "I want a peanut." It is also common for the children to avoid pronouns altogether by referring to themselves by name ("Erik wants to take a break"). Second, those children who do learn to speak seldom participate in conversations and generally do not speak spontaneously (Charlop, Schreibman, & Thibadeau, 1985). Third, the speech of initially mute children who acquire speech through training is often characterized by dysprosody. Thus the modulation, intonation, stress, rhythm, pitch, loudness, and articulation may be incorrect (Baltaxe, 1981). These children often sound like speaking deaf children. Fourth, even skilled autistic speakers demonstrate difficulty with abstractions, metaphors, and subtle associations.

RITUALISTIC BEHAVIOR AND INSISTENCE UPON SAMENESS

According to Rutter (1978), there are four ritualistic behaviors commonly seen in autistic children. First, autistic children often engage in a very limited and rigid type of play. They may repeatedly line up toys or parts of a game or collect objects of a special shape or texture. Second, the child may become overly attached to a specific item and want it with him or her at all times. If the object is taken away, the child will usually protest and have a tantrum. Third, an autistic child may have an unusual preoccupation with, for example, numbers, geometric shapes, bus routes, and colors. Fourth, the children display a marked resistance to change in their environment. They maintain a rigid routine and tantrum if a small change is made in their environment. The child may become quite upset if the furniture is rearranged or if a different route to the supermarket is taken.

APPARENT SENSORY DEFICIT

Many parents of autistic children complain that their children seem to be "living in a world of his own" or "not tuned in to reality" (Koegel & Schreibman, 1976). Often, autistic children appear to have a sensory deficit and are unresponsive to external stimulation (Ornitz & Ritvo, 1976b; Schreibman & Mills, 1983; Wing, 1976). Because of the apparent sensory deficit, as young children they are often suspected of being deaf or blind. However, their vision and audition are intact and, at times, the child does respond in a normal manner. It is interesting that a child who does not flinch when presented with a loud noise will pursue the crinkling of a candy wrapper on the other side of the room.

SELF-STIMULATION

Self-stimulatory behavior is repetitive, stereotyped movement that seems to serve no other purpose than to provide sensory input. These bizarre mannerisms include flapping hands or arms repeatedly (often in front of the eyes), rhythmic rocking or swaying of the torso, turning around in circles, body posturing, head rolling, and toe walking. Each child usually has a repertoire of self-stimulatory behaviors. There are also more subtle forms of this type of behavior such as staring at lights or rubbing hands along surfaces. Autistic children may engage in self-stimulation using other people (e.g., smelling hair) or objects (e.g., flapping a toy in front of the eyes). In addition, self-stimulatory behavior can be of a verbal nature in which the child repeats sounds or words again and again. Self-stimulatory behavior is quite problematic in that not only does it make the child appear especially bizarre, but it makes him or her even more unresponsive to the environment (Lovaas, Litrownik, & Mann, 1971; Schreibman & Mills, 1983). This behavior is difficult to eliminate in that it appears to be a preferred activity of these youngsters, who often engage in self-stimulatory behavior most of their waking hours.

SELF-INJURIOUS BEHAVIOR

Few of the behaviors seen in childhood autism are as dramatic as self-injurious behavior (SIB). SIB involves any behavior in which the individual inflicts physical damage to his or her own body (Tate & Baroff, 1966). For autistic children, the two most common forms of SIB are head banging and biting of hand or wrist (Rutter & Lockyer, 1967). Other common SIBs are hair pulling, face scratching, slapping of face or sides, eye gouging, and arm or leg banging (Schreibman & Mills, 1983).

INAPPROPRIATE AFFECT

Autistic children may display inappropriate affect. Some have unusual and profound mood swings from cheerful laughing at one moment to intense crying or tantrums the next. Others display a flattened affect, seldom showing any emotional behavior at all (Rimland, 1964; Schreibman, & Mills, 1983).

Their emotions are often inappropriate to the situation (i.e., laughing while being punished or crying while being tickled). Additionally, autistic children tend to display inappropriate fear responses. They may lack fear when there is real danger (i.e., running out into the middle of the street) or be terrified of harmless situations or objects (i.e., a specific toy) (Wing, 1976).

ADDITIONAL COMMON CHARACTERISTICS

Autistic children also may be healthy and attractive (Dunlap, Koegel, & Egel, 1979; Kanner, 1943). Although initially thought to be quite intelligent because of the serious expression on their faces, no physical anomalies, good rote memory, and areas of average or above average performance (Eisenberg & Kanner, 1956; Kanner, 1943), normal or above normal intelligence is not associated with autism today (Rutter, 1978). In fact, approximately 60% of autistic children have IQs below 50 (Ritvo & Freeman, 1978). Occasionally, however, islets of superior ability in such areas as music, mechanics, or mathematics are observed (Applebaum, Egel, Koegel, & Imhoff, 1979; Rimland, 1964).

HISTORY AND DEVELOPMENT

In 1943, Leo Kanner first described the syndrome that he called early infantile autism. Based on 11 cases, he presented a specific type of childhood psychosis that differed markedly from other types of childhood disorders, yet still maintained many similarities with what was known at the time as childhood schizophrenia. He described the syndrome as the manifestation of the following characteristics.

1. *Extreme autistic aloneness.* This was considered to be from birth and was indicated by the failure to develop normal relationships with

parents during infancy, general unresponsivity to people, failure to play with other children, and failure to notice the presence and absence of parents and others.

2. *Language abnormalities.* This included mutism, immediate and delayed echolalia, pronominal reversals, and the ability in verbal children to repeat names of objects, nursery rhymes, songs, and lists requiring an excellent rote memory.

3. *Obsessive desire for the maintenance of sameness.* The children were upset by changes in daily routine, furniture or objects arrangement, wording of requests, and broken objects. This also included stereotypic, self-stimulatory behaviors, and preoccupation with certain objects.

4. *Good cognitive potential.* This was indicated by intelligent and serious facial expressions, excellent rote memory, and good performance on the Seguin Form Board.

5. *Normal physical development.* This included the presence of good fine-motor skills.

6. *Highly intelligent, obsessive, and cold parents.* Most parents were professionals with advanced degrees, appeared aloof and withdrawn, and reported unhappy marriages.

Although such "clear and careful" prose (Schopler, 1978; Rutter, 1978) as a manner to delineate characteristics of autism reflects psychiatry during that time (Newsom & Rincover, 1982), it presents difficulties in that clear, objective criteria were not proposed. Since the initial paper (Kanner, 1943), the criteria for autism have undergone numerous changes. Three major areas of controversy existed: (a) whether autism was indeed separate from other kinds of childhood psychosis, (b) what the diagnostic criteria were, and (c) the role of the parents in etiology and as a diagnostic factor.

Kanner continued to present autism as a similar but separate syndrome from other childhood disorders (Eisenberg & Kanner, 1956; Kanner, 1943, 1949). Others, however, described children similar to Kanner's cases as those with "atypical development" (Rank, 1955), symbiotic psychosis (Mahler, 1952), or childhood schizophrenia (Bender, 1942; Creak, 1961; Goldfarb, 1961). Rutter (1968), however, clearly delineated the characteristics in which autistic children and psychotic or schizophrenic children differ, and today autism is viewed as a distinct developmental disability that can be diagnosed differentially from psychoses, retardation, and other childhood disorders.

After Kanner's initial description of autism (Kanner, 1943), he reduced the essential symptoms of autism to extreme aloneness and preoccupation with preservation of sameness (Eisenberg & Kanner, 1956). It is interesting to note that language abnormalities, which were stressed in the earlier papers, were no longer considered essential characteristics (Rutter, 1978).

Later the British Working Party, as summarized by Creak (1961), proposed nine points for the diagnosis of "childhood schizophrenia" (including autism):

1. Gross and sustained impairment of emotional relationships with people
2. Apparent unawareness of personal identity (for example, pronominal reversals, self-stimulation, and self-injurious behavior)
3. Pathological preoccupation with particular objects or certain characteristics of them
4. Resistance to change
5. Abnormal perceptual experience—unpredictable response to sensory stimuli or insensitivity to pain or temperature
6. Acute, excessive, and seemingly illogical anxiety (inappropriate or absence of appropriate fear)
7. Speech abnormalities
8. Distortion in motility patterns (self-stimulatory behavior)
9. A background of serious retardation in which islets of normal, near normal, or exceptional intellectual function or skill may appear

The British Working Party's nine points are of great importance in that, unlike Kanner, they continued to recognize the importance of abnormalities in speech. In addition, unlike Kanner, they proposed that the children's intellectual functioning was quite impaired.

Finally, it is important to note the change in the emphasis on parental pathology as a condition for the diagnosis of autism. In Kanner's 1949 paper, he continued to stress psychogenic factors in autism. He described mothers of autistic children as mechanistic, lacking in warmth toward their children, unemotional, obsessive, and perfectionistic. Others (e.g., Goldfarb, 1961; Kaufman, Rosenblum, Heims, & Willer, 1957) and especially Bettelheim (1967) concurred. Empirical evidence was later provided that contradicted psychogenic factors in association with autism (Creak & Ini, 1960; Koegel, Schreibman, O'Neill, & Burke, 1983; Kolvin, 1971; Rutter, 1968).

CURRENT DIAGNOSTIC CRITERIA

Over the years, then, the definition of autism changed from Kanner's (1943) original description. In addition to the need to specify more precisely the nature of autism and how it differed from other childhood disorders, the change in diagnostic characteristics also functioned to increase the number of children who would be considered autistic. If autism was defined in strict agreement with Kanner, then too few children would maintain the diagnosis of such "classic" autism. This would make research on the syndrome quite difficult as too few subjects would be available (Newsom & Rincover, 1982). In addition, parents and educators needed larger numbers in order to justify the need for special education for autistic youngsters and to qualify for government funding.

Today there is still much disagreement as to the criteria for diagnosing autism (see Newsom & Rincover, 1982, for a synopsis of a variety of diagnostic criteria employed in major research and treatment centers). Two main sets of diagnostic criteria are currently in use. Rutter (1978) devised his definition of autism based on previous definitions and research. Rutter's definition of autism consists of

1. Onset before the age of 30 months
2. Impaired social development that is not due to the child's impaired intellectual level. This includes lack of affection and eye contact
3. Delayed and deviant language development. This includes lack of comprehension, immediate and delayed echolalia, pronominal reversal, and lack of conversational speech
4. Insistence on sameness which is indicated by stereotypic actions, preoccupations with certain objects or activities, rigid routines, and resistance to environmental change

Although Rutter's (1978) criteria are based on a summation of research, the other prominent diagnostic criteria, proposed by the National Society for Autistic Children (NSAC) (Ritvo & Freeman, 1978), were devised to serve administrative and legislative purposes. These five criteria are based on clinical observation and professional consensus rather than a summation of the literature (Newsom & Rincover, 1978). The NSAC criteria are

1. Age of onset before 30 months
2. Disturbances of developmental rates and sequences in the areas of motor, social-adaptive, and cognitive skills
3. Disturbances of responses to sensory stimuli. This includes hyper- or hypo-reactivity in audition, vision, tactile stimulation, motor, smell, and taste. Self-stimulatory behavior is included here
4. Disturbances of speech, language-cognition, and nonverbal communication. This includes mutism, immediate and delayed echolalia, and failure to use abstract terms

5. Disturbances of the capacity to appropriately relate to people, events, and objects. This includes lack of social behavior, affection, and appropriate play. Interruption of the idiosyncratic or perseverative use of objects will result in upsetting the child. There may be an awareness of the sequence of events with interruption of the sequence resulting in discomfort or panic

Although the two definitions overlap, sufficient differences exist. For example, Rutter (1978) highlighted insistence on sameness as a necessary characteristic, whereas NSAC emphasized developmental delays and sensory disturbances. Schopler (1978) proposed that both sets of criteria have their place in the diagnostic arena. The American Psychiatric Association's (1980) definition of autism, as presented in the *Diagnostic and Statistical Manual* (DSM-III), more closely resembles Rutter's (1978) definition. The DSM-III criteria are

1. Onset before the age of 30 months
2. Pervasive lack of responsiveness to other people ("autism")
3. Gross deficits in language development
4. If speech is present, peculiar speech patterns such as immediate and delayed echolalia, and pronominal reversal
5. Bizarre responsiveness to the environment. This includes resistance to change and unusual attachments to particular objects
6. Absence of delusions, hallucinations, loosening of associations, and incoherence (as in schizophrenia)

A comparison of the different sets of diagnostic criteria used for autism since 1943 is summarized in Table 1. The left column lists the various behaviors/characteristics that would be tapped by the various sets of criteria. The various diagnostic criteria are listed along the top of the table.

DIFFERENTIAL DIAGNOSIS

Given the disparate opinions regarding behavioral characteristics required for an autism diagnosis, it is not surprising that the application of different criteria has resulted in considerable heterogeneity in the population. One reason for this heterogeneity is an overlap with other childhood disorders (Schreibman & Mills, 1983). Thus autism shares several central features with other disorders (e.g., impaired cognitive ability is also found in mental retardation and developmental aphasia). However, it now appears that autism can be clearly differentiated from at least four major categories of disability. These include childhood

TABLE 1. CHARACTERISTICS OF AUTISM AND VARIOUS DIAGNOSTIC CRITERIA

Characteristics	Kanner, 1943	British Working Party, 1961	Rutter, 1978	NSAC, 1978	DSM-III, 1981	Erik: case description
Extreme autistic aloneness (impaired social development)	X	X	X	X	X	0
Language & speech abnormalities	X	X	X	X	X	0
Obsessive desire for maintenance of sameness	X	X	X	X	X	0
Good cognitive potential	X					0
Normal physical development	X					0
Highly intellectual, obsessive, cold parents	X					
Preoccupation with particular objects	X	X	X	X	X	0
Abnormal response to sensory stimuli (i.e., pain, temperature)		X		X		
Inappropriate fears and anxieties		X				
Self-stimulatory behavior		X	X	X		0
Background of retardation with islets of normal functioning		X		X	X	
Onset before 30 months			X	X	X	0

schizophrenia, developmental aphasia, mental retardation, and environmental deprivations.

In distinguishing autism from childhood schizophrenia, several features can be considered (Schreibman & Mills, 1983). In autism, there is an early onset of symptoms (before 30 months) with no initial period of normal development, no history of mental illness in the family, normal or above average motor development, good physical health, and a failure to develop complex language and social skills. In contrast, in childhood schizophrenia, the onset is later (after age 5), often following a family history of mental illness, poor physical health and poor motor performance (Rimland, 1964; Rutter, 1972; Wing, 1976).

Contrasting autism with developmental aphasia, it has been noted that the language difficulties of autistic children are more severe and widespread (Churchill, 1972; Rutter, Bartak, & Newman, 1971) than in aphasic children. Also, unlike autistic children, aphasics can achieve meaningful communication through use of gestures (Wing, 1976), exhibit emotional intent (Griffith & Ritvo, 1967), and show imaginative play (Wing, 1976).

Autistic and retarded children share impaired intellectual functioning that persists throughout the life span (Lockyer & Rutter, 1969). Also, many retarded children exhibit some autistic symptomology (Wing, 1976). Differences between the two are that (a) many retarded children are quite sociable and communicative (e.g., Schreibman & Mills, 1983); (b) retarded children often do not have normal physical development, whereas classically autistic youngsters do (e.g, Schreibman & Mills, 1983; and (c) retarded children exhibit poor performance on all aspects of functioning, whereas autistic children exhibit more variable functioning with the most severe problems being in the use of meaning and concepts (Rutter, 1978), with occasional outstanding abilities in nonlanguage skills (e.g., rote memory, music, mathematics, manual performance) (Rimland, 1964).

There is a consensus that autism is not a product of environmental neglect or deprivation. Deprived children (maternal deprivation, anaclitic depression, hospitalism) demonstrate developmental delays in areas of social responsiveness, speech, motor skills, and toy play. However, when placed in an enriched environment such children typically "catch up" in these areas (Ornitz & Ritvo, 1976a). Also, neglected children do not display the repetitious, stereotyped play, echolalia, pronominal reversal, and complete social withdrawal characteristic of autism (Ornitz & Ritvo, 1976a).

STRATEGIES FOR EVALUATION

CLINICAL INTERVIEW AND INFORMAL OBSERVATIONS

Much of the information gathered during diagnostic evaluation is obtained from an interview with the parents and informal observations of the child. Information obtained from the parents includes:

1. Developmental history of the childbirth complications, childhood illnesses, presence of apparent sensory deficit (suspicion of deafness or blindness), developmental milestones, affect during infancy (e.g., molding to parents when held).

2. Social behavior—How responsive to people was the child as an infant? Did the child seem "different" or disinterested when held? Did he or she look at people? Did the child cry or demand attention, or was he or she content to be left alone? Is the child "attached" to the mother and/or father? Is the child affectionate, and does he or she seek parents' comfort? Is the child a "loner"? Does the child interact with other children or avoid them? Is the child shy of strangers?

3. Speech acquisition—presence or absence of speech, echolalia, present extent of speech and language abilities as perceived by the parents.

4. Self-stimulatory or self-injurious behavior (SIB)—What self-stimulatory behaviors does the child engage in? Does he or she engage in any SIB?

5. Inappropriate emotions—Does the child have any irrational fears? Does the child have appropriate fear (fear of running out into a busy street)? Does he or she have tantrums or laugh for no apparent reason?

6. What (if any) compulsive rituals or fetishes does the child have?

7. Does the child appear to be quite skilled in one particular area? Is he or she good at puzzles? Is the child musical? Does the child appear to have a good memory?

8. What are the child's social and play behaviors like at home? In school?

9. Behavior problems—Is the child toilet-trained? Does he or she have feeding problems? Is the child aggressive, noncompliant, manipulative?

Informal observations of the child can be made during the clinical interview. The interviewer will:

1. Observe the child's spontaneous eye contact and attempt to engage the child in eye contact.

2. Observe the child for appropriate behaviors, such as play, interactions with parents, speech, and compliance to requests made by parents and the interviewer.

3. Observe the child for inappropriate behaviors, such as self-stimulation, echolalia, SIB, tantrums, and noncompliance.

4. Observe affect toward parents—Does the child approach the parents? Does he or she notice and/or seem concerned when the parents leave the room? Does the child ask the parents for assistance when needed? Does he or she put his or her arms around the parent when

asked for a hug, or does he or she squirm and give an "autistic hug"? Does the child appear to be engaging in self-stimulatory behavior while hugging? Will he or she hug the interviewer?

5. Does the child demonstrate any appropriate speech and language? Does he or she know the names of objects receptively/expressively? Can the child label (receptively/expressively) body parts? Colors?

BEHAVIOR CHECKLISTS AND OBSERVATIONAL SCHEMES: DESCRIPTIONS AND RESEARCH FINDINGS

In addition to the preceding sets of diagnostic criteria and assessment procedures, several evaluation checklists and observational schemes have been developed by various research groups. Although some have been used rather widely (e.g., Rimland's E-2 checklist), they are most appropriately employed as a screening measure in conjunction with additional assessment procedures. Descriptions of major checklists and discussion of reliability and validity measures follow.

Rimland's Diagnostic Checklist for Behavior-Disturbed Children consists of questions to be answered by the parents about their child's behavior and development. The original form, Form E-1, was revised to include questions applying to the child after the age of 5 years (Form E-2) (Rimland, 1964). The checklist consists of questions on topics such as birth history, symptoms, and speech. It is scored like a test with a plus given for each response characteristic of autism and with a minus for each response that is considered nonautistic. Rimland provided scores from 2,218 forms, ranging from −42 to +45, with a score of +20 as indicative of autism (Rimland, 1971).

Interrater reliability has not been assessed for Rimland's checklist. Reliability between parents' and teachers' reports suggested that teachers score the children as more abnormal than parents (Prior & Bence, 1975). Internal consistency, test–retest reliability, content validity, and concurrent validity have not been specifically addressed (Parks, 1983). Discriminant validity is still questionable (Davids, 1975; DeMeyer, Churchill, Pontius, & Gilkey, 1971).

Ruttenberg and colleagues have developed the Behavior Rating Instrument for Autistic and Atypical Children (BRIAAC). This evaluation instrument is based on observations in a psychoanalytically oriented day-care unit (Ruttenberg, Dratman, Fraknoi, & Wenar, 1966; Ruttenberg, Kalish, Wenar, & Wolf, 1977). The checklist consists of eight scales that measure relationship to an adult, communication, drive for mastery, vocalization and expressive speech, sound and speech reception, social responsiveness, body movement, and psychosexual development.

Interrater reliabilities have ranged from .85 to .93 for the eight scales of the BRIAAC (Wenar & Ruttenberg, 1976). Internal consistency and content validity of the instrument have been demonstrated. However, concurrent validity, discriminant validity, and construct validity remain questionable (Parks, 1983).

The Autism Behavior Checklist, part of the Autism Screening Instrument for Educational Planning (ASIEP), was developed by using behaviors selected from a variety of checklists and instruments for identifying autism, including Rimland's checklist (Form E-2), the nine points of the British Working Party, the BRIAAC, and Kanner's original criteria (Krug, Arick, & Almond, 1981). Fifty-seven behaviors were selected, weighted in terms of prediction ability, and grouped into the five symptom areas of sensory, relating, body and object use, language, and social and self-help. The ASIEP also contains components to obtain samples of vocalizations, an interaction assessment, an educational assessment, and a prognosis of learning rate.

Initial interrater reliability reports are high but based on the ratings of only 14 children. Internal consistency, test–retest reliability, content validity, concurrent validity, discriminant validity, and construct validity have been questioned (Parks, 1983).

The Behavior Observation Scale for Autism (Freeman, Ritvo, Guthrie, Schroth, & Ball, 1978) combines a checklist with direct observations. The instrument consists of 67 operationally defined behaviors. The rater observes the child in a room with toys and records the occurrence of the 67 behaviors in nine 3-minute intervals. The scale is based on the premise that because autistic children are still developing, they are continuously changing clinically. Thus the children should often be reevaluated and compared to normal and mentally retarded populations.

Interrater reliability is acceptable for 55 of the 67 behaviors. Attention to the other kinds of reliability and validity issues is needed.

The Childhood Autism Rating Scale (Schopler, Reichler, DeVeblis, & Daly, 1980) also combines observations with a checklist. The child is first observed in a structured session and then scored, on a scale ranging from *normal* to *severely abnormal*, for each of 15 subscales. Total scores can range from 15 to 60 with a score of 30 or less considered not autistic. The scale is based on the diagnostic criteria of Kanner, the British Working Party, Rutter, and NSAC.

Interrater reliability has been reported at .71 (Schopler *et al.*, 1980). Internal consistency has been demonstrated to be high, but test–retest reliability, content validity, discriminant validity, and construct validity need to be examined. Reported correlations for concurrent validity are high (Parks, 1983).

BEHAVIORAL ASSESSMENT

Although the information obtained from the use of checklists can lead to a diagnosis of autism, there are some limitations inherent in their use. First, due to the hetereogeneity among these children, a label of *autism* does not necessarily specify the behaviors of a particular child. For example, a high-functioning autistic child who has speech and language and a minimum of self-stimulatory behavior is quite different from a child whose behavioral repertoire consists primarily of inappropriate responses. Second, the diagnosis of autism does not imply a specific treatment. Although professionals may agree on a treatment approach (e.g., behavior modification), treatment techniques are generally employed for a specific symptom or characteristic of autism (e.g., removal of attention for tantrums), not for the syndrome as a whole. Finally, a label of autism does not provide a specific prognosis. Some children may make great improvement with treatment, whereas others do not (Lovaas, Koegel, Simmons, & Long, 1973; Schreibman & Koegel, 1981).

In order to ameliorate the previously mentioned problems, behavioral assessment provides a functional definition of the syndrome as it is specific to an individual child. Schreibman and Koegel (1981) have suggested three steps in the behavioral assessment of autism. First, individual behaviors displayed by a particular child are operationally defined. Not only are the autistic characteristics of the child noted, but specific behaviors comprising the characteristic are delineated. For example, for a particular child, self-stimulatory behavior means the child flaps his or her hands, walks on toes, and swishes saliva.

The second step in behavioral assessment consists of identifying the variables that control the specific behaviors. For example, children may engage in tantrums only when demands are made of them as an attempt to get out of working on a task. A child may engage in self-injurious behavior in the presence of his or her mother who attends to such behavior, whereas he or she may sit quietly in the classroom where the behavior is ignored.

The third step involves grouping the specific behaviors according to common controlling variables. Those responses that appear to serve no other purpose than to provide sensory feedback (e.g., hand flapping, toe walking, and saliva swishing in the earlier example) would comprise the child's self-stimulatory behaviors. A child's whining, crying, and throwing of toys constitute his or her tantrum behavior.

Behavioral assessment of autism is immediately useful because it has implications for treatment. It specifies exactly what the child does and does not do, identifies variables controlling behaviors, and suggests environmental alterations required for the child's improvement. Information regarding the specific behaviors can be obtained from several sources. These include parental interviews, interviews with teachers, behavior checklists, and what is most important, direct observations of the child. The use of a structured observation system is excellent for determining behavioral deficits and excesses and for subsequent treatment evaluation.

STRUCTURED OBSERVATIONS

The structured observation procedure, initially described by Lovaas *et al.* (1973), consists of continuous recording of behaviors observed during a 30-minute session. The child's behaviors are grouped into eight categories that are considered important in the assessment and treatment of autism (Lovaas *et al.*, 1973): appropriate verbal behavior, inappropriate vocalizations (e.g., echolalia), social/nonverbal behavior (i.e., affection, compliance), self-stimulation, appropriate play, exploratory play (interacting with toys—holding or carrying), noncompliance, and tantrums. Behaviors in each of the categories are operationally defined for each child.

The 30-minute session is divided into three 10-minute conditions. During an "alone" condition, the child is observed while alone in a room with toys. During the "attending" condition, an adult is present but does not initiate any interactions. In the "inviting" condition, an adult attempts to interact with the child by playing with him or her, conversing with the child, and providing requests for him or her to carry out (i.e., "Get me the ball"; "Touch your nose"). All behaviors pertinent to the eight categories are recorded using a continuous 10-second partial-interval recording procedure. Thus one or several occurrences of a specific behavior within a 10-second interval would be recorded as occurring once. Two raters observe the child to obtain interrater reliability. It is suggested that the session be videotaped so that observers can view the tape several times and score a subset of the eight behaviors at different viewings to enhance accuracy and interrater reliability. The sessions are conducted with the child's mother as the adult, with a stranger as the adult, and later with a therapist as the adult to assess the stimulus control of specific individuals on the child's behavior.

After behavioral assessment is completed, the clinician has a profile of the child's behavioral deficits and excesses. Once identified, the clinician can now select appropriate treatment targets for the child and, through analyses of present environmental contingencies, appropriate treatment procedures. For example, if a specific child is mute, has a high incidence of self-stimulatory behavior, shows severe difficulty in learning simple tasks, and engages in head banging, the clinician is directed toward designing appropriate treatments. The behavioral excesses (self-stimulation, self-injury) need to be reduced or eliminated, and the behavioral deficits (lack of language, attentional deficits) need to be improved. There is an arsenal of behavioral procedures available to the clinician that can be used to treat these behaviors. Further, by repeating the behavioral assessment at regular intervals (or after specific interventions), the researcher or clinician can evaluate the child's behavioral changes. The range of detail provided by this analysis is limited only by the range of the behaviors identified and included in the assessment. The advantage of a comprehensive behavioral analysis is that it allows for a very detailed picture of specific as well as more global changes. The clinician can again use this information to delineate the direction of further treatment.

CASE DESCRIPTION

Erik was 8 years old when he was referred to our behaviorally oriented treatment and research program for autistic children. Erik is the oldest of three boys (older than his fraternal twin brother by only seconds). Erik's twin is a normal child with an unusually high IQ (140), who is participating in the gifted children's program at school. Erik's younger brother, a 3-year-old, is also unusually bright. He could read and spell before he could talk. Erik's father is a shy and quiet computer programmer, and his mother is an outgoing and gregarious housewife with a bachelor's degree in art. The family lives in a middle-class neighborhood where the two older boys attend public school. Here Erik attends a classroom for autistic children.

A description of Erik's autistic characteristics is provided later. The reader is referred once again to Table 1 where a comparison of characteristics included in the various diagnostic criteria with Erik's can be made.

Extreme autistic aloneness. From birth, Erik was considered an "easy" child. He preferred to be left by himself in his crib, or later, in his room. As an infant, he appeared to merely tolerate his mother's holding and cuddling and would remain stiff and motionless until put down. As Erik grew older, he actually fought being hugged and would run away from such contact. Erik did not display spontaneous eye contact. Currently, after much training, Erik will provide only fleeting eye contact upon command. Erik prefers to be alone, does not stay with other children, and resists attempts at social interaction. Often he seems oblivious to his environment and does not seem to notice if others are present. Because of his unresponsivity to his surroundings, Erik's mother once suspected that he was deaf. However, subsequent evaluations indicated that Erik's hearing is normal.

Language abnormalities. Erik's mother reported that he was mute until the age of 5. At that time, he started echoing words and phrases, particularly those he heard on television.

Due to intensive speech therapy, Erik now has an excellent receptive and expressive vocabulary. He can speak in full sentences but will only speak appropriately when it is demanded of him. He seldom initiates any speech, and he does not continue conversations. During conversational speech training, he will echo what was just said. Most of his spontaneous verbalizations are delayed echoes. Usually, they are of something that he has heard from a game show on television. For example, after making a correct response on a task, Erik will chant, "You're right again. Let's go for the tie breaker!" On one occasion, Erik pointed to the food tray and said, "I'll go with the popcorn to block!" When Erik does speak, his pronouns are usually reversed. In order to get around this problem, Erik will often refer to himself as "Erik" and another individual by name rather than using I-You.

Obsessive desire for the maintenance of sameness. Erik insists on traveling down one parkway during cloudy weather and another during sunny weather. He lines up his toys and becomes agitated if any are out of place. When at the clinic, he lines up chairs to make "cars" and adds a specific configuration of blocks on the seats as "push-button seat belts." If either the chairs or the seat belts are slightly altered, he will become agitated and refuse to do anything before he can "fix" them. If a peanut accidentally is put in with the chocolate chips in the food tray, Erik will fuss until the food is again segregated. Erik must have his shirt cuffs buttoned and will not allow others to roll up their sleeves. He engages in specific rituals, such as touching the first and last steps in a stairway.

Preoccupation with particular objects. Erik becomes preoccupied with specific toys for a period of a few months and then will switch to a new toy. He does not play with these toys appropriately but stares at them through crossed eyes or flaps them back and forth before his eyes (self-stimulatory behavior).

Erik is also obsessed with game shows on television and will repetitively write all the names in the credits. He assigns television-related responses to other events in his life. For example, he might say, "Stay tuned for the Cub Scouts," whenever he is on his way to a scout meeting. He also favors three specific situation-comedy television shows. Erik is preoccupied with decks of cards manufactured only by the Hallmark Company. Although Erik is quite artistic, he will only draw pictures of buses using green or purple crayons.

Good cognitive potential. Erik's IQ, as measured by the WISC-R is 100. He has an excellent rote memory (as evidenced by his ability to list all of the credits of his favorite television shows) and generally maintains a serious expression on his face. He is also quite skillful at puzzles and arithmetic.

Normal physical development. Erik's developmental milestones (except for speech) were normal. He has good fine and gross motor skills and is a gold medal winner in the Special Olympics. He is healthy looking and is considered "gorgeous with a perfect complexion."

Onset before 30 months of age. Erik's parents noticed peculiar behavior at about 8 months but did not suspect autism or retardation until he was 2 years of age.

Self-stimulatory behavior. Erik's self-stimulation is primarily in the visual mode (e.g., flapping objects in front of his eyes). He often crosses his eyes and walks on his toes. In addition, Erik will repetitively page through the phone book (Yellow Pages only).

SUMMARY

Because of the heterogeneity of the autistic population and the historical debate as to the specifics of the syndrome, the psychological evaluation of these children remains complicated. The path a researcher/clinician may take in an evaluation is best determined by the function such an evaluation is to serve. If one seeks to determine whether an autism diagnosis is appropriate, there are several diagnostic instruments and criteria mentioned in this chapter that will be useful. Perhaps the inclusion of more than one instrument will provide reliability for the diagnostic decision. If one seeks to evaluate the child for purposes of designing treatment strategies, the emphasis of the evaluation shifts from diagnostic to prescriptive. Thus a thorough assessment of the child's behavioral excesses and deficits is needed in order to decide specific treatment procedures. Obviously, the researcher/clinician must have a clear idea what function the evaluation is to provide. Then, the choice of evaluation techniques can be made.

ACKNOWLEDGMENTS

The authors are grateful to Holly Sadeghian for her assistance in the preparation of this chapter. Appreciation is also extended to Karen Laski, N. Jennifer Oke, and Alison Stanley for their helpful comments on an earlier draft.

REFERENCES

American Psychiatric Association (1980). *Diagnostic and statistical manual of mental disorders (3rd ed.).* Washington, D. C.: Author.

Applebaum, E., Egel, A. L., Koegel, R. L., & Imhoff, B. (1979). Measuring musical abilities of autistic children. *Journal of Autism and Developmental Disorders, 9,* 279–285.

Baltaxe, C. A. M. (1981). Acoustic characteristics of prosody in autism. In P. Mittler (Ed.), *Frontiers of knowledge in mental retardation, Vol. 1: Social, educational and behavioral aspects* (pp. 223–233). Baltimore: University Park Press.

Bender, L. (1942). Childhood schizophrenia. *The Nervous Child, 1*, 138–140.

Bettleheim, B. (1967). *The empty fortress*. New York: Free Press.

Carr, E. G., Schreibman, L., & Lovaas, O. I. (1975). Control of echolalic speech in psychotic children. *Journal of Abnormal Child Psychology, 3*, 331–351.

Charlop, M. H., & Cugliari, C. P. (1984). *Environmental effects on the delayed echolalia of autistic children*. Unpublished manuscript.

Charlop, M. H., Schreibman, L., & Thibadeau, M. G. (1985). The use of a time delay procedure to teach spontaneous speech to autistic children. *Journal of Applied Behavior Analysis, 18*, 155–166.

Churchill, D. W. (1972). The relation of infantile autism and early childhood schizophrenia to developmental language disorders of childhood. *Journal of Autism and Childhood Schizophrenia, 2*, 182–197.

Creak, M. (1961). Schizophrenic syndrome in childhood: Progress report of a working party. *Cerebral Palsy Bulletin, 3*, 501–504.

Creak, M. & Ini, S. (1960). Families of psychotic children. *Journal of Child Psychology and Psychiatry, 1*, 156–175.

Davids, A. (1975). Childhood psychosis: The problem of differential diagnosis. *Journal of Autism and Childhood Schizophrenia, 5*, 129–138.

DeMyer, M. K., Churchill, D. W., Pontius, W., & Gilkey, K. M. (1971). A comparison of five diagnostic systems for childhood schizophrenia and infantile autism. *Journal of Autism and Childhood Schizophrenia, 1*, 175–189.

Dunlap, G., Koegel, R. L., & Egel, A. L. (1979). Autistic children in school. *Exceptional Children, 45*, 552–558.

Egel, A. L., Koegel, R. L., & Schreibman, L. (1980). A review of educational treatment procedures for autistic children. In L. Mann & D. Sabatino (Eds.), *Fourth review of special education* (pp. 109–149). New York: Grune & Stratton.

Eisenberg, L., & Kanner, L. (1956). Early infantile autism: 1943–1955. *American Journal of Orthopsychiatry, 26*, 55–65.

Freeman, B. J., Ritvo, E. R., Guthrie, D., Schroth, P., & Ball, J. (1978). The Behavior Observation Scale for Autism: Initial methodology, data analysis, and preliminary findings on 89 children. *Journal of the American Academy of Child Psychiatry, 17*, 576–588.

Goldfarb, W. (1961). *Childhood schizophrenia*. Cambridge: Harvard University Press.

Griffith, R., & Ritvo, E. R. (1967). Echolalia: Concerning the dynamics of the syndrome. *Journal of the American Academy of Child Psychiatry, 6*, 184–193.

Kanner, L. (1943). Autistic disturbances of affective contact. *The Nervous Child, 3*, 217–250.

Kanner, L. (1949). Problems of nosology and psychodynamics of early infantile autism. *American Journal of Orthopsychiatry, 19*, 416–426.

Kaufman, I., Rosenblum, E., Heims, L., & Willer, L. (1957). Childhood schizophrenia: Treatment of children and parents. *American Journal of Orthopsychiatry, 27*, 683–690.

Koegel, R. L., & Schreibman, L. (1976). Identification of consistent responding to auditory stimuli by a functionally "deaf" autistic child. *Journal of Autism and Childhood Schizophrenia, 6*, 147–156.

Koegel, R. L., Schreibman, L., O'Neill, R. E., & Burke, J. C. (1983). The personality and family-interaction characteristics of parents of autistic children. *Journal of Consulting and Clinical Psychology, 51*, 683–692.

Kolvin, I. (1971). Studies in the childhood psychoses, I. Diagnostic criteria and classification. *British Journal of Psychiatry, 118,* 381–384.

Krug, D. A., Arick, J. R., & Almond, P. J. (1981). Autism Screening Instrument for Educational Planning: Background and development. In J. E. Gilliam (Ed.), *Autism: Diagnosis, instruction, management, and research* (pp. 64–78). Springfield, IL: Charles C Thomas.

Lockyer, L., & Rutter, M. (1969). A five to fifteen year follow-up study of infantile psychosis, III. Psychological aspects. *British Journal of Psychology, 115,* 865–882.

Lovaas, O. I., Koegel, R. L., Simmons, J. Q., & Long, J. S. (1973). Some generalization and follow-up measures on autistic children in behavior therapy. *Journal of Applied Behavior Analysis, 6,* 131–166.

Lovaas, O. I., Litrownik, A., & Mann, R. (1971). Response latencies to auditory stimuli in autistic children engaged in self-stimulatory behavior. *Behavior Research and Therapy, 9,* 39–49.

Mahler, M. S. (1952). On sadness and grief in infancy and childhood. In A. Freud (Ed.), *Psychoanalytic study of the child* (pp. 332–352). New York: International University Press.

Miller, L. N. (1969). *The effects of fear on delayed echolalia in autistic children.* Unpublished manuscript.

Newsom, C., & Rincover, A. (1982). Autism. In E. J. Marsh & L. G. Terdal (Eds.), *Behavioral assessment of childhood disorders* (pp. 397–439). New York: The Guilford Press.

Ornitz, E. M., & Ritvo, E. R. (1976a). Medical assessment. In E. R. Ritvo, B. J. Freeman, & P. T. Tanguay (Eds.), *Autism: Diagnosis, current research and management* (pp. 7–23). New York: Spectrum.

Ornitz, E., & Ritvo, E. (1976b). The syndrome of autism: A critical review. *The American Journal of Psychiatry, 133,* 609–621.

Parks, S. L. (1983). The assessment of autistic children: A selective review of available instruments. *Journal of Autism and Developmental Disorders, 3,* 255–267.

Prior, M., & Bence, R. (1975). A note on the validity of the Rimland Diagnostic Checklist. *Journal of Clinical Psychology, 31,* 510–513.

Rank, B. (1955). Intensive study and treatment of preschool children who show marked personality deviations of "atypical development" and their parents. In G. Caplan (Ed.), *Emotional problems of early childhood* (pp. 491–501). New York: Basic Books.

Rimland, B. (1964). *Infantile autism.* New York: Appleton-Century-Crofts.

Rimland, B. (1971). The differentiation of childhood psychoses: An analysis of checklists for 2,218 psychotic children. *Journal of Autism and Childhood Schizophrenia, 1,* 161–174.

Ritvo, E. R., & Freeman, B. J. (1978). National Society for Autistic Children definition of the syndrome of autism. *Journal of Autism and Childhood Schizophrenia, 8,* 162–167.

Ruttenberg, B. A., Dratman, J. L., Fraknoi, J., & Wenar, C. (1966). An instrument for evaluating autistic children. *Journal of the American Academy of Child Psychiatry, 5,* 453–478.

Ruttenberg, B. A., Kalish, B. I., Wenar, C., & Wolf, E. G. (1978). *Behavior Rating Instrument for Autistic and Other Atypical Children* (BRIACC). Chicago: Stolting.

Rutter, M. (1968). Concepts of autism: A review of research. *Journal of Child Psychology and Psychiatry, 9,* 1–25.

Rutter, M. (1972). Childhood schizophrenia reconsidered. *Journal of Autism and Childhood Schizophrenia, 2,* 315–337.

Rutter, M. (1978). Diagnosis and definition of childhood autism. *Journal of Autism and Childhood Schizophrenia, 8,* 139–161.

Rutter, M., & Lockyer, L. (1967). A five to fifteen year follow-up study of infantile psychosis, I. Description of sample. *British Journal of Psychiatry, 113,* 1169–1182.

Rutter, M., Bartak, L., & Newman, S. (1971). Autism—A central disorder of cognition or language? In M. Rutter (Ed.), *Infantile autism: Concepts, characteristics and treatment* (pp. 148–171). London: Churchill-Livingstone.

Schopler, E. (1978). On confusion in the diagnosis of autism. *Journal of Autism and Childhood Schizophrenia, 8,* 137–138.

Schopler, E., Reichler, R. J., DeVellis, R. F., & Daly, K. (1980). Toward objective classification of childhood autism: Childhood Autism Rating Scale (CARS). *Journal of Autism and Developmental Disorders, 10,* 91–103.

Schreibman, L., & Koegel, R. L. (1981). A guideline for planning behavior modification programs for autistic children. In S. M. Turner, K. S. Calhoun, & H. E. Adams (Eds.), *Handbook of clinical behavior therapy* (pp. 500–526). New York: Wiley.

Schreibman, L., & Koegel, R. L. (1982). Multiple cue responding in autistic children. In J. Steffen & P. Karoly (Eds.), *Advances in child behavior analysis and therapy: Vol. II* (pp. 81–99). Lexington, MA: D. C. Heath.

Schreibman, L., & Mills, J. I. (1983). Infantile autism. In T. J. Ollendick & M. Hersen (Eds.), *Handbook of child psychopathology* (pp. 123–149). New York: Plenum Press.

Schreibman, L., Koegel, R. L., Charlop, M. H., & Egel, A. (1982). Autism. In A. S. Bellack, M. Hersen, & A. E. Kazdin (Eds.), *International handbook of behavior modification and therapy* (pp. 891–915). New York: Plenum Press.

Schreibman, L., Charlop, M. H., & Britten, K. R. (1983). Childhood autism. In R. J. Morris and T. R. Kratochwill (Eds.), *The practice of child therapy* (pp. 221–251). New York: Pergamon Press.

Tate, B. G., & Baroff, G. S. (1966). Aversive control of self-injurious behavior in a psychotic boy. *Behaviour Research and Therapy, 4,* 281–287.

Wenar, C. & Ruttenberg, B. A. (1976). The use of BRIACC for evaluating therapeutic effectiveness. *Journal of Autism and Childhood Schizophrenia, 6,* 175–191.

Wing, L. (1976). Diagnosis, clinical description, and prognosis. In L. Wing (Ed.), *Early childhood autism* (pp. 15–48). London: Pergamon Press.

8

Developmental Retardation

JOHN T. NEISWORTH AND STEPHEN J. BAGNATO

INTRODUCTION

Psychologists and other professionals collect relevant information about children in order to make decisions concerning placement and treatment. The process can include direct testing, *in-situ* observation, and interviews of and reports from significant others. Regardless of the mode employed (testing, observation, interview), appraisal is always *descriptive*; that is, it attempts to characterize the child's status on some dimension(s) of concern. In turn, these descriptions are then used for a variety of purposes: screening and identification, diagnosis, therapeutic and instructional treatment, and child progress and program evaluation (Bagnato & Neisworth, 1981). In short, we describe children in order to place, predict, and/or prescribe.

DIAGNOSIS VERSUS ASSESSMENT

Assessment traditionally has been carried out in order to place a child within some already established clinical category (e.g., mental retardation). When the child's assessment picture fits certain criteria, a diagnostic label is attached, and the child's status is thus diagnosed. In brief, we are able to give a name to the child's condition or syndrome.

JOHN T. NEISWORTH • Division of Special Education, Pennsylvania State University, University Park, Pennsylvania 16802. STEPHEN J. BAGNATO • Children's Hospital, University of Pittsburgh, School of Medicine, Pittsburgh, Pennsylvania 15213.

Of course, children do not always completely fit a diagnostic category. Further, the parameters of clinical categories vary with respect to their inclusiveness and clarity. (DSM-III attempts to provide syndrome criteria of greater clarity and specificity in order to facilitate reliable diagnosis.) Assessment conducted for purposes of diagnosis is nomothetic in that it employs generalizations that apply to many cases (Powers, 1984), in contrast to idiographic assessment, which provides individualized data not selectively gathered in order to determine categorical fit (Powers, 1984). Further, assessment for diagnostic purposes may be *genotypic* rather than *phenotypic* (Bagnato & Neisworth, 1981). Assessment that attempts to delineate the child's "condition" or underlying state is genotypic; it describes what the child (allegedly) *is*. This is in contrast to phenotypic assessment wherein descriptions are provided concerning what the child can *do* and *not do*. In diagnosis, we attempt to test, observe, interview, and rate in order to ascertain how well a child conforms to the syndromal boundaries provided by whatever diagnostic system is being employed. How much of the condition or syndrome does the child have? Is he or isn't he? On the other hand, idiographic, phenotypic assessment refers to a close-up of the diagnosed child's current capabilities across relevant dimensions and offers valuable information for program planning and treatment.

Idiographic, phenotypic reports provide the child's "entry behaviors" so that starting points for therapy and instruction can be determined. In addition, the child's strengths and weaknesses are identified to help guide selection of intervention techniques.

A further distinction arises when contrasting assessment of the syndrome of mental retardation (MR) versus assessment of the child's (retarded) developmental functioning. When diagnosing mental retardation, usually "psychological" variables are measured. In practice, this usually means cognitive functioning or IQ. Regardless of other dimensions that are included in definitions of MR (e.g., social competence), IQ determination is the major consideration for the diagnosis. In fact, recent research and proposals advocate reliance on IQ because we have no better measures of intellectual functioning (Zigler, Balla, & Hodapp, 1984).

Although IQ is central to a diagnosis of mental retardation, it does not survey the scope of the child's developmental status. Rather, wide spectrum developmental assessment is necessary for program planning and treatment. Developmental assessment looks at functioning across the several domains of development. Instead of providing only a summary of the child's cognitive status, developmental assessment produces a profile of strengths and weaknesses within speech and language, personal-social, fine and gross motor as well as intellectual functioning. This comprehensive developmental assessment recognizes that cognitive abilities do not stand alone but are interrelated to other areas of development (Stroufe, 1979; Thomas, 1981). The interrelation influences both the development and expression of cognitive skills. Clearly, for example, serious deficits in relating to others may not only limit stimulus and response opportunities important to intellectual development but also performance on (socially administered) assessment instruments. Likewise, perceptual-motor difficulties can delay and distort cognitive development as well as depress scores on standardized instruments that demand motoric responses (Dubose, 1981).

STRATEGIES FOR DIAGNOSIS OF DEVELOPMENTAL RETARDATION

The phases involved in diagnostic appraisal include (a) selection of a definition of the syndrome in question, in this case mental retardation; (b) choice of instruments that appraise characteristics required by the definition; and (c) determination of the congruence of the appraisal and diagnostic criteria.

DEFINING MENTAL RETARDATION

Retardation is a construct variously defined by different cultures and professions. Because the judgment of retardation is relative to the standards of a culture, there is no single, accepted definition. Even within contemporary Western culture, physicians, psychologists, and educators have differing conceptions and, thus, definitions of mental retardation. One's philosophic/theoretical position also influences the definitions proposed; thus an environmentalist conception of retardation stresses the meagerness of the child's behavior repertoire that results from restrictions in stimulus and response opportunities (Bijou, 1966). A sociological position (Mercer, 1973) defines retardation in terms of social roles and relative status. Among the many definitions, those advocated by the American Association of Mental Deficiency (AAMD) (Grossman, 1977, 1983) and the American Psychiatric Association (DSM-III) have the most professional support. The AAMD definition, by far the most accepted and widely used, is based on criteria published in the *Manual on Terminology and Classification in Mental Retardation* (Grossman, 1977) and originally proposed by Heber (1961):

> Mental retardation refers to subaverage general intellectual functioning existing concurrently with deficits in adaptive behavior, and manifested during the developmental period. (p. 11)

Each criterion is further operationalized to provide for clarity and reliability. Subaverage intellectual functioning is operationalized to mean measured performance two or more standard deviations below the mean on a standardized instrument. Adaptive behavior deficit refers to problems in coping and personal independence when compared with age norms for personal and social responsibility. Finally, developmental period is defined as the time between birth and 18 years of age. A critical aspect of the AAMD definition is the requirement that both cognitive and adaptive functioning be significantly deficient. Serious deficits in intellectual performance not accompanied by difficulties in adaptive behavior would not warrant the MR diagnosis (although these two dimensions usually co-vary). Note, also, that the definition is based on present functioning and does not purport to estimate potential or to cite etiology. Further, the definition does not insist on the irreversibility or transsituationality of retardation. A child might be diagnosed as mentally retarded at five years of age but not later, and during schooling but not in a vocational setting.

Four levels or degrees of mentally retarded are described within the AAMD manual: mild, moderate, severe, and profound. Mild retardation requires two standard deviations below the mean (100), with the other levels each involving an additional standard deviation of 15 or 16 points (see Table 1).

TABLE 1. LEVELS OF MENTAL RETARDATION AND CORRESPONDING IQ

	Level	*SD*s below the mean	Measured IQ: Stanford-Binet	Measured IQ: Wechsler scales
ORGANICITY ↓	Mild	2–3	52–67	55–69
	Moderate	3–4	36–51	40–54
	Severe	4–5	20–35	25–39
	Profound	5 or more	Below 20	Below 25

SELECTING INSTRUMENTS AND DETERMINING CONGRUENCE

An array of measures is available for estimating intellectual status and describing adaptive behavior (Salvia & Ysseldyke, 1981; Sattler, 1982). In addition to choosing devices that are of satisfactory reliability and validity (.90 or better), instruments normed on representative populations are essential. Standardizations that include the type of child in question are preferred, although available for only a few measures. Intelligence measures, such as the Stanford-Binet and the Wechsler Intelligence Scale for Children—Revised (WISC-R), are frequently employed because of their thorough standardization and wide-base norms.

Estimates of adaptive behavior can be obtained through interviews with parents and teachers and by naturalistic observation. Informal techniques are often helpful, but the use of standardized scales is increasing. The AAMD Adaptive Behavior Scale and the Vineland Adaptive Behavior Scale are two measures that can be used with a minimum of time and effort (see "Prominent Measures for Diagnosis and Assessment of Developmental Retardation" section).

STRATEGIES FOR EVALUATION

Comprehensive developmental assessment that provides the base for program planning has been referred to as the *diagnostic-prescriptive* model (see Figure 1). Screening and identification (diagnosis) necessarily depend on the use of nomothetic, classificatory devices. After determining the child's diagnostic "ball park," a closer inspection of his or

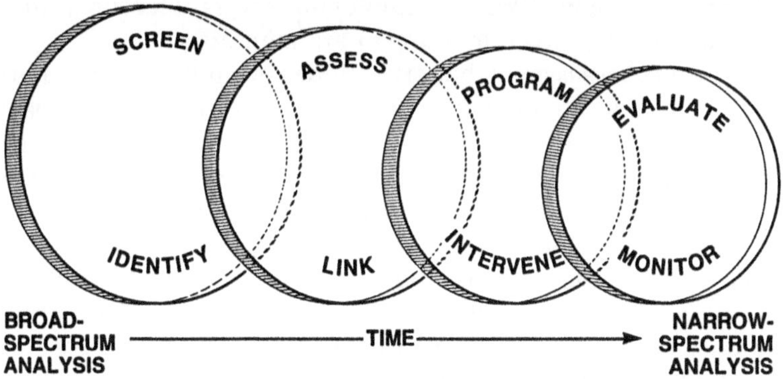

FIGURE 1. Linking assessment–intervention goals.

her strengths and weaknesses (idiographic information) permits the design of a treatment program. The detailed developmental assessment conducted in this step can also become the base for evaluating child progress and program effectiveness.

PURPOSE OF ASSESSMENT

The mission of assessment is seldom psychometric description for the sake of mere description. Assessment is usually sought for the purpose of helping the child to receive services matched to his or her specific needs. Diagnosis, *per se*, falls short of providing the detail and meaningful information that teachers and therapists need. Knowing that the diagnosis is "moderately retarded" provides some guidance for intervention but certainly not for tailoring the child's program.

To plan and deliver an optimal program, assessment must yield a profile of specific strengths and weaknesses. The results constitute a blueprint for the child's program. The blueprint is then used to generate specific entry points and treatment objectives.

If the agency or preschool program uses a particular curriculum, that information can be a guide in the selection of assessment measures. By matching assessment devices to therapeutic/instructional materials and approaches existing within a program, the developmental assessment is immediately meaningful to the staff and links directly to program materials.

When the specific curriculum or materials to be employed are not established or known, the best procedure is to select devices that provide a full and reliable appraisal of the child's entire developmental status. To provide the most treatment-relevant information, a multimeasure approach is recommended (Bagnato & Neisworth, 1981; Simeonsson, Huntingdon, & Parse, 1980). By employing several measures, the possible limitations of a given instrument are minimized.

An optimal assessment battery includes norm-based, criterion (curricular)-based, and adaptive measures that may include neuropsychological scales. Standardized, norm-based devices provide the context or larger picture of how the child functions when compared to age peers. This information is essential in the diagnostic appraisal.

Criterion (curricular)-based and adaptive measures offer several advantages. First, they provide the detail and articulation with the program. Second, tasks can be altered to suit the child's stimulus or response limitations. Standardized norm-based instruments, of course, do not allow for changes in their administration, as this would violate standardization and obviate the advantage of a norm-based device. Criterion- or curricular-based items, however, are open to modification in both their presentation and response modes. Handles affixed to puzzle pieces, eye localization or head pointers, and communication boards may be substituted and thus permit the child to demonstrate knowledge and skills not apparent on the standardized measures.

Greater validity can be achieved when assessment is carried out in more than one setting and when information is obtained from more than one source (Bagnato & Neisworth, 1985). Assessment can be conducted not only in "the testing room" but also within the child's context—classroom, cottage, home, and the like. Input from parents and teachers should be sought to augment the assessment picture.

SUMMARY

The process and strategies for evaluating developmental retardation vary depending on the purpose of the assessment. Thus, purpose, goals, and strategies must be viewed as interrelated. The types of measures selected and the kinds of information emphasized will differ if the purpose is diagnosis (classification) versus program and treatment planning. However, a comprehensive assessment model underscores that diagnostic (nomothetic) and prescriptive (idiographic) measures are "linked" and that evaluation is continuous and increasingly fine-focused in operation. The appropriate design of batteries to assess and program for developmental retardation incorporates measures for general diagnosis as well as measures for individualized treatment planning.

PROMINENT MEASURES FOR DIAGNOSIS AND ASSESSMENT OF DEVELOPMENTAL RETARDATION

Three major types of assessment strategies are available to guide the comprehensive evaluation of developmental retardation: (a) norm-based assessment, (b) criterion-based assessment, and (c) neuropychological assessment.

NORM-BASED ASSESSMENT: COMPARATIVE EVALUATION

The most frequently employed evaluation strategy involves the use of norm-based or norm-referenced scales. Norm-based measures provide a comparative evaluation of children in that they compare an individual's performance and skills to those of other children who are presumably similar along several different dimensions (i.e., age, gender, socioeconomic status, race). Norm-based scales are standardized on large groups of individuals across different age and grade levels; their primary purpose is to appraise the relative performances of children rather than to analyze the acquisition or mastery of specific skills. Such measures are valuable for differential diagnosis (e.g., determining the existence and degree of cognitive developmental retardation). Yet norm-based scales are available to assess current relative performance levels in all major developmental domains. The comprehensive evaluation originally mandated in Public Law 94-142 can be ensured most effectively when measures are selected that estimate performance levels in each functional area (i.e., cognitive, communication, socioemotional and adaptive, learning, and neuromotor).

COGNITIVE

Assessment of the cognitive and adaptive capabilities of infants and toddlers suffering developmental disabilities requires the use of scales that survey multiple dimensions. Two traditional norm-referenced measures fulfill this need particularly well, namely the Bayley Scales of Infant Development (BSID) (Bayley, 1969) and the Gesell Developmental Schedules (GDS) (Ames, Gillespie, Haines, & Ilg, 1979; Knobloch, Stevens, & Malone, 1980). Although these traditional developmental scales have been criticized for being unable to predict adequately later intellectual functioning of normal children (Yang & Bell, 1975), research demonstrates that they are reliable measures of current cognitive/adaptive functioning as well as accurate predictors of the later functioning of moderately to severely retarded children (Dubose, 1981; Knobloch & Pasamanick, 1974). The Bayley scales are the most technically adequate of the traditional cognitive developmental measures. The separate Mental and Motor subscales survey 244 sensorimotor, language, and social tasks across the 2- to 30-month age range. The BSID was standardized on 1,262 infants and reports performances in terms of developmental ages and developmental quotients (Mental Development Index [MDI]; Psychomotor Development Index [PDI]).

The Gesell schedules are more appropriately referred to as norm-based measures because they have a normative "reference" group (i.e., between 107 and 320, and 927 preschoolers in different studies) but have no standardized sample to guide scoring as with the BSID. However, the GDS samples 350 to 400 behaviors over a birth to 72-month age range within five developmental domains: language, fine motor, gross motor, adaptive (cognitive), and personal-social. Developmental age scores and ratio developmental quotients are derived to guide differential diagnosis of retardation and neurological dysfunctions.

As children progress developmentally, the content of cognition changes from predominantly sensorimotor capabilities to verbally mediated problem-solving behaviors (McCall, Hogarty, & Hurlburt, 1972). Similarly, the content of tasks that assess "intelligence" changes with a premium placed upon concept knowledge and language understanding and use. The Stanford-Binet Intelligence Scale (SBIS) (Terman & Merrill, 1972) and the Wechsler Intelligence Scale for Children—Revised (Wechsler, 1974) are the most frequently used intellectual assessment measures with school-aged children. The Stanford-Binet historically has been considered an age scale because items were grouped at levels in which the majority of children could complete that item or cluster. However, the recent restandardization of the scale has altered this assumption. Nevertheless, the SBIS represents the best traditional example of a verbal intelligence scale. It surveys cognitive capabilities across the two-year to superior-adult age range with performances represented by mental ages and deviation IQs ($M = 100$; $SD = 16$). Researchers have attempted to classify the clusters of general intellectual behaviors that the scale samples. Sattler (1965) constructed an arbitrary grouping of Binet items reflected in the Binetgram that clustered items in the following manner: language, memory, conceptual thinking, reasoning, numerical reasoning, visual-motor, and social intelligence. Also, Valett (1964) grouped Binet items into the domains of general comprehension, visual-motor ability, arithmetic reasoning, memory and concentration, vocabulary and verbal fluency, and judgment and reasoning. Finally, the SBIS was standardized on approximately 2,100 children. Yet some questions have arisen regarding the technical adequacy of this process (Salvia & Ysseldyke, 1981). Reliability and validity data on the current revision are lacking, although research on previous editions were sufficiently strong.

Although the SBIS clusters various intellectual tasks according to age level, the WISC-R is a point scale that organizes 10 primary and 2 supplementary subtests into two major scales: Verbal (e.g., Information, Similarities, Arithmetic, Vocabulary, Comprehension, Digit Span) and Performance (e.g., Picture Completion, Picture Arrangement, Block Design, Object Assembly, Coding, Mazes). Standardized on 2,200 children according to the 1970 census, the WISC-R surveys cognitive skills across a 6-year to 6-year, 11-month age range through three deviation IQs, Verbal, Performance, and Full Scale—a composite of the verbal-performance indexes. Test-age equivalents also are available to more practically define a child's performance, although "mental age" conceptions on the WISC-R are minimized. The WISC-R displays excellent reliability and adequate validity as a general measure of intellectual functioning in children.

SPECIALIZED COGNITIVE MEASURES

One of the most frustrating problems confronting diagnostic specialists is the accurate assessment of the intellectual capabilities of children who suffer sensori- and neuromotor disorders. Most scales such as the SBIS and the WISC-R do not include either retarded or disabled children in their normative groups. Moreover, the presentation of items and the response mode required are inappropriate for multihandicapped children and penalize them during the assessment process. Psychologists have attempted a variety of techniques to modify these scales so that children with sensory and neuromotor disorders could be validly assessed. Common strategies have involved physically altering the items or tasks themselves, excluding items that require motor responses, or allowing eye localization, gesturing, and yes-no or multiple-choice alternative responses. However, any of these methods renders the use of the standardization group inappropriate. Another strategy that is gaining wide popularity again after years of neglect is the design and use of handicap-appropriate assessment instruments (i.e., those scales that are standardized upon specific groups of disabled children—cerebral palsied, blind, hearing impaired) and/or contain standardized stimulus-response adaptations for such children who also may be mentally retarded. The Pictorial Test of Intelligence (PTI) (French, 1964) was originally developed as a measure of general cognitive abilities (comprehension) for both normal and physically handicapped children ages 3 to 8 years, although no children with neuromotor impairments were included in the standardization sample. The PTI uses oversized picture cards and accommodates any response mode (e.g., eye localization, head pointing) to allow the child to reveal his or her concept knowledge in six specific areas of information: picture vocabulary, form discrimination, information and comprehension, similarities, size and number, and immediate recall. A diagnostic profile of the child's process abilities (intact prerequisite psychological processes like recall memory) and product abilities (acquired knowledge like number concepts) is generated through mental ages for each of the subtests and a deviation IQ. The PTI stands as one of the best standardized norm-referenced adaptive measures available. It includes 1,830 children and has established reliability and validity data for both normal and handicapped populations.

Designed to analyze the global cognitive abilities of hearing-impaired, speech/language-disordered, bilingual, and non-English-speaking individuals, the Leiter International Performance Scale (LIPS) (Leiter, 1969) requires no verbal instructions but includes demonstrations to sample various process-dominant skills in the 2- to 18-year age range.

The LIPS requires a unique response mode involving essentially match-to-sample behaviors with blocks and a stimulus card. A wooden frame holds a stimulus card that reveals an array of color patterns, pictures, and geometric designs. The child responds by matching blocks with pictures to corresponding pictures on the stimulus card contained in the response *gate*. Although the LIPS is motivating and ingenious in design, its standardization is poorly done and nonrepresentative because it is based on only 289 children. Although reliability and validity data are needed, the scale's mental age and ratio IQ indexes provide a functionally appropriate screening of the intellectual abilities in certain handicapped children.

For hearing-impaired or deaf children, the Hiskey-Nebraska Test of Learning Aptitude (HNTLA) (Hiskey, 1966) is the overall test of choice for defining general intellectual functioning, although the Performance subtests of the WISC-R are now normed on hearing-impaired children. The HNTLA was standardized on 1,079 deaf and 1,074 hearing children across the 3- to 16-year age range. It provides pantomime administration of items for deaf children and verbal directions with hearing children and separate norm structures, "learning ages," and "learning quotients" for deaf children. The scale encompasses 12 creatively developed subtests to assess various prerequisite acquired learning abilities (e.g., visual attention span, picture analogies, memory for digits). The use of plastic digits for the child to indicate his or her recall of numbers in a series is an example of its unique and adaptive quality. The scale has adequate reliability and validity for assessment and placement of mentally retarded, hearing-impaired children.

Finally, the Blind Learning Aptitude Test (BLAT) (Newland, 1969) was developed to assess the learning aptitude of blind children 6 to 20 years of age, although 6 to 12 years is a more effective range. The BLAT uses a raised dot braillelike format to assess various prerequisite psychological abilities such as discrimination, sequencing, and pattern completion. The BLAT was normed on 961 blind children in both day and residential schools in the United States. Internal consistency and test–retest reliability data of .93 and .87, respectively, attest to the scale's capacity for differential diagnosis. The scale's stimulus characteristics and response mode as well as normative qualities make it the most appropriate intellectual assessment measure for school-aged blind children.

COMMUNICATION

Dysfunctions in both language comprehension and production are common in mentally retarded children. Given the strong interrelationships among language-mediated thinking and self-control capabilities, assessment of speech and language abilities is essential in the comprehensive evaluation of developmental retardation.

Language measures are available that analyze both language competence (i.e., reception) and performance (i.e., expression). The association between the child's conceptual knowledge and his or her understanding and use of language is strong. Receptive language scales frequently are used to evaluate competence by requiring the child to point to a particular picture to indicate his or her understanding of certain linguistic concepts. The Peabody Picture Vocabulary Test—Revised (PPVT-R) (Dunn & Dunn, 1981) is perhaps the most frequently employed receptive language test. The PPVT-R can be used with individuals from 2 1/2 to 40 years of age. Through a series of black-and-white picture plates, both normal and handicapped children can be assessed through their comprehension of pictures depicting nouns, verbs, and adjectives. The scale was standardized on 5,028 individuals (4,200 children and adolescents) on both age and grade reference groups. Reliability and validity data support the measure's use as a screening device for detecting language comprehension difficulties. Other receptive language measures are more sophisticated in the linguistic structures that they analyze. The Test of Auditory Comprehension of Language (Carrow, 1973) measures three separate aspects of language: vocabulary, morphology, and syntax. The use of age scores and percentiles aid in the treatment-based analysis of results for children 3 to 8 years of age. Strong test–retest reliability data are available as well as concurrent validity information for deaf children, retarded children, and dysphasic children.

The most widely used instrument for comprehensive identification of language disorders in school-aged children is the Clinical Evaluation of Language Functions (CELF) (Semel & Wiig, 1980). This multidimensional measure assesses the relationship between language and learning disorders in kindergarten through the 12th grade. The CELF effectively merges assessment and treatment goals by integrating evaluation of receptive and expressive language dimensions through 13 subtests: six scales for language processing, five scales for language production, and two supplementary scales for auditory discrimination and phonology. The scales were standardized on a sample of 159 children in grades kindergarten through 12 with grade-level norms being the index for differential diagnosis of disorders. A treatment manual accompanies the scale so that individualized program planning can be promoted. In order to assess those language disorders that are associated with various degrees of learning disabilities, the CELF surveys such skills as auditory memory and recall of words, auditory comprehension and sequencing, and word retrieval or word-finding skills.

ADAPTIVE AND SOCIOEMOTIONAL

The ability of a child to demonstrate a level of "personal independence and social responsibility" (i.e, adaptive behavior) is an important dimension of the AAMD definition of mental retardation (Grossman, 1977). However, as mentioned previously, the usefulness and validity of this definition for accurately classifying children is questionable (Zigler *et al.*, 1984). In addition, comprehensive assessment of the affective domain requires that a child's mood characteristics and behavior disorders be described.

Perhaps the most widely used developmental measure of social competence has been the Vineland Social Maturity Scale (Doll, 1953/1985). Although reliability and validity data on the original scale were adequate, concerns about item placement and the data quality of the norms have led researchers to emphasize the need for a substantial revision of the scale. The recent revision of the Vineland Adaptive Behavior Scales (VABS) (Sparrow, Balla, & Cicchetti, 1984) is a positive change to address these concerns. The VABS consists of three forms (i.e., Interview Edition Survey, Expanded Forms, and the Classroom Edition) and surveys social competence and adaptive behavior across the birth to 18-year, 11-month age range. Through standard scores ($M = 100$; $SD = 15$), percentiles and age equivalents skills are assessed in four major domains (communication, daily living skills, socialization, and motor) with an Adaptive Behavior Composite score and a survey of maladaptive behaviors. Standardization data are available on 4,000 handicapped and nonhandicapped individuals. Standard scores also describe different "adaptive levels": high, moderately high, adequate, moderately low, and low. The classroom edition covers the 3-year to 12-year, 11-month age range and is normed on 3,000 children. Initial reliability and concurrent validity data appear strong. The scales are viewed as valuable in the continuous process of individual diagnostic evaluations and program placement and goal planning. Like the Vineland scale, the Developmental Profile (DP) (Alpern, Boll, & Shearer, 1982) is a norm-referenced measure of developmental capabilities that relies on a structured interview with the parents to estimate a child's current level of functioning. The DP, however, is unique among interview screening measures in that it is multidimensional, technically adequate, and relatively well standardized on a sample of 3,008, newborn to 9-year-old children. The measure contains 217 tasks that are clustered into five functional domains: physical, self-help, social, academic, and communication. Developmental ages are derived for each domain, and "developmental lags" are then determined from the norm tables. The scale is a valuable adjunct to a comprehensive battery that seeks to incorporate parent judgments in the assessment of developmental retardation.

The American Association on Mental Deficiency Adaptive Behavior Scale (ABS) (Nihara, Foster, Shellhaas, & Leland, 1974) was developed to rate the behavioral and affective competencies of mentally retarded, emotionally maladjusted, and developmentally disabled institutionalized individuals. The ABS was standardized on 4,000 institutionalized persons in the United States and covers the 3- to 69-year range. Part I surveys 10 behavioral domains (e.g., independent functioning, language development, physical development, self-direction), whereas Part II assesses aspects of behavior and personality (e.g., stereotyped mannerisms, self-abusive behavior, violent destructive behavior). This behavioral assessment is accomplished through a combination of interview and naturalistic observation methods. Despite the scale's practical appeal, its limited residential norms and lack of adequate reliability and validity limit its application, especially with retarded children in public-school settings.

Because of the drawbacks presented by the residential norms for the 1974 ABS, it was restandardized for use with children in grades 2 through 6. The resulting ABS-Public School Version (Lambert, Windmiller, Cole, & Figueroa, 1975) was normed on a sample of 2,600 children age 7 to 13 years. Some scales not relevant to typical behaviors in school settings were eliminated, whereas the remaining sections are similar to the original. Reliability and validity data on the scale are still limited. Other adaptive behavior scales have been developed for special populations, such as the TMR (Trainable Mentally Retarded) School Competency Scales (Levine, Elzey, Thormahlen, & Cain, 1976) for moderately retarded children, the Wisconsin Behavior Rating Scale (Song & Jones, 1980) and the Balthazar Scales of Adaptive Behavior (Balthazar, 1976) for severely and profoundly mentally retarded individuals.

Behavior problem checklists frequently are employed with parents, teachers, and specialists in applied settings to describe a child's most prevalent types and styles of behaviors. They are designed to screen for problems that affect socioemotional functioning by highlighting behaviors that appear to cluster into categories that indicate psychopathology. Three such measures can be useful with mentally retarded children: Revised Behavior Problem Checklist (RBPC) (Quay & Peterson, 1983), Child Behavior Checklist (CBCL) (Achenbach & Edelbrock, 1982), and the Preschool Behavior Questionnaire (Behar & Stringfield, 1974). The RBPC is the most established behavior checklist for use by teachers. The scale's items group into the following six factors: Conduct Disorder, Socialized Aggression, Attention Problems-Immaturity, Anxiety-Withdrawal, Psychotic Behavior, and Motor Excess. Research with various populations indicates that children can be reliably and validly classified, particularly if parent and teacher ratings are combined (Mattison, Cantwell, & Baker, 1982). The CBCL is a more recently developed instrument that is available in forms for both teachers and parents. The scale consists of 138 items grouped through factor analytic studies into factor profiles for each sex and age group: 4 to 5, 6 to 11, 12 to 16. Sample behavior factors are Anxiety, Depression, Overactivity, Aggression, Social Withdrawal, and Inattention. Classification of child psychopathology is based on cutoff scoring ($M = 50$; $SD = 10$) with a t greater than 70 on any scale as the severity index. Broad scoring in terms of externalizing and internalizing dimensions is also useful. Recent normative and reliability/validity research support the system's wide use in various school programs for exceptional children. Finally, few systematic studies have been conducted on the behavior problems of developmentally disabled preschool children. The most frequently used behavior problem checklist with disabled preschoolers is the Preschool Behavior Questionnaire (PBQ). Teacher and/or parent ratings are focused on 30 items that cluster into three subscales: Hostile-Aggressive, Anxious, and Hyperactive-Distractible. Percentiles with a cutoff of 90 and above for a severity index are available for each subscale and a total score. Although additional research is needed to establish the scale's technical adequacy, it is useful for classifying the behavior problems of mildly disabled children. Clinically, however, the PBQ does not contain the types of behaviors needed to rate the severity of disorders (e.g., stereotypies) seen in moderate to severely handicapped young children.

LEARNING

Assessment of a child's acquired academic skills invariably provides the most practical picture of his or her strengths and weaknesses that signal success or failure in the school setting. Norm-referenced measures of various learning abilities (i.e., reading, spelling, math) are useful to diagnose skill levels that differ from grade- and age-level expectancies. Also, variations in one's own pattern of abilities can be detected. However, norm-based measures are not sufficiently detailed in scope and content to plan curricular goals. Their primary purpose is to describe and profile current levels of academic skills, which then provide a starting point for more fine-focused instructional evaluation. Two of the most popular screening measures of general learning skills are the Wide Range Achievement Test—Revised (WRAT-R) (Jastak & Wilkinson, 1984) and the Peabody Individual Achievement Test (PIAT) (Dunn & Markwardt, 1970).

The PIAT screens academic skills expected in kindergarten through high school by the use of age- and grade-level scores in five areas:

mathematics, reading recognition, reading comprehension, spelling, and general information. Children respond to this scale solely through a pointing response that indicates their comprehension or recognition of acquired learning rather than their ability to perform on paper-and-pencil tasks. This quality makes the PIAT useful with children suffering neuromotor disabilities and language problems. For example, the child indicates through any means one of four words that is correctly spelled or identifies the picture in an array of four pictures that correctly depicts the action in a sentence that the child reads silently. Age and grade equivalents, percentile ranks, and standard scores provide the basis for determining current abilities. Standardization of the test is based upon a 1969 national sample of approximately 200 students at each grade level from 29 school districts throughout the United States. Normative data on the PIAT are excellent, although it is becoming dated and is in need of restandardization. Reliability and validity research support its confident use for detecting major areas of academic weakness.

In contrast to the PIAT, the WRAT-R is a paper-and-pencil achievement test that analyzes basic learning abilities in the areas of reading (i.e., pronunciation of increasingly difficult single words), spelling, and arithmetic. The current revision of the WRAT-R was standardized in a national sample on 5,600 individuals across the 5-year to 74-year, 11-month age range. The major scoring change is that the derived scores are now directly transformed into standard scores (M = 100, SD = 15) instead of being converted to grade equivalents first. Minor item changes are evident on the arithmetic tasks. Technical adequacy data still need to be established. Yet the scale provides a quick estimate of general academic "performance" skills and, when compared with a comparable IQ score, helps to detect basic learning difficulties.

The Woodcock-Johnson Psychoeducational Battery (WJPEB) (Woodcock, 1978) represents the recent trend in test development toward multiple skill batteries with assessments of cognitive and academic abilities based on the same standardization group. The WJPEB evaluates 27 different skill areas clustered into the areas of cognitive ability, scholastic aptitude, academic achievement, and interests. The battery was normed on 4,732 children in 49 communities in the United States covering the 3- to 80-year age range. Inter- and intraindividual skill comparisons are possible through the use of "cluster scores," age and grade equivalents, percentiles, and standard scores. Many of the subtests are valuable in sampling memory and selective attention skills (e.g., Visual-Auditory Learning) as well as the ability to learn new material. Reliability and validity data are adequate for differential diagnosis of learning disorders. However, some caution should be observed in viewing the reading tasks as representative of specific reading skills required in school (e.g., the Passage Comprehension subtest uses a CLOZE technique). However, the battery should be viewed as the most comprehensive and detailed norm-referenced cognitive and achievement test available.

SPECIFIC ACHIEVEMENT MEASURES

One of the most frequently used criterion-based, multiskill learning inventories in the Brigance Diagnostic Inventory of Basic Skills (BDIBS) (Brigance, 1977) and the Brigance Diagnostic Inventory of Essential Skills (BDIES) (Brigance, 1980). Each inventory is a detailed sequence of specific learning and survival skills that can be used for assessment and programming of children in grades kindergarten through sixth and secondary programs, respectively. A particularly unique aspect of both inventories is that each has norms (grade levels) for when material and skills are initially taught in school. The BDIBS surveys 140 skill sequences (e.g., Word Recognition, Language, and Mathematics subscales), whereas the BDIES surveys 165 essential skill patterns (e.g., oral reading and comprehension, functional word recognition, reference skills, completing forms, measurements, telephone skills)—academic and applied skills. Both inventories have strong content validity and represent invaluable guides for special educators in planning and implementing individualized programs for children with special needs.

The Woodcock Reading Mastery Tests (WRMT) (Woodcock, 1973) provide a detailed survey of various reading skills and processes through its combination of norm- and criterion-referenced dimensions. The WRMT is a diagnostic battery of five measures covering skills expected in kindergarten through grade 12 in the following areas: letter identification, word identification, word attack, word comprehension, and passage comprehension. Performances are reported in grade scores that reflect "reading grade scores," "easy reading level," and "failure reading level." A "mastery score" is available that provides an index of skill change and acquisition that is more accurate than the percentiles or grade scores provided. Unlike other criterion-based measures, the WRMT also was normed on a sample of over 5,000 children from 141 schools in the United States. Evidence for validity is good, whereas the individual subtest reliabilities vary. The total battery score appears to be a more confident index of current functioning.

Similar to the WRMT, the KeyMath Diagnostic Arithmetic Test (Connolly, Nachtman, & Pritchett, 1971) encompasses both norm- and criterion-referenced features in analyzing increasingly complex arithmetic skills expected in kindergarten through the eighth grade. The battery contains 15 subtests divided into three major areas: content (Numeration, Fractions, Geometry, and Symbols), operations (Addition, Subtraction, Multiplication, Division, Mental Computation, Numerical Reasoning), and applications (Word Problems, Missing Elements, Money, Measurement, Time). Individual items and grade scores serve to target "behavioral objectives" to evaluate mastery. The KeyMath was normed on 1,222 children in the United States. The adaptive format of the KeyMath with its easel, flipcard organization, and limited need for reading and writing makes it appropriate for diverse developmental/learning disabilities. Reliability and validity are acceptable but need greater refinement, particularly in terms of significance of differences among subtest scores.

NEUROMOTOR

Developmentally disabled children often experience concomitant dysfunctions in two or more developmental processes. Thus assessments of interrelated areas of functioning (e.g., language, motor, cognitive) are vital with such children. Evaluations of the perceptual and neuromotor capabilities of disabled children provide not only information on the general integrity of the nervous system but also on such characteristics as attention, self-regulation, goal and motor planning, and behavioral organization. Various measures are available to assess neuromotor status as it influences school behavior.

The Developmental Test of Visual-Motor Integration (DTVMI) (Beery & Buktenica, 1967/1982) assesses the child's emerging ability to coordinate visual perceptual and drawing skills. Children 2 through 15 years of age copy increasingly complex geometric designs in an enclosed response box modeling a stimulus design. The use of the response box provides impulsive children with more structure than is usually available on such measures. Norms are currently available on 3,090 children from 2 years, 9 months to 19 years, 8 months. A child's total raw score can be converted to percentiles, standard scores (M = 10; SD = 3), and developmental age equivalents. The DTVMI is particularly useful to screen the perceptual and neuromotor skills of preschool children and those functioning in the 0- to 8-year age range.

A more comprehensive evaluation of motor functioning is provided by the Bruininks-Oseretsky Test of Motor Proficiency (BOTMP) (Bruininks, 1978). The BOTMP was standardized on 765 children throughout the United States and Canada. It assesses both gross and fine motor skills in eight subareas across the 4 1/2- to 14 1/2-year age range (e.g., running speed and agility, balance, bilateral coordination, strength, upper limb coordination, response speed, visual-motor control, and upper limb speed and dexterity). The scale reports performances in fine motor, gross motor, and composite areas through percentiles and standard scores (Subtest $M = 15$; $SD = 5$; Composite $M = 50$; $SD = 10$). Reliability and validity research support the battery's wide administration to plan and evaluate the efficacy of neuromotor training programs.

The Peabody Developmental Motor Scales (PDMS) (Folio & Fewell, 1983) is a unique package of materials designed to both assess and individually program for neuromotor strengths and weaknesses. The PDMS is appropriate for children from birth to 83 months and was standardized on 617 children in 20 states. Two major scales (e.g., Gross Motor and Fine Motor) encompass a variety of functional dimensions to be analyzed: manual dexterity, reflexes, balance, nonlocomotor, locomotor, receipt and propulsion, grasping, hand use, and eye–hand coordination. Performance is indexed by various standard scores, such as developmental age and rate quotients and *t* and *z* scores. The availability of the PDMS Activity Cards ensures that accurate diagnostic assessment will lead to need-specific programming for a particular child.

CRITERION-BASED ASSESSMENT: SKILL-MASTERY EVALUATION

With the increasing need to individualize learning for developmentally disabled children, more professionals and programs rely upon criterion-referenced assessment techniques. Criterion- or curriculum-based assessment strategies allow specialists to merge testing, teaching, and progress evaluation into one continuous process. Unlike norm-referenced techniques, which compare a child's performance and abilities to those of his or her peers, criterion-referenced assessment compares a child to him- or herself (i.e., baseline performance levels) in order to monitor learning and mastery of specific sequences of developmental and behavioral skills. Such techniques allow specialists to assess changes in the quality of the child's behavior. Curriculum-based instruments represent the most prominent criterion-referenced measures because they contain detailed "task analyses" of skill sequences that a child must learn in order to progress. Initial, baseline performance assessments allow educators to enter a child within a particular curriculum sequence, at his or her individual level of skill development and to individualize instruction so that progress occurs. Norm-referenced assessment techniques serve to diagnose functional levels, whereas criterion-referenced measures ensure that instruction and treatment are tailored to the child's needs within a particular diagnostic group.

Many criterion-based assessment techniques are commercially available that task-analyze specific areas of learning and developmental functioning.

Developmental Curriculum Measures

Intervention programs for young exceptional children and children with severe and profound developmental retardation increasingly use structured curricula in which the content and objectives are developmentally sequenced and the methods of management and instruction are behaviorally based. Some curricula are appropriate for generalized developmental disorders, whereas others are targeted for the needs of specific handicapped populations (e.g., severely profound retarded, blind, cerebral palsied).

Several curricula have been developed and field tested by various federally funded model preschool programs for handicapped children. Three curricula, in particular, represent this type of criterion-referenced measure: the HICOMP Preschool Curriculum (Willoughby-Herb & Neisworth, 1982), Learning Accomplishment Profile (LAP) (Sanford, 1978), and Developmental Programming for Infants and Young Children (Schafer & Moersch, 1981). The HICOMP is a developmentally sequenced curriculum that emphasizes specific behavior management strategies that can be used to teach clusters of related skills to both normal and handicapped preschoolers across the birth to 60-month age range. Over 700 behavioral and developmental objectives are clustered into four functional domains: communication, own-care, motor, and problem solving. This system emphasizes the use of a diagnostic-prescriptive model to "link" developmental assessment and individualized curriculum planning. Similarly, the LAP sequences skills in five developmental domains: fine motor, gross motor, language, cognition, and self-help. It enables the individualization of goal planning for young disabled children by task-analyzing skills across the birth to 72-month age range. One of the most adaptive developmental curricula now available is the diagnostic-prescriptive system called Developmental Programming for Infants and Young Children. The system contains structured methods for modified tasks and their presentation to children who are visually impaired, hearing impaired, and motorically impaired. This curriculum is divided into two sections, Early Intervention Developmental Profile (birth to 36 months) and Preschool Developmental Profile (36 to 72 months). The curriculum also blends developmental research on attachment, Piagetian theory, and neuromotor development into its content.

Although not a curriculum as such, the Brigance Diagnostic Inventory of Early Development (Brigance, 1978) is an excellent criterion-referenced sequence of developmental tasks covering the birth to 72-month age range. It enables the assessment of skills in 11 different subdomains, which sample traditional areas like fine motor and speech/language skills but also analyzes readiness skills, basic reading, and math skills. The tasks are organized so that adaptive modifications can be accommodated as needed and multisource assessment emphasized (i.e., observation, report, performance).

SPECIALIZED CURRICULUM MEASURES

Various curricula have been designed and field tested for distinct groups of developmentally disabled children. The Uniform Performance Assessment System (Haring, White, Edgar, Affleck, & Hayden, 1981) is designed to comprehensively evaluate the skills of moderately and severely handicapped individuals who are functioning at levels comparable to the birth to 72-month range. Assessments lead directly to IEP goals and objectives as the system measures criterion skills in five functional areas: preacademic/fine motor, communication, social/self-help, gross motor, and behavior management. The Programmed Environments Curriculum (PEC) (Tawney, Knapp, O'Reilly, & Pratt, 1979) focuses on functional living skills in the birth to 36-month age range that are appropriate for individuals with moderate, severe, and profound developmental disabilities. The program emphasizes an intensive, behavioral, direct instruction model to teach skills in either individual or small-group settings. The PEC consists of 79 programs detailing skills in cognitive, motor, self-help domains and blends assessment, programming, and the monitoring of child progress by continuous data recording. Finally, the Oregon Project Curriculum for Visually Impaired and Blind Preschool Children (Brown, Simmons, & Methvin, 1979) is an example of a specialized curriculum that incorporates skills that are developmentally appropriate for children with both vision and multiple impairments. Tactile, language, and cue-directed object manipulation behaviors are emphasized whereas motor and visually directed exploratory skills are deemphasized. This diagnostic-prescriptive system covers the birth to 72-month age range.

NEUROPSYCHOLOGICAL ASSESSMENT: PROCESS EVALUATION

Encouraged by ongoing research into brain–behavior relationships, psychologists believe that measures that sample various "neuropsychological processes" (e.g., attention, memory, sequential and simultaneous learning, perception and motor control) can be potentially valuable in comprehensively assessing the capabilities and needs of children with developmental/learning disabilities (Hynd & Obrzut, 1981). For example, neuropsychological tests may prove helpful in (a) defining a child's strongest individual modality for learning, (b) monitoring the effects of medication, (c) assessing the status and progress or deterioration in children suffering traumatic brain injuries, and (d) increasing our understanding of how the brain mediates control of behavior (e.g., verbal mediation and self-control). Many of these instruments are in the formative stages of development and must be viewed in research or experimental terms because their reliability and validity are still being established. Other measures are more traditional tests that exhibit features that are neuropsychological in character. Two types of instruments are representative of this assessment approach. These include measures that presumably are based on theories of brain organization and function and those that tap various cognitive and neurodevelopmental functions that reflect the integrity of the child's nervous system.

PROCESS ANALYSIS

The Luria-Nebraska Neuropsychological Battery for Children (LNNBC) (Golden, 1980) is perhaps the most prominent instrument for surveying alleged brain–behavior relationships in children ages 8 to 12 years. Based upon Luria's theory of interactive, functional systems within the brain that coordinate to produce behavior, the LNNBC attempts to tap selected dimensions of brain functioning through 11 subtests: Motor Skills, Rhythm, Tactile, Visual, Receptive Speech, Expressive Language, Writing, Reading, Arithmetic, Memory, and Intelligence. Total scores for each subtest or scale are determined and then transformed into t scores (M = 50; SD = 10) in order to facilitate differential diagnostic comparisons among subscales that reflect lateralization of brain function. Preliminary research shows that the scales distinguish between matched groups of normal children and those with documented damage to the tertiary frontal area. Also, data on 50 children show that the LNNBC effectively predicts both IQ and WRAT reading levels as indicated in multiple correlations of .70 to .85. The scales are used with a variety of child populations exhibiting developmental disabilities (i.e., mental retardation, specific learning disabilities, neurological impairments).

Several other measures purport to measure primary cognitive, attentional, and neurodevelopmental processes that reflect specific brain functions. One such instrument is the Kaufman Assessment Battery for Children (K-ABC) (Kaufman & Kaufman, 1983). The K-ABC is based on recent developments in cognitive and neuropsychological research. It assesses a child's range of capabilities in solving increasingly complex problems using two primary processes that are available to the brain to deal with information: simultaneous and sequential. Simultaneous processing taps the child's ability to integrate multiple inputs at the same time to solve a problem that frequently involves spatial, analogic, and organizational skills to form a "gestalt" of the entire problem. In contrast, sequential processing focuses on the arrangement of arrays of information in serial order to solve problems. The K-ABC encompasses 16 subtests covering the 2 1/2- to 12 1/2-year age range. The battery includes such global scales as Sequential Processing, Simultaneous Processing, and the Achievement cluster. The global subscales are scored on the basis of a mean of 100 and standard deviation of 15. The entire battery was standardized on 2,000 children across the United States using 1980 census figures. A nonverbal scale of the K-ABC is excellent for assessing hearing-impaired and language-disordered children. Initial evidence for reliability and validity appears quite good for diagnostic purposes. However, much criticism has been directed at the lack of research support for using such diagnostic information to plan individualized programs for children (Salvia & Hritcho, 1984).

The McCarthy Scales of Children's Abilities (MSCA) (McCarthy, 1972) is conceptualized as a measure of cognitive functioning in preschool children. However, ongoing research and clinical work with the instrument suggest that it may be better viewed as an effective measure of developmental and learning readiness that taps various prerequisite functions such as attention, memory, information processing, language, and neuromotor functions. Results with handicapped children on the MSCA often are much lower than those on the SBIS and WISC-R intellectual scales (Sattler, 1982). The MSCA covers the 2 1/2- to 8 1/2-year age range as it samples strengths and weaknesses across 18 subtests and six global scales: Verbal, Perceptual-Performance, Quantitative, Memory, Motor, and General Cognitive. Each subtest is scored with a mean of 50 and standard deviation of 10, whereas the General Cognitive Index (GCI) (Composite) has a mean of 100 and standard deviation of 16. The scale was normed on 1,032 children and stratified on multiple variables. Reliability and validity data are excellent for individual diagnosis. Analysis of neurodevelopmental strengths and weaknesses is aided by the derivation of developmental age scores for each subtest and the GCI.

Diagnostic specialists often feel the need to assess the processes of sustained and selective attention in developmentally disabled children. One frequently employed measure of such attentional processes in the visual mode is the Matching Familiar Figures Test (MFFT) (Kagan, 1966). The MFFT is a measure of selective and sustained visual attention that requires the child to inspect a stimulus picture presented alone (e.g., cowboy) and then to shift attention to discriminate among an array of six other pictures to detect the one that is identical to the stimulus picture. Each set of pictures shows an increasing complexity of detail so that discriminations become finer and require greater inspection or "decision time." Performance is scored according to the amount of time required for the child to make a decision (i.e., latency) and the number of errors made (up to a limit of five) before the correct picture is selected. Scores are compared to the mean latency and error scores for clinical samples of children and the norm group of over 1,000 children to determine the child's "cognitive style" (e.g., reflective, impulsive, mixed). The MFFT often is used in studies to evaluate the effects of medication. It also is valuable in determining the types and frequency of behavioral cues and strategies that are needed in an instructional situation to promote attention and more organized visual inspection, waiting, and problem solving.

One of the most controversial models for assessment and intervention with retarded learners is the Feuerstein approach (Feuerstein, 1970). This "dynamic assessment and instruction model" is purportedly designed to diagnose and remediate the cognitive deficits of mentally retarded children and adolescents. The model assumes that the assessment approach described can provide a "cognitive map" of the process deficits of retarded children and then match this map with individualized instructional procedures to remediate the mediational disorders of such children. This diagnostic-prescriptive model has been criticized as another "ability-training" method with unsupported reliability, validity, and efficacy (Bradley, 1983; Salvia & Ysseldyke, 1974). Critical reviews of published research studies with this model currently do not provide the needed validation.

INTERACTIVE ANALYSIS

Specialists who serve developmentally disabled children, particularly those with severe handicaps, have stressed the need for assessment strategies that (a) are functionally appropriate to the child's disabilities, (b) provide a description of the child's ability to use adaptive skills to interact with people and objects, and (c) are sensitive for monitoring developmental and behavioral progress (Bagnato, 1984; Bagnato & Neisworth, 1981; Simeonsson *et al.*, 1980). Thus diagnostic specialists have begun to incorporate the use of structured "clinical judgment" scales into their diagnostic batteries as a method of detecting subtle changes in behavioral style and interactive skills. Originally designed for newborn and premature infants, the Brazelton Neonatal Behavioral Assessment Scale—Revised (BNBAS-R) (Brazelton, 1984) is increasingly used with severely disabled young children who have acquired or congenital neurodevelopmental deficits. The newly revised scale contains 37 items that tap various interactive and neurophysiological capabilities as well as items that survey primitive reflexes. The BNBAS is organized into six factor clusters (e.g., Habituation, Orientation, Motor, State Variation, State Regulation, and Autonomic Stability) and has been normed on various groups of children from which can be derived approximate functioning levels in terms of gestational and postterm developmental ages. Through presentation of scale items, an infant's interactive behavior with objects and people using his or her sensori- and neuromotor capabilities is progressly rated in quality through various state changes (e.g., asleep, drowsy, alert, agitated). Optimal performance is the focus of these 1 to 9 rating scales that also place a premium on emerging self-regulatory abilities.

Clinical judgment and other adaptive, interactive measures attempt to stress assessments that describe reciprocal effects between the child and his or her environment. The Carolina Record of Individual Behavior (CRIB) (Simmeonsson, Huntington, Short, & Ware, 1982) provides a clinical rating of the young severely handicapped child's developmental and behavioral capabilities similar to that provided by the BNBAS. It examines such dimensions as social communication, participation, object orientation, activity level, reactivity, and goal-setting skills, and includes ratings of the severity of various rhythmic habit patterns (e.g., head banging, body rocking). Similarly, the Perceptions of Developmental Skills (Bagnato, Neisworth, & Eaves, 1978) was designed to allow an interdisciplinary team to provide a multisource clinical screening of the status and progress of normal and disabled preschool children across such dimensions as motivation, activity, communication, socioemotional, sensory, neuromotor, and problem-solving areas. Finally, the Home Observation for Measurement of the Environment (HOME) (Caldwell & Bradley, 1978) is very useful for describing qualities of the child, parent, and physical environment that are related to child status and progress. With two scales covering the birth to 36-month to 72-month age ranges, the HOME rates such dimensions as emotional and verbal responsivity of the mother, avoidance of restriction and punishment, organization of the environment, provision of appropriate play materials, interaction with the child, and opportunities for daily stimulation.

Studies with various diagnostic groups have repeatedly demonstrated the relationship between child and progress and the quality of interactions and the home environment.

CASE STUDY

Tom, age 6 years 11 months, is a child with severe developmental disabilities involving developmental retardation, physical deficits, visual impairments, neurological dysfunctions, and stereotyped and self-injurious behaviors. He was admitted to the hospital for extensive neurodevelopmental therapies, the construction of an adaptive wheelchair, and the design of behavioral and developmental management programs.

Tom lives at home with his mother, stepfather, and normal 9-year-old sister. According to his mother, Tom was normal until 3 months of age, at which time he suffered meningoencephalitis. A neurological evaluation indicated mental retardation, spastic quadriplegia, seizure disorder (presently controlled with phenobarbital), and other abnormalities, all of which are secondary to the meningoencephalitis. Tom is also visually impaired, the degree to which is uncertain (i.e., reports vary and include references to "cortical blindness," "spotty vision," and normal vision in the left and impaired in the right eye). The mother reports that Tom's vision on the left appears good, that he cannot see well at a distance, and that his eyes cross at times. Tom's hearing is reportedly normal. Tom is currently enrolled in a class for the severely and profoundly retarded. Tom is nonambulatory. His wheelchair is broken beyond repair, and he has been without one since April of this year.

The mother states that up until 19 months ago, Tom had grand mal seizures two or three times a day, lasting 5 to 6 minutes. Only after the seizures were brought under control did his mother note significant developmental progress. She reports that Tom did not become interested in toys until 5 years of age and that he did not begin reaching until almost 6 years of age. At present, Tom reaches for objects and secures them by the perimeter without fumbling (therefore, suggesting adequate vision), turns to sounds, recognizes family members, responds to tone of voice, makes fleeting eye contact, and plays pat-a-cake. Self-stimulating behaviors are prominent, and Tom has recently begun evidencing temper tantrums, during which he will scream and cry uncontrollably for an hour or longer. If caught early enough, Tom's father and sister are able to interrupt screaming by firmly saying, "No!" However, once Tom loses control, he cannot be distracted, and the tantrums must run their course. Tantrums are precipitated by disturbing events or sounds (e.g., running water in a bathtub or a vacuum cleaner) or if Tom is thwarted (e.g., made to do something he does not want to do).

DEVELOPMENTAL DIAGNOSIS AND CURRICULUM PLAN

The following battery of diagnostic measures was used to provide a comprehensive assessment of Tom's range of cognitive, adaptive, sensorimotor, and behavioral capabilities and needs as a guide to individualized programming and developmental stimulation: Bayley Scales of Infant Development (BSID), Early Intervention Development Profile (EIDP), Carolina Record of Individual Behavior (CRIB), and Uniform Performance Assessment System (UPAS).

According to Tom's performance across all developmental measures, he presently is functioning overall at the 8-month level with a chronological age of 6 years 11 months. This places him in the profoundly retarded range ($DQ = 10$). Tom's deficits are in the areas of vocalizations and human relatedness, and his strength is in the area of object exploitation. Tom's test performance was characterized by some scatter. His earliest failures were at the 2-month level (personal-social and vocal items) and highest passes at 18 months (both involving the manipulation of objects). Tom's development is described according to the following areas:

1. *Preverbal*. During admission, Tom was heard to utter two different syllables (i.e., "ah" and "huh"), placing him at 2 to 3 months. Tom expressed his feelings (e.g., pleasure and displeasure) through facial expressions, body movements, and vocalizations (4 to 5 months). Receptively, Tom recognizes family voices (6 months), responds differently to tone of voice (5 to 6 months), but does not yet comprehend any words (8 months).

2. *Auditory*. Tom turns his head to sounds in all fields and responds differentially to familiar sounds (e.g., with pleasure to a bell and with displeasure to the sound of running water).

3. *Visual*. Although Tom's eyes were noted to wander without his control, he does appear to have vision in both, with vision best in the left. Tom tends to exclude his right visual field, but he will track and inspect objects on the right if his attention is captured by noise or movement. Tom displays eye–hand coordination in reaching and secures near objects deftly and directly. Tom does not appear to inspect objects or his environment several feet away from him, but he will explore visually when objects are close. Therefore, his range of vision appears limited. Table 2 presents a curriculum-based developmental task analysis of visual attention, tracking, and processing for Tom's individualized program. This outlines a sample task analysis for stimulating visual-motor processes.

4. *Perceptual and Fine Motor*. Tom evidences a significant right-side weakness and his right hand often was fisted. However, he did occasionally use this hand assisitively (e.g., to brace objects). Tom also uses his mouth assistively to position or hold objects. Tom passed such perceptual-motor and adaptive items as pulling a string to secure a ring, lifting a cup by its handle, hitting a squeaky toy, manipulating and ringing a bell, and playing a clapping game. Tom did not imitate the examiner's motor movements unless such behaviors were already in his repertoire.

TABLE 2. A CURRICULUM-BASED DEVELOPMENTAL TASK ANALYSIS OF VISUAL ATTENTION, TRACKING, AND PROCESSING FOR TOM'S INDIVIDUALIZED PROGRAM

Developmental objectives
Demonstrates ability to attend to visual stimuli
Turns eyes toward light
Eyes fix on object momentarily
Demonstrates ability to follow moving object with eyes
Horizontally tracks within 90° arc (not crossing midline)
Horizontally tracks past midline (greater than 90° arc)
Diagonally tracks past midline (greater than 90° arc)
Horizontally tracks within 180° arc—eyes and head
Moves eyes independently of head in 180° arc
Follows vanishing stimulus with eyes
Follows object moving in circular path
Follows moving object held 18 inches from eyes
Follows moving object along floor 10 feet away
Follows object dangling on string 10 feet away
Demonstrates ability to fixate eyes on objects
Identifies familiar objects by sight
Identifies objects as same when position/settings change
Demonstrates ability to make visual discriminations
Matches objects, colors, lengths, size, shape
Sorts objects, size, shape, color
Differentiates between before and after, in and out, left and right
Makes fine visual discrimination between objects such as colors, sizes, shapes, and letters.
Identifies fine differences in pictures

5. *Play Patterns*. Tom's preferred modes of object exploitation are indiscriminate schemata, such as mouthing, banging, waving, shaking, swatting, and rubbing. These patterns are consistent with Tom's mental age and place him at about 6 months. Tom does not yet adapt schemata to the specific properties of objects (11 months), and mouthing is still prominent (usually fading out at 9 months). Some of Tom's play patterns are fairly complex and ritualized (e.g., placing a toy in his mouth and repeatedly hitting it to experience the vibrations).

6. *Gross Motor*. Tom pulls to sit from supine and lowers himself from sitting to supine. Tom does not yet crawl or stand with support. As in the upper extremities, a right-side weakness is noted.

7. *Social*. Tom smiles and responds enthusiastically to direct tactile and kinesthetic stimulation from others. However, during admission, he did not respond to indirect social contact (e.g., the arrival or departure of a person or a social smile without auditory input). Eye contact was very limited.

BEHAVIOR ANALYSIS AND MANAGEMENT PLAN

Tom is a delightful, happy, and active child whose presence was thoroughly enjoyed by the hospital staff. Direct interactions with Tom (e.g., tickling, touching, frolic play, offering him toys, etc.) were met with immediate, pleasurable, and rewarding responses. When toys were readily accessible and opportunities to explore the environment were intrusive, Tom entertained himself enthusiastically and at a level appropriate to his developmental stage. However, when stimulation opportunities were not intrusive, Tom resorted to self-stimulating behaviors, including pressing his fingers against his eyes, mouthing his hands and occasionally his foot, grinding his teeth, hitting his head lightly, rocking and grunting, and visual fixation on his moving hand. When Tom was engaged in self-stimulating behavior, he was totally self-absorbed and tuned out his environment and others. However, he could be easily distracted and responded to alternate, appropriate forms of stimulation when initiated by an adult.

1. It is important to initially focus on the self-stimulatory behaviors that are injurious to Tom (i.e., pressing fingers against his eyes, grinding teeth, and occasional chewing on hands or feet). Whenever he engages in such behaviors, immediately say, "No!" and restrain him by holding him firmly under the chin for 10 seconds. At the hospital, this was effective in interrupting and reducing the incidence of these behaviors.

2. If one senses that Tom is in a beginning stage of a temper tantrum, one should use the previously described technique to prevent the tantrum from escalating. At the hospital, if the staff intervened quickly enough, the tantrums could be averted. However, once Tom loses control, the tantrum must run its course. Tom should then be placed in an area where he will not disturb others and be left there until the trantrum subsides and he regains self-control. One should ignore Tom during the tantrum and not attempt to distract him because this would inadvertently reinforce the tantrum. If a tantrum is precipitated by his noncompliance concerning a necessary task (e.g., feeding himself at the hospital), it is important to bring him back to the activity after the trantrum and make him comply. In this way, the tantrums will gradually fade out because they are not serving any useful purpose for Tom.

3. Tom plays energetically and contentedly with toys when they are intrusive and readily available. Therefore, when he is in the wheelchair, the mobile bar made at the hospital should be attached, with a variety of toys hung from it. Tom particularly enjoys shiny, sound-producing toys (e.g., two aluminum pie tins taped together with paper clips inside) and those that can be batted, waved, fingered, and explored orally. A mobile rack could also be constructed for use when Tom is on the floor (i.e., a 3-foot bar on two 3-foot legs, which can be placed over him). Additionally, a wheelchair is important because Tom may then sit at a table (with the wheelchair slightly under it) and have ready access to toys close to him or the tabletop.

4. Once the self-injurious stimulatory behaviors are eliminated, one may want to focus on other self-stimulatory actions (e.g., rocking) and eliminate them using the procedure recommended previously (i.e., a firm "No!" and restraining Tom by the chin for 10 seconds). At present, one should immediately interrupt Tom when he engages in self-stimulating behaviors and provide an appropriate substitute (e.g., give him a toy or engage him in a social game). The goal is to make appropriate activities more pleasurable and meaningful for Tom so that they will naturally replace the self-stimulating behaviors. Many of Tom's self-stimulating behaviors can be converted into appropriate actions. For example, if Tom is rocking, join him by playing, "Row, Row, Row Your Boat," or if he is indiscriminately hitting an object, turn this into a game of pat-a-cake. Again, the goal is to have these higher level, adaptive behaviors substitute for the pattern of self-stimulation.

5. To increase Tom's play skills, one should expand upon the actions currently in his repertoire by introducing slight variation and encouraging him to imitate. For example, if he is waving his squeaky toy or hitting it against himself, show him how to hit it against another object (e.g., one dangling from his mobile bar) to create a new sound or visual display. Another objective is to help him adapt his play to specific properties of different objects, instead of using the same action for all toys.

An infant busy box and easily activated toys (e.g., a toy top with a wide base requiring only slight pressure on the plunger to spin it) are good resources. Through demonstrations, Tom will learn to discriminate among response opportunities (e.g., on the busy box, the door is for sliding, the wheel is for turning, the bell activator for pressing, etc.). By stressing these imitation activities, his degree of awareness and ability to learn from demonstrations also will improve.

6. Tom enjoys social interaction, particularly tactile and kinesthetic stimulation. When interacting with Tom, keep your face close to his to stimulate eye contact and to allow him to see you clearly (because Tom's distance vision is impaired). Whenever he looks into your eyes, respond enthusiastically with hugs, praise, laughing, and the like. Direct methods of stimulating eye contact can also be devised, such as holding a snack (e.g., bit of cookie) in front of your face and waiting until Tom makes eye contact before giving it to him. A verbal cue (i.e., "Tom" or "Look") should always be paired with the treat, so that he will eventually learn to respond to the request for eye contact alone.

7. At present, Tom readily indicates his feelings and needs by expressing pleasure or displeasure. The next step is to help him become more active and adaptive in expressing his wants (e.g., reaching toward something you have, instead of fussing, to indicate his desire for it). This can be accomplished through demonstrations (e.g., guiding Tom through the reaching movement and then rewarding him with the object) or by contriving situations to foster communication (e.g., temporarily interrupting a pleasurable activity, such as a tickling game, and waiting for Tom to lean toward you, reach out, grap your hand, or make eye contact before

resuming the game). In this way, Tom will learn that he can influence the behavior of others through direct communication efforts.

8. Any vocalizations on Tom's part should be dramatically reinforced, and one should imitate his sounds (e.g., "ah" and "huh") in an attempt to engage him in vocal play.

9. Greater use of Tom's right visual field should continue to be encouraged (e.g., attracting his attention to the right by moving objects or using sound-producing toys). Inventive strategies such as those the mother currently uses (i.e., offering food on Tom's right side) are excellent.

SUMMARY

Developmental assessment of retardation describes developmental functioning and thus provides not only a status report but also objectives for education and treatment. *Diagnosis* of retardation usually employs psychological constructs (e.g., intelligence) and is aimed only at assignment to a clinical (genotypic) category, (i.e., "mental retardation"). The diagnosis of mental retardation involves three phases. First, one must select the definition of retardation and the criteria to be evaluated. For example, the AAMD definition includes IQ and adaptive behavior criteria. Next, instruments are chosen to measure the criteria, in this case, intelligence and adaptive behavior. Finally, the results of diagnostic testing determine the presence and degree of retardation in reference to the definition. A developmental assessment battery includes not only measures for general diagnosis but scales that yield a blueprint for individualized treatment planning. Norm-based, criterion-referenced, and, when necessary, adaptive-process measures analyze functioning in the basic developmental domains (cognitive, communication, sensori- and neuromotor, social-emotional, and academic learning).

Assessment of the child's capabilities in each of these developmental areas provides a detailed picture of functional strengths and weaknesses. The content items of the assessment battery can then be compared with the content of the treatment or teaching programs to select instructional/therapeutic objectives. Assessment that profiles strengths and weaknesses transcends diagnosis and yields developmental pinpoints for therapy.

REFERENCES

Achenbach, T. M., & Edelbrock, C. S. (1982). *Manual for the Child Behavior Checklist and Revised Child Behavior Profile*. Burlington: University of Vermont, Department of Psychiatry.

Alpern, G., Boll, T. J., & Shearer, M. (1982). *Developmental Profile II*. Aspen, CO: Psychological Development Corporation.

Ames, L. B., Gillespie, C., Haines, J., & Ilg, F. (1979). *The Gesell Institute's child from 1 to 6: Evaluating the behavior of the preschool child*. New York: Harper & Row.

Bagnato, S. J. (1984). Team congruence in developmental diagnosis: Comparing clinical judgment and child performance measures. *School Psychology Review, 13*(1), 7–16.

Bagnato, S. J., & Neisworth, J. T. (1981). *Linking developmental assessment and curricula: Prescriptions for early intervention*. Rockville, MD: Aspen.

Bagnato, S. J., & Neisworth, J. T. (1985). Efficacy of interdisciplinary assessment and treatment for infants and preschoolers with congenital and acquired brain injury. *Analysis and intervention in developmental disabilities, 5*, 81–102.

Bagnato, S. J., Neisworth, J. T., & Eaves, R. C. (1978). A profile of perceived capabilities for the preschool child. *Child Care Quarterly, 7*(4), 327–335.

Balthazar, E. E. (1976). *Bathazar Scales of Adaptive Behavior*. Palo Alto, CA: Consulting Psychologists Press.

Bayley, N. (1969). *Manual for the Bayley Scales of Infant Development*. San Antonio, TX: Psychological Corporation.

Beery, K. E., & Buktenica, N. (1982). *Revised administration, scoring, and teaching manual for the Developmental Test of Visual-Motor Integration*. Cleveland, OH: Modern Curriculum Press. (Original publication in 1967)

Behar, L., & Stringfield, S. (1974). A behavior rating scale for the preschool child. *Developmental Psychology, 10*, 601–610.

Bijou, S. (1966). A functional analysis of retarded development. In N. R. Ellis (Ed.), *International review of research in mental retardation* (Vol. 1, pp. 89–114). New York: Academic Press.

Bradley, T. B. (1983). Remediation of cognitive deficits: A critical appraisal of the Feuerstein model. *Journal of Mental Deficiency Research, 27*, 79–92.

Brazelton, B. (1984). *Brazelton Neonatal Behavioral Assessment Scale—Revised*. Philadelphia, PA: Lippincott.

Brigance, A. (1977). *Brigance Diagnostic Inventory of Basic Skills*. North Billerica, MA: Curriculum Associates.

Brigance, A. (1978). *Brigance Diagnostic Inventory of Early Development*. North Billerica, MA: Curriculum Associates.

Brigance, A. (1980). *Brigance Diagnostic Inventory of Essential Skills*. North Billerica, MA: Curriculum Associates.

Brown, D., Simmons, V., & Methvin, J. (1979). *Oregon project curriculum for visually impaired and blind preschool children*. Eugene, OR: Jackson County Education Service District.

Bruininks, R. H. (1978). *Bruininks-Oseretsky Test of Motor Proficiency*. Circle Pines, MN: American Guidance Service.

Caldwell, B., & Bradley, R. (1978). *Home observation for measurement of the environment*. Little Rock: University of Arkansas.

Carrow, E. (1973). *Test of Auditory Comprehension Language*. Austin, TX: Learning Concepts.

Connolly, A., Nachtman, W., & Pritchett, E. (1971). *Manual for the KeyMath Diagnostic Arithmetic Test*. Circle Pines, MN: American Guidance Service.

Doll, E. A. (1985). *Vineland Social Maturity Scale*. Circle Pines, MN: American Guidance Service. (Original publication in 1953)

Dubose, R. (1981). Assessment of severely impaired young children: Problems and recommendations. *Topics in Early Childhood Special Education, 1*(2), 9–22.

Dunn, L., & Dunn, L. (1981). *Peabody Picture Vocabulary Test—Revised*. Circle Pines, MN: American Guidance Service.

Dunn, L., & Markwardt, F. C. (1970). *Peabody Individual Achievement Test*. Circle Pines, MN: American Guidance Service.

Feuerstein, R. (1970). A dynamic approach to the causation, prevention, and alleviation of retarded performance. In H. C. Haywood (Ed.), *Social-cultural aspects of mental retardation* (pp. 185–224). New York: Appleton-Century-Crofts.

Folio, M. R., & Fewell, R. R. (1984). *Peabody Developmental Motor Scales and Activity Cards*. Allen, TX: Developmental Learning Materials/Teaching Resources.

French, J. L. (1964). *The Pictorial Test of Intelligence*. Boston: Riverside.

Golden, C. J. (1980). *Luria-Nebraska Neuropsychological Battery for Children*. Unpublished experimental test. Omaha: University of Nebraska Medical Center.

Grossman, H. (Ed.). (1977). *Manual on terminology and classification in mental retardation* (rev. ed.). Washington, DC: American Association on Mental Deficiency.

Grossman, H. (1983) *Classification in mental retardation*. Washington, DC: American Association on Mental Deficiency.

Haring, N. G., White, O. R., Edgar, E. B., Affleck, J. Q., & Hayden, A. A. (1981). *Uniform performance assessment system*. Columbus, OH: Charles E. Merrill.

Heber, R. (1961). A manual on terminology and classification in mental retardation. *American Journal of Mental Deficiency, 65*, (Monograph suppl. rev.).

Hiskey, M. (1966). *Hiskey-Nebraska Test of Learning Aptitude*. Lincoln: Union College Press.

Hynd, G. W., & Obrzut, J. E. (1981). *Neuropsychological assessment and the school-age child: Issues and procedures*. New York: Grune & Stratton.

Jastak, S., & Wilkinson, G. S. (1984). *Wide Range Achievement Test—Revised administration manual*. Wilmington, DE: Jastak Associates.

Kagan, J. (1966). *Matching Familiar Figures Test*. Cambridge: Harvard University Press.

Kaufman, A. S., & Kaufman, N. L. (1983). *Kaufman Assessment Battery for Children*. Circle Pines, MN: American Guidance Service.

Knobloch, H., & Pasamanick, B. (1974). *Developmental diagnosis*. New York: Harper & Row.

Knobloch, H., & Stevens, F., & Malone, A. F. (1980). *Manual of developmental diagnosis*. New York: Harper & Row.

Lambert, N., Windmiller, M., Cole, L., & Figueroa, R. (1975). *Manual for AAMD Adaptive Behavior Scale—Public School Version*. Washington, DC: AAMD.

Leiter, R. G. (1969). *General instructions for the Leiter International Performance Scale*. Chicago: Stoelting.

Levine, S., Elzey, F. F., Thormahlen, P., & Cain, L. F. (1976). *Manual for the TMR School Competency Scales*. Palo Alto, CA: Consulting Psychologists Press.

Mattison, R. E., Cantwell, D. P., & Baker, L. (1982). A practical method for screening psychiatric disorder in children with speech and language disorders. *Journal of Abnormal Child Psychology, 10*(1), 25–32.

McCall, R. B., Hogarty, P. S., & Hurlburt, N. (1972). Transitions in infant sensorimotor development and the prediction of childhood IQ. *American Psychologist, 27*, 728–748.

McCarthy, D. (1972). *Manual for the McCarthy Scales of Children's Abilities*. New York: Psychological Corporation.

Mercer, J. (1973). *Labeling and the mentally retarded* Berkeley: University of California Press.

Newland, T. E. (1969). *Manual for the Blind Learning Aptitude Test: Experimental Edition*. Urbana, IL: T. Ernest Newland.

Nihira, K., Foster, R., Shellhass, M., & Leland, H. (1974). *AAMD Adaptive Behavior Scale manual*. Washington, DC: American Association on Mental Deficiency.

Powers, M. (1984). Syndromal diagnosis and the behavioral assessment of childhood disorders. *Child and Family Behavior Therapy, 6*(3), 1–15.

Quay, H. C., & Peterson, D. R. (1983). *Manual for the Revised Behavior Problem Checklist*. Coral Gables: University of Miami.

Salvia, J., & Hritcho, T. (1984). The K-ABC and ability training. *Journal of Special Education, 18*(3), 345–356.

Salvia, J., & Ysseldyke, J. E. (1981). *Assessment in special and remedial education* (2nd ed.). Boston: Houghton-Mifflin.

Salvia, J., & Ysseldyke, J. E. (1974). Diagnostic-prescriptive teaching: Two models. *Exceptional Children, 41*, 181.

Sanford, A. (1978). *Learning Accomplishment Profile*. Winston-Salem, NC: Kaplan School Supply.

Sattler, J. M. (1965). Analysis of functions of the 1960 Stanford-Binet Intelligence Scale, Form L-M. *Journal of Clinical Psychology, 21*, 173–179.

Sattler, J. M. (1982). *Assessment of Children's Intelligence and Special Abilities*. Philadelphia: W. B. Saunders.

Schafer, D. S., & Moersch, M. S. (1981). *Developmental programming for infants and young children* (Vols. 1–5). Ann Arbor: University of Michigan Press.

Semel, E. M., & Wiig, E. H. (1980). *Clinical evaluation of language functions*. Columbus: Charles E. Merrill.

Simeonsson, R. J., Huntingdon, E. S., & Parse, S. A. (1980). Assessment of children with severe handicaps: Multiple problems—multivariate goals. *Journal of Association for the Severely Handicapped, 5*, 55–72.

Simeonsson, R. J., Huntingdon, G. S., Short, R. J., & Ware, W. B. (1982). The Carolina Record of Individual Behavior. *Characteristics of Handicapped Infants and Children, 2*(2), 43–55.

Song, A., & Jones, S. E. (1980). *Wisconsin Rating Scale*. Madison: Center for Developmentally Disabled.

Sparrow, S. S., Balla, D. A., & Cicchetti, D. V. (1984). *Vineland Adaptive Behavior Scales*. Circle Pines, MN: American Guidance Service.

Stroufe, L. (1979). The coherence of individual development: Early care, attachment, and subsequent issues. *American Psychologist, 34*(10), 834–841.

Tawney, J., Knapp, D., O'Reilly, C., & Pratt, S. (1979). *Programmed environments curriculum*. Columbus: Charles E. Merrill.

Terman, L., & Merrill, M. (1972). *Stanford-Binet Intelligence Scale* (norms ed.). Boston: Houghton-Mifflin.

Thomas, A. (1981). Current trends in developmental theory. *American Journal of Orthopsychiatry, 51*(4), 580–609.

Valett, R. E. (1964). A clinical profile for the Stanford-Binet. *Journal of School Psychology, 2*, 49–54.

Wechsler, D. (1974). *Manual for the Wechsler Intelligence Scale for Children—Revised*. New York: Psychological Corporation.

Willoughby-Herb, S. J., & Neisworth, J. T. (1982). *HICOMP preschool curriculum*. Columbus: Charles E. Merrill.

Woodcock, R. W. (1973). *Woodcock Reading Mastery Tests*. Circle Pines, MN: American Guidance Service.

Woodcock, R. W. (1978). *Woodcock-Johnson Psychoeducational Battery*. Boston: Teaching Resources.

Yang, R. K., & Bell, R. Q. (1975). Assessment of infants. In P. McReynolds (Ed.), *Advances in psychological assessment* (Vol. 3). San Francisco: Jossey-Bass.

Zigler, E., Balla, D., & Hodapp, R. (1984). On the definition and classification of mental retardation. *American Journal of Mental Deficiency, 89*(3), 215–230.

9

Hyperactivity, Attention Deficit Disorders, and Learning Disabilities

STEPHEN P. HINSHAW

INTRODUCTION

The psychological evaluation of attention deficit disorders, hyperactivity, and learning disabilities encompasses a vast domain. In addition to such standard assessment procedures as clinical interviews, completion of rating scales by significant adults, and administration of intellectual and achievement measures, the assessor may profitably employ a diversity of nontraditional tools, including peer sociometric ratings, neuropsychological test batteries, and observations of classroom, playground, and parent–child interactions. Furthermore, a host of specific measures of the key constructs of attention, impulsivity, motor activity, and learning have been developed, yielding a wide (and potentially confusing) array of assessment instruments. The focus of this chapter will be on those evaluation procedures that demonstrate the greatest utility for defining key characteristics, identifying homogeneous subgroups, planning for intervention, and assessing treatment outcome.

A major issue pertinent to evaluation efforts involves the diagnostic validity of the categories of attention deficit disorder/hyperactivity and learning disability. Indeed, whether true syndromes of hyperactivity and

STEPHEN P. HINSHAW • Department of Psychology, University of California, Los Angeles, California 90024.

learning disorders exist has been intensively debated (e.g., Aman, 1984; Barkley, 1981b; Quay, 1979; Rutter, 1982, 1983a; Shaffer, 1980). A major controversy centers around the distinctiveness of hyperactivity and attentional deficits, on the one hand, and conduct problems and aggression, on the other (see Lahey, Green, & Forehand, 1980; Milich, Loney, & Landau, 1982; Prinz, Connor, & Wilson, 1981; Sandberg, Rutter, & Taylor, 1978). Although strict medically defined syndromes in these areas have not been validated, consensus is emerging that (a) they are partially independent and (b) assessment and evaluation strategies must be able to separate their key features (Hinshaw, 1987; Quay, 1986). Another point of consensus is that children within the categories of either attentional problems/hyperactivity or learning difficulties are far from homogeneous (Ross & Ross, 1982; Rourke, 1985). As will be highlighted throughout this chapter, the potential identification of meaningful subgroups of these children is receiving considerable attention (see also Milich & Pelham, 1986). Overall, the conception of the disorders in question is continually evolving. Not only are evaluation procedures determined by prevailing diagnostic and conceptual paradigms, but the results of clinical evaluations help to shape the evolution of new diagnostic conceptions.

DESCRIPTION

I will initially consider the definitions of hyperactivity/attention deficits and learning disorders that are presented in the third edition of the *Diagnostic and Statistical Manual of Mental Disorders* (DSM-III; American Psychiatric Association, 1980). In keeping with the bulk of current research, this classification system separates attentional problems and hyperactivity from learning disabilities.

ATTENTION DEFICIT DISORDERS

Replacing such terms as hyperactivity, hyperkinesis, and minimal brain dysfunction is the DSM-III category of Attention Deficit Disorder (see Table 1). Attention Deficit Disorder without Hyperactivity (ADD) requires the presence of three of the five listed symptoms of inattention and three of the six of impulsivity; the addition of two of the five symptoms of hyperactivity warrants the diagnosis of Attention Deficit Disorder with Hyperactivity (ADDH). Thus the current scheme reflects the seminal work of such researchers as Douglas (1972, 1983; Douglas & Peters, 1979), which holds that the core symptomatology lies in the area

TABLE 1. DSM-III DIAGNOSTIC CRITERIA FOR ATTENTION DEFICIT DISORDER WITH HYPERACTIVITY[a]

A. Inattention
   1. Often fails to finish things he or she starts
   2. Often does not seem to listen
   3. Easily distracted
   4. Has difficulty concentrating on schoolwork or other tasks requiring sustained attention
   5. Has difficulty sticking to a play activity

B. Impulsivity
   1. Often acts before thinking
   2. Shifts excessively from one activity to another
   3. Has difficulty organizing work (this not being due to cognitive impairment)
   4. Needs a lot of supervision
   5. Frequently calls out in class
   6. Has difficulty awaiting turn in games or group situations

C. Hyperactivity
   1. Runs about or climbs on things excessively
   2. Has difficulty sitting still or fidgets excessively
   3. Has difficulty staying seated
   4. Moves about excessively during sleep
   5. Is always "on the go" or acts as if "driven by a motor"

[a]Taken from *Diagnostic and Statistical Manual of Mental Disorders* (3rd ed.), American Psychiatric Association (1980), p. 43–44. Reprinted with permission.

of dysfunctional attention, particularly in structured, adult-directed environments. Hyperactivity *per se* is considered to be a secondary feature.[1]

Diagnosis requires a certain duration (6 months) and age of onset (before 7 years) of the symptoms, as well as their "developmental inappropriateness." (This last qualification is, unfortunately, not elaborated.) The exclusion of other major diagnostic categories—in particular, severe or profound mental retardation, affective illness, and schizophrenia—is also a prerequisite.

[1]The diagnostic changes incorporated in DSM-III have added to the current terminologic profusion (and confusion) in the field. Whereas the term *hyperactivity* has traditionally denoted the entire symptom cluster of attentional, impulse control, and motor activity problems, it currently refers only to the behaviors of restlessness and overactivity that may accompany attention deficit disorder. Because of its historical usage and because of the awkwardness of continually specifying the long-winded term of *attention deficit disorder with or without hyperactivity, hyperactivity* will often be used in the former sense, to refer to the entire disorder. The reader's tolerance for the confusing and evolving terminology of the field is solicited.

Hyperactivity is among the most prevalent categories of childhood psychopathology, comprising nearly half of the referrals to outpatient treatment clinics for children and families (Stewart, Cummings, Singer, & deBlois, 1981). Conservative prevalence estimates have been set at 1% to 2% of school-aged children (Bosco & Robin, 1980; Sandoval, Lambert, & Sassone, 1980). These figures rise to over 5% when less stringent definitions are employed. Boys are considerably more likely than girls to be diagnosed (American Psychiatric Association, 1980). Interestingly, a large percentage of hyperactive children—as many as 17%—are adopted (Deutsch, Swanson, Bruell, Cantwell, Weinberg, & Baren, 1982).

A complete elucidation of the key features of the disorder is beyond the scope of the chapter (see, particularly, Barkley, 1981a; Pelham, 1982a; Ross & Ross, 1982; Whalen, 1983). Yet several pertinent considerations bear comment. First, children with ADD or ADDH are likely to exhibit a variety of noncompliant, socially inappropriate, vigorous, and poorly modulated behaviors, many of which are bothersome to adults and peers alike (Barkley, 1981b). The vast majority of these children, however, display no major intellectual or neurological problems, yielding a puzzling picture for the parent, teacher, diagnostician, researcher, or therapist (see Whalen, 1983). Second, there are a host of frequently associated problems, with aggression and conduct disturbance, peer difficulties, decrements in academic achievement, emotional lability, and lowered self-esteem being among the most commonly cited (Cantwell & Satterfield, 1978; Cunningham & Barkley, 1978; Milich & Landau, 1982; Safer & Allen, 1976). Next, etiology is largely unknown. Although a number of temperamental, perinatal, and biological/biochemical variables are posited to be precursors (Kanter, 1982; Ross & Ross, 1982), socioeconomic and familial-environmental factors may shape behavioral content, especially in the domain of aggression (Paternite & Loney, 1980).

Fourth, the category is unique among major childhood disorders in that a pharmacologic intervention, stimulant medication, shows short-term efficacy for ameliorating several key symptoms in a majority of cases (Cantwell & Carlson, 1978; Conners & Werry, 1979; Gittelman, 1983). The sufficiency and long-term efficacy of such intervention is, however, openly questioned (Barkley, 1981b; Barkley & Cunningham, 1978; Pelham & Murphy, 1986; Whalen & Henker, 1980). Finally, contrary to considerable initial speculation, the disorder is persistent (Aman, 1984; Helper, 1980). Although some symptoms may diminish or change in form during adolescence, problems of attention, impulse control, restlessness, self-esteem, and poor peer relationships are likely to last through adolescence or young adulthood (e.g., Gittelman, Mannuzza, Shenker, & Bonagura, 1985; Weiss, Hechtman, Perlman, Hopkins, &

Wener, 1979). (DSM-III, in fact, lists the category of Attention Deficit Disorder, Residual Type, for adults with continuing attentional problems.) Furthermore, there is a greatly increased risk for delinquency in adolescence among children initially diagnosed as hyperactive (Satterfield, Hoppe, & Schell, 1982). In short, the disorder is prone to persist, at least in some form.

An area of crucial importance for psychological evaluation is the association of hyperactivity with conduct disorders/aggression. As noted earlier, the separate status of these two categories is controversial. Indeed, previous research has demonstrated a strong statistical association between the two types of symptoms (see Quay, 1979). Influential investigations by Milich, Loney, and colleagues (Milich & Loney, 1979; Milich *et al.*, 1982; Loney, Kramer, & Milich, 1981; Loney, Langhorne, & Paternite, 1978; Paternite & Loney, 1980), however, point to the independence of the two classes of behaviors (see review by Hinshaw, 1987). Most impressive is the finding of the differential predictive validity of inattention and overactivity, on the one hand, and aggressive conduct problems, on the other. Indeed, the presence of aggressive behaviors in diagnosed hyperactive children during middle childhood was found to strongly predict conduct problems, school failure, and delinquency at the time of adolescent follow-up, whereas the severity of the children's hyperactive and inattentive behaviors themselves showed little predictive power for such outcomes (Loney *et al.*, 1981). Thus assessment of aggression is of prime importance for the evaluator.

In summary, the attention deficit disorders encompass a diverse set of symptoms, marked chiefly by a lack of age-appropriate self-control in areas of attention deployment, behavioral inhibition, compliance to demands for structured learning, and interpersonal interactions (see Barkley, 1981a,b). Whether certain features of the current diagnostic system—particularly, the separation into subgroups with and without hyperactivity—will withstand empirical validation is unknown (see Edelbrock, Costello, & Kessler, 1984; Lahey, Schaughency, Strauss, & Frame, 1984; Werry, Methven, Fitzpatrick, & Dixon, 1983). Improved diagnostic criteria have been proposed (Barkley, 1982), and sophisticated research efforts that refine our understanding of the situational specificity, social contexts, and transactional nature of the component behaviors have been undertaken (e.g., Barkley & Cunningham, 1979; Jacob, O'Leary, & Rosenblad, 1978; Whalen, Henker, & Dotemoto, 1980, 1981). Because of their prevalence, salience, and persistence, and through their generation of diverse assessment, treatment, and research strategies, the attention deficit disorders truly constitute a major category of childhood psychopathology.

LEARNING DISABILITIES (SPECIFIC DEVELOPMENTAL DISORDERS)

A confusing array of descriptive and diagnostic terms permeates the field of learning disorders. Dyslexia, perceptual handicaps, dysgraphia, strephosymbolia, underachievement, specific reading retardation, dyscalculia, and specific learning disabilities are but a few of the many labels still used to describe the general problem of substandard academic achievement that is not accounted for by low intellect, overt organicity, or clear-cut cultural or school-related factors. DSM-III has categorized such problems in learning and achievement as Specific Developmental Disorders, which are coded on Axis II.[2] Reading, arithmetic, language, and articulation disorders as well as mixed and atypical subtypes are listed in the nomenclature; the present chapter will consider only those disorders relating to academic subject matter.

Regardless of the specific diagnostic term or classification system, the key elements in defining learning disorders pertain to (a) exclusionary criteria and (b) the degree of discrepancy between actual and expected academic performance. First, most definitions exclude children with overt sensory or motor delays or impairments, mental retardation, demonstrable organic involvement, or cultural deprivation or disadvantage. Furthermore, children who lack access to appropriate educational resources are often removed from consideration. Whereas the learning problems of children in these various categories are, of course, noteworthy and deserving of attention, much of the conceptualization about learning disabilities has focused on the problems of children without readily apparent causes of academic underachievement (see Critchley, 1970; U.S. Office of Education, 1977; see also the review by Rutter, 1978).[3]

Next, most definitions require some measure of disparity between (a) either age level, grade level, or intellectual potential, and (b) actual academic performance. (Unfortunately, neither DSM-III nor many recent federal and state guidelines provide specific operational definitions of

[2]Although placement on Axis II attempts to (a) denote developmental, as opposed to mental, disorders, and (b) foster more frequent inclusion of the problems when they do occur, controversy exists regarding the inclusion of deficits in learning and achievement in a psychiatric classification. For discussion, see Rapoport and Ismond (1984).

[3]Critics of such definitions point out that children from impoverished backgrounds or children with mild to moderate mental retardation may also have specific difficulties with certain academic subject matter. As stated by Rutter and Yule with regard to the exclusionary nature of the diagnosis of specific developmental dyslexia: "It suggests that if all the known causes of reading disability can be ruled out, the unknown (in the form of "dyslexia") should be invoked. A counsel of despair, indeed" (1975, p. 192). The search for useful operational definitions of learning disorders continues (see Schere, Richardson, & Bialer, 1980).

such disparity.) Different types and amounts of discrepancy can have far-reaching implications. For example, in the classic epidemiological study undertaken on the Isle of Wight by Rutter and colleagues (Rutter, Tizard, & Whitmore, 1970), the presence of reading disabilities was determined in two ways. If reading scores were simply 2 1/3 years or more below those expected for the child's chronological age, signifying *low* achievement, a diagnosis of "general reading backwardness" was made. This group constituted approximately 10% of the population. If, however, reading scores were at least 2 1/3 years below the level predicted (via regression equations) from a combination of chronological age plus IQ, "specific reading retardation," or *under*achievement, was assessed. This latter category constituted, with few exceptions, a subgroup of the former; the key difference was the discrepancy between the child's reading level and his or her own intellectual potential.

Children with specific reading retardation (4% of the population) differed from the remainder of the general reading backwardness group on a number of dimensions. They were higher in intelligence (an artifact of the selection process); they were much more likely to be boys; they had many fewer neurodevelopmental delays and neurological disorders; but, despite their higher intelligence and favorable neurodevelopmental status, they had a much *worse* prognosis for outcome in reading and spelling, as assessed at 4- to 5-year follow-up (Rutter & Yule, 1975; Yule, Rutter, Berger, & Thompson, 1974). (See Silva, McGee, & Williams, 1985, for an empirical investigation of this distinction.) Thus differential selection criteria can yield vastly different types and rates of "learning-disabled" children. One implication for assessment is that administration of an individual intelligence measure is nearly a necessity for accurate evaluation of specific learning disabilities. Another is that discrepancy scores can be extremely unreliable, particularly when the tests yielding the discrepancies are correlated (see Salvia & Ysseldyke, 1985). Thus, caution must be used when defining learning disabilities by means of achievement-intelligence differences (Berk, 1984).

Depending on the stringency of the defining criteria, prevalence estimates of learning disabilities vary enormously, from less than 1% to over 25% of the school-aged population (Tucker, Stevens, & Ysseldyke, 1983). A conservative, representative range for reading disability is 3% to 5% (Badian, 1984; Rutter & Yule, 1975), although this figure may be higher in inner-city areas (Berger, Yule, & Rutter, 1975). Less is known about specific spelling and arithmetic disabilities (see Gaddes, 1980, Chapter 9; Rourke & Strang, 1983; Sweeney & Rourke, 1985). Boys outnumber girls on the basis of nearly all reports (American Psychiatric Association, 1980; Rutter, 1978). As in the case of hyperactivity, a number of secondary problems are associated with learning disabilities; among the most salient are decrements in self-esteem, problems in social skill development, and presence of conduct disturbances, attentional deficits, overactivity, and, in some cases, school phobias (Barkley, 1981c; Bryan, 1976; Dykman, Ackerman, Clements, & Peters, 1971; Kinsbourne & Caplan, 1979; La Greca, 1981; Peter & Spreen, 1979). Furthermore, the achievement problems of a majority of learning-disabled children tend to persist into adolescence and adulthood (see reviews by Helper, 1980; Schonhaut & Satz, 1983), and there is an association between early development of reading problems, in particular, and juvenile delinquency (e.g., Rutter, 1978). With respect to treatment, well-controlled studies documenting the short-term efficacy of educational intervention for LD children are extremely rare (Gittelman & Feingold, 1983); stimulant medication is not generally regarded as enhancing standardized measures of achievement (Barkley & Cunningham, 1978; Gittelman, Klein, & Feingold, 1983); and the long-range efficacy of any intervention strategy is not established. Thus, despite terminologic confusion and definitional problems, learning disorders clearly comprise an educational, psychological, and social problem of major proportions, and they are notably refractory to significant amelioration.

As the reader may well have noted, the similarity of learning disabilities and attention deficit disorders with respect to prevalence rates, sex ratio, poor prognosis, and associated problem behaviors is striking. In fact, the diagnostic overlap between ADD and LD is high. Lambert and Sandoval (1980), for example, reported that 53% of a stringently defined sample of hyperactive children met objective criteria for learning disabilities. Taking the reverse approach, Silver (1980) assessed 26% of a school-defined group of learning-disabled children as hyperactive. The overlap is not complete, however, and there is consensus that the disorders merit separate consideration (see review by Aman, 1984; see also Lahey, Stempniak, Robinson, & Tyroler, 1978). Several research groups have recently begun to study the characteristics of overlapping subgroups—that is, those children with both hyperactivity and learning disabilities (Copeland & Weissbrod, 1983; Halperin, Gittelman, Klein, & Rudel, 1984). There is likely to be continued interest in the attentional problems of LD children as well as the achievement difficulties of children with ADD.

More thorough descriptions of the complex topic of learning disabilities are found in the reviews of Barkley (1981c), Bryan and Bryan (1980), Denckla (1979), and Rutter (1978); see also the volumes by Benton and Pearl (1978), Goldberg, Shiffman, and Bender (1983), and Mosse (1982). In closing, it should be reemphasized that many different types of children fall into the LD category. Thus, merely assessing the amount or level of underachievement in reading, spelling, or arithmetic constitutes only the beginning of competent evaluation. Analysis of the *patterns* and *profiles* of deficit across these three achievement areas (Rourke & Finlayson, 1978), observation of the *types* of errors that are made (Boder, 1971; Sweeney & Rourke, 1978), and assessment of the strengths and weaknesses in underlying *neuropsychological* processing areas (e.g., Rourke, 1981, 1985) all show promise as useful evaluation strategies for identifying meaningful subgroups of these children and for specifying appropriate treatment modalities. These topics will be explored further in later sections.

HISTORY AND DEVELOPMENT

Space permits only brief consideration of the history of the disorders in question (see Kessler, 1980, for an interesting historical account through the mid-1970s). Although the origins of current thinking about learning disorders can be traced to the neurological work of Broca and others in the nineteenth century (see also Morgan, 1896) and although clinical descriptions of hyperactive children can also be traced to the nineteenth century (see Barkley, 1981a) and early twentieth century (Still, 1902), a commonly agreed-upon starting point for "modern" diagnostic conceptualization was the identification of a postencephalitic syndrome in the United States during and after World War I. The syndrome included such diverse behavioral symptoms as impaired attention, emotional instability, overactivity, depression, and various forms of conduct and learning disturbance (see, for example, Ebaugh, 1923). Given this association between neural impairment and behavioral symptomatology, it was not long before the directionality of the causal reasoning was reversed: Presence of the behavioral manifestations alone led to inference of a brain damage syndrome. Because of the variable and somewhat milder symptomatology displayed by many children with the purported syndrome, the phrasing was later softened to "minimal brain damage" (see Straus & Kephart, 1948). Thus an underlying neurological malfunction was held to be the common etiological precursor to the various behavioral, perceptual, and learning difficulties of a vast array of non-retarded children, despite the circular reasoning and undocumented inference involved.

So-called minimal brain damage encompassed a wide range of symptoms. Some experts were, however, identifying narrower clusters of deviant behavior or below-expected school performance. Orton (1937) conceptualized the tendency to reverse written symbols (strephosymbolia) as related to learning disorders. Such reversals and associated perceptual distortions were held to reflect incomplete cortical dominance. Kahn and Cohen (1934) posited that "organic driveness," characterized chiefly by overactivity, reflected brain stem dysfunction. Two decades later, Laufer and Denhoff (1957) coined the term *hyperkinetic impulse disorder* to refer to children with the common presenting symptoms of inappropriate motor overactivity, poor impulse control, lack of attention to task, academic underachievement, and visual motor problems. It is clear from the neurological theorizing involved that these "narrower band" disorders were viewed as subclasses of minimal brain damage (see Kessler, 1980).

By the 1960s, dissatisfaction was growing with regard to the implicit and explicit references to neural damage in the diagnostic terminology. In an attempt to soften further the presumption of actual brain lesion, Clements and Peters (1962) christened the term *minimal brain dysfunction* (MBD) as a replacement for minimal brain damage. Despite the widespread acceptance of this term (see Clements, 1966; Wender, 1971), the same problems of overinclusiveness (nearly 100 symptoms were held by Clements, 1966, to characterize the disorder) and presumption of neurological deficit continued to plague its utility. Furthermore, research evidence accumulated, demonstrating that (a) the majority of children with the characteristic behavioral features do not display observable organic involvement (see review by Satz & Fletcher, 1980), and (b) the majority of children with demonstrable brain damage do not display impulsivity, inattention, motor restlessness, and the like (Rutter, 1982). Thus, in the words of Satz and Fletcher:

> The term MBD represents an inference concerning an unknown deviation in the brain based on unexpected academic failure and/or signs of behavioral disturbance (primarily hyperactivity). This inference is reckless and unwarranted. (1980, p. 674)

Indeed, the overwhelming conclusion of the many contributors to a relatively recent volume on MBD is that the term should be abandoned (Rie & Rie, 1980; see also Taylor, 1983).[4]

Two important developments occurred in 1968. First, the second edition of the American Psychiatric Association's *Diagnostic and Statistical Manual* (DSM-II; American Psychiatric Association, 1968) was published.

[4]Whether subtle neurophysiological or electroencephalographic abnormalities underlie or co-vary with the behavioral manifestations of *some* of these children is still under active investigation (e.g., Calloway, Halliday, & Naylor, 1983; see also Rutter, 1983b).

It listed Hyperkinetic Reaction of Childhood as a major category for children. Second, the federally sponsored National Advisory Committee on the Handicapped formally defined "specific learning disabilities" and provided an impetus for the passing of subsequent legislation mandating programs for LD students. Thus formal recognition was being given to narrower categories, and emphasis was shifting from presumptive neural etiology to descriptive symptom clusters.

Yet reliance on these and other descriptive definitions in the last 19 years has not, unfortunately, led to automatic clarification of matters. For one thing, operational criteria are often lacking. Neither definition from 1968 incorporated operationally defined inclusionary criteria, and even DSM-III fails to specify a precise level of achievement-intelligence disparity in its definition of Specific Developmental Disorders. Furthermore, a large and perplexing array of terms is still in use to describe the various behavioral excesses and learning problems associated with these children. This plethora of labels and titles reflects the lack of consensus in the field regarding both common core symptoms and preferred modes of evaluation; it has rendered comparison of findings across many studies in the field to be virtually impossible. An important "message" to be taken from this current state of affairs is the necessity for careful assessment within the framework of clearly thought-out evaluation strategies, both to facilitate diagnostic accuracy and to plan for proper interventions.

STRATEGIES FOR EVALUATION

In the pages that follow, a host of assessment tools and evaluation strategies will be surveyed. Throughout, pertinent research findings regarding the major procedures will be discussed. Because thorough descriptions of each measure and procedure would require an extremely lengthy format, the review will, of necessity, be selective. For purposes of organization, measures are organized with regard to diagnosis, ADD versus LD. This division is somewhat arbitrary, however, given the considerable overlap in problem behaviors and learning difficulties across the two groups. Finally, in reading the following pages, the reader must keep in mind the *goals* of the evaluation to be performed. That is, certain assessment procedures may aid in making a formal diagnosis but provide little guidance in monitoring outcome; others may be useful in planning for psychosocial or psychoeducational treatment despite a lack of normative data. Multiple modes of assessment are therefore a virtual necessity.

ATTENTION DEFICIT DISORDERS

There is no single test or test battery that specifies a diagnosis of ADD or hyperactivity (Cantwell, 1975; Sleator & Ullman, 1981). In addition, there are no unequivocal positive markers or infallible pathognomonic signs. Rather, diagnostic evaluation demands a careful consideration of information from observers in the natural environment, chiefly parents and teachers. Although not essential for diagnostic purposes, test and interview data obtained directly from the child may be of great value in gaining rapport and in facilitating psychosocial, pharmocological, and educational interventions. Although increasingly employed, laboratory measures of attention, activity level, and impulsivity are quite limited in terms of their utility for most clinical assessment.

Rating Scales. The situational nature of hyperactive children's attentional and behavioral problems is such that they rarely are displayed in a 1:1 assessment situation, particularly the office of a doctor or assessor (Sleator & Ullman, 1981). Thus information from outside informants, particularly parents and teachers, is absolutely essential for proper evaluation. In order to provide a standardized means of obtaining pertinent information about the child's social and behavioral functioning in the natural environment, a number of rating scales have been developed. The importance of such scales in current psychological evauation is underscored by the fact that several authoritative sources (e.g., Barkley, 1981a,b; Guy, 1976) require deviant scores (usually 1.5 or 2 standard deviations above norms) on standardized rating scales for establishing a diagnosis of hyperactivity.

The best known and most widely used rating scales for hyperactivity and attention deficits are the parent and teacher scales of Conners (Conners, 1969, 1970, 1973). The most recent versions include the 28-item Conners Teacher Rating Scale (CTRS), 48-item Conners Parent Rating Scale (CPRS), and 10-item Conners Abbreviated Parent-Teacher Questionnaire (CAPTQ), also known as the Hyperkinesis Index (see Goyette, Conners, & Ulrich, 1978). Factors entitled Conduct Problem, Learning Problem, Psychosomatic, Impulsive-Hyperactive, and Anxiety have been extracted from the CPRS; the revised CTRS yielded factors of Conduct Problem, Hyperactivity, and Inattentive-Passive. Scores on the scale items and factors range from 0 (*Not at All*) to 3 (*Very Much*). The scales have impressive psychometric properties, including good test–retest stability, the ability to discriminate between hyperactive and control children, sensitivity to intervention effects, and established norms in several regions of the United States and foreign countries. It is noteworthy that (a) the brief Hyperkinesis Index, composed of the 10 most frequently endorsed and treatment-sensitive items from the CPRS and CTRS, is an acceptable substitute for the longer scales when repeated assessment is required, and (b) age and sex of the child and sex of the parent—but not SES—significantly relate to the scores obtained from the scales. A detailed critique of item content and factor score interpretation is found in Ross and Ross (1982).

A problem with the Conners scales—particularly the 10-item Hyperkinesis Index—is that dimensions of hyperactivity and conduct problems are confounded (Hinshaw, 1987; Loney & Milich, 1982). As a result, samples selected on the basis of these scales will inevitably contain a preponderance of hyperactive plus aggressive children (Ullmann, Sprague, & Sleator, 1985). To "unconfound" the Conners scales, Loney and Milich (1982) retained items from the original CTRS that correlated with chart ratings of either hyperactivity or aggression—but not both—in a clinic-referred sample. The resultant IOWA Conners scale thus comprises two relatively independent subscales: five items encompassing Inattention/Overactivity and five items tapping Aggression. Scores on these subscales can be used to distinguish subgroups of hyperactive, aggressive, and aggressive-hyperactive children (Loney & Milich, 1982). The independence of such dimensions and subgroups has been documented by Milich and Fitzgerald (1985) and Johnston and Pelham (1986).

In devising another relatively recent scale that is specific for hyperactivity, Swanson, Nolan, and Pelham (1981) used the exact items from the DSM-III criteria for ADDH (see also Swanson, Sandman, Deutsch, & Baren, 1983). A subscale pertaining to peer difficulties was also included. The SNAP questionnaire thus yields quantitative scores for the dimensions of Inattention, Impulsivity, Hyperactivity, and Peer Interaction, using the same 0 to 3 metric as the Conners scales.

Data from the SNAP provided by Pelham, Atkins, and Murphy (1981) and by Swanson *et al.* (1981) present an interesting picture of the changing developmental norms for the component behaviors of ADDH. Between the ages of 6 and 11, there are decreasing trends for the amounts of inattention, impulsivity, and hyperactivity displayed by most children; in addition, boys consistently display higher frequencies of the behaviors than do girls. Thus in order to surpass the traditional cutoff of 2 standard deviations above the normative average *for his own age cohort*, a 6- to 7-year-old boy would require an overall average score (across all three DSM-III dimensions) of 2.77 out of a possible 3.00—close to *very much* for all the component behaviors. A 10- to 11-year-old boy, on the other hand, would require a score of 1.96, signifying *pretty much* of the symptoms, and a 10- to 11-year-old girl would need an average of only 1.28, closer to *just a little* of the behaviors. These striking differences highlight the need to consider *developmentally inappropriate* levels of inattention, impulsivity, and overactivity in diagnosing ADDH. Although DSM-III gives lip service to such a consideration, its defining criteria for ADD and ADDH require the same number of symptoms regardless of the child's age or sex (American Psychiatric Association, 1980). It is thus probable that younger children and boys would be overdiagnosed and older children and girls underdiagnosed by DSM-III criteria. Some investigators are now requiring the more stringent standards of deviance in comparison with same-age and same-sex norms for inclusion in a hyperactive sample (Barkley, 1982). In sum, the SNAP rating scale quantifies the defining criteria for ADDH and points out a shortcoming of categorical, nonquantitative diagnostic schemes like DSM-III.

Two major rating scales that assess a wide range of both internalizing and externalizing behaviors will be considered briefly. First, the Child Behavior Checklist (CBCL) of Achenbach and Edelbrock (1983) has undergone extensive standarization and validation (e.g., Achenbach, 1978). A recent teacher version is now available to supplement the original parent form (Edelbrock & Achenbach, 1984). The CBCL is noteworthy for its inclusion of social competence items in addition to the usual pathology questions, as well as for the patterns or "profiles" across different symptom clusters that it yields for the individual child. Among the large number of narrow-band factors of psychopathology that have been extracted, independent factors termed Inattentive, Aggressive, and Nervous/Overactive have emerged from the teacher form, supporting the independent status of these three symptom areas. Interestingly, recent research with the teacher form supports the diagnostic separation of ADD from ADDH (Edelbrock *et al.*, 1984).

Second, Quay and Peterson (1983) have provided data on their Revised Behavior Problem Checklist (RBPC). The RBPC can be completed by parents or teachers; it yields independent, orthogonal factors of Attentional Problem, Conduct Disorder, and Socialized Aggression (the latter referring to adolescent, gang-related conduct problems). Thus, like the CBCL, the RBPC supports the independence of attentional deficits and aggressive conduct problems; the validity of this distinction has been established in a kindergarten sample (Hinshaw, Morrison, Carte, & Cornsweet, in press). Furthermore, Quay and Peterson report a minor factor entitled Motor Tension-Excess—orthogonal to the Attentional Problem factor—again yielding tentative support for the DSM-III separation of attentional problems from overactivity. In terms of clinical practicality, whereas both the CBCL (over 100 items) and the RBPC (89 items) are longer than such scales as the Conners, the Iowa Conners, and the SNAP, they yield more comprehensive symptom pictures across a variety of dimensions of pathology.

An even broader questionnaire that has received recent empirical investigation with hyperactive children is the Personality Inventory for Children (PIC; Wirt, Lachar, Klinedinst, & Seat, 1977). The 600-item PIC is completed by parents; it yields three validity scales and twelve clinical scales. Breen and Barkley (1983) and Voelker, Lachar, and Gdowski (1983) provide evidence that the PIC usefully discriminates hyperactive from control children and separates favorable from poor responders to stimulant medication treatment. The PIC is likely to be increasingly employed in research endeavors.

In an attempt to elucidate the situational nature of hyperactivity, Barkley (1981a,b) has devised the Home Situations Questionnaire (HSQ) for clinical and research use with hyperactive children. This measure assesses parental perceptions of the kinds of settings and situations at home that elicit problems in behavior or compliance. In his stringent criteria for diagnosis of hyperactivity, Barkley (1982) requires that families rate at least 8 of the 16 situations as problematic. He also comments on the utility of the questionnaire for specifying intervention strategies during parent education and training.

Finally, several other scales will receive extremely brief mention. Initially devised as a measure of motor overactivity to be filled out by professionals while interviewing parents, the Werry-Weiss-Peters Activity Scale (see Werry, 1968) has been used most often as a parent questionnaire. It tends to correlate more highly with measures of behavioral disturbance or inappropriateness than with assessments of overactivity *per se* (see Werry, 1978). The Davids Rating Scale for Hyperkinesis (Davids, 1971) assesses several dimensions of hyperactivity and conduct disturbance. It can be completed by parents and teachers. Reliability and validity data have been provided only relatively recently (Zentall & Barack, 1979). In addition, Ullmann, Sprague, and Sleator (1984) and Shaywitz, Schnell, Shaywitz, and Towle (1986) have published data on newly developed rating scales that promise to separate relevant dimensions of inattention, hyperactivity, aggression, and learning problems. Please refer to Ross and Ross (1982) and Werry (1978) for a more comprehensive list of rating scales for hyperactive children; see also Edelbrock and Rancurello (1985).

A few comments about the general use of rating scales are in order. First, by their very nature, rating scales are subject to bias, halo effects, and other artifacts of the observer's personality and percepts. Because of this inherent subjectivity, different raters will display unequal thresholds for detection of deviant behavior (Pelham *et al.*, 1981). Thus there is grave doubt as to whether a deviant score on a rating scale should be a central criterion for a diagnosis of hyperactivity; certainly, it should not be the only criterion (Atkins, Pelham, & Licht, 1985; Conger, Conger, Wallander, Ward, & Dygdon, 1983; Pelham, 1982a).[5] Second, whereas ratings provide a low-cost means of evaluation, their utility is limited unless extensive normative data are available (in this regard, the CBC is clearly the best-normed instrument). Furthermore, item and factor scores from most scales do not specify the situational contexts of maladaptive behavior; thus their usefulness for treatment planning is quite limited (Barkley, 1981a). Finally, the validity of parent and teacher ratings is controversial. Different "sources" of ratings often fail to correlate with one another (e.g., Langhorne, Loney, Paternite, & Bechtoldt, 1976; see also Rutter, 1983a). Such a finding may well be expected, however, given the situational specificity of behavior. Yet there is also an often-reported lack of association between scores on rating scales and those from more objective measures, behavior observations, or psychometric tests (e.g., Conger *et al.*, 1983; Gittelman-Klein & Klein, 1975; but see Schachar, Sandberg, & Rutter, 1986). (For discussion of such issues, see Rutter, 1983a, and Whalen and Henker, 1976.) In sum, rating scales provide a first step in the evaluation process; they can often be sent to parents and teachers prior to an initial interview, in order to obtain a broad picture of current symptomatology.

Interviews. Clinical interviews with parents are a sine qua non for the evaluation of hyperactivity. Although reliability is always a concern with interview data, there is no substitute for the detailed questioning about such areas as the situational specificity of the child's behaviors, breadth of symptomatology, developmental history, parental concerns and attitudes, and family background that an interview can provide. Furthermore, the rapport engendered via the interview process will facilitate the close working relationship needed for treatment planning. Systematic guidelines for comprehensive parent interviews are provided in Cantwell (1975) and Barkley (1981b).

Two aspects—from among many—of the data obtainable from parent interviews will be highlighted. One pertains to the familial history of psychiatric illness. Whereas such information may provide a corroboration of the general finding of increased risk for alcoholism, sociopathy, and histrionic personality disorder—the "antisocial spectrum"—

[5]There is an additional problem associated with the use of a first-time rating as the sole index of behavioral deviance. Milich, Roberts, Loney, and Caputo (1980) report on the often-cited tendency for adults' initial ratings of children on the Conners APTQ to be more extreme than any subsequent ratings. In order to counter such effects, which Milich *et al.* attribute to statistical regression, initial ratings should probably be repeated soon, and the earliest rating ignored or discarded (see Whalen, 1983).

in the families of children with hyperactivity (e.g., Cantwell, 1978), recent research has identified the possibility of subgroup identification based on such familial background. August and Stewart (1983) have noted that the presence of these antisocial spectrum disorders in a biological parent of a hyperactive child is associated with a significantly increased presence of conduct disturbance in the child and his or her siblings but does not relate to the severity of overactivity or inattention *per se*. Thus, two subtypes of hyperactivity, one with a positive family history of antisocial behavior and one without, have been identified, each with different concurrent characteristics. August and Stewart (1983) hypothesize a basic independence between the two subtypes and highlight the importance of identifying the "positive" group because of the poor prognosis typically associated with aggressive and conduct-disordered behavior patterns.

Second, Barkley (1981b) recommends that interviewers employ detailed questioning with respect to the specific antecedents and consequences of the noncompliant behaviors displayed by most hyperactive children. Such assessment is of particular benefit for devising behavioral interventions that attempt to circumvent the family's vicious cycle of coercive interactions, which typically serve to escalate and maintain the problem behavior (Patterson, 1976). The key is to have parents specify precisely the interaction patterns that occur; the interviewer must take an active role in prompting and guiding the discussion. The interview format can therefore provide a wealth of detailed clinical information untapped by rating scales.

Interviews with teachers are also recommended, when possible and feasible. When combined with behavioral observations (see next section), such interview data can provide an excellent picture of the child's academic, social, and behavioral performance in the classroom (see Barkley, 1981b).

The epidemiological work on the Isle of Wight, noted earlier, also spurred interest in structured interviews with the child (see Rutter & Graham, 1968). Whereas it has typically been claimed that the child's own accounts of problem behavior are inaccurate, several structured interviews for children that include questions about hyperactivity and conduct problems have demonstrated acceptable reliability and validity (Herjanic & Reich, 1982; Hodges, Kline, Stern, Cytryn, & McKnew, 1982; Hodges, McKnew, Cytryn, Stern, & Kline, 1982; Reich, Herjanic, Welner, & Gandhy,1982; Rutter & Graham, 1968). A thorough discussion of the pros and cons of diagnostic interviews with children is beyond the scope of this chapter. It is clear, however, that parallel forms of the same basic interview schedule—one for children, one for adults—are necessary to ensure comprehensive coverage of symptomatology and to enhance validity (see Costello, Edelbrock, & Costello, 1985). In this regard, Herjanic and Reich (1982) state that children are likely to "overreport," in comparison with their mothers' accounts, such subjective symptoms as worries, anxieties, somatic concerns, psychotic symptoms, and depression, but they "underreport" school-related problem behavior and noncompliance at home. (Contrary to expectation, children were also found to overreport severe antisocial behavior if not yet discovered by authorities.) The implication for evaluation is clear: Information from both children and parents is needed in order to prevent a one-sided account of either inattentive/noncompliant problem behavior or important "internalizing" symptoms.

It would be a mistake, however, to conceive of child interviews as important only in terms of diagnostic considerations. The evaluator may gain a wealth of knowledge about the child's maturity level, interests, self-esteem, and attitudes from a thoughtful interview. With respect to attitudes, the importance of the child's conceptions about his or her label of hyperactivity and about the treatments, particularly stimulant medication, that he or she may receive has been highlighted by Whalen and Henker (1976) and Henker and Whalen (1980). In brief, the child's acceptance of a diagnosis of hyperactivity and successful treatment with medication may reinforce a belief that problem behaviors are essentially beyond personal control, fostering the attitude that personal effort is unimportant with respect to successful outcomes. Periodic interviews with the child throughout the assessment and treatment period can help the key adults to gain insight into the child's perceptions and to clarify misconceptions and distortions about the diagnostic and treatment process (see also Whalen & Henker, 1980).

Behavioral Observations. Systematic observations of children's behavior in classroom or playground settings or within parent–child interaction situations are typically associated with large-scale research efforts (e.g., Abikoff, Gittelman, & Klein, 1980; Barkley & Cunningham, 1979; Hinshaw, Henker, & Whalen, 1984; Pelham & Bender, 1982; Whalen, Collins, Henker, Alkus, Adams, & Stapp, 1978). Indeed, coordinating a crew of playground observers or nonobtrusively observing an entire classroom involves considerable practical and logistic problems, not to mention financial outlay. Nonetheless, observational strategies have yielded valuable information with regard to hyperactivity, and some smaller scale observation efforts are within the means of most evaluators.

Within classrooms, several rather intricate observation systems have reliably distinguished hyperactive from control children (Abikoff, Gittelman-Klein, & Klein, 1977; Abikoff *et al.*, 1980) as well as medicated from nonmediated hyperactive children (Whalen *et al.*, 1978; Whalen,

Henker, Collins, Finck, & Dotemoto, 1979). The distinguishing variables have been observations of on versus off task behavior, in addition to multiple categories of disruptive, noncompliant, and low-frequency but salient problem behaviors. One problem facing users of observational systems pertains to the difficulty in establishing acceptable reliability for the important latter group of rarely occurring behavioral categories (Whalen *et al.*, 1979). (For a general review of reliability issues with behavioral observation systems, see Kent & Foster, 1977.) Despite limitations in the number of categories that individual evaluators can observe, such assessors are encouraged to make direct observations in classrooms, to avoid seeing the child solely through the filter of the teacher's perceptions and to gain a better appreciation of the situational determinants of problem behavior. Only the "target" child, and perhaps a randomly selected classmate, need to be observed, and even a relatively simple count of on versus off task behaviors—plus a general category of "disruption"—can yield important data. Such behavioral information can not only document the distinguishing behaviors of the hyperactive child but can also aid in treatment planning, particularly when the observer notes the task parameters that accompany the deviant behaviors. Indeed, it is felt that school districts would be wise to hire, train, and monitor districtwide teams of observers, who could rotate through classrooms and schools on a periodic basis, to supplement their predominant mode of office-based psychometric assessment.

Playground observation is another important option, especially given the previously highlighted importance of hyperactive children's social interactions and peer relationships. Such procedures as scan sampling, which involves the repeated, brief observation of individual children in sequential fashion, are better suited than traditional time or event sampling approaches to the "wide open spaces" of a play yard (Altmann, 1974; Hinshaw *et al.*, 1984; Whalen, Henker, Swanson, Granger, Kliewer, & Spencer, in press). Yard monitors or college student volunteers in public schools could be trained to provide reliable observations of aggression and noncompliance as well as of cooperation and prosocial behavior. These data would be valuable with respect to treatment monitoring, at both an individual and schoolwide level.

A viable option for the typical office-based evaluation is the observation of parent–child interactions or peer groups. Employing the observational procedures of Mash, Terdal, and Anderson (1973), Barkley (1981b) and Barkley and Cunningham (1979) describe an approximately 40-minute mother–child interaction sequence encompassing both unstructured interchanges and specific task demands intended to elicit problem behavior. The tasks are designed to simulate the everyday interactions of a home setting. Observers rate interaction sequences from behind a one-way mirror; videotaping can also be performed. In combination with information from the Home Situations Questionnaire and from parent interviews, the observational data can provide the assessor with valuable "raw material" for the planning of specific behavioral interventions to modify problematic parent–child interactions. Of concern with respect to all such office-based procedures is their representativeness or "ecological validity," despite attempts to simulate naturalistic interchanges.

In sum, large-scale observation systems require considerable time, money, and effort. Smaller scale alternatives for naturalistic observation of classroom and playground behavior patterns were suggested, and observation of office-based interactions between parent and child can be obtained relatively easily with the use of one-way mirrors or videotape. Whereas normative data with respect to such specific interactional patterns are typically lacking, fine-grained behavioral observations are of particular benefit for assessing situational influences on behavior and thus for designing intervention strategies. They are also, typically, sensitive to treatment effects (Barkley, 1981b). Above all, they provide a necessary "behavioral anchor" to supplement the parent and teacher perceptions that constitute the bulk of the evaluation information.

Peer Sociometric Ratings. Although peer ratings are not often included in the psychological evaluation of hyperactivity and attention deficits, their increasing importance in the field merits their inclusion in the present discussion. This importance parallels the increased emphasis on the interpersonal and social difficulties of hyperactive children (Milich & Landau, 1982; Pelham & Bender, 1982; Whalen & Henker, 1985). The relevance of peer evaluations to the field of child psychopathology in general was highlighted by the often-cited study of Cowen, Pederson, Babigian, Izzo, and Trost (1973). These investigators reported that negative peer nominations in early elementary grades surpassed teacher and clinician ratings, school records, and a wide range of standardized psychometric tests in predicting psychiatric status in young adulthood. Peers were clearly "picking up" on some sorts of behavioral deviance in an important fashion, spurring renewed interest in the diagnostic and prognostic significance of peer evaluations.

Typical sociometric procedures involve children's nominating or rating their peers within such categories as popularity, social competence, or more specific behavioral descriptors (see Pekarik, Prinz, Liebert, Weintraub, & Neale, 1976). When elementary-aged children are asked to rate their hyperactive classmates, the latter are overwhelmingly disliked, rejected, and unpopular (see review of Milich & Landau, 1982). Furthermore, peers are able to assess the behaviors of their hyperactive compatriots along dimensions that are similar to adult characterizations—for example, inattentive, overactive, disruptive (Glow & Glow, 1980). Recent investigations have demonstrated that sociometric ratings are useful in discriminating hyperactive from control boys quite accurately (Johnston, Pelham, & Murphy, 1985). Furthermore, the negative appraisals received by hyperactive children appear to be stable across the elementary years (Johnston *et al.*, 1985) and are extremely refractory to otherwise beneficial interventions, like stimulant medication (Pelham & Bender, 1982). Thus peer ratings may prove to be useful in future diagnostic procedures for hyperactivity, and investigators wishing to ameliorate the social/interpersonal problems of hyperactive children will need to devise creative treatment combinations in order to alter peer status.

The growing literature on the sociometric assessment of child psychopathology in general and of ADD in particular has only been touched upon (see, for example, Dodge, 1983; Putallaz, 1983). It is predicted that the area of peer evaluation will continue to increase in importance for the field.

Medical Evaluation. Despite the present volume's concern with psychological evaluation, a few words pertaining to medical assessment are in order. Under this broad heading is included such procedures as general medical screening, physical examination, office neurological workup, and more extensive electroencephalographic and psychophysiologic evaluation. Experts in the hyperactivity field concur on several points. First, a general medical examination/physical checkup is always a good idea for the initial evaluation of hyperactivity, in order to rule out the small—but real—chance of uncovering a specific medical etiology (e.g., lead poisoning) or sensory deficit (Cantwell, 1975). In addition, if stimulant medication is indicated, baseline height and weight measurements must be taken, given the possibility of side effects that inhibit growth (see Mattes & Gittelman, 1983). Second, as described by Cantwell (1975), "a careful pediatric neurological examination should be part of the standard work-up of every hyperactive child, if only to rule out a treatable or progressive neurological disease" (p. 43). It should be noted, however, that a positive neurological examination is *not* a prerequisite for a diagnosis of hyperactivity, despite the fact that some hyperactive children display "hard" neurological signs and still more show evidence of "soft" signs (Mikkelsen, Brown, Minichiello, Millican, & Rapoport, 1982). Indeed, if positive neurological signs are required for diagnosis, as they were in many school districts nationwide during the heyday of the MBD diagnosis, the true prevalence of hyperactivity will be greatly underestimated. Finally, EEG examinations as well as metabolic/biochemical studies cannot be justified in routine evaluations unless the history or preliminary neurological examination is sufficiently suggestive to warrant the expense and time (Cantwell, 1975). In sum, careful medical examination is certainly a key part of the evaluation of the hyperactive child (see also Ross & Ross, 1982; Werry, 1978), although positive findings will occur in only a minority of cases.

Projective Measures. Many authoritative sources either virtually or entirely ignore the area of projective assessment of ADD. This lack of attention no doubt reflects, at least in part, the troubling lack of established reliability and validity for projective measures (e.g., Gittelman, 1980). Yet, as noted earlier, inattentive and overactive behavior patterns probably represent the "final common pathway" of multiple causal factors, and the possibility of biochemical or constitutional underpinnings for such behavior does not preclude the presence of concurrent intrapsychic conflict and/or troubled family interaction. Furthermore, understanding of secondary features (e.g., low self-esteem, aggression) may be aided by assessment strategies that focus on the uncovering of latent images and fantasies in addition to overt behavior. The question thus remains as to whether projective assessment can aid in the evaluation process.

The answer will, in all likelihood, be determined largely by the theoretical orientation of the evaluator. Although several experts (Satterfield, Satterfield, & Cantwell, 1980, 1981) advocate dynamically oriented individual therapy as a central facet of multimodality intervention for hyperactivity, the pendulum has certainly swung in the direction of behavioral and cognitive-behavioral modes of assessment and treatment for such children (Mash & Dalby, 1979, Mash & Terdal, 1981). As regards specific projective measures, Exner and Weiner (1982) have attempted to provide a more solid empirical basis for the scoring and interpretation of the Rorschach. In addition, children's norms are available for this instrument (e.g., Exner & Weiner, 1982; Levitt & Truumaa, 1972). The TAT has fared poorly with children, however (Gittelman, 1980), and projective techniques are, in general, all too likely to direct attention solely to within-child variables and constructs, belying the situational and transactional nature of the component behaviors. In addition, the vagueness and nonverifiability of diagnostic formulations that emanate from projective measures are felt to limit their utility for treatment planning. The interested reader is invited to consult Gittelman (1980), Mash and Terdal (1981), and Palmer (1983) for discussion of pertinent issues.

Measures of Attention, Impulsivity, Activity Level, and Learning. The multitude of individually administered measures for assessing attention, impulse control, motor activity, and learning capacity in children could easily constitute a chapter-length or book-length review. Some of these measures, however, are impractical to administer in a clinical setting; others are limited by inadequate reliability and validity; and the majority lack normative data, diminishing their contribution to diagnosis and treatment planning. This vast area will therefore receive only brief coverage.

In considering such individual assessment tools, it is essential to bear in mind the multidimensional nature of the key constructs of attention, impulsivity, activity, and learning. To take one example, "attention" is felt to encompass at least three independent (or partially independent) elements: (a) selective attention, or the ability to attend to a task in the face of distraction; (b) attentional capacity, measured by the "load" of information to which one can attend; and (c) sustained attention, often denoted by such terms as *attention span* or *vigilance* (Posner & Boies, 1971). Deficits in the latter area of sustained attention have been posited as crucial for hyperactive children (Douglas & Peters, 1979). In an attempt to determine the relative importance of these three domains for children diagnosed as ADDH, Pelham (1982b) discovered that measures of both sustained attention and attentional capacity differentiated the hyperactive children from controls. Despite these differences, however, discriminant functions did not predict group membership with great accuracy, and age was a moderator variable. Furthermore, the attention capacity task was lengthy and expensive; its test–retest reliability was also quite variable. Thus a host of considerations render the clinical utility of the various measures premature at best. Pelham (1982b), however, highlights the potential for specific measures of attention to aid in research diagnostic efforts to isolate subgroups of "attentional deficits."

Several commonly employed measures in the domains under consideration will be presented. The most frequently used assessments of sustained attention are the "family" of Continuous Performance Tests (CPT; see Kupietz & Richardson, 1978). In these vigilance tasks, children view a lengthy list of stimulus numerals or figures and attempt to recognize and indicate the presence of certain rarely occurring "signals" (e.g., the child is instructed to circle the 5s or to press a button when a 3 follows a 7). Errors of omission (neglecting to indicate a "signal" stimulus) as well as commission (incorrectly indicating any other stimulus) are scored. As indicated before, such measures have reliably distinguished hyperactive from normal children (e.g., Rapoport *et al.*, 1980). Computerized versions are now available (Gordon, 1986; Klee & Garfinkel, 1983). Whether these tasks, however, more specifically assess sustained attention as opposed to motivation or compliance to the tedious task requirements is indeterminate. As well, such tasks do not adequately represent the full domain of attentional/cognitive demands for a hyperactive child in a classroom.

Regarding impulsivity, the Matching Familiar Figures Test (MFF) is the most frequently employed assessment tool (Kagan, 1966; see also Milich & Kramer, 1984, for a review of the construct of impulsivity). In this task, children attempt to identify, from among six complex drawings, the one stimulus figure that exactly matches a sample. Thus visual discrimination and attention span, as well as impulsivity *per se,* influence performance. Scores are determined for latency (response time to choice) and accuracy (error rate). Although hyperactive children are frequently found to be "impulsive"—quick to respond—and inaccurate in comparison with controls, the MFF has received considerable criticism on conceptual and psychometric grounds (Messer, 1976). Despite improvements in format and scoring (Cairns & Cammock, 1978), the MFF is likely to be useful only as an adjunctive measure for assessing hyperactivity.

A variety of ingenious and unusual devices and measurement tools have been designed to assess the elusive construct of activity level. Actometers, pedometers, "wiggle cushions" in chairs, pneumatic floor pads, and gridded playrooms have all been employed to measure the amount of movement a child displays. Although some promising results have been obtained, these measures are often limited by their artificiality, unreliability, and lack of concurrent validity (Barkley, 1981b; Whalen & Henker, 1976). Furthermore, hyperactive children seem to be differentiated from their peers more by the quality and situational inappropriateness of their activity than by its amount *per se* (Whalen & Henker, 1976; Whalen, 1983). In a more recent study, however, Porrino, Rapoport, Behar, Sceery, Ismond, and Bunney (1983) assessed the activity level of both hyperactive and normal children in the natural environment with portable, solid-state monitors, which the children unobtrusively wore 24 hours per day. Reliable differences in activity level were found between the groups across nearly all activities, raising once again the issue of the primary versus secondary status of activity level in the conceptualization of attention deficit disorders. Yet again, the clinical utility of such an instrument is far from established.

The area of learning is perhaps the broadest and most conceptually confusing of the lot. No attempt will be made to delve into a comprehensive definition of "learning" or the multitude of assessment issues that surround the topic. Mention will be given to one influential measure, the paired-associate learning (PAL) task of Swanson, Kinsbourne, Roberts, and Zucker (1978). In this measure of new learning, children attempt to associate pictures of animals with the zoos of various cities (e.g., the bear belongs in St. Louis) or with numerals (the lion goes with 8). The number of items incorrectly remembered during recall periods subsequent to the initial presentation is the chief outcome measure. Swanson *et al.* (1978) and Swanson and Kinsbourne (1976) report that the measure is particularly beneficial for distinguishing good from poor responders to stimulant medication. That is, whereas relatively simple measures of attention or memory are drug sensitive in an overwhelming majority of both hyperactive and normal children (see Rapoport *et al.*, 1980), performance on the PAL is enhanced by stimulants in only about 60% of hyperactive children. The PAL thus leads to a more conservative criterion of medication responsiveness, and one presumably based on the important construct of the learning of new material. The relationship of this individual learning measure with established achievement and learning tasks requires further exploration.

To summarize, the many assessment tools available to the clinician and researcher have been only briefly accounted for in the present review. A pervasive issue for all such instruments is the multidimensionality of the constructs they purport to assess. Because neither attention, impulsivity, activity level, nor learning is a homogeneous "entity," different measures of a given area may well assess different components of the construct, leading to confusion in interpretation of results. In general, until such measures are better developed along conceptual, psychometric, and normative dimensions, they are likely to provide the individual assessor with only limited diagnostic or treatment-related information. Their continued development, however, should aid research investigators in understanding the fine-grained cognitive characteristics of hyperactive children.

LEARNING DISABILITIES

In this section, the focus will be on psychometric assessment of academic deficits in reading, spelling, and arithmetic and on neuropsychological evaluation of underlying processing areas. It should be remembered, however, that most of the strategies in the previous section are also pertinent to the evaluation of learning disabilities. For instance, behavioral observations are important for assessment of LD children; observers would probably wish to focus more on counts of academic task attempts and completion than on inattentive or off-task behavior alone. Parent interviews are also critical, particularly when emphasis is placed on the child's achievement history throughout schooling. Furthermore, because of the frequency of learning problems in hyperactive children, it is recommended that the latter group receive intellectual and achievement tests as part of a complete evaluation (Barkley, 1981a; Cantwell, 1975). In short, the categorization of the measures by diagnostic category is somewhat arbitrary, as both groups of children require thorough, multi-modal assessment.

Achievement and Intelligence Tests. It is impossible to survey the large number of achievement and intelligence measures available for administration to children. For comprehensive reviews of such tests, see Compton (1984) and Salvia and Ysseldyke (1985). The reader is referred to these reviews and to the test manuals referenced within each book for description of test format, testing procedures, and an overview of norming procedures, reliability, and validity. The present discussion will focus instead on some principles of learning disabilities assessment, the properties of several key measures, and interpretation of patterns of results.

As discussed at some length earlier in the chapter, a preliminary diagnosis of learning disability depends chiefly on detection of disparity between intellectual potential and actual achievement. Group tests of intelligence require children to read instructions and items; they are therefore of dubious value in determining a valid "anchor" from which to assess reading deficits. Among individual intelligence measures, the Stanford-Binet, the revised Wechsler Intelligence Scale for Children (WISC-R), the McCarthy Scales of Children's Abilities, and the Kaufman Assessment Battery for Children (K-ABC) are the most carefully normed instruments. All of these tests correlate significantly with academic achievement; the choice of which specific test to employ entails consideration of the child's age, the purposes of the assessment, and the scale's psychometric properties. Assessors must be thoroughly familiar with test procedures and scoring criteria to ensure the validity of scores obtained. In addition, given the generalized aversion to testing displayed by many children with learning problems, examiners should attempt to elicit maximum performance on these tests, through use of frequent praise for effort (but not, of course, for correctness of response; see Barkley, 1981c; Rourke, 1976).

Although the lengthy debate about both the nature of intelligence and the ethical and psychometric basis for intelligence testing cannot be covered here, there is growing discomfort with use of an overall intelligence "score" to represent a child's learning potential or capacity (see, for example, Anastasi, 1982). That is, the overall intelligence quotient used as the standard by which to assess discrepancies in academic achievement may represent a difficult-to-interpret average of discordant abilities. The patterns and interrelationships among subtest scores of intellectual measures have therefore received considerable empirical investigation. Caution is required, however, in interpreting such subtest "scatter." For example, take the commonly used Verbal-Performance discrepancy from the WISC-R. Whereas a 10-point V-P difference is often interpreted as indicative of underlying learning disabilities, it is noteworthy that (a) the *average* discrepancy across all children in Wechsler's standardization sample was nearly 10 points and (b) a 12-point difference occurred in over 33% of this sample (Kaufman, 1979). Furthermore, a host of factors—of which learning disabilities is but one—may contribute to "real" V-P discrepancies.

Problems are multiplied when the individual subtests of the WISC-R or McCarthy scales are compared with one another. Indeed, Kavale and Forness (1984) provide a scathing critique of the entire process of scatter interpretation and "profile analysis." Certainly, evaluators must consider current validational evidence regarding significant subtest scatter and current factor analytic work with respect to scale interrelationships to make valid interpretations (Kaufman, 1979). In addition, the limitations of intelligence scores in estimating the learning potential of minority and language-delayed children must be realized (Mercer, 1979).

Several comments about the four tests mentioned by name are in order. Although the Stanford-Binet is the "grandfather" of individual intelligence measures and although it can be used from ages 2 1/2 to adult, it yields only one overall IQ score, diminishing its utility for assessing meaningful components of intellectual functioning. Furthermore, it is heavily weighted with items that are verbal in nature. The McCarthy Scales display good reliability and promising validity; they contain items that may be particularly useful for children suspected of learning disabilities. The ceiling age is only 8 1/2, however, so the test is limited to use with preschool and early primary children.

The best-researched intelligence test for children is the WISC-R. It is appropriate for children from 6 1/2 to 17 years of age, rendering it useful for most assessment purposes with school-aged children. (The Wechsler Preschool and Primary Scale of Intelligence, or WPPSI, is used for children from 4 to 6 1/2.) The WISC-R has a well-defined standardization sample, excellent reliability, and established validity. It yields subtest scores, which have been the subject of extensive clinical speculation and research (see Kaufman, 1979). Factor analytic work (Kaufman, 1975) roughly corroborates the basic Verbal-Performance distinction on the WISC-R. A third factor, comprising the Arithmetic, Coding, and Digit Span subtests and variously titled Freedom from Distractibility, Freedom from Anxiety, or Sequencing, has also been identified. Kaufman (1979) provides a guide to the voluminous research on this instrument.

Finally, the K-ABC is a relatively new addition to children's intelligence measures. More than other intelligence tests considered here, the K-ABC makes an intentional separation of achievement-related items from those tapping allegedly more basic information processing. Thus the battery yields both achievement scores, comprising 6 tests of reading, arithmetic, and verbal comprehension, and a mental-processing composite score of up to 12 tests of memory, perceptual organization, and spatial abilities. These latter tests yield two major factors, entitled Sequential and Simultaneous processing. This distinction is claimed to be of benefit for determination of underlying processing deficits of learning-disabled children (see Das, Leong, & Williams, 1978); a significant disparity between either or both processing scales and the achievement scores may be indicative of learning disability.

The K-ABC is appropriate for children from 2 1/2 to 12 1/2 years. It has been vigorously normed, and the standardization sample includes adequate numbers of handicapped, minority, and preschool children. Reliability appears quite good. Interestingly, racial differences on the Mental Processing Composite score are only half those of traditional IQ scores. Limitations include the lack of coverage of important verbal and visual motor skills in the mental-processing scales. Furthermore, Sternberg (1984) has recently provided a major conceptual critique of the K-ABC, highlighting in particular its questionable construct validity as an intelligence scale. In short, the test is in its infancy, and only future research will determine the utility of the K-ABC for learning-disabled children.[6]

The achievement scale of the K-ABC is actually an abridgment of a longer achievement battery, the Kaufman Test of Educational Achievement (K-TEA). This instrument is but one of many available tests of academic functioning. Salvia and Ysseldyke (1985) organized the particularly large group of reading tests by means of a useful tree diagram, which incorporates the dimensions of the tests' purpose (screening vs. diagnostic), mode of administration (individual vs. group), and type of

[6]Before leaving the topic of intelligence testing, the reader should be aware of some of the current legal issues pertaining to such testing in schools. As reviewed by Bersoff (1984), court decisions in the 1960s and 1970s have constrained the use of intelligence testing in several regions of the country. These decisions—particularly *Larry P. vs. Riles* in California—have been based largely on claims of the cultural bias of IQ tests, as evidenced by the disproportionate numbers of minority children placed in special classes on the basis of test performance. Appeals of these decisions and other judgments with nearly opposite findings and interpretations have confused the overall picture (Bersoff, 1984). As an example of an extreme ramification, the San Francisco Unified School District has disallowed use of the WISC-R for special education placement decisions. Despite its lack of established validity, only the K-ABC is permitted, allegedly because of its less culturally influenced Mental Processing Composite (as opposed to IQ) score. Readers are advised to keep abreast of the current and complex legal decisions in their respective regions.

validation employed (norm vs. criterion referenced). The reader is referred to this organizational scheme and to the descriptions of specific reading, spelling, and arithmetic tests for guidelines in instrument selection.

Each of the three major achievement domains is broad. In assessing reading, for example, one must consider the dimension of decoding (word recognition) versus comprehension (understanding of the content of the written material). Both skills are obviously required for literacy, and assessment of comprehension is particularly important for older schoolchildren. Furthermore, whereas most tests assess silent reading, learning-disabled children may have particular difficulties with oral reading (see Boder, 1971). In discussing screening instruments, Barkley (1981c) recommends use of both the Peabody Individual Achievement Tests (PIAT), which include measures of silent reading, decoding, and comprehension, and the Gray Oral Reading Test, a speeded measure of oral reading skills. Without such multiple assessment, key areas of deficit may be missed.

The PIAT also includes tests of mathematics, factual knowledge, and spelling; it is thus a screening device with coverage of the major achievement areas. A multiple-choice format is employed on most of the subtests, however, so that children need only recognize the correct response. Particularly in the domain of spelling, actual recall of words (and writing them) is a far more difficult and important endeavor.

The often-employed Wide Range Achievement Test (WRAT), which has recently been revised (WRAT-R), is another broad screening test that surveys the major achievement areas. What is important is that its spelling test does require written responses. Yet the WRAT reading test merely assesses sight word recognition—a partial estimate, at best, of the complex process of reading. Overall, despite its popularity, the WRAT-R has been challenged with respect to its lack of sensitivity and its questionable psychometric characteristics (Witt, 1986).

Such measures as the PIAT and WRAT yield grade-equivalent scores and standard scores; they are useful chiefly for establishing a child's standing relative to the standardization samples in the assessed domains. Caution is indicated in interpreting grade-equivalent scores, which some experts have recommended abandoning (see Compton, 1984). In addition, because of the differences in format, content domains, and standardization across different achievement tests, the "same" grade or standard score may reflect different abilities (e.g., Prasse, Siewert, & Breen, 1983).

Longer and more finely differentiated diagnostic tests (e.g., Key Math Diagnostic Arithmetic Test; Gates-McKillop Reading Diagnostic Test; Stanford Diagnostic Reading Test) provide specific assessment information with direct implications for treatment planning. When time is available for thorough individual testing to help with intervention decisions, such diagnostic instruments provide a far more comprehensive data base than do screening instruments. Readers are again invited to consult Salvia and Ysseldyke (1985) and Compton (1984) for consideration of the wide group of diagnostic tests. It must be noted, however, that a great number of screening *and* diagnostic achievement tests suffer from unestablished reliability and validity and from poorly established norms. In addition, several diagnostic tests purport to assess processing areas of questionable validity. Evaluators are strongly encouraged to investigate prospective tests thoroughly. Criterion-referenced tests should be considered, particularly when one is aware of the curriculum by which the child is taught and when determination of the relative standing of children with respect to norms is not of utmost importance.

Evidence is increasing that merely specifying a given *level* of low achievement or underachievement in reading, spelling, or arithmetic is insufficient for accurately portraying learning disabilities. As highlighted by the review of Rourke and Gates (1981), children with low levels of achievement are extremely heterogeneous, and children with precisely the same degree of underachievement in a given area of functioning may display vastly different kinds of cognitive and neuropsychological characteristics. It is the *pattern* or configuration of deficits across different achievement domains that must be ascertained. Rourke and Finlayson (1978), for example, compared three groups of LD children who differed in their WRAT achievement configurations. In one key finding, two groups, equated for arithmetic disability but diverging in reading and spelling skills, yielded entirely different levels of linguistic and visual-spatial skills. Such a finding highlights the need to assess all three areas of academic functioning; it should provide a cautionary note to those who proclaim the equivalence of children with the same level of underachievement in any one academic domain.

In closing, I must reiterate that the present review does not intend to provide comprehensive coverage of intelligence and achievement tests. Rather, a framework for considering the many tests available has been presented (see Berk, 1984, for thorough treatment of the testing of learning disabled children). Examiners must not only choose and administer appropriate tests but also evaluate the properties and capabilities of the child's teacher, school, and home, as these factors will influence choice of treatment modalities. In all, if the reader has been motivated to examine more closely the psychometric, educational, and normative properties of tests to be selected for evaluation purposes, a major aim will have been achieved.

Neuropsychological Assessment. As noted earlier, most definitions of learning disabilities exclude children with clear psychosocial, cultural, or emotional etiologies. It is therefore presumed by many that subtle constitutional/neurological deficits or delays underlie the academic difficulties of a majority of these children. Indeed, interest in the application of neuropsychological evaluation strategies to LD children has surged (see reviews and volumes by Benton & Pearl, 1978; Chadwick & Rutter, 1983; Hynd & Obrzut, 1981; Knights & Bakker, 1976; Rourke, 1981; Rourke, Bakker, Fisk, & Strang, 1983). The presumption is that specification of deficits in major processing areas will lead both to finer differentiation of the heterogeneous group of learning-disabled children and to development of specific intervention strategies matched to the profiles of strengths and weaknesses. In addition, findings from neuropsychological evaluations may contribute to theoretical models of brain-behavior relationships in children (e.g., Rourke, 1982).

The field of child neuropsychology has developed into a major area of study; no attempt will be made here to describe its main tenets and procedures thoroughly. In brief, neuropsychological assessment with children entails the administration of a "large number of tests known to be sensitive to the functional integrity of the cerebral hemispheres" (Rourke, 1981, pp. 454–455). The battery used by Rourke and colleagues, for example, is based largely on the work of Reitan and Davison (1974); it includes the processing of areas of tactile-perceptual, visual-perceptual, auditory and language-related, conceptual/reasoning, and motor/psychomotor skills. Profiles of scores in these various areas are examined in comparison with norms and with one another to determine areas of strength and weakness and to provide a basis for neural specification of deficit. Although important for theoretical reasons, such wide coverage is, in practical terms, lengthy and costly, limiting the routine clinical administration of neuropsychological batteries. Furthermore, the reliability, validity, and standardization of many commonly used neuropsychological tools is not adequately established for children. In addition, because of the rapid developmental changes that all children undergo, test results will differ in meaning at different ages. Evaluators are once again encouraged to investigate carefully the instruments they wish to employ.

Many investigators have recently attempted to determine subgroups of learning-disabled children based on multivariate clustering procedures that are employed with neuropsychological test data (see reviews by Fisk & Rourke, 1983; Lyon, 1985; McKinney, 1984; Satz & Morris, 1981; see also Rourke, 1985). Although results are complex and although the statistical procedures of cluster analysis and Q factor analysis are not foolproof (Satz & Morris, 1981), there is some convergence across studies with respect to fundamental "types" of reading disability, in particular. One often-replicated subgroup displays deficits in oral-linguistic skills but shows normal visuospatial processing (cf. the dysphonetic subgroup of Boder, 1971). Another reveals deficits in visual-perceptual-motoric skills but displays relatively normal language functioning (cf. Boder's dyseidetic group). Pervasive language *and* "spatial" difficulties are evidenced in a third, "mixed" subgroup. (See Rourke and Strang, 1983, and Sweeney and Rourke, 1985, for recent evidence pertaining to subtypes of arithmetic and spelling disabilities.) Such findings, presented in their barest form here, should indicate caution to those who posit a unitary group of learning-disabled children. Investigators are now attempting to validate such putative subgroups on the basis of independent measures of achievement and differential response to intervention (see Rourke, 1985).

In sum, the neuropsychological assessment of children is a burgeoning area. Evaluators will need to keep abreast of current developments in the field, both to monitor the promising developments and to avoid "jumping on the bandwagon" of expensive, time-consuming assessment procedures that may lack sufficient psychometric rigor. Neuropsychological evaluation cannot take the place of the other assessment procedures outlined in this chapter; as indicated by Barkley (1981c) and Gaddes (1980), neuropsychological assessment can profitably be linked with interview and rating scale data and with the functional analysis of poor achievement afforded by direct observations of classroom interactions. Future reviews of the evaluation of learning disabilities will, in all likelihood, devote considerably more attention to the topic of neuropsychological assessment.

CASE DESCRIPTION

The following paragraphs describe the results of a variety of evaluation procedures employed with a boy who shows evidence of attentional deficits, hyperactivity, learning disability, and conduct problems. The case was chosen to highlight the clinical reality of assessment with a child who does not display the clear-cut, unidimensional symptomatology so often portrayed in textbooks. The reader is invited to attend to the blending of "soft" interview data with "harder" test and rating scale scores in the case conceptualization, as well as to the partial independence of the child's behavioral, educational, and psychological problems (see Keogh & Barkett, 1980).

At the time of his referral to the outpatient clinic of a community mental health center, George D. was 8 years, 0 months old. A right-handed, Caucasian boy, he was referred by his mother, who was increasingly concerned with reports of poor academic performance and behavioral disruption at school and with lying, stealing, and noncompliance at home. George attends public school, where he is a second-grader in a regular classroom. He is an only child, living with his mother, grandmother, and an elderly great-aunt in a working-class neighborhood of a large East Coast city.

Extensive parental interviews revealed, first, a nonremarkable developmental history. With regard to family history of mental disorder, it is noteworthy that George's father was alcoholic (the mother and father divorced when George was an infant) and that substance abuse, delinquency, and histrionic traits characterize George's relatives. The mother reported feeling extremely close to George throughout his childhood, actively depending on the closeness of their relationship to help her deal with the divorce. She recalled no major problems with George until kindergarten (age 5), when the teacher complained of inattention and acting out. The family pediatrician, who reported a negative physical and neurological examination, recommended counseling after further school problems were reported in first grade, but Mrs. D. terminated after one session because the therapist's questions were "too personal."

Initial interviews with George revealed a personable, friendly boy, who willingly told the interviewer about his hobbies and his friends at school. He largely denied having significant problems at school or home, and he reacted with extreme defensiveness when any attempt was made to have him do anything remotely resembling schoolwork. No evidence of affective illness, phobias, thought disorder, or intellectual impairment was noted during a structured child interview, although some aspects of separation anxiety were evident.

Conners and SNAP ratings were obtained from the current teacher and, retrospectively, from the first-grade teacher. George's overall first-grade score on the SNAP (for inattention, impulsivity, and hyperactivity combined) was 2.73; his second grade score was 2.60. Thus he was close to the *very much* rating of 3.00, attaining scores 2 standard deviations above same-age and same-sex norms for attention deficit disorder with hyperactivity. His scores on the Conner Hyperkinesis Index were somewhat lower, 2.4 and 2.1, but still in the range considered deviant by most investigators. The second-grade teacher's comments during an initial phone interview were sprinkled with such phrases as "George is able, but not performing as well as he could be," "he craves one to one attention," "peers don't like him, because he bothers them," "inconsistent," and "constantly out of his seat." She noted, as well, that George was not usually aggressive with classmates, just "out of touch" or "obnoxious." Based on the interview and rating scale data, it became clear that George met inclusionary and exclusionary criteria for ADDH.

Additional data were gathered during the initial phases of treatment. In individual therapy sessions, the mother disclosed that she had recently become pregnant by a long-term boyfriend whom she did not plan to marry. She was also becoming alarmed with George's escalating temper tantrums, his stealing of amounts up to $50 from her or her mother, and his play with matches (he had nearly started a living room fire in recent months). It was also revealed that George had been enuretic three to five nights per week for several years and that he was increasingly adamant about his refusal to comply with his mother's commands. It was therefore evident that significant oppositional and conduct problems also marked George's symptom picture and that the family system was at a point of extreme distress. It is important, however, that there was no evidence of aggression directed toward peers or adults, save for his lashing out at his mother when disciplined. Finally, informal observations of parent–child interactions revealed a persistent pattern of maternal criticism of her son even in absence of problem behavior. Punishments at home were reported to be frequent (and largely ineffectual).

Because of George's academic problems at school, individual assessment of intelligence and achievement was undertaken. Table 2 displays the WISC-R and WRAT scores that George attained at age 8 years, 1 month. Immediately apparent are the above average intelligence scores, particularly on the Verbal scales. In fact, however, George's Verbal score probably underestimates his "true" verbal potential for two reasons: (a) the Arithmetic scaled score (8), which may actually lie on another factor, depresses the verbal total; and (b) significant intratest scatter, not apparent from the

TABLE 2. INTELLIGENCE AND ACHIEVEMENT TEST RESULTS FOR 8-YEAR-OLD BOY

WISC-R

Verbal	Scaled score	Performance	Scaled score
Information	13	Picture Completion	14
Similarities	16	Picture Arrangement	11
Arithmetic	8	Block Design	10
Vocabulary	13	Object Assembly	12
Comprehension	15	Coding	5
	Verbal IQ: 118	Performance IQ: 102	
	Full Scale IQ: 112		

WRAT

Achievement area	Grade equivalent	Standard score	Percentile
Reading	2.3	81	10
Spelling	2.6	88	21
Arithmetic	2.5	85	16

table, also prevented higher scores on many tests (that is, George often missed easy items before accurately answering more difficult questions, decreasing his numerical scores). Indeed, if the three-factor "solution" to the WISC-R of Kaufman, Bannatyne, and others is employed, George is found to perform most poorly on two of the three tests (Arithmetic, Coding) that comprise the Freedom from Distractibility factor, suggesting attentional difficulties. Given his strong intellectual capacity, the below-average WRAT achievement scores—particularly in reading—are suggestive of a diagnosis of specific reading retardation or specific learning disability. Tests of oral reading skill and more comprehensive diagnostic assessments of academic subject matter would be necessary for complete evaluation.

Formal neuropsychological evaluation was unfortunately not performed with George. Informal assessment and observation, however, revealed a pattern of phonetically *accurate* misspellings of words (see Sweeney & Rourke, 1978), of letter reversals, of depressed visual-motor skills, and of difficulty in keeping his place in column addition, suggesting "dyseidetic" (Boder, 1971), poor visual motor, and/or sequential-processing difficulties (Lyon, 1985). The relatively lower Performance IQ on the WISC-R seems to corroborate such spatial difficulties. Behavior observations in the classroom revealed a virtual absence of task attention and task completion during independent desk work. Thus, in addition to any underlying processing deficits, George's classroom behavior made learning nearly impossible.

These briefly presented evaluation data led to speculation regarding prognosis and treatment planning. The severity of George's attentional problems, hyperactivity, and oppositional conduct disorder, along with the hostile and often chaotic interactions of the family, were felt to bode poorly for his eventual outcome. Indeed, the establishment of such "covert" antisocial behaviors as stealing and lying (particularly by age 8) is associated with poor prognosis (see Loeber & Schmaling, 1985). On the positive side, George was not aggressive with peers, he was bright, and his mother showed strong motivation for treatment.

Among the many questions in this case is the association between George's symptoms of ADDH and his learning and achievement difficulties: Do the clear problems in attention span and impulse control "cause" his academic deficits, or is there an independent set of learning difficulties, which may, in fact, trigger inattentive behavior? Regardless, it seemed clear that intervention should focus on direct enhancement of academic work as well as on reduction of inattentive and impulsive classroom behavior. Furthermore, observation of mother–son interactions pointed to the need for Mrs. D. to focus more on the positive behaviors that George did display and to "disengage" from a possibly overinvolved relationship with her son. In short, multimodal interventions were indicated.

Whereas space limitations prevent thorough description and analysis of the treatment procedures that were instituted, it should be noted that a "package" of individual therapy for both mother and son, conjoint family therapy sessions, and home–school reinforcement procedures was instituted. As the mother began to deal more actively with her pregnancy, to gain perspective on her relationships with significant others, and to distance herself appropriately from George, many of his home-related symptoms began to diminish. In addition, whereas slight improvements in school and behavior performance accompanied the institution of the contingency system, the addition of stimulant medication later in the school year witnessed a dramatic increase in attention and task completion. Furthermore, in order to promote generalization and maintenance of behavioral gains, George was encouraged to perform the cognitive-behavioral procedures of self-monitoring and self-evaluation. By the end of the school year, follow-up achievement testing yielded small but important improvement, suggesting that enhanced attention (via medication) and increased motivation for task completion (via the reinforcement system) were contributing to academic "catch up." Furthermore, life at home was marked by more positive interactions, more consistent and timely punishment, and a near cessation of stealing. It is, of course, impossible to specify the "active ingredients" leading to this short-term success, and the maintenance of gains is not yet ascertained. As in any clinical venture, timely reevaluation of behavioral, achievement-related, and family interactional domains will be a crucial aspect of the total intervention process.

SUMMARY

Thorough evaluation of hyperactivity, attentional deficits, and learning disabilities encompasses multiple modes of assessment. Elucidation of pertinent aspects of these closely related disorders requires reports and ratings from parents and teachers, elicitation of information directly from the child, observation of family and classroom interactions, and, in most cases, individual intelligence and achievement testing. Supplementary procedures—sociometric assessment, laboratory measures, neuropsychological evaluation—may also be profitably employed. The chapter has provided guidelines for implementation of these diverse tools.

Throughout the preceding pages, evaluators have been encouraged to investigate actively the psychometric properties of the rating scales, interview formats, observation systems, and tests they are considering. Without incorporating such information, evaluators risk using instruments that may, at worst, lack reliability, validity, or appropriate standardization, or at best, relate only tangentially to the goals of the assessment. In all, despite the youth of the scientific study of childhood psychopathology, intelligent use of evaluation strategies can help to integrate current research knowledge with the pressing clinical needs of children and families.

REFERENCES

Abikoff, H., Gittelman-Klein, R., & Klein, D. F. (1977). Validation of a classroom observation code for hyperactive children. *Journal of Consulting and Clinical Psychology, 45*, 772–783.

Abikoff, H., Gittelman, R., & Klein, D. F. (1980). Classroom observation code for hyperactive children: A replication of validity. *Journal of Consulting and Clinical Psychology, 48*, 555–565.

Achenbach, T. M. (1978). The Child Behavior Profile: I. Boys aged 6–11. *Journal of Consulting and Clinical Psychology, 46*, 478–488.

Achenbach, T. M., & Edelbrock, T. S. (1983). *Manual for the Child Behavior Checklist and Revised Child Behavior Profile*. Burlington, VT: University of Vermont, Department of Psychiatry.

Altmann, J. (1974). Observational study of behavior: Sampling methods. *Behaviour, 49*, 227–267.

Aman, M. G. (1984). Hyperactivity: Nature of the syndrome and its natural history. *Journal of Autism and Developmental Disorders, 14*, 39–56.

American Psychiatric Association (1968). *Diagnostic and statistical manual of mental disorders* (2nd ed.). Washington, DC: Author.

American Psychiatric Association (1980). *Diagnostic and statistical manual of mental disorders* (3rd ed.). Washington, DC: Author.

Anastasi, A. (1982). *Psychological testing* (5th ed.). New York: Macmillan.

Atkins, M. S., Pelham, W. E., & Licht, M. E. (1985). A comparison of objective classroom measures and teacher ratings of attention deficit disorder. *Journal of Abnormal Child Psychology, 13*, 155–167.

August, G. J., & Stewart, M. A. (1983). Familial subtypes of childhood hyperactivity. *Journal of Nervous and Mental Disease, 171*, 362–368.

Badian, N. A. (1984). Reading disability in an epidemiological context: Incidence and environmental correlates. *Journal of Learning Disabilities, 17*, 129–136.

Barkley, R. A. (1981a). *Hyperactive children: A handbook for diagnosis and treatment*. New York: Guilford.

Barkley, R. A. (1981b). Hyperactivity. In E. J. Mash & L. G. Terdal (Eds.), *Behavioral assessment of childhood disorders* (pp. 127–184). New York: Guilford.

Barkley, R. A. (1981c). Learning disabilities. In E. J. Mash & L. G. Terdal (Eds.), *Behavioral assessment of childhood disorders* (pp. 441–482). New York: Guilford.

Barkley, R. A. (1982). Guidelines for defining hyperactivity in children: Attention deficit disorder with hyperactivity. In B. B. Lahey & A. E. Kazdin (Eds.), *Advances in clinical child psychology* (Vol.5, pp. 137–180). New York: Plenum Press.

Barkley, R. A., & Cunningham, C. E. (1978). Do stimulant drugs improve the academic performance of hyperkinetic children? *Clinical Pediatrics, 17*, 85–92.

Barkley, R. A., & Cunningham, C. E. (1979). The effects of methylphenidate on the mother-child interactions of hyperactive children. *Archives of General Psychiatry, 36*, 201–208.

Benton, A., & Pearl, D. (Eds.). (1978). *Dyslexia: An appraisal of current knowledge*. New York: Oxford University Press.

Berger, M., Yule, W., & Rutter, M. (1975). Attainment and adjustment in two geographical areas: II. The prevalence of specific reading retardation. *British Journal of Psychiatry, 126*, 510–519.

Berk, R. A. (1984). *Screening and diagnosis of children with learning disabilities.* Springfield, IL: Charles C. Thomas.

Bersoff, D. N. (1984). Psychological assessment in the schools. In N. D. Reppucci, L. A. Weithorn, E. P. Mulvey, & J. Monahan (Eds.), *Children, mental health, and the law* (pp. 259–287). Beverly Hills, CA: Sage.

Boder, E. (1971). Developmental dyslexia: Prevailing diagnostic concepts and a new diagnostic approach. In H. R. Mykleburst (Ed.), *Progress in learning disabilities* (Vol. 2, pp. 293–321). New York: Grune & Stratton.

Bosco, J. J., & Robin, S. S. (1980). Hyperkinesis: Prevalence and treatment. In C. K. Whalen & B. Henker (Eds.), *Hyperactive children: The social ecology of identification and treatment* (pp. 173–187). New York: Academic Press.

Breen, M. J., & Barkley, R. A. (1983). The Personality Inventory for Children (PIC): Its clinical utility with hyperactive children. *Journal of Pediatric Psychology, 8*, 359–366.

Bryan, T. (1976). Peer popularity of learning disabled children: A replication. *Journal of Learning Disabilities, 9*, 49–53.

Bryan, T., & Bryan, J. H. (1980). Learning disorders. In H. E. Rie & E. D. Rie (Eds.), *Handbook of minimal brain dysfunctions: A critical view* (pp. 456–482). New York: Wiley.

Cairns, E., & Cammock, T. (1978). The development of a more reliable version of the Matching Familiar Figures Test. *Developmental Psychology, 14*, 555–560.

Calloway, E., Halliday, R., & Naylor, H. (1983). Hyperactive children's event-related potentials fail to support underarousal and maturational lag theories. *Archives of General Psychiatry, 40*, 1243–1248.

Cantwell, D. P. (1975). Diagnostic evaluation of the hyperactive child. In D. P. Cantwell (Ed.), *The hyperactive child: Diagnosis, management, current research* (pp. 17–50). New York: Spectrum.

Cantwell, D. P. (1978). Hyperactivity and antisocial behavior. *Journal of the American Academy of Child Psychiatry, 17*, 252–262.

Cantwell, D. P., & Carlson, G. A. (1978). Stimulants. In J. S. Werry (Ed.), *Pediatric psychopharmacology: The use of behavior modifying drugs in children* (pp. 171–207). New York: Brunner/Mazel.

Cantwell, D. P., & Satterfield, J. H. (1978). The prevalence of academic underachievement in hyperactive children. *Journal of Pediatric Psychology, 3*, 168–171.

Chadwick, O., & Rutter, M. (1983). Neuropsychological assessment. In M. Rutter (Ed.), *Developmental neuropsychiatry* (pp. 181–212). New York: Guilford.

Clements, S. D. (1966). *Minimal brain dysfunction in children—Terminology and identification* (USPHS Publication No. 1415). Washington, DC: U.S. Government Printing Office.

Clements, S. D., & Peters, J. E. (1962). Minimal brain dysfunction in the school-aged child. *Archives of General Psychiatry, 6*, 185–197.

Compton, C. (1984). *A guide to 75 tests for special education.* Belmont, CA: Pitman Learning.

Conger, A. J., Conger, J. C., Wallander, J., Ward, D., & Dygdon, J. (1983). A generalizability study of the Conner's Teacher Rating Scale-Revised. *Educational and Psychological Measurement, 43*, 1091–1031.

Conners, C. K. (1969). A teacher rating scale for use in drug studies with children. *American Journal of Psychiatry, 126*, 884–888.

Conners, C. K. (1970). Symptom patterns in hyperactive, neurotic, and normal children. *Child Development, 41*, 667–682.

Conners, C. K. (1973). Rating scales for use in drug studies with children [Special Issue: Pharmacotherapy of Children]. *Psychopharmacology Bulletin*, 24–84.

Conners, C. K., & Werry, J. S. (1979). Pharmacotherapy. In H. C. Quay & J. S. Werry (Eds.), *Psychopathological disorders of childhood* (2nd ed., pp. 336–386). New York: Wiley.

Copeland, A. P., & Weissbrod, C. S. (1983). Cognitive strategies used by learning disabled children: Does hyperactivity always make things worse? *Journal of Learning Disabilities, 16*, 473–477.

Costello, E. J., Edelbrock, C. S., & Costello, A. J. (1985). Validity of the NIMH Diagnostic Interview Schedule for Children: A comparison between psychiatric and pediatric referrals. *Journal of Abnormal Child Psychology, 13*, 579–595.

Cowen, E. L., Pederson, A., Babigian, H., Izzo, L. D., & Trost, M. A. (1973). Long-term follow-up of early detected vulnerable children. *Journal of Consulting and Clinical Psychology, 41*, 438–446.

Critchley, M. (1970). *The dyslexic child.* Springfield, IL: Charles C Thomas.

Cunningham, C. E., & Barkley, R. A. (1978). The role of academic failure in hyperactive behavior. *Journal of Learning Disabilities, 11*, 15–21.

Das, J. P., Leong, C. K., & Williams, N. H. (1978). The relationship between learning disability and simultaneous-successive processing. *Journal of Learning Disabilities, 11*, 618–625.

Davids, A. (1971). An objective instrument for assessing hyperkinesis in children. *Journal of Learning Disabilities, 4*, 499–501.

Denckla, M. B. (1979). Childhood learning disabilities. In K. M. Heilman & E. Valenstein (Eds.), *Clinical neuropsychology* (pp. 535–573). New York: Oxford University Press.

Deutsch, C. K., Swanson, J. M., Bruell, J. H., Cantwell, D. P., Weinberg, F., & Baren, M. (1982). Overrepresentation of adoptees in children with the attention deficit disorder. *Behavior Genetics, 12*, 231–238.

Dodge, K. A. (1983). Behavioral antecedents of peer social status. *Child Development, 54*, 1386–1399.

Douglas, V. I. (1972). Stop, look, and listen: The problem of sustained attention and impulse control in hyperactive and normal children. *Canadian Journal of Behavioral Science, 4*, 259–282.

Douglas, V. I. (1983). Attentional and cognitive problems. In M. Rutter (Ed.), *Developmental neuropsychiatry* (pp. 280–329). New York: Guilford.

Douglas, V. I., & Peters, K. G. (1979). Toward a clearer definition of the attentional deficit of hyperactive children. In G. A. Hale & M. Lewis (Eds.), *Attention and cognitive development* (pp. 173–247). New York: Plenum Press.

Dykman, R. A., Ackerman, P. T., Clements, S. D., & Peters, J. E. (1971). Specific learning disabilities: An attentional deficit syndrome. In H. R. Mykleburst (Ed.), *Progress in learning disabilities* (Vol. 2, pp. 56–93). New York: Grune & Stratton.

Ebaugh, F. G. (1923). Neuropsychiatric sequelae of acute epidemic encephalitis in children. *American Journal of Diseases of Children, 25*, 89–97.

Edelbrock, C., & Achenbach, T. M. (1984). The teacher version of the Child Behavior Profile: I. Boys aged 6–11. *Journal of Consulting and Clinical Psychology, 52*, 207–217.

Edelbrock, C., & Rancurello, M. D. (1985). Childhood hyperactivity: An overview of rating scales and their applications. *Clinical Psychology Review, 5*, 429–445.

Edelbrock, C., Costello, A. J., & Kessler, M. D. (1984). Empirical corroboration of attention deficit disorder. *Journal of the American Academy of Child Psychiatry, 23*, 285–290.

Exner, J. E., & Weiner, E. B. (1982). *The Rorschach: A comprehensive system: Vol. 3. Assessment of children and adolescents.* New York: Wiley.

Fisk, J. L., & Rourke, B. P. (1983). Neuropsychological subtyping of learning-disabled children: History, methods, implications. *Journal of Learning Disabilities, 16*, 529–531.

Gaddes, W. H. (1980). *Learning disabilities and brain function: A neuropsychological approach.* New York: Springer-Verlag.

Gittelman, R. (1980). The role of psychological tests for differential diagnosis in child psychiatry. *Journal of the American Academy of Child Psychiatry, 19,* 413–438.

Gittelman, R. (1983). Hyperkinetic syndrome: Treatment issues and principles. In M. Rutter (Ed.), *Developmental neuropsychiatry* (pp. 437–449). New York: Guilford.

Gittelman, R., & Feingold, I. (1983). Children with reading disorders—I. Efficacy of reading remediation. *Journal of Child Psychology and Psychiatry, 24,* 167–191.

Gittelman, R., Klein, D. F., & Feingold, I. (1983). Children with reading disorders—II. Effects of methylphenidate in combination with reading remediation. *Journal of Child Psychology and Psychiatry, 24,* 193–212.

Gittleman, R., Mannuzza, S., Shenker, R., & Bonagura, N. (1985). Hyperactive boys almost grown up: I. Psychiatric status. *Archives of General Psychiatry, 42,* 937–947.

Gittelman-Klein, R., & Klein, D. F. (1975). Are behavioral and psychometric changes related in methylphenidate-treated, hyperactive children? *International Journal of Mental Health, 4,* 182–198.

Glow, P. H., & Glow, R. A. (1980). Peer and self-rating: Children's perception of behavior relevant to hyperkinetic impulse disorder. *Journal of Abnormal Child Psychology, 8,* 471–490.

Goldberg, H. K., Shiffman, G. B., & Bender, M. (1983). *Dyslexia: Interdisciplinary approaches to reading disabilities.* New York: Grune & Stratton.

Gordon, M. (1986). Microprocessor-based asessment of attention deficit disorders. *Psychopharmacology Bulletin, 22,* 288–290.

Goyette, C. H., Conners, C. K., & Ulrich, R. F. (1978). Normative data on revised Conners Parent and Teacher Rating Scales. *Journal of Abnormal Child Psychology, 6,* 221–236.

Guy, W. (1976). *ECDEU assessment manual for psychopharmacology* (rev. ed.) (DHEW Publication No. ADM 76-338). Washington, DC: U.S. Government Printing Office.

Halperin, J. M., Gittelman, R., Klein, D. F., & Rudel, R. G. (1984). Reading-disabled hyperactive children: A distinct subgroup of attention deficit disorder with hyperactivity? *Journal of Abnormal Child Psychology, 12,* 1–14.

Helper, M. M. (1980). Follow-up of children with minimal brain dysfunctions: Outcomes and predictors. In H. E. Rie & E. D. Rie (Eds.), *Handbook of minimal brain dysfunctions: A critical view* (pp. 75–114). New York: Wiley.

Henker, B., & Whalen, C. K. (1980). The many messages of medication: Hyperactive children's perceptions and attributions. In S. Salzinger, J. Antrobus, & J. Glick (Eds.), *The ecosystem of the "sick" child: Implications for classification and treatment* (pp. 141–166). New York: Academic Press.

Herjanic, B., & Reich, W. (1982). Development of a structured psychiatric interview for children: Agreement between child and parent on individual symptoms. *Journal of Abnormal Child Psychology, 10,* 307–324.

Hinshaw, S. P. (1987). On the distinction between attentional deficits/hyperactivity and conduct problems/aggression in child psychopathology. *Psychological Bulletin, 101,* 443–463.

Hinshaw, S. P., Henker, B., & Whalen, C. K. (1984). Cognitive-behavioral and pharmacologic interventions for hyperactive boys: Comparative and combined effects. *Journal of Consulting and Clinical Psychology, 52,* 739–749.

Hinshaw, S. P., Morrison, D. C., Carte, E. T., & Cornsweet, C. (1987). Factorial dimensions of the Revised Behavior Problem Checklist: Replication and validation in a kindergarten sample. *Journal of Abnormal Child Psychology, 15,* 309–327.

Hodges, K., Kline, J., Stern, L., Cytryn, L., & McKnew, D. (1982). The development of a child assessment interview for research and clinical use. *Journal of Abnormal Child Psychology, 10,* 173–189.

Hodges, K., McKnew, D., Cytryn, L., Stern, L., & Kline, J. (1982). The Child Assessment Scale (CAS) diagnostic interview: A report on reliability and validity. *Journal of the American Academy of Child Psychiatry, 21,* 468–473.

Hynd, G. W., & Obrzut, J. E. (Eds.). (1981). *Neuropsychological assessment and the school-age child: Issues and procedures.* New York: Grune & Stratton.

Jacob, R. G., O'Leary, K. D., & Rosenblad, C. (1978). Formal and informal classroom settings: Effects on hyperactivity. *Journal of Abnormal Child Psychology, 6,* 47–59.

Johnston, C. J., & Pelham, W. E. (1986). Teacher ratings predict peer ratings of aggression at 3-year follow-up in boys with attention deficit disorder. *Journal of Consulting and Clinical Psychology, 54,* 571–572.

Johnston, C., Pelham, W. E., & Murphy, H. A. (1985). Peer relationships in ADDH and normal children: A developmental analysis of peer and teacher ratings. *Journal of Abnormal Child Psychology, 13,* 89–100.

Kagan, J. (1966). Reflection-impulsivity: The generality and dynamics of conceptual tempo. *Journal of Abnormal Psychology, 71,* 17–24.

Kahn, E., & Cohen, L. H. (1934). Organic driveness: A brain stem syndrome and an experience. *New England Journal of Medicine, 210,* 748–756.

Kanter, D. R. (1982). Etiological considerations in childhood hyperactivity. In P. Karoly, J. J. Steffen, & D. J. O'Grady (Eds.), *Child health psychology: Concepts and issues* (pp. 211–227). Elmsford, NY: Pergamon.

Kaufman, A. S. (1975). Factor analysis of the WISC-R at eleven age levels between 6 1/2 and 16 1/2 years. *Journal of Consulting and Clinical Psychology, 43,* 135–147.

Kaufman, A. S. (1979). *Intelligent testing with the WISC-R.* New York: Wiley.

Kavale, K. A., & Forness, S. R. (1984). A meta-analysis of the validity of Wechsler Scale profiles and recategorizations: Patterns or parodies? *Learning Disability Quarterly, 7,* 136–156.

Kent, R. N., & Foster, S. L. (1977). Direct observational procedures: Methodological issues in naturalistic settings. In A. R. Ciminero, K. S. Calhoun, & H. E. Adams (Eds.), *Handbook of behavioral assessment* (pp. 279–324). New York: Wiley.

Keogh, B. K., & Barkett, C. J. (1980). An educational analysis of hyperactive children's achievement problems. In C. K. Whalen & B. Henker (Eds.), *Hyperactive children: The social ecology of identification and treatment* (pp. 259–282). New York: Academic Press.

Kessler, J. W. (1980). History of minimal brain dysfunctions. In H. E. Rie and E. D. Rie (Eds.), *Handbook of minimal brain dysfunctions: A critical view* (pp. 18–51). New York: Wiley.

Kinsbourne, M., & Caplan, P. J. (1979). *Children's learning and attention problems.* Boston: Little, Brown.

Klee, S. H., & Garfinkel, B. D. (1983). The computerized Continuous Performance Task: A new measure of inattention. *Journal of Abnormal Child Psychology, 11,* 487–496.

Knights, R. M., & Bakker, D. J. (Eds.). (1976). *The neuropsychology of learning disorders.* Baltimore: University Park Press.

Kupietz, S. S., & Richardson, E. (1978). Children's vigilance performance and inattentiveness in the classroom. *Journal of Child Psychology and Psychiatry, 19,* 155–160.

La Greca, A. M. (1981). Social behavior and social perception in learning-disabled children: A review with implications for social skills training. *Journal of Pediatric Psychology, 6,* 395–416.

Lahey, B. B., Stempniak, M., Robinson, E. J., & Tyroler, M. J. (1978). Hyperactivity and learning disabilities as independent dimensions of child behavior problems. *Journal of Abnormal Psychology, 87*, 333–340.

Lahey, B. B., Green, K. D., & Forehand, R. (1980). On the independence of ratings of hyperactivity, conduct problems, and attention deficits in children: A multiple regression analysis. *Journal of Consulting and Clinical Psychology, 48*, 566–574.

Lahey, B. B., Schaughency, E. A., Strauss, C. C., & Frame, C. L. (1984). Are attention deficit disorders with and without hyperactivity similar or dissimilar disorders? *Journal of the American Academy of Child Psychiatry, 23*, 302–309.

Lambert, N. M., & Sandoval, J. (1980). The prevalence of learning disabilities in a sample of children considered hyperactive. *Journal of Abnormal Child Psychology, 8*, 33–50.

Langhorne, J. E., Jr., Loney J., Paternite, C. E., & Bechtoldt, H. P. (1976). Childhood hyperkinesis: A return to the source. *Journal of Abnormal Psychology, 85*, 201–209.

Laufer, M. W., & Denhoff, E. (1957). Hyperkinetic behavior syndrome in children. *Journal of Pediatrics, 50*, 463–473.

Levitt, E. E., & Truumaa, A. (1972). *The Rorschach technique with children and adolescents: Application and norms*. New York: Grune & Stratton.

Loney, J., & Milich, R. (1982). Hyperactivity, inattention, and aggression in clinical practice. In M. Wolraich & D. K. Routh (Eds.), *Advances in developmental and behavioral pediatrics* (Vol. 2, pp. 113–147). Greenwich, CT: JAI Press.

Loney, J., Langhorne, J. E., & Paternite, C. E. (1978). An empirical basis for subgrouping the hyperkinetic/MBD syndrome. *Journal of Abnormal Psychology, 87*, 431–441.

Loney, J., Kramer, J., & Milich, R. (1981). The hyperkinetic child grows up: Predictors of symptoms, delinquency, and achievement at follow-up. In K. D. Gadow, & J. Loney (Eds.), *Psychosocial aspects of drug treatment for hyperactivity* (pp. 381–415). Boulder, CO: Westview Press.

Lyon, G. R. (1985). Educational validation studies of learning disability subtypes. In B. Rourke (Ed.), *Neuropsychology of learning disabilities: Essentials of subtype analysis* (pp. 228–253). New York: Guilford.

Mash, E. J., & Dalby, J. T. (1979). Behavioral interventions for hyperactivity. In R. L. Trites (Ed.), *Hyperactivity in children: Etiology, measurement, and treatment implications* (pp. 161–216). Baltimore: University Park Press.

Mash, E. J., & Terdal, L. G. (1981). Behavioral assessment of childhood disturbance. In E. J. Mash & L. G. Terdal (Eds.), *Behavioral assessment of childhood disorders* (pp. 3–76). New York: Guilford.

Mash, E. J., Terdal, L. G., & Anderson, K. (1973). The response class matrix: A procedure for recording parent-child interactions. *Journal of Consulting and Clinical Psychology, 41*, 163–164.

Mattes, J. A., & Gittelman, R. (1983). Growth of hyperactive children on maintenance regimen of methylphenidate. *Archives of General Psychiatry, 40*, 317–321.

McKinney, J. D. (1984). The search for subtypes of specific learning disability. *Journal of Learning Disabilities, 17*, 43–50.

Mercer, J. (1979). *Technical Manual: SOMPA*. New York: Psychological Corporation.

Messer, S. B. (1976). Reflection-impulsivity: A review. *Psychological Bulletin, 83*, 1026–1052.

Mikkelsen, E. J., Brown, G. L., Minichiello, M. D., Millican, F. K., & Rapoport, J. L. (1982). Neurologic status in hyperactive, enuretic, encopretic, and normal boys. *Journal of the American Academy of Child Psychiatry, 21*, 75–81.

Milich, R., & Fitzgerald, G. (1985). Validation of inattention/overactivity and aggression ratings with classroom observations. *Journal of Consulting and Clinical Psychology, 53*, 139–140.

Milich, R., & Kramer, J. (1984). Reflections on impulsivity: An empirical investigation of impulsivity as a construct. In K. D. Gadow (Ed.), *Advances in learning and behavioral disabilities* (Vol. 3, pp. 57–94). Greenwich, CT: JAI Press.

Milich, R., & Landau, S. (1982). Socialization and peer relations in hyperactive children. In K. Gadow & I. Bialer (Eds.), *Advances in learning and behavioral disabilities* (Vol. 1, pp. 283–339). Greenwich, CT: JAI Press.

Milich, R., & Loney, J. (1979). The role of hyperactive and aggressive symptomatology in predicting adolescent outcome among hyperactive children. *Journal of Pediatric Psychology, 4,* 93–112.

Milich, R., & Pelham, W. E. (1986, August). Differentiating valid subgroups of hyperactive and aggressive children. In W. E. Pelham (Chair), *Subgrouping research in externalizing disorders of childhood: Toward an integration.* Symposium presented at the annual meeting of the American Psychological Association, Washington, DC.

Milich, R., Roberts, M. A., Loney, J., & Caputo, J. (1980). Differentiating practice effects and statistical regression on the Conners Hyperkinesis Index. *Journal of Abnormal Child Psychology, 8,* 549–552.

Milich, R., Loney, J., & Landau, S. (1982). Independent dimensions of hyperactivity and aggression: A validation with playroom observation data. *Journal of Abnormal Psychology, 91,* 183–198.

Morgan, W. P. (1896). A case of congenital word blindness. *British Medical Journal, 2,* 1378.

Mosse, H. L. (1982). *The complete handbook of children's reading disorders: A critical evaluation of their clinical, educational, and social dimensions.* New York: Human Sciences Press.

Orton, S. T. (1937). *Reading, writing, and speech problems in children.* New York: Norton.

Palmer, J. O. (1983). *The psychological assessment of children.* (2nd ed.). New York: Wiley.

Paternite, C. E., & Loney, J. (1980). Childhood hyperkinesis: Relationships between symptomatology and home environment. In C. K. Whalen & B. Henker (Eds.), *Hyperactive children: The social ecology of identification and treatment* (pp. 105–141). New York: Academic Press.

Patterson, G. R. (1976). The aggressive child: Victim and architect of a coercive system. In E. J. Mash, L. A. Hammerlynck, & L. C. Handy (Eds.), *Behavior modification and families* (pp. 267–316). New York: Brunner/Mazel.

Pekarik, E. G., Prinz, R. J., Liebert, D. E., Weintraub, S., & Neale, J. M. (1976). The Pupil Evaluation Inventory: A sociometric technique for assessing children's social behavior. *Journal of Abnormal Child Psychology, 4,* 83–97.

Pelham, W. E. (1982a). Childhood hyperactivity: Diagnosis, etiology, nature, and treatment. In R. J. Gatchel, A. Baum, & J. E. Singer (Eds.), *Clinical psychology and behavioral medicine: Overlapping disciplines* (pp. 261–327). Hillsdale, NJ: Erlbaum.

Pelham, W. E. (1982b, August). Laboratory measures of attention in the diagnosis of hyperactivity/attention deficit disorder. In W. Pelham (Chair), *Identification and diagnosis of children with attention deficit disorder/hyperactivity.* Symposium presented at the meeting of the American Psychological Association, Washington, DC.

Pelham, W. E., & Bender, M. E. (1982). Peer relationships in hyperactive children: Description and treatment. In K. Gadow & I. Bialer (Eds.), *Advances in learning and behavioral disabilities* (Vol. 1, pp. 365–436). Greenwich, CT: JAI Press.

Pelham, W. E., & Murphy, H. A. (1986). Attention deficit and conduct disorders. In M. Hersen (Ed.), *Pharmacological and behavioral treatments: An integrative approach* (pp. 108–148). New York: Wiley.

Pelham, W. E., Atkins, M. S., & Murphy, H. A. (1981, August). Attention deficit disorder with and without hyperactivity: Definitional issues and correlates. In W. Pelham (Chair), *DSM-III category of attention deficit disorder: Rationale, operationalization, and correlates*. Symposium presented at the meeting of the American Psychological Association, Los Angeles.

Peter, B. M., & Spreen, O. (1979). Behavior rating and personal adjustment scales of neurologically and learning handicapped children during adolescence and early adulthood: Results of a follow-up study. *Journal of Clinical Neuropsychology, 1*, 17–37.

Porrino, L. J., Rapoport, J. L., Behar, D., Sceery, W., Ismond, D. R., & Bunney, W. E. (1983). A naturalistic assessment of the motor activity of hyperactive boys: I. Comparison with normal controls. *Archives of General Psychiatry, 40*, 681–687.

Posner, M., & Boies, S. (1971). Components of attention. *Psychological Review, 78*, 391–408.

Prasse, D. P., Siewert, J. C., & Breen, M. J. (1983). An analysis of performance on reading subtests from the 1978 Wide Range Achievement Test and Woodcock Mastery Test with the WISC-R for learning disabled and regular education students. *Journal of Learning Disabilities, 16*, 458–461.

Prinz, R. J., Connor, P. A., & Wilson, C. C. (1981). Hyperactive and aggressive behaviors in childhood: Intertwined dimensions. *Journal of Abnormal Child Psychology, 9*, 191–202.

Putallaz, M. (1983). Predicting children's sociometric status from their behavior. *Child Development, 54*, 1417–1426.

Quay, H. C. (1979). Classification. In H. C. Quay & J. S. Werry (Eds.), *Psychopathological disorders of childhood* (2nd ed., pp. 1–42). New York: Wiley.

Quay, H. C. (1986). Classification. In H. C. Quay & J. S. Werry (Eds.), *Psychopathological disorders of childhood* (3rd ed., pp. 1–34). New York: Wiley.

Quay, H. C., & Peterson, D. R. (1983). *Interim manual for the Revised Behavior Problem Checklist* (1st ed.). Unpublished manuscript, University of Miami.

Rapoport, J. L., & Ismond, D. R. (1984). *DSM-III training guide for diagnosis of childhood disorders*. New York: Brunner/Mazel.

Rapoport, J. L., Buchsbaum, M. S., Weingartner, H., Zahn, T. P., Ludlow, C., & Mikkelsen, E. J. (1980). Dextroamphetamine—Its cognitive and behavioral effect in normal and hyperactive boys and normal men. *Archives of General Psychiatry, 37*, 933–943.

Reich, W., Herjanic, B., Welner, Z., & Gandhy, P. R. (1982). Development of a structured interview for children: Agreement on diagnosis comparing child and parent interviews. *Journal of Abnormal Child Psychology, 10*, 325–336.

Reitan, R. M., & Davison, L. A. (1974). *Clinical neuropsychology: Current status and applications*. Washington, DC: V. H. Winston.

Rie, H. E., & Rie, E. D. (Eds.). (1980). *Handbook of minimal brain dysfunctions: A critical view*. New York: Wiley.

Ross, D. M., & Ross, S. A. (1982). *Hyperactivity: Current issues, research, and theory*. New York: Wiley.

Rourke, B. P. (1976). Issues in the neuropsychological assessment of children with learning disabilities. *Canadian Psychological Review, 17*, 89–102.

Rourke, B. P. (1981). Neuropsychological assessment of children with learning disabilities. In S. B. Filskov & T. J. Boll (Eds.), *Handbook of clinical neuropsychology* (pp. 453–478). New York: Wiley.

Rourke, B. P. (1982). Central processing deficiencies in children: Toward a developmental neuropsychological model. *Journal of Clinical Neuropsychology, 4*, 1–18.

Rourke, B. P. (Ed.). (1985). *Neuropsychology of learning disabilities: Essentials of subtype analysis*. New York: Guilford.

Rourke, B. P., & Finlayson, M. A. J. (1978). Neuropsychological significance of variations in patterns of academic performance: Verbal and visual-spatial abilities. *Journal of Abnormal Child Psychology, 6,* 121–133.

Rourke, B. P., & Gates, R. D. (1981). Neuropsychological research and school psychology. In G. W. Hynd & J. E. Obrzut (Eds.), *Neuropsychological assessment and the school-age child* (pp. 3–25). New York: Grune & Stratton.

Rourke, B. P., & Strang, J. D. (1983). Subtypes of reading and arithmetical disabilities: A neuropsychological analysis. In M. Rutter (Ed.), *Developmental neuropsychiatry* (pp. 473–488). New York: Guilford.

Rourke, B. P., Bakker, D. J., Fisk, J. L., & Strang, J. D. (1983). *Child neuropsychology: An introduction to theory, research, and clinical practice.* New York: Guilford.

Rutter, M. (1978). Prevalence and types of dyslexia. In A. L. Benton & D. Pearl (Eds.), *Dyslexia: An appraisal of current knowledge* (pp. 5–28). New York: Oxford University Press.

Rutter, M. (1982). Syndromes attributed to "minimal brain dysfunction" in childhood. *American Journal of Psychiatry, 139,* 21–33.

Rutter, M. (1983a). Behavioral studies: Questions and findings on the concept of a distinctive syndrome. In M. Rutter (Ed.), *Developmental neuropsychiatry* (pp. 259–279). New York: Guilford.

Rutter, M. (Ed.). (1983b). *Developmental neuropsychiatry.* New York: Guilford.

Rutter, M., & Graham, P. (1968). The reliability and validity of the psychiatric assessment of the child: I. Interview with the child. *British Journal of Psychiatry, 114,* 563–579.

Rutter, M., & Yule, W. (1975). The concept of specific reading retardation. *Journal of Child Psychology and Psychiatry, 16,* 181–197.

Rutter, M., Tizard, J., & Whitmore, K. (Eds.). (1970). *Education, health, and behavior.* London, Longmans.

Safer, D. J., & Allen, R. P. (1976). *Hyperactive children: Diagnosis and management.* Baltimore: University Park Press.

Salvia, J., & Ysseldyke, J. E. (1985). *Assessment in special and remedial education* (3rd ed.). Boston: Houghton Mifflin.

Sandberg, S. T., Rutter, M., & Taylor, E. (1978). Hyperkinetic disorder in psychiatry clinic attenders. *Developmental Medicine and Child Neurology, 20,* 279–299.

Sandoval, J., Lambert, N. M., & Sassone, D. (1980). The identification and labeling of hyperactivity in children: An interactive model. In C. K. Whalen & B. Henker (Eds.), *Hyperactive children: The social ecology of identification and treatment* (pp. 145–171). New York: Academic Press.

Satterfield, J. H., Satterfield, B. T., & Cantwell, D. P. (1980). Multimodality treatment: A two-year evaluation of 61 hyperactive boys. *Archives of General Psychiatry, 37,* 915–918.

Satterfield, J. H., Satterfield, B. T., & Cantwell, D. P. (1981). Three-year multimodality treatment study of 100 hyperactive boys. *Journal of Pediatrics, 98,* 650–655.

Satterfield, J. H., Hoppe, C. M., & Schell, A. M. (1982). A prospective study of delinquency in 110 adolescent boys with attention deficit disorder and 88 normal adolescent boys. *American Journal of Psychiatry, 139,* 795–798.

Satz, P., & Fletcher, J. M. (1980). Minimal brain dysfunctions: An appraisal of research concepts and methods. In H. E. Rie & E. D. Rie (Eds.), *Handbook of minimal brain dysfunctions: A critical view* (pp. 669–714). New York: Wiley.

Satz, P., & Morris, R. (1981). Learning disability subtypes: A review. In F. J. Pirozzolo & M. C. Wittrock (Eds.), *Neuropsychological and cognitive processes in reading* (pp. 109–141). New York: Academic Press.

Schachar, R., Sandberg, S., & Rutter, M. (1986). Agreement between teachers' ratings and observations of hyperactivity, inattentiveness, and defiance. *Journal of Abnormal Child Psychology, 14,* 331–345.

Schere, R. A., Richardson, E., & Bialer, I. (1980). Toward operationalizing a psychoeducational definition of learning disabilities. *Journal of Abnormal Child Psychology, 8,* 5–20.

Schonhaut, S., & Satz, P. (1983). Prognosis for children with learning disabilities: A review of follow-up studies. In M. Rutter (Ed.), *Developmental neuropsychiatry* (pp. 542–563). New York: Guilford.

Shaffer, D. (1980). An approach to the validation of clinical syndromes in childhood. In S. Salzinger, J. Antrobus, & J. Glick (Eds.), *The ecosystem of the "sick" child* (pp. 31–45). New York: Academic Press.

Shaywitz, S. E., Schnell, C., Shaywitz, B. A., & Towle, V. R. (1986). Yale Children's Inventory (YCI): An instrument to assess children with attentional deficits and learning disabilities I. Scale development and psychometric properties. *Journal of Abnormal Child Psychology, 14,* 347–364.

Silva, P. A., McGee, R., & Williams, S. (1985). Some characteristics of 9-year-old boys with general reading backwardness or specific reading retardation. *Journal of Child Psychology and Psychiatry, 26,* 407–421.

Silver, L. B. (1980). The relationship between learning disabilities, hyperactivity, distractibility, and behavioral problems: A clinical analysis. *Journal of the American Academy of Child Psychiatry, 20,* 385–397.

Sleator, E. K., & Ullman, R. K. (1981). Can the physician diagnose hyperactivity in the office? *Pediatrics, 67,* 13–17.

Sternberg, R. J. (1984). The Kaufman Assessment Battery for Children: An information-processing analysis and critique. *Journal of Special Education, 18,* 269–279.

Stewart, M. A., Cummings, C., Singer, S., & deBlois, C. S. (1981). The overlap between hyperactive and unsocialized aggressive children. *Journal of Child Psychology and Psychiatry, 22,* 35–45.

Still, G. F. (1902). Some abnormal psychical conditions in children. *Lancet, 1,* 1077–1082.

Straus, A. A., & Kephart, N. C. (1948). *Psychopathology and education of the brain injured child* (Vol. 1). New York: Grune & Stratton.

Swanson, J. M., & Kinsbourne, M. (1976). Stimulant-related state-dependent learning in hyperactive children. *Science, 192,* 1354–1357.

Swanson, J., Kinsbourne, M., Roberts, W., & Zucker, K. (1978). Time response analysis of the effect of stimulant medication on the learning ability of children referred for hyperactivity. *Pediatrics, 61,* 21–29.

Swanson, J., Nolan, W., & Pelham, W. (1981, August). *The SNAP rating scale for the diagnosis of the attention deficit disorder.* Paper presented at the meeting of the American Psychological Association, Los Angeles.

Swanson, J. M., Sandman, C. A., Deutsch, C., & Baren, M. (1983). Methylphenidate hydrochloride given with or before breakfast: I. Behavioral, cognitive, and electrophysiologic effects. *Pediatrics, 72,* 49–55.

Sweeney, J. E., & Rourke, B. P. (1978). Neuropsychological significance of phonetically accurate and phonetically inaccurate spelling errors in younger and older retarded spellers. *Brain and Language, 6,* 212–225.

Sweeney, J. E., & Rourke, B. P. (1985). Spelling disability subtypes. In B. P. Rourke (Ed.), *Neuropsychology of learning disabilities: Essentials of subtype analysis* (pp. 147–166). New York: Guilford.

Taylor, H. G. (1983). MBD: Meanings and misconceptions. *Journal of Clinical Neuropsychology, 5*, 271–287.

Tucker, J., Stevens, L. J., & Ysseldyke, J. E. (1983). Learning disabilities: The experts speak out. *Journal of Learning Disabilities, 16*, 6–14.

Ullmann, R. K., Sleator, E. K., & Sprague, R. L. (1984). A new rating scale for diagnosis and monitoring of ADD children. *Psychopharmacology Bulletin, 20*, 160–164.

Ullmann, R. K., Sleator, E. K., & Sprague, R. L. (1985). A change of mind: The Conners Abbreviated Rating Scales reconsidered. *Journal of Abnormal Child Psychology, 13*, 553–565.

U.S. Office of Education (1977). Assistance to states for education of handicapped children: Procedures for evaluating specific learning disabilities. *Federal Register, 43*, 65082–65085.

Voelker, S., Lachar, D., & Gdowski, C. L. (1983). The Personality Inventory for Children and response to methylphenidate: Preliminary evidence for predictive utility. *Journal of Pediatric Psychology, 8*, 161–169.

Weiss, G., Hechtman, L., Perlman, T., Hopkins, J., & Wener, A. (1979). Hyperactives as young adults: A controlled prospective ten-year follow-up of 75 children. *Archives of General Psychiatry, 36*, 675–681.

Wender, P. H. (1971). *Minimal brain dysfunction in children*. New York: Wiley.

Werry, J. S. (1968). Developmental hyperactivity. *Pediatric Clinics of North America, 15*, 581–599.

Werry, J. S. (1978). Measures in pediatric psychopharmacology. In J. S. Werry (Ed.), *Pediatric psychopharmacology: The use of behavior modifying drugs in children* (pp. 29–78). New York: Brunner/Mazel.

Werry, J. S., Methven, R. J., Fitzpatrick, J., & Dixon, H. (1983). The interrater reliability of DSM-III in children. *Journal of Abnormal Child Psychology, 11*, 341–354.

Whalen, C. K. (1983). Hyperactivity, learning problems, and the attention deficit disorders. In T. H. Ollendick & M. Hersen (Eds.), *Handbook of child psychopathology* (pp. 151–199). New York: Plenum Press.

Whalen, C. K., & Henker, B. (1976). Psychostimulants and children: A review and analysis. *Psychological Bulletin, 83*, 1113–1130.

Whalen, C. K., & Henker, B. (1980). The social ecology of psychostimulant treatment: A model for conceptual and empirical analysis. In C. K. Whalen & B. Henker (Eds.), *Hyperactive children: The social ecology of identification and treatment* (pp. 3–51). New York: Academic Press.

Whalen, C. K., & Henker, B. (1985). The social worlds of hyperactive (ADDH) children. *Clinical Psychology Review, 5*, 447–478.

Whalen, C. K., Collins, B. E., Henker, B., Alkus, S. R., Adams, D., & Stapp, J. (1978). Behavior observations of hyperactive children and methylphenidate (Ritalin) effects in systematically structured classroom environments: Now you see them, now you don't. *Journal of Pediatric Psychology, 3*, 177–187.

Whalen, C. K., Henker, B., Collins, B. E., Finck, D., & Dotemoto, S. (1979). A social ecology of hyperactive boys: Medication effects in systematically structured classroom environments. *Journal of Applied Behavior Analysis, 12*, 65–81.

Whalen, C. K., Henker, B., & Dotemoto, S. (1980). Methylphenidate and hyperactivity: Effects on teacher behaviors. *Science, 208*, 1280–1282.

Whalen, C. K., Henker, B., & Dotemoto, S. (1981). Teacher response to the methylphenidate (Ritalin) versus placebo status of hyperactive boys in the classroom. *Child Development, 52*, 1005–1014.

Whalen, C. K., Henker, B., Swanson, J. M., Granger, D., Kliewer, W., & Spencer, J. (in press). Natural social behaviors of hyperactive children: Dose effects of methylphenidate. *Journal of Consulting and Clinical Psychology*.

Wirt, R., Lachar, D., Klinedinst, J., & Seat, P. (1977). *Multidimensional description of child personality: A manual for the Personality Inventory for Children*. Los Angeles: Western Psychological Services.

Witt, J. C. (1986). Review of the Wide Range Achievement Test-Revised. *Journal of Psychoeducational Assessment, 4*, 87–90.

Yule, W., Rutter, M., Berger, M., & Thompson, J. (1974). Over- and under-achievement in reading: Distribution in the general population. *British Journal of Educational Psychology, 44*, 1–12.

Zentall, S. S., & Barack, R. S. (1979). Rating scales for hyperactivity: Concurrent validity, reliability, and decisions to label for the Conners and Davids Abbreviated Scales. *Journal of Abnormal Child Psychology, 7*, 179–190.

10

Speech and Language Disorders

ELLIN SIEGEL-CAUSEY, ED SCHULTE, AND DOUG GUESS

INTRODUCTION

The process of communication is a highly complex and multifaceted developmental skill. Communicative competence can be viewed as "the development of separable but interdependent systems" (Hollos, 1977, p. 211) that allow persons to represent and express their needs, ideas, emotions, and beliefs in a variety of forms and levels. This chapter will present discernible aspects appropriate to assessing the dynamic, complex processes of communication, speech, and language.

Communication, speech, and language are often assumed to be synonymous. It is, however, important to make the following distinctions between these terms when evaluating communication disorders.

Communication may be viewed as the transmission of a message (idea, thought, feeling, or intent) from one person to another. One can communicate by using words, a smile, an outstretched hand, a photograph, or a giggle. *Language* is defined as a learned, arbitrary symbol system used to convey messages. Language may take such forms as spoken or written words, sign language, or graphic symbols. The element that binds language systems is their use of representational symbols to convey meaning. *Speech* is the oral-motor production of an audible sound pattern taking the form of a language code. Verbal behavior is extremely flexible because an infinite number and variety of communicative messages may be conveyed by manipulating surface content and production features.

ELLIN SIEGEL-CAUSEY • Special Education Department, University of Kansas, Lawrence, Kansas 66045. ED SCHULTE • Kansas University Affiliated Facility, Lawrence, Kansas 66045. DOUG GUESS • Special Education Department, University of Kansas, Lawrence, Kansas 66045.

Although speech and language are the most commonly recognized forms of expression, communication can and does exist on a number of levels; both verbal and nonverbal, linguistic and nonlinguistic. It is the focus of this chapter to present a broad perspective of communication evaluation. This will include a continuum of development (Figure 1) from prelinguistic (prior to language acquisition) to linguistic and acquired communication disorders.

The common definition of a communication disorder warranting evaluation is one that (a) interferes with the transmission of messages, (b) stands out as being unusually different, (c) produces negative feelings within the communicator (Taylor, 1982), and (d) is potentially harmful to the speech mechanism.

PURPOSE OF COMMUNICATION EVALUATION

The evaluation process requires detailed analysis of information relevant to specific assessment purposes or outcomes. The process begins with an evaluation purpose and concerns including questions of why assess (goals), what to assess (content), and how to assess (method) (Miller, 1978). Language and communication evaluation involve different assessment levels. These are prescreening, screening, diagnostic assessment, and assessment for programming.

There is enormous variability in acquisition of communication strategies, communication environments, and patterns of delay or deviance in communication skills. In addition, the responsibility for assessment may vary, depending on the type of service delivery approach utilized and the professional staff available. Generally, the responsibility is shared between a communication disorders specialist (usually a speech-language pathologist), the primary service provider (e.g., educator, classroom teacher, primary care physician), the psychologist, and/or members of other related disciplines when available.

An effort will be made to synthesize the various purposes of evaluation, using the format of initial identification (prescreening), general evaluation (screening), nature and extent of problem (diagnosis), and baseline and progress (assessment for programming). Each will focus on specific aspects of communication or language behavior. The

Nonlinguistic skills ——→ Prelinguistic skills ——→ Linguistic skills ——→ Acquired communication disorders

Birth ——→ 9 months ——→ 12–15 months ——→ 7 years ——→

FIGURE 1. Continuum of communication development.

complexity of this task is clear; "there is no single, all-purpose format for language assessment" (Schiefelbusch & McCormick, 1984, p. 118).

INTERDISCIPLINARY EVALUATION NEEDS

An adequate evaluation of communication and language skills must occur in conjunction with other assessments in the areas of vision, hearing, neurological status, perceptual motor skills, social competency, and behavioral deviance. This is because processes in a communication system are based on real physiological and psychological events. From a physical standpoint, the act of communicating entails the production of raw stimuli, such as sound, movement, or gesture. These may in turn be detected through the receptive modalities of another individual (primarily visual, auditory, or tactile channels). This information is then transformed into a neural code by the individual receiver and interpreted on the basis of this individual's stored knowledge. Deficits in any of the areas of production, reception, or cognitive processing will result in a loss of information and the increased likelihood that the message will not be communicated successfully. Assessment of a communication disorder must be carried out on an individual basis with consideration of the overall functioning level of each person. Recommendations and considerations from other chapters in this volume should be integrated into communication evaluation.

Specific aspects that provide adequate assessment of communication and language are offered by Stremel-Campbell (1982, p. 215):

1. Behaviors within each component of speech, language, and communication must be assessed and skill level determined.
2. Assessment should be directly related to training and provide more than an intelligence score or mental age; an assessment of general student functioning should be conducted.
3. Assessment should show not only what the student cannot do (needs) but also what the student can do (skills).
4. Assessment should be current.
5. Assessment must be continuous and constantly provide input into the training process.

DESCRIPTION OF FORMAT

The format of the chapter takes into consideration the range of communication expressions that might be exhibited by a person with developmental or physical disorders. Consequently, the evaluation format includes information regarding vocal and nonvocal langage modes.

A brief overview of the following categories will be provided:

1. Prespeech behaviors
2. Speech disorders: articulation, phonation-resonance, disfluency, and prosody
3. Language components: semantics, syntax, morphology, and pragmatics
4. Nonvocal communication modes

Table 1 provides a synthesis of the chapter content. A thorough communication evaluation includes all levels of assessment purposes (why), processes (what), and procedures (how). The table is structured by addressing the basic components of evaluation: Why assess, what to assess, and how to assess.

DEVELOPMENT AND COMPONENTS OF COMMUNICATION SYSTEMS

NONLINGUISTIC ASPECTS OF COMMUNICATION

It is not uncommon for assessment of communication and language to focus strictly on the aspects of verbal (production of words) or vocal (production of sounds) usage. Communication can be viewed as the transmission and reception of a message from one person to another. This can be done with symbols (e.g., through speech, sign language, pictures) or without using symbols (e.g., vocal sounds, eye contact, facial expression). Given the varied transmission modes, Irwin (1982, p. 22) provides a diagram of the process of communication:

Sender → Message → Receiver

Prior to the development of speech, there are nonlinguistic elements that form the basis for future language acquisition. Many persons experiencing physical or mental disabilities may exhibit delay in the early, nonlinguistic development stages. In addition, some persons may not develop adequate verbal communication skills or may lose basic skills as a result of traumatic injury. It is therefore important that language and speech evaluation encompass the nonlinguistic variables of communication development, including responses to sensory and social input, and interactions with objects.

Purposes of Early, Nonlinguistic Acquisition. The foundation of language development originates at the nonlinguistic level as infants interact

TABLE 1. PROCESSES IN ASSESSMENT OF COMMUNICATION AND LANGUAGE

Why	What	How
I. Prescreening: initial identification of individuals/groups requiring screening for communication impairment. II. Screening: general evaluation of communicative functioning and related competencies to identify presence of a problem. III. Diagnostic assessment: identification of nature and extent of communicative problem IV. Assessment for programming: A. Establish baseline functioning; identify current performance levels in natural environments and in relationship to specific objectives B. Assessment of progress; establish nature of behavioral change during and following intervention	I. Processes in communication systems A. Sensory/receptive functioning B. Cognitive functioning C. Productive modalities D. Alternative or augmentative capabilities II. Development and components of communication systems A. Nonlinguistic B. Prelinguistic C. Linguistic structure D. Linguistic content III. Environmental factors A. Pragmatics: context of use B. Communication environments C. Communication needs of the individual D. Personnel involved; service delivery model	I. Procedures and techniques A. Standardized tests B. Nonstandardized tests C. Developmental scales D. Behavioral observation

Note. From "Assessing Children's Language Behavior: A Developmental Process Approach," (pp. 269–318) by J. Miller. In R. Schiefelbusch (Ed.), *Bases of Language Intervention*, 1978, Baltimore: University Park Press. Copyright 1978 by University Park Press. Adapted by permission.

with persons and events in their environment. Caregivers consistently respond to early, nonlinguistic behavior as if they were intentional communicative attempts. Infants and young children learn to communicate nonliguistically with their eyes, facial expressions, and body movements. The success of their communication is dependent on learning they have something to communicate about (content), a means of expression (nonlinguistic form), and a reason to communicate (Bloom, 1970). Some of the outcomes of this initial, nonlinguistic stage are the development of cause and effect, social awareness, engagement of attention, separation of self from environment and persons, desire to communicate, responsiveness to communication, and signaling of communication. Deficits in these early behaviors may impair communication development, inhibit progress, and prolong preverbal stages. It is imperative that diagnostic assessment, baseline functioning assessment, and assessment of progress begin with orientation to these prerequisite behaviors.

"Long before they speak their first words, infants communicate with people around them" (Ziajka, 1981, p. 81). In the same manner that the nonlinguistic infant communicates, the nonlinguistic individual may engage in interactions. It is important that assessment focus on the nonlinguistic individual's display of nonverbal expressions (without words) of pleasure, displeasure, hunger, thirst, protest, request, greeting, and preference. The importance of nonlinguistic communication in infancy in relationship to later language acquisition is recognized by many researchers (Elliott, 1984; McClean & Snyder-McClean, 1978; Rogers-Warren & Warren, 1984; Rogow, 1984; Ziajka, 1981). Infants and children learn to use their body movements, eyes, facial expression, touch, laughter, and gestures to communicate. Early communication outcomes include mutual attention, turn taking, synchrony of signals, and initiation and sustaining interactions. These early communicative behaviors transmit messages to others and form the basis for future language development.

Nonlinguistic Skills and Assessment. "Random vocalizations, hand movements, or body posture can be transformed into effective social signals when adults respond in meaningful consistent ways" (Rogow, 1984, p. 69). By recognizing the importance of early nonlinguistic development and utilizing assessment formats, service providers may identify the nature and extent of the client's nonverbal behavior, determine current performance levels, and evaluate the changes resulting from communication intervention. This type of an evaluation process promotes an awareness of nonlinguistic skill acquisition and the possible focus of intervention.

An extensive review of the multifaceted behaviors included in nonlinguistic development is not within the scope of this chapter. Some of the potentially important nonlinguistic behaviors are visual fixation and tracking, auditory discrimination and localization, participation in familiar routines, imitation of gestures and actions, initiation of attention of others by utilizing eye contact, smiles, and/or vocalizations. Table 2 displays these behaviors and their approximate acquisition age. This table may aid the evaluation process in focusing on the scope and ontongeny of nonlinguistic development. (Similar behaviors may also be important in evaluating basic competencies in severe acquired disorders such as global aphasia.) Specific assessments that contain evaluation components of nonlinguistic development are displayed in the Appendix.

PRELINGUISTIC ASPECTS OF COMMUNICATION

The nonlinguistic behaviors displayed in the left portion of Table 2 include nonverbal behaviors normally acquired between birth and 9 months of age. At approximately the 9-month developmental age, children have acquired intentionality and the ability to utilize nonverbal behaviors to produce desired responses or interactions (e.g., gesturing for "no," getting attention of others, indicating displeasure). Prelinguistic development is not comprised of symbolic representation or rules for sequencing symbols. Instead, at the prelinguistic level, the child from 9 months of age to approximately 12 to 15 months continues to learn important communicative behaviors prior to speaking the first words. "Formal language use is one point on a continuum of communication behaviors that begins in nonverbal social exchanges during infancy and extends through the use of written language" (Rogers-Warren & Warren, 1984, p. 8). The prelinguistic behaviors on this continuum consist of the refinement of nonverbal (without words) behaviors to express wants, needs, feelings, and preferences. The communication evaluation at the prelinguistic level includes assessment of (a) expressive development with refinements of *nonverbal* behaviors and additional *vocal* (production of sounds) behaviors; and (b) receptive development with attention to verbal aspects (response to words) and nonverbal aspects (gestures, facial expression).

Prelinguistic Skills and Assessment. Early prelinguistic expressive and receptive processes allow the child to refine the communication skills that began at birth. Utilization of assessment instruments that focus on the prelinguistic levels provides a broader perspective of what communication development encompasses. Service providers may identify the nature and extent of an individual's expressive and receptive

TABLE 2. NONLINGUISTIC AND PRELINGUISTIC COMMUNICATIVE DEVELOPMENT

Sensory responses	Fixation on familiar person or object. Visually tracks side to side. Visually searches for sound.	Localizes sound by head or eye movement. Turns head to localize familiar sounds.	Tries to gain attention through eye contact, smile, vocalizations.	Follows trajectory of a moving object and moves to look for it.
Social interactions	Smiles to familiar voice and to adult's smile. Turns or quiets to personal contact.	Laughs when engaged in pleasurable activity—alone or with others. Participates in familiar movements. Smiles at familiar person interacting with them.	Continues familiar movement when contact is maintained. Extends arms to be picked up. Resists by pushing or refusing.	Indicates displeasure vocally or motorically. Imitates action. Anticipates and demonstrates next action in a series.
Object interactions		Increases/decreases activity level on seeing interesting object. Looks back and forth between two objects.	Demonstrates four or more actions on objects. Reaches and takes objects partially hidden. Recognizes two familiar objects as part of activity using contextual cues.	Acts on objects differentially.
Expressive development: nonvocal		Anticipates a familiar event from whole body and contextual cues.	Utilizes and associates several familiar objects with specific actions.	
Vocal/verbal	Prelanguage vocalizations: cooing, throaty sounds. Differentiated cry.		Vocalizes states such as contentment, fear, anger, etc.	
Receptive development: nonvocal				
Vocal/verbal				
Age range in months[a]	0 to 2	2 to 4	4 to 6	6 to 8

[a]Age ranges are approximate; many ages and categories overlap as a child matures and communication develops.
Note. Sources for this table are Everington *et al.*, 1982; McCormick, 1984; Stillman, 1978; Stremel-Campbell *et al.*, 1984.

TABLE 2. *(Continued)*

Imitates familiar gestures or scheme. Responds to "no" Gestures for "no" in response to "do you want ———?"	Repeats behavior that others laugh at. Uses gestures to direct adult attention (pointing, etc.)	Shows/points out objects to others to elicit attention and intention.	Exchanges roles in motor/vocal game (initiator and responder). Waves bye-bye appropriately (with prompting).
Demonstrates two or more complex actions with objects. Reaches and takes objects entirely hidden.	Gives objects on request.	Pulls strings vertically or horizontally to obtain object at end of string.	Uses object within reach (rake, stick, etc.) in order to obtain object out of reach.
Places adults hand on object of desire. Displays repertoire of actions or gestures to activate object or initiate action. Imitates unfamiliar visible gestures.	Initial demonstration of social use of objects. Shakes head for "no."	Gestures for "help," "yes," etc. in context. Gives toy or object to adult when action stops and waits for help.	Demonstrates awareness of usual whereabouts of familiar persons or objects and notices their absence.
Displays five different babbling combinations. Mama or Dada specific. Imitates nonspeech sounds (cough, tongue, click, etc.).	Imitates sounds initiated by adult. Displays five different babbling combinations (nonrepetitive).	First word, holophrastic speech. Vocalizes words in jargon utterances. Imitates word approximations (two syllable).	Production of 10 words. Labels 4 familiar objects. Uses word *no*. Two-word phrases, telegraphic speech.
Responds to "come here" presented verbally and gesturally. Ceases activity at "no", "stop", etc. Follows a pointing cue used by adult.	Anticipates familiar events from contextual cues. Gesture serves as representation of object not present. Responds to "look."	Responds to own name. Locates two body parts. Points to familiar persons, animals, toys on request.	Identifies familiar people by looking at, pointing to, or touching. Responds to requests for play actions ("kiss the baby" "push the car").
	Vocalizes familiar sounds on hearing novel ones.	Jargon shows comprehension on syntax. Imitates novel sound sequences.	Follows four commands without gestures. Uses intonation that sound like sentences.
8 to 10	10 to 12	12 to 15	15 to 20

behaviors, determine overall communication performance levels, and evaluate changes during intervention. In addition, a thorough assessment at the early developmental stages of nonlinguistic and prelinguistic skills provides a starting point for initiating augmentative nonverbal modes among persons for whom verbal language (production of words) may not be feasible (see "Nonvocal Augmentation" section of this chapter).

Potentially important prelinguistic behaviors that form the foundation for symbolic use include development of "yes" and "no" gestures and vocalizations, repertoire of actions or gestures displayed to activate objects or initiate interactions, ceasing activity to such verbal directions as "no" or "stop," anticipating familiar events, and taking turns in interactions. The far right portion of Table 2 displays some of these behaviors and their corresponding acquisition age. This table may aid the evaluation process in focusing on the scope and progression of prelinguistic development. Specific assessments that contain evaluation components of prelinguistic development are included in the Appendix.

COMMUNICATION ASSESSMENT: SPEECH AND LANGUAGE

Spoken language represents communication in its most complex yet viable form. To communicate efficiently and effectively using speech as the medium, the subelements comprising verbal production and linguistic meaning must be produced in a manner that is conventional, recognizable, and acceptable. Verbal communication requires following predetermined rules of language (linguistic knowledge) as well as accurate realization of speech targets in the expression of a linguistic intent. Analysis of the speech and language components of verbal communication is a central concern in speech and language assessment. As Nation and Aram (1977) suggest, the overt speech/language product is both accessible for direct observation and manipulation. Further, it reflects the status of internal processes of a cognitive, structural, or physiologic nature.

To facilitate discussion and to provide a format for systematic observation, the processes of speech and language production are often viewed as a dichotomy comprised of levels of speech production versus levels of linguistic content. In this instance the levels are defined as follows:

Dimensions of Speech Production

1. Phonation-resonance: aspects of voice production (pitch, quality, loudness, or flexibility)

2. Articulation: the movements of the articulators in the production of speech sounds
3. Fluency: the rate, ease, and efficiency of sound production
4. Prosody: variations in pitch, loudness, duration, and silence resulting in characteristics of rhythm, rate, stress, and intonation

Dimensions of Language

1. Phonology: the rules for production or perception of speech sound patterns
2. Syntax/morphology: the grammatical rules relating to the structure of words and the ways in which words are organized to form sentences
3. Semantic skills: word meaning and the relationships among words in connection speech
4. Pragmatics: the relationship between communicative context and language use

Verbal communication is multiphasic and multidimensional and is therefore difficult to describe or assess from a wholistic viewpoint. The dichotomy and descriptive levels are presented as a simplified illustration and should not be construed as support for the functional independence of the processes listed. Assessment procedures are most often designed to isolate specific behaviors for purposes of systematic analysis. Complete assessment should, however, include interpretation of behavioral measurements from a framework of integration rather than separation.

ASSESSMENT LEVELS

Just as speech/language behaviors are composed of multiphasic, interrelated components resulting in a verbal product, the evaluation process also represents a multidimensional procedure designed to assess communication abilities. Several levels of assessment are discussed in relation to specific goals of evaluation (see Why column of Table 1). The levels include prescreening, screening, diagnostic assessment, and assessment for programming. Although each assessment level is most closely associated with specific goals, formats, and procedures, there is often considerable overlap in application. Also, elements of each level are present in most clinical situations. Differences between screening, diagnostic assessment, and assessment for programming represent a shift in purpose and interpretation. Similarly, an assessment tool or procedure may be used at more than one level of assessment (i.e., screening, diagnosis) and provide information relative to answering several types of evaluation questions. The remainder of this section will describe basic considerations in assessment of speech–language skills, and the manner in which procedures are used to provide pertinent information at each level of evaluation.

PRESCREENING

The general goal of prescreening is to identify individuals in need of subsequent screening for disorders of speech and language. Three general behavioral patterns are noted that may signal difficulty with verbal communication skills (see Rice, 1978, pp. 48–49):

1. Individuals with related handicaps such as hearing loss, mental retardation, physical impairments (e.g., cleft palate), or neurological impairments (central or peripheral), such as stroke or cerebral palsy
2. Individuals referred for impairment by parents, teachers, physicians, or others concerned with delayed development, low intelligibility, poor social acceptability, or loss of communication skills
3. Individuals exhibiting subtle patterns of communication failure, such as low socialization with peers, avoidance of verbal interactions, limited verbalization (especially when accompanied by sophisticated compensatory communication), or deliberate monitoring of verbal communication for minimal length and complexity constraints

Specific segments of the general population may also require screening as a means of assessing a broad range of needs and abilities, including communication. Examples of such populations include preschool children, college freshmen, new military recruits, and the elderly.

An important component of prescreening is providing relevant information to potential referral agents, administrators of programs servicing high-risk populations, and authorities responsible for screening large populations. This information may focus on the incidence, type, effects, and efficacy of treating communication disorders.

SCREENING

The primary goals of speech and language screening are to (a) provide a general evaluation of communicative functions and (b) determine the presence of a problem severe enough to warrant further evaluation or referral to another discipline. Screening protocols range from informal assessments based on observation of contextual communication to formal assessments of a range of abilities in predetermined categories. As Muma (1978) notes, informal strategies assume a correspondence to typical behaviors, and evidence and conclusions are therefore more representative and relevant to actual communication abilities. Conversely, formal strategies assume predetermined categories of behavior to be relevant to the individual's communicative behaviors, with the rates, sequence, and level of development serving to quantify performance relative to norms. Accurate clinical decisions involved in screening should be based both on normative and descriptive data, taking into account individual differences and needs within natural communication contexts.

EXAMPLES OF SCREENING PROTOCOLS

Productive aspects of speech are often screened using a combination of conversational samples and formal assessment devices. A conversational sample of speech may be sufficient to determine informally that phonation/resonance, articulation, and prosodic elements appear disordered but may not be sufficient to demonstrate that these processes are adequate for communication purposes. A more complete assessment is provided by sampling a number of predetermined tasks, which may reveal a disorder manifested in a communication context not sampled in conversation. In addition, these tasks may identify individuals who modify verbal or linguistic content to avoid exhibiting errors of voice, articulation, or fluency. In this example, informal assessment of productive components of speech might be supplemented by

1. Application of a general speech behavior rating scale (Darley, Aronson, & Brown, 1975; Spriestersbach & Morris, 1978)
2. An oral-peripheral or motor speech examination of the structural-functional integrity of the speech-vocal mechanism in a variety of contexts (Darley, 1978; Spriestersbach, Morris, & Darley, 1978)
3. An articulation screening test of the sounds of English in varying phonetic contexts, positions in words, and connected speech (Goldman-Fristoe Test of Articulation [Goldman & Fristoe, 1969]; A Screening Deep Test of Articulation [McDonald, 1968])
4. An evaluation of fluency/prosodic elements in a number of predetermined speech contexts (The Stuttering Interview [Ryan, 1974])

Similarly, an informal screening assessment of linguistic content variables might be supplemented by such measures as the following:

1. A comprehensive language test, providing information relative to a range of content areas and language processes (e.g., Sequential Inventory of Communication Development [Hedrick, Prather, & Tobin, 1975]; The Bankson Language Screening Test [Bankson, 1977]; Western Aphasia Battery [Kirtesz, 1979]; Aphasia Language Performance Scales [Keenan & Brassell, 1975])
2. Objective measures of syntactic-morphological development (Carrow Ellicited Language Inventory [Carrow, 1974]; Test for Auditory Comprehension of Language [Carrow, 1973]; Developmental Sentence Analysis [Lee, 1974])
3. Measures of lexical/semantic functions (Peabody Picture Vocabulary Test [Dunn, 1965]; Test of Language Development [Newcomer & Hammill, 1977])
4. Orientation and general information (Wertz, 1978)

When possible, intake information (case history, referral summary, detailed observations) should be used to focus the screening procedure. This information should include an introduction to areas in question (origin, status, and development of perceived communication problems) and provide a context for assessment and interpretation. (See Darley & Spriestersbach [1978] for a discussion and specific examples of case history utilization with several types of disorders.)

Obviously, extensive assessments and detailed case histories cannot be used routinely in screening for speech/language disorders. The type and extent of evaluation should in each instance be determined by the need for making optimal use of clinical time, the characteristics of the population to be screened (especially incidence of specific disorder types), and the consequences of failing to identify a significant problem during screening (Will the individuals be available for further observation, referral, or treatment once dismissed?). Screening requires a balanced view of these issues. Rice (1978) states that

> the identification process usually involves the collection of some normative data, the observation of some particular language performances in both structured and nonstructured circumstances, and the gathering of aforementioned characteristic behavioral patterns, which are deemed pertinent. (p. 49)

In summary, the issues of *what* to assess, *how* to assess, and interpretation of information gained from screening must be based on knowledge of normal and disordered communication as well as considerable clinical intuition and judgment. The screening process serves both to identify individuals with a speech/language/communication problem and to initiate the diagnostic process.

DIAGNOSTIC ASSESSMENT

Once a communication problem is identified (at the prescreening or screening stages), the assessment issue becomes one of specifying the nature and extent of the problem. The primary goals of diagnostic assessment are to (a) accurately measure and describe the behaviors in question, (b) organize and analyze data to provide the most accurate profile of the client's disorder, (c) rule out concomitant disorders that may affect communication skills, and (d) interpret assessment data for prognostic and management decisions.

Diagnostic assessment initially demands that available information (screening data, intake information) be scanned to determine the reason for referral, the preliminary hypothesis as to the type and extent of the problem, the specific diagnostic questions to be addressed, and the assessment procedures and materials that appear most appropriate. Assessment should be designed to be both discriminative (i.e., identifying the most pertinent behavioral variables) and descriptive (i.e., providing an appropriate level of systematic, valid, and reliable data).

Rather than selection of test procedures based on test name, purported purpose, or catagorical labels provided, evaluation tools must be carefully matched to client characteristics and to critical diagnostic questions based on content and methodological issues. Awareness of such variables as manner and mode of stimulus presentation and client response, maturity level, complexity and content of stimulus items, and overall face validity are extremely important in assessing communication abilities. Assessment strategies must be flexible enough to allow both modification for specific situational demands (e.g., altering standard protocols to incorporate an available response mode) and shifts in the focus of assessment (diagnostic hypothesis) based on newly available data.

Finally, assessment must provide information that is relevant to the communication abilities of the individual in natural contexts. Optimal methods of acquiring representative data are a topic of considerable debate. Highly structured procedures offer numerous psychometric advantages (standardized materials and procedures, control of contextual variables, specification of target responses) but may lack relevance to functional communication. Minimally structured procedures utilizing more natural contexts may sample representative behaviors but are typically more time consuming and difficult to interpret. In most cases, both structured and minimally structured evaluation procedures are needed in assessment of communication function. Decisions as to the clinical efficacy of specific procedures may depend on the disorder type, sophistication of available assessment tools, the specific diagnostic questions to be answered, and expectations as to subsequent management goals.

ASSESSMENT FOR PROGRAMMING: BASELINE AND PROGRESS

The evaluation methodology employed in screening and diagnostic assessment should provide the basic data for determining current performance levels, treatment strategies, and goals/objectives of remediation. Obtaining valid and reliable measures of ongoing progress and generalization of abilities requires designing performance measures related to specific treatment objectives as well as to functional communication environments. According to McReynolds (1981, p. 245), assessment for programming may require adequate samples of several behaviors:

1. Performance on target exemplars used in training contexts
2. Performance on similar but untrained stimuli (within-class generalization)
3. Performance on related but dissimilar targets that are anticipated to be influenced by treatment (cross-class generalization)
4. Performance on targets within typical communication settings (extraclinical generalization)

CLASSIFICATION OF DISORDERS

Specific assessment strategies often are guided by using basic methods to classify the behaviors in question. Most pertinent to diagnostic assessment of speech and language abilities are classification schemes that are descriptive in nature, promoting development of accurate profiles of communicative performance. A basic concern is distinguishing between disorders with an organic versus a functional etiology. *Organic disorders* are those that appear related to a known pathophysiological condition, such as neurological or structural anomalies (e.g., cortical trauma, cleft palate) affecting one or more levels of verbal performance. *Functional disorders* refer to communicative disorders for which no organic cause can be readily identified (e.g., developmental delays, emotional factors, faulty learning, slow maturation, environmental deprivation). Table 3 provides a description of verbal production hierarchies, their organization, components, and functions.

TABLE 3. VERBAL PRODUCTION HIERARCHIES

Level of organization	Components	Function
1. Cognitive/ linguistic	Entire cerebrum but primarily referring to cortical levels of function	Comprehension and formulation of communicative events. Perceptual, psychological, linguistic and learning substrates as basis for rules governing semantics, phonology, syntax-morphology, and pragmatic competence.
2. Motor programming	Present at but not limited to prefrontal areas of cortex	Transform abstract communicative intent into neuromuscular code. Requires spatial-temporal planning and integration of speech mechanism positions and states with the simultaneous and sequential movements involved in speech production.
3. Neuromotor transmission	Central and peripheral nervous system components	Transfer and refinement of neuromotor commands from control centers (cerebrum) to end organ (speech mechanism).
4. Performance	Speech mechanism components: muscles and structures of the abdomen, diaphragm, chest wall, larynx, pharynx, palate, tongue, teeth, mandible, lips, and face	Mechanical and aerodynamic events. Muscular contractions and structural movements resulting in (a) shape and volume changes, (b) air pressures and air flows that result in respiration, phonation, resonance, articulation, and prosody.
5. Feedback	Components of auditory, visual, tactile-kinesthetic, and somatosensory systems	Perception, integration, monitoring, and modification of systems function.

Assessment of individuals with obvious organic deficits may focus on the manner and degree to which impairments effect function. This includes the prognosis for physical management, return or development of abilities, and compensatory, alternative, or augumentative strategies. Evaluation of functional disorders may initially involve ruling out organic variables and then proceed with careful analysis and description of relevant behavioral variables and/or environmental factors that might contribute to the disorder.

ASSESSMENT: DISORDERS OF SPEECH PRODUCTION

Disorders of speech production refer to communication aberrations involving phonation-resonance, articulation, fluency, or prosody that are judged to be abnormal on the basis of acoustical standards, cultural norms, or vocal hygiene. Speech production impairments play a crucial role in the everyday conduct of an individual's life. Disorders may impact on the efficiency and effectiveness of message transmission (i.e., intelligibility and success in conveying a desired intent). They may contribute to psychological, socioemotional, and economic status (i.e., personality formation, social competence and acceptance, vocational aspirations, and interpersonal relations). Finally, speech disorders may change the physical and functional integrity of certain anatomical structures (i.e., parameters of use affect speech mechanism components involved in respiration, phonation, resonance, and articulation).

Diagnostic assessment of speech production disorders will be concerned with those etiological, perceptual, and kinesiologic attributes that are most helpful in defining behaviors, guiding management decisions, and structuring intervention. As is illustrated in Table 3, the functional organization of verbal behaviors is quite complex, and a number of factors must be considered simultaneously in assessment. McReynolds and Elbert (1982) underscore the dynamic aspects of assessment noting that strategies chosen are determined in part by (a) the model adhered to by the clinician, (b) the degree to which behaviors appear defective, and (c) the clinician's opinion of the extent to which the disorder needs to be described before training goals can be determined.

Articulation Assessment. Articulation disorders have long been recognized as a significant type of communication impairment. Disordered articulation may be of a developmental or acquired nature, relate to a wide variety of etiological conditions, and may range in severity from mild sound distortions to severe, almost unintelligible productions. An articulation error exists when a "normal" listener perceives a target sound (e.g., the /p/ sound in "*p*lot") as a substitution (e.g., "*b*lot"), a distortion (e.g., a nasalized /p/ in "*p*lot"), an omission (e.g., "__lot"), or addition (e.g., "*p*alot"); or when productions are perceived as unintelligible. Articulation is considered disordered when sound production skills are not appropriate for an individual's age or level of cognitive development.

Diagnostic assessment of articulation disorders necessitates use of a varety of measures in addition to information provided in the case history and screening procedures. The diagnostic battery typically will include samples of spontaneous connected speech, an index of functional articulation, phonetic inventories designed to elicit the sounds of a language in the word positions in which they naturally occur, stimulability testing, to assess motor production abilities and the level of complexity at which errors occur, and tests of phonetic context to probe the variability of articulation as influenced by adjacent sounds. Numerous types of supplemental measures also may be appropriate to enhance the reliability of measurement, rule out conflicting hypotheses, and focus subsequent management. Examples are tests of auditory acuity, auditory discrimination (general or phoneme specific), oral-peripheral or motor-speech exams, and tests of general language function.

Basis analysis of data from articulation exams involves evaluation of the consistency, type, phonetic context, and stimulability of individual error sounds; the number and type of errors taken as a whole; and overall intelligibility in communication contexts (Darley, 1978). Errors of young children may be compared to normative data (e.g., Sanders, 1972; Templin, 1957). Interpretation, however, is necessarily restricted due to variability in rate and/or sequence of acquisition for any one individual. Normative data are largely irrelevant in interpreting the articulatory errors of individuals past age 10 or when deviations are confounded by differences in culture or dialect.

Analysis also may focus on evaluating patterns of errors, particularly in regard to more complex disorders. A place/manner/voicing analysis (e.g., Fischer & Logemann, 1971) allows review of production parameters according to place of articulation, presence or absence of voicing, and manner of production (e.g., plosives, fricatives). These factors may be related to disordered learning patterns or organic deficits. Distinctive-feature approaches (McReynolds & Engemann, 1975) categorize errors according to the basic elements of phonemes (i.e., distinctive features are the abstract components of sound targets that distinguish one sound from another). The rationale is that maximal changes in phonological organization may be achieved by addressing feature error patterns that are most prevalent. Phonological process analyses (Ingram, 1976) represent a fairly recent area of assessment providing description of errors in terms of simplification patterns (processes) resembling those of children in early stages of phonological acquisition. Errors may relate to inappropriate retention of processes or may represent adaptive behaviors related to an acquired disorder.

Phonation/Resonance Assessment. Phonation and resonance comprise the basic components in the production of voice. Specifically, *phonation* refers to the physical act of sound production through interaction of the vocal chords and the exhaled airstream. *Resonance* refers to modification of sound production through changes in cavity size, shape, and vibratory characteristics of the speech mechanism (see Table 3). Vocal production presents both a set of complex physiological processes and a behavioral manifestation of personality, identity, emotion, and general state of being.

Disorders of phonation/resonance may be defined in terms of psychological, perceptual, or acoustic characteristics. Vocal disturbances are typically identified in terms of pitch, loudness, quality, and flexibility. Listeners judge these parameters in relation to a speaker's age, sex, cultural background, and contextual appropriateness. As organic etiologies are more frequent and potentially serious (e.g., vocal nodules, laryngeal cancer), assessment is typically skewed toward identification of causal factors.

Diagnostic assessment often begins with a careful voice history (Aronson, 1980) to describe pertinent variables, including the genesis of the problem (e.g., onset, duration, variation), environmental factors (e.g., daily use of voice in personal and vocational settings, potential situations of vocal abuse or irritation), and medical factors (e.g., diagnosis, treatment, illnesses). Vocal evaluation procedures may be used to assess the parameters of pitch, loudness, quality, and flexibility in a variety of contexts. Descriptions may be facilitated by the use of standard assessment protocols (Wilson, 1979) and comparison to normative data (Aronson, 1980). Yet professional judgment, training, and experience remain the most important criteria.

Perceptual measures may be supplemented by physiological assessment. Medical evaluation of structural/functional parameters is a necessary component of every voice disorder assessment. Other measures of physiological parameters may include objective measures of airflow (rate and volume), wave forms, duration, pitch, and intensity. In complex cases, subtle acoustic characteristics such as voice onset and decay and harmonic amplitudes may be quantified to provide an additional source of data.

Documentation of vocal behaviors in baseline will be influenced by whether treatment involves medical/surgical modification of structures, modification of negative environmental factors, or direct behavior modification to reduce the disorder and improve the voice. Management of organic impairments resulting in voice disorders may be primarily medical, remedial, or may require a combination of efforts. Psychogenic or functional voice disorders necessitate integrated management by medical, psychological, and speech language personnel.

Disfluency Assessment. Verbal production requires that a vast number of mechanical adjustments be made at an extremely rapid rate. Darley *et al.* (1975) estimate that connected speech requires over 140,000 neuromuscular events per second. Not surprisingly, disfluencies are typical of all normal speakers and are especially prevalent during the early childhood years. A fluency disorder exists when speech behaviors are judged as abnormal on the basis of frequency, duration, or the bizarre nature of production (Van Riper, 1971).

Stuttering behaviors are composed of audible features, such as sound repetitions, prolongations, silent pauses, and insertions, and/or visible characteristics (e.g., struggle behaviors, inappropriate articulatory postures, extraneous movements). These effect the smooth initiation of, or transitions between, speech sounds. In addition, other nonspeech behaviors used to avoid stuttering may become secondary symptoms of the disorder (e.g., head jerk, arm movements, foot stomp).

General assessment strategies consist of a case history and analysis of the number, type, and duration of disfluencies across a number of different linguistic and environmental contexts. Specific concerns may vary significantly according to the remedial approach utilized. Environmental manipulation strategies, which are an indirect treatment approach often used with young children, involve a detailed analysis of contextual communication dynamics and require some form of environmental observation. Treatments designed to directly modify stuttering behaviors usually require development of extensive quantitative and qualitative profiles of behavioral and contextual parameters of stuttering (see Ryan, 1974). Remedial programs that focus on training of fluent modes of production (e.g., Shames & Florance, 1980) are less concerned with symptomatic variables as they involve development of strategies to bypass disfluencies.

Prosody Assessment. Prosody refers to vocal effects resulting from variations in pitch, loudness, duration, and silence, which are manifested as suprasegmental elements of rhythm, stress, and intonation. The critical role of prosody in verbal communication has only recently been addressed in the literature. Therefore, assessment currently is at rudimentary levels of development. This is rather surprising when, as Freeman (1982) notes, every major category of disordered speech is characterized by some degree of disrupted prosody. Also, abnormal production or perception of prosody is a primary salient characteristic of several specific communication impairments, such as dysarthria, apraxia of speech, speech of the deaf, stuttering, and right-hemisphere language impairments.

Freeman has suggested (1982) two interrelated ways in which prosody may function in perception and production: (a) as a segmentation device for dividing the flow of speech into coherent linguistic structures suitable for processing and (b) as an integration device providing structural integrity, and therefore predictability, in the organization of spoken language.

At present there is a striking lack of procedures available for assessment of prosodic encoding and decoding abilities. Major goals of current research are to (a) devise adequate methodologies for describing variables related to prosodic function (Allen, 1984), (b) provide adequate nomenclature for characterizing prosodic disturbances (Kent, 1979), and (c) describe patterns of performance associated with specific disorder types (Kent & Rosenbeck, 1982).

EVALUATION OF LANGUAGE DISORDERS

In contrast to the more observable nature of speech processes, assessment of linguistic abilities must focus on the abstract, predetermined rules for transforming meaning into language and language into meaning. Language impairments represent a large and complex class of behaviors in which the rules governing language use may be delayed, distorted, or impaired. Disorders may range in nature from mild to profound, in form from general to specific, and in occurrence from impaired acquisition during early development to traumatic dissolution of language functions (aphasia) occurring at any age. A plethora of classification schemes exist to describe language impairments (Davis, 1983). This discussion will center on three dimensions of language function: form, content, and use (Bloom & Lahey, 1978).

The concept of linguistic form includes the mode, organization, and structure of utterances, relating primarily to the dimensions of phonology and syntax-morphology. Specifically, phonological rules pertain to the relationship between abstract linguistic units (distinctive features), their organization into a system of discrete elements (phonemes), and their realization in sound (phonetic production). Phonology encompasses disorders of articulation and discrimination at the phonetic level but that also may be impaired at the phonemic level. For example, individuals with aphasia often demonstrate phonemic errors in production or reception of words (e.g., boos, boat, bug, boot, bot, for "book"), evidence that phonological rules of selection and combination are misrepresented (Davis, 1983). Considerable debate exists as to whether another disorder type, apraxia of speech, is based in phonological deficit or is a motor-speech programming error (Lessor, 1978).

Disorders of syntax-morphology are another type of form error. *Morphology* involves rules for combining morphemes (single units of meaning) into word forms resulting in greater specificity (e.g., marking tense, number, possession, case). *Syntax* refers to the ordering and arranging of words in an utterance to facilitate decoding of a verbal intent. Grammatical errors involving syntax-morphology are a common characteristic of developmental and acquired language impairments.

The dimension of linguistic content refers primarily to the area of semantics: the conceptual meanings conveyed by words (lexical semantics) and the relationships between words in utterances (relational semantics). Semantic abilities comprise more than the learning of nominal labels for certain stimuli. They also entail the refinement of a set of associations contributing to a specific sense of word meaning within a linguistic context. Semantic disorders may result in impaired development of conceptual categories or semantic features, disrupt the interrelated organization of word meanings, or effect the ability to retrieve lexical labels for well-known stimuli.

Finally, dimensions of use relate closely to pragmatic behaviors that are the dynamic attributes of language within a communicative environment. From a pragmatic view, elements of form and content are constantly modified to match situational demands (the setting, participants, intent, topic, occasion.). The recent focus on pragmatics in the field has broadened the view of language function to include social and contextual effects. This has resulted in a closer approximation to true communicative competence (Prutting, 1982; Roth & Spekman, 1984). As such, pragmatic abilities are of prime concern in assessment of developmental and acquired language disorders (Roth & Spekman, 1984; Wilcox & Davis, 1984).

LANGUAGE ASSESSMENT

Diagnostic assessment of language abilities usually entails administration of global measures of language performance. Such measures are selected to provide a broad information base relative to the major area of diagnostic concern, to allow differential diagnosis of language disorders from other types of impairments, and to suggest fruitful avenues for exploring individual aspects of performance. Two general types of procedures are commonly used. Highly structured standardized tests often are used to provide clinicians an opportunity to analyze responses across modalities (receptive and expressive); levels of complexity; different stimulus, processing, or response variables; and levels of language function (dimensions of form, content, and use). Performance scores may be compared to specific test data from normal and/or language-disordered groups or to more general performance criteria, such as mean length of utterance, type-token ratio, and the like, that serve as a general indicator of performance. (For examples of comprehensive tests of language, refer to the section on screening.) However, few structured language tests provide the depth of information needed for addressing specific abilities of the client. More detailed analyses clearly are required.

Spontaneous language sampling procedures provide a measure of global language skills that may be representative of functional language abilities. Analysis procedures vary, and guidelines for eliciting and transcribing the sample should be closely followed (Lee, 1974; Tyack & Gottsleben, 1974). Development of computerized analysis procedures may greatly enhance the efficiency, practicality, and scope of linguistic analysis. For example, Lingquest (see Mordecai, Palin, & Palmer, 1982) provides a detailed quantitative and qualitative analysis of grammatical form, lexicon, syntactic structure, and verb tense for 50 utterance samples with minimal computer entry preparation. Such procedures hold great promise for improving the efficacy of assessment and extending the data base relative to language disorders.

Extension Testing. Subsequent to identification of the more global behavioral symptoms of language disorder, focal measures are used to explore pertinent variables in more depth, to provide a sufficient sample of behaviors to establish patterns of behaviors, and as preliminary baseline data relative to programming. Probes of language behaviors may be chosen from the existing test literature when appropriate or are developed for the individual case. For example, probes of an aphasic individual's phonological abilities might include a series of select word production tasks, providing an adequate number of trials for assessment of a particular phonological process such as cluster reduction. Given an adequate sample of contexts and opportunities for use, a more complete description of disorder parameters can be constructed. Analysis of the frequency, type, and pattern of errors may allow development of a specific hypothesis as to the primary language deficit underlying the symptom complex. This hypothesis will guide subsequent management decisions and should be continuously tested in ongoing interactions. Finally, baseline functioning can be inferred from identifying performance levels in relation to specific goals of therapy and intra- or extratherapy sampling procedures.

In summary, evaluation of speech/language impairments is a complex process necessitating a comprehensive analysis of communication behaviors. A review of general considerations in assessment may provide some insight into the reasons certain protocols are employed. For more specific information relative to particular disorder types and evaluation tools, the reader is referred to texts by Darley and Spriestersbach

(1978), Lass, McReynolds, Northern, and Yoder (1982), and Shames and Wiig (1982).

NONVOCAL COMMUNICATION MODES—ALTERNATIVE AND AUGMENTATIVE SYSTEMS

Determination of the need for nonvocal communication modes may occur at any point along the continuum of communication development between the acquisition of nonlinguistic skills and acquired communication disorders. As proposed in previous sections of this chapter, current performance levels of the client's communication systems are determined at the nonlinguistic, prelinguistic, and/or linguistic levels by utilizing screening and diagnostic assessments. At the completion of these evaluation components, it is possible that the evaluation will establish that the primary expressive and/or receptive modes of communication are nonvocal. Upon that determination, a thorough speech and language evaluation will include assessment of alternative or augmentative nonvocal systems.

Individuals who display physical or mental disabilities may not receive an adequate communication evaluation utilizing traditional methods of speech and language assessment. Clients may appear to lack communicative behavior due to sensory impairments, cognitive deficits, neuromotor dysfunction, or behavioral disorders. The evaluator must ascertain what modes the individual employs to express needs, wants, preferences, and feelings and determine the appropriateness of alternatives to traditional speech output and input.

The evaluation components included in the nonlinguistic and prelinguistic section of this chapter would be the first step in the evaluation process. Next, the evaluation would include linguistic diagnostic assessment to determine the nature and extent of the current display of the productive components of speech. On completion of the nonlinguistic and prelinguistic screening, diagnostic assessment, evaluation of baseline functioning, and linguistic diagnostic assessment, enough information will be available to ascertain the need of nonvocal programming using alternative and augmentative communication systems.

Nonvocal programming may be utilized for verbal facilitation, augmentation of verbal output, or as an alternative to verbal expression. The nonvocal system selected for verbal facilitation is a temporary system that emphasizes an outcome of verbal competence. Nonvocal systems that emphasize programming as an alternative or augmentation to verbal output focus on communicative competence using the selected system itself. These distinctions are important to direct-care providers as they

TABLE 4. ELECTION DECISION MATRIX

LEVEL I Cognitive Factors
- At least Stage V sensorimotor intelligence?
- At least 18 months mental age, or ability to recognize at least at photograph level?
  - YES → Go to II
  - NO → Delay

LEVEL II Oral Reflex Factors
- Persistent (1) rooting; (2) gag; (3) bite; (4) suckle/swallow; or (5) jaw extension reflex?
  - YES → ELECT → Go to X
  - NO → Continue to III

LEVEL III Language and Motor Speech Production Factors
- A. Is there a discrepancy between receptive and expressive skills?
  - YES → Go to III B
  - NO → Go to V
- B. Is the discrepancy explained predominantly on the basis of a motor speech disorder?
  - YES → Go to V
  - NO → Go to III C
  - UNCERTAIN → Go to IV
- C. Is the discrepancy explained predominantly on the basis of an expressive language disorder?
  - YES → Go to VII
  - NO → GO to VI
  - UNCERTAIN → Go to V

LEVEL IV Motor Speech—Some Contributing Factors
- Presence of neuromuscular involvement affecting postural tone and/or postural stability?

LEVEL VI Emotional Factors
- A. History of precipitous loss of expressive speech?
  - YES → Go to VIII
  - NO → Go to VI B
- B. Speaks to selected persons or refuses to speak?
  - YES → Go to VIII
  - NO → Go to V

LEVEL VII Chronological Age Factors
- A. Chronological age less than 3 years?
  - YES → Go to VIII A
- B. Chronological age between 3 and 5 years?
  - YES → Go to VIII A
- C. Chronological age greater than 5 years?
  - YES → Go to VIII A

LEVEL VIII Previous Therapy Factors
- A. Has had previous therapy?
  - YES → Go to VIII B
  - NO → Go to IX, weigh evidence • (DELAY with Trial Therapy or ELECT) Go to X
- B. Previous therapy appropriate?
  - YES → Go to VIII C
  - NO → DELAY with Trial Therapy
- C. Therapy progress too slow to enable effective communication?
  - YES → ELECT → Go to X
  - NO → DELAY → continue therapy
- D. Therapy appropriately withheld?
  - YES → ELECT → Go to X
  - NO → DELAY with trial therapy

Presence of praxic disturbance?
Vocal production consists primarily of vowel production?
Vocal production consists primarily of undifferentiated sounds?
History of eating problems?
Excessive drooling?
Yes → Evidence to support motor speech involvement (Go to V)
No → Evidence against motor speech involvement (Go to V)

LEVEL V Production—Some Contributing Factors
Speech unitelligible except to family and immediate friends?
Predominant mode of communication is through pointing, gesture, facial–body affect?
Predominance of single word utterances?
Frustration associated with inability to speak?
YES → (Evidence to ELECT) Go to VII
NO → Evidence to DELAY or REJECT) Go to VII

LEVEL IX Previous Therapy—Some Contributing Factors
Able to imitate (with accuracy) speech sounds or words; gross motor or oral motor movements?
YES → (Evidence to DELAY) Go to VIII
NO → (Evidence to ELECT) Go to VIII

LEVEL X Implementation Factors—Environment
Family willing to implement (use, allow to be introduced) Augmentative Communication System recommendation?
YES → IMPLEMENT
NO → COUNSEL

Note: From "Election Criteria for the Adoption of an Augmentative Communication System: Preliminary Considerations," by H. C. Shane and A. S. Baskir, 1980, *Journal of Speech and Hearing Disorders, 45*, p. 409. Copyright 1980 by the American Speech-Language-Hearing Association. Reprinted by permission.

assess progress during nonvocal intervention programs. The decision-making process in determining the type of emphasis on nonvocal modes of communication focuses on both input and output. The client who is nonvocal may receive messages (input) through the verbal mode (speech) and transmit messages (output) through a nonvocal mode (e.g., communication board, sign language) (Musslewhite & St. Louis, 1982). It is suggested that both vocal and nonvocal components be incorporated into the communication program. Consequently, it is important that these input/output considerations be included in the nonvocal assessment of nonvocal alternative and augmentative systems.

Initial decision making during nonvocal assessment may be facilitated by a formalized system such as the decision-making matrix presented by Shane and Bashir (1980) and shown in Table 4. This formalized system aids the evaluation in basing information on clusters of factors rather than limited information and by appropriately assessing individuals for vocal or nonvocal systems.

Upon completion of a decision process such as the Shane-Bashir matrix (Table 4) or other appropriate decision scheme, alternative and augmentative programming may be needed. The evaluation process is then focused on determining the emphasis on unaided or aided systems (Mathy-Laikko, Ratcliff, Villarruel, & Yoder, 1986). Unaided or gestural systems "necessitate movement of the body, typically the arms and hands, but do not require access to equipment or devices separate from the body" (Musslewhite & St. Louis, 1982, p. 90). Aided systems may be electronic (e.g., microcomputers, voice synthesizers, typewriters) or nonelectronic (e.g., communication boards, books, charts).

Unaided augmentative assessment includes determining use of gestural codes or sign language systems. Both of these types of unaided systems differ from speech "in that the input system is visual rather than auditory, and the output medium is a motor response" (Mathy-Laikko *et al.*, 1986, p. 185). Therefore, the assessment for unaided systems includes determining motor control, comprehension of gestures, visual discrimination, and receptive language. As suggested by Musslewhite and St. Louis (1982) unaided or gestural analysis should include sign language, gestural language codes, educational sign systems, and natural gestural systems.

Aided augmentative assessment includes determining the use of nonelectronic or electronic aids. Use of either aided system generally includes representational symbol systems and language codes. Therefore, in addition to determining electronic or nonelectronic systems, further analysis includes: reception and expression of symbols; determining motor control; visual discrimination; and visual tracking, scanning, and matching. A means of indication, input modes, organization of sytems, and determination of content to include must also be assessed. A nonvocal alternative or augmentative assessment entails many levels of diagnosis. Further information is provided by the tools listed in Nonlinguistic and Prelinguistic Assessment (see Appendix as well as Halle, Alpert, & Anderson, 1984; McCormick & Schiefelbusch, 1984; Mathy-Laikko *et al.*, 1986; McLean & Snyder-McLean, 1978; Miller, 1978; Musslewhite & St. Louis, 1982; Schiefelbusch, 1978; and Silverman, 1980).

SUMMARY

This chapter has presented evaluation formats that take into consideration the complex processes of communication. The transmission of messages (communication) occurs in both verbal and nonverbal modes and at nonlinguistic or linguistic levels. It is important to recognize that there are distinctions between analyzing communication disorders (interference with the transmission of a message), language disorders (impaired utilization of arbitrary symbol systems), and speech disorders (disruption of production of oral-motor behavior).

A systematic format for addressing the complex nature of communication was provided. Prior to initiation of assessment procedures, the evaluator should address the *purpose* of the communication assessment (why), the *content* and *processes* to assess (what), and the *method* to utilize (how). An adequate evaluation must occur with assessments of other developmental skills, such as vision, hearing, neurological status, and perceptual-motor skills.

Of all aspects of human existence, communication may be one of the most significant behaviors affecting one's life. Communication behaviors exist in all individuals regardless of physical or mental disability and may be displayed in vocal, verbal, or nonverbal ways. As noted by Shames and Wiig (1982):

> Human communication and its disorders are a part of the overall human condition. Each of us lives and exists as a uniquely synthesized unit. We express ourselves to one another, and relate to one another, not as a mouth or a tongue or an ear, but as individual thoughtful, caring, feeling people. (p. xii)

The multifaceted expressions of communication demand an evaluation that is thorough and systematic. This chapter has provided a format that follows a broad perspective of communication assessment from nonlinguistic development to linguistic and acquired disorders. The role of the evaluator is to determine those impairments that negatively influence communication and to devise ways to maximize each individual's potential for conveying messages to others. The variety and complexity of communication and its importance in human interaction makes this an endeavor that is both challenging and rewarding.

REFERENCES

Allen, G. (1984, November). *Transcribing the prosodic (suprasegmental): Features of English.* Paper presented at the American Speech-Language-Hearing Convention, San Francisco.

Aronson, A. E. (1980). *Clinical voice disorders.* New York: Thieme Stratton.

Bankson, N. (1977). *The Bankson Language Screening Test.* Baltimore: University Park Press.

Bloom, L. (1970). *Language development: Form and function in emerging grammars.* Cambridge: M.I.T. Press.

Bloom, L., & Lahey, M. (1978). *Language development and language disorders.* New York: Wiley.

Carrow, E. (1973). *Test for Auditory Comprehension of Language* (5th ed.). Austin, TX: Learning Concepts.

Carrow, E. (1974). *Carrow Elicited Language Inventory.* Austin, TX: Learning Concepts.

Darley, F. L. (1978). Appraisal of articulation. In F. L. Darley & D. C. Spriestersbach (Eds.), *Diagnostic methods in speech pathology* (pp. 222–255). New York: Harper & Row.

Darley, F. L., & Spriestersbach, D. C.(Eds.). (1978). *Diagnostic methods in speech pathology.* New York: Harper & Row.

Darley, F. L., Aronson, A. E., & Brown, J. R. (1975). *Motor speech disorders.* Philadelphia: W. B. Saunders.

Dunn, L. M. (1965). *Peabody Picture Vocabulary Test.* Circle Pines, MN: American Guidance Services.

Dunst, C. (1980). *A clinical and educational manual for use with the Uzgiris and Hunt scales for infant psychological development.* Baltimore: University Park Press.

Elliott, N. (1984). Communicative development from birth. *Western Journal of Speech Communication, 48,* 184–196.

Everington, C., Heckert, S., Jones, S., Pierce, J., Stith-Richards, E., Thomas E., Worley, L., & Yaraheski-Domme, S. (1982). *Los Lunas Curricular System.* Los Lunas, NM: Education Department, Los Lunas Hospital and Training School.

Fischer, H. B., & Logemann, J. A. (1971). *The Fischer-Logemann Test of Articulation Competence.* Boston: Houghton-Mifflin.

Freeman, F. J. (1982). Prosody in perception, production, and pathologies. In N. Lass, L. McReynolds, J. Northern, & D. Yoder (Eds.), *Speech, language, and hearing* (pp. 652–672). Philadelphia: W. B. Saunders.

Goldman, R., & Fristoe, M. (1969). *Goldman-Fristoe Test of Articulation.* Circle Pines, MN: American Guidance Service.

Halle, J. W., Alpert, C. L., & Anderson, S. R. (1984). Natural environment language assessment and intervention with severely impaired preschoolers. *Topics in Early Childhood Special Education, 4*(2), 36–56.

Hedrick, P. L., Prather, E. M., & Tobin, A. R. (1975). *Sequenced Inventory of Communication Development*. Seattle: University of Washington Press.

Hollos, M. (1977). Comprehension and use of social rules in pronoun selection by Hungarian children. In S. Ervin-Tripp & C. Mitchell-Kernan (Eds.), *Child discourse* (pp. 211–223). New York: Academic Press.

Ingram, D. (1976). *Phonological disability in children*. New York: Elselvier.

Irwin, J. (1982). Human language and communication. In G. H. Shames & E. H. Wiig (Eds.), *Human communication disorders: An introduction* (pp. 21–44). Columbus, OH: Charles Merrill.

Keenan, J. S., & Brassell, E. G. (1975). *Aphasia Language Performance Scales*. Murfreesboro, TN: Pinnacle Press.

Kent, R. D. (1979, November). *Prosodic disturbance and neurological lesion*. Paper presented at the American Speech-Language-Hearing Convention, Atlanta, GA.

Kent, R. D., & Rosenbeck, J. (1982). Prosodic disturbance and neurological lesion. *Brain and Language, 15*, 259–291.

Kirtesz, A. (1979). Western Aphasia Battery. In A. Kirtesz (Ed.), *Aphasia and associated disorders: Taxonomy, localization, and recovery*. New York: Grune & Stratton.

Klein, M. D., Wulz, S. V., Hall, M. K., Waldo, L. J., Carpenter, S. A., Lathan, D. A., Myers, S. P., Fox, T., & Marshall, A. M. (1981). *Comprehensive communication curriculum guide*. Lawrence: Early Childhood Institute, University of Kansas.

Lass, N., McReynolds, L., Northern, J., & Yoder, D. (Eds.). (1982). *Speech, language, and hearing: Vol. II. Pathologies of speech and language*. Philadelphia: W. B. Saunders.

Lee, L. L. (1974). *Developmental sentence analysis*. Evanston, IL: Northwestern University Press.

Lessor, R. (1978). *Linguistic investigations of aphasia*. New York: Elselvier.

Mathy-Laikko, P., Ratcliff, A. E., Vallarreul, F., & Yoder, D. E. (1986). Augmentative communication systems. In M. Bullis (Ed.), *Communication development in young children with deaf-blindness: Literature review III* (pp. 183–219). Monmouth, OR: Communication Skills Center for Young Children with Deaf-Blindness.

McClowry, D. P., Guilford, A. M., & Richardson, S. O. (Eds.). (1982). *Infant communication: Development, assessment and intervention*. New York: Grune & Stratton.

McCormick, L. (1984). Review of normal language acquisition. In L. McCormick & R. Schiefelbusch (Eds.), *Early language intervention* (pp. 35–88). Columbus, OH: Charles Merrill.

McCormick, L., & Schiefelbusch, R. (Eds.). (1984). *Early language intervention*. Columbus, OH: Charles Merrill.

McCormick, L., & Shane, H. (1984). Augmentative communication. In L. McCormick & R. Schiefelbusch (Eds.), *Early language intervention* (pp. 325–356). Columbus, OH: Charles Merrill.

McDonald, E. T. (1968). *A Screening Deep Test of Articulation*. Pittsburg: Stanwix House.

McLean, J. E., & Snyder-McClean (1978). *A transactional approach to early language training*. Columbus, OH: Charles Merrill.

McReynolds, L. V. (1981). Generalization in articulation training. *Analysis and intervention in developmental disabilities, 1*, 245–258.

McReynolds, L. V., & Elbert, M. F. (1982). Articulation disorders of unknown etiology and their remediation. In N. Lass, L. McReynolds, J. Northern, & D. Yoder (Eds.), *Speech, language, and hearing* (pp. 591–610). Philadelphia: W. B. Saunders.

McReynolds, L. V., & Engemann, D. L. (1975). *Distinctive feature analysis of misarticulations*. Baltimore: University Park Press.

Miller, J. (1978). Assessing children's language behavior: A developmental process approach. In R. Schiefelbusch (Ed.), *Bases of language intervention (Vol. 1*; pp. 269–318). Baltimore: University Park Press.

Mordecai, D. R., Palin, M. W., & Palmer, C. B. (1982). *Lingquest 1: Language Sample Analysis*. Napa, CA: Linqest Software.

Muma, J. R. (1978). *Language handbook. Concepts, assessment, intervention*. Englewood Cliffs, NJ: Prentice-Hall.

Musselwhite, C., & St. Louis, K. W. (1982). *Communication programming for the severely handicapped: Vocal and non-vocal strategies*. San Diego: College Hill Press.

Nation, J., & Aram, D. (1977). *Diagnosis of speech and language disorders*. St. Louis: C. V. Mosby.

Newcomer, P., & Hammill, D. D. (1977). *Test of language development*. Austin, TX: Pro-Ed.

Prutting, C. A. (1982). Pragmatics as social competence. *Journal of Speech and Hearing Disorders, 47*, 123–133.

Rice, M. (1978). Identification of children with language disorders. In R. L. Schiefelbusch (Ed.), *Language intervention strategies* (pp. 19–55). Baltimore: University Park Press.

Rogers-Warren, A. K., & Warren, S. F. (1984). The social basis of language and communication in severely handicapped preschoolers. *Topics in Early Childhood Special Education, 4*(2), 57–72.

Rogow, S. (1984). The uses of social routines to facilitate communication in visually impaired and multihandicapped children. *Topics in Early Childhood Special Education, 3*(4), 64–70.

Roth, F., & Spekman, N. (1984). Assessing the pragmatic abilities of children. *Journal of Speech and Hearing Disorders, 49*, 2–17.

Ryan, B. (1974). Evaluation. In *Programmed therapy for stuttering in children and adults*. Springfield, IL: Charles C Thomas.

Sanders, E. (1972). When are speech sounds learned? *Journal of Speech and Hearing Disorders, 37*, 55–63.

Santa Cruz County Superintendent of Schools (1973). *BCP-Behavior Characteristics Progression*. Palo Alto, CA: Vort Corporation.

Schiefelbusch, R. (Ed.). (1978). *Bases of early language intervention* (Vol. 1). Baltimore: University Park Press.

Schiefelbusch, R., & McCormick, L. (1984). Initial and ongoing assessment. In L. McCormick & R. Schiefelbusch (Eds.), *Early language intervention* (pp. 117–156). Columbus, OH: Charles Merrill.

Shames, G. H., & Florance, C. L. (1980). *Stutter-free speech, a goal for therapy*. Columbus, OH: Charles Merrill.

Shames, G. H., & Wiig, E. H. (Eds.). (1982). *Human communication disorders: An introduction*. Columbus, OH: Charles Merrill.

Shane, H. C., & Bashir, A. S. (1980). Election criteria for the adoption of an augmentative communication system: Preliminary considerations. *Journal of Speech and Hearing Disorders, 45*, 408–414.

Silverman, F. H. (1980). *Communication for the speechless*. Englewood Cliffs, NJ: Prentice-Hall.

Spriestersbach, D. C., & Morris, H. L. (1978). General evaluation of oral communication. In F. Darley & D. Spriestersbach (Eds.), *Diagnostic methods in speech pathology* (pp. 97–101). New York: Harper & Row.

Spriestersbach, D. C., Morris, H., & Darley, F. (1978). Examination of the speech mechanism. In F. Darley & D. Spriestersbach (Eds.), *Diagnostic methods in speech pathology* (pp. 322–345). New York: Harper & Row.

Stillman, R. (Ed.). (1978). *The Callier-Azusa Scale—Form G.* University of Texas at Dallas, Callier Center: South Central Regional Center for Services to Deaf-Blind Children.
Stillman, R. & Battle, C. W. (1985). The Callier-Azusa Scale (H) Scales for the assessment of communicative abilities. University of Texas at Dallas: Callici Center for Communication Disorders.
Stremel-Campbell, K. (1982). The development of language in the mentally retarded hearing impaired child: Instructional methods. In D. Tweedie & E. H. Shroyer (Eds.), *The multiply handicapped hearing impaired: Identification and instruction* (pp. 211–248). Washington, DC: Gallaudet College Press.
Stremel-Campbell, K., Johnson-Dorn, N., & Clark-Guida, J. (1984) *Communication placement assessment manual.* Monmouth, OR: Teaching Research.
Templin, M. C. (1957). Certain language skills in children, their development and interrelationships. *Institute of Child Welfare Monograph Series,* No. 26. Minneapolis: University of Minnesota Press.
Tyack, D., & Gottsleben, R. (1974). *Language sampling, analysis, and training: A handbook for teachers and clinicians.* Palo Alto, CA: Consulting Psychological Press.
Van Riper, C. (1971). *The nature of stuttering.* Englewood Cliffs, NJ: Prentice-Hall.
Wertz, R. T. (1978). Neuropathologies of speech and language. In D. Johns (Ed.), *Clinical management of neurogenic communication disorders* (pp. 1–102). Boston: Little, Brown.
Wilcox, M., & Davis, G. (1984). *Pragmatics, PACE, and adult aphasia.* San Diego, CA: College-Hill Press.
Wilson, D. K. (1979). *Voice problems of children.* Baltimore: Williams & Wilkins.
Ziajka, A. (1981). *Prelinguistic communication in infancy.* New York: Praeger Publishers.

APPENDIX: SELECTED NONLINGUISTIC AND PRELINGUISTIC ASSESSMENT TOOLS

	BCP (Behavioral Characteristics Progression)[a]	*Comprehensive Communication Curriculum Guide (CCC)*[b]	*The Callier-Azusa Scale (H) Scales for the Assessment of communicative abilities*[c]
Population designed for	Mentally and behaviorally exceptional children	Students who are severely/profoundly retarded, physically handicapped with little or no communication	Deaf/blind, multihandicapped severely/profoundly handicapped
Age range	Not stated; presents behavioral characteristic	Not stated (birth-adolescent)	Not stated, developmental levels birth to twenty-four months
Criterion; norm referenced; development scale; other	Developmental and criterion combination	Other (interview, questionnaire)	Norm; developmental scale
Interpretation	Profile of skill attainments	Outcome is organized information of student's current communicative performance	Developmental profile with approximate age equivalencies
Tool objective	Diagnostic, establish baseline, assess progress	Diagnostic assessment and establish baseline functioning	Comprehensive, developmentally based framework for viewing communication abilities
Administrator	Special educator and related team personnel	Adult service providers who are very familiar with the student being assessed; primary caregiver and/or parent	Persons familiar with student (teacher, paraprofessional, clinician) in familiar environments/activities
Type of response	Verbal and nonverbal responses during structured and naturally occuring situation	Observation of child in *all* natural environments	Verbal and nonverbal responses during spontaneous interactions in natural environment
		Assessment Areas	
Sensory	Sensory perception; auditory perception	Physical condition; general health	Incorporated into items within all domains (representa-

			tional development, receptive communication, intentional communication, reciprocity)
Social interactions	Interpersonal relations	Attending behavior, reinforcers, communicative environment	Within all domains
Object interactions	Visual motor I & II	No	Within all domains
Vocal development	Prearticulation	Vocal development	Within all domains
Receptive communication	Language comprehension	Indirectly reported	Within all domains
Expressive communication	Language development	Communicative function; communicative responses	Within all domains
Prelanguage	Within other strands	Prelanguage	Within all domains
Language	Within other strands	Language	On items relating to speech or sign language
Speech	Speech reading; articulation; attention to verbal communication (listening)	Speech	Within all domains
Manual signs	Sign language, finger spelling	Child responses may be signs	Within all domains
Communication devices	—	In the guide but not the questionnaires	—
Comments	Easily used; provides visual (chart) output for training skill areas; sequential list of items	Caregiver interview; questionnaire and teacher questionnaire are the assessment tools included; guide includes curriculum and training procedures; thrust is functional	Profile summary sheet provided; examples provided of each skill level assessed; accommodates nonverbal and nonvocal child

[a]Santa Cruz County Superintendent of Schools (1973); VORT Corporation, P.O. Box 11132, Palo Alto, CA 94306.
[b]Klein *et al.* (1981); Early Childhood Institute, University of Kansas, Lawrence, KS 66045.
[c]Stillman & Battle (1985); The University of Texas at Dallas, Callier Center, 1966 Inwood Road, Dallas, TX 75235.

Appendix (*Continued*)

	Communication Placement Assessment Manual[a]	*A Clinical and Educational Manual for Use with Uzgiris and Hunt Scales of Infant Psychological Development*[b]	*Los Lunas Curricular System*[c]
Population designed for	Severe and/or profound handicapping conditions	Normal infants, children beyond 3 years with retardation or other handicaps	Severely profoundly handicapped
Age range	Younger range 0–30 months; older range not specified (estimate 4–6 year mental age)	Birth to 2 years	Birth to 6 years
Criterion; norm referenced; development scale; other	Developmental scale	Ordinal scale with hierarchical steps	Criterion and developmental scale
Interpretation	Communication Assessment Profile (developmental level) and IEP Planning Worksheet (objectives)	Profile	Individual profile bar graph and percentage correct/incorrect
Tool objective	Instructional planning, establishing baseline functioning	Diagnostic, establish baseline functioning for program planning	Diagnostic, establish baseline functioning, assess progress
Administrator	Educator and related team personnel	Any person trained to use the scale	Educator and related team personnel used as resources
Type of response	Direct observation, arranging situations, reports by familiar person/nonvocal and vocal child responses	Verbal and nonverbal responses during structured and spontaneous tasks/situations	Verbal and nonverbal responses during natural and structured situations, group & individual settings
		Assessment Areas	
Sensory	Responses to sensory input	Sensory (cognitive, visual pursuit, object permanence)	Awareness of environment
Social interactions	Responses to social input	Social interaction	Awareness of people; identification of body parts
Object interactions	Interactions with objects	Object interaction (spatial relationships, operational causality)	Identification of objects

Vocal development	Vocal development; oral-motor development	Vocal development, vocal imitation	Vocabulary comprehension, prelinguistic skills
Receptive communication	Receptive communication	Receptive communication	Complete subsection verbal and nonverbal
Expressive communication	Expressive communication	Expressive communication	Complete subsection verbal and nonverbal
Prelanguage	Expressive communication; prelanguage	Prelanguage	Prelanguage
Language	Expressive communication; communication functions	Language	Identification of pictures, prepositions, pronouns, morphemes
Speech	Expressive communication; Language Modality Supplement: speech	—	Sound production
Manual signs	Expressive communication; language; Language Modality Supplement; manual signs	Manual signs (gestures)	Gestures, mode selection within Communication Skills Summary
Communication devices	Language Modality Supplement: communication devices and systems	Communication devices	Can be used for most expressive items
Comments	Comprehensive format incorporating prelanguage vocal and nonvocal skill development; incorporates language vocal and nonvocal skill development; direct application to service providers	Profile summary sheet and activity suggestions included; 2–3 day assessment; cognitive section includes communication skills	Scoring accomodates neutral; skill impossible due to physical impairment (blindness: exclusively visual items; cerebral palsy: contractures) Communication Skills Summary flow chart: (language prerequisites, mode selection, symbolic language, communication board pretraining)

[a]Stremel-Campbell, Johnson-Dorn and Clark-Guida (1984); Teaching Research, Monmouth, OR 97361.
[b]Carl Dunst (1980); University Park Press, 233 East Redwood Street, Baltimore, MD 21202.
[c]Everington *et al.* (1982); Los Lunas Hospital and Training School, Box 1269, Los Lunas, NM 87031.

11

Craniocerebral Trauma in Children

Ralph E. Tarter and Kathleen L. Edwards

INTRODUCTION

The nervous system is the primary means by which the human organism communicates with the environment. Trauma to the nervous system in children often results in complex morphological, biochemical, and physiological disturbances. Not surprisingly, such disruption compromises adaptational potential. This is evidenced at the psychological level of analysis as cognitive deficits, emotional dysregulation, motivational difficulties, and interpersonal maladjustment in school, at home, and in the social macroenvironment.

Trauma, all types combined, is the leading cause of death in children who are over 1 year of age (Gratz, 1979). In the United States, trauma to the head is the most common cause of fatal injuries, being responsible annually for approximately 4,000 deaths (Raphaely, Swedlow, Downes, & Bruel, 1980). Approximately 200,000 children are hospitalized each year as the result of a head or brain injury, of whom 15,000 require prolonged institutional care (Mealey, 1968; Raphaely *et al.*, 1980). It is estimated that 10% of children in the population suffer at least one episode of head trauma that is of sufficient severity to cause unconsciousness (Melchior, 1961).

Males are at higher risk than females to suffer head trauma. In a recent large-scale study of incidence rates spanning four decades, males were found to outnumber females in a ratio of 2:1 (Annegers, Grabow,

Ralph E. Tarter and Kathleen L. Edwards • Western Psychiatric Institute and Clinic, 3811 O'Hara Street, Pittsburgh, Pennsylvania 15213.

Kurland, & Laws, 1980). In addition, the peak age of risk for suffering a head injury differs between the sexes: Males are at the highest and second highest risk between 15 to 24 and 5 to 9 years of age, whereas females are at greatest risk between 10 to 14 years of age and secondly between 15 to 24 years of age (Jennett, 1972).

The factor most likely to be responsible for the traumatic injury changes with age. Cerebral trauma occurring at the time of childbirth has been estimated to have fatal consequences in about three births per 1,000 (Butler & Bonham, 1963). Since this finding was published, innovations in medical technology have undoubtedly produced a lower rate of fatalities consequential to cerebral trauma. However, whereas the mortality rate from cerebral trauma occurring at birth may have declined, it is also likely because of advances in medical technology that there is a larger proportion of surviving children who have a chronic neurologic disability. In the preschool child, the most frequent cause of craniocerebral trauma is from a fall (Annegers *et al.*, 1980). Traffic accidents, on the other hand, are the most likely cause of trauma for older children, particularly for severe injuries (Heiskanen & Kaste, 1974; Rutter, Chadwick, Shaffer, & Brown, 1980).

Trauma incurred from a sport activity and from assaults are the third and fourth leading causes of brain injury (Annegers *et al.*, 1980). With respect to assaults, increasing attention has been directed by both professionals and the media to child abuse as a cause of brain trauma. In the absence of epidemiological research, however, the extent to which parental violence contributes to the prevalence of craniocerebral trauma in children is unknown. McHenry, Girdany, and Elmer (1963) reported that 25% of physically abused children admitted to hospital were found to have a subdural hematoma. Six percent of the cases resulted in the death of the child. Thus, although the population rates of head trauma from parental abuse have yet to be studied, it is possible to conclude, at the very least, that those who suffer such abuse are at risk for experiencing very deleterious neurological consequences and even death. Certain children are at particularly high risk to suffer a brain injury from physical abuse. Children of alcoholic fathers, for example, suffer a loss of consciousness from physical abuse as well as from other factors more than children of nonalcoholics (Tarter, Hegedus, Goldstein, Shelly, & Alterman, 1984).

One point that needs to be underscored is that traumatically brain-injured children do not constitute a random sample in the population. Children who have a preexisting behavioral disturbance, a factor possibly accounting for the uneven sex distribution because conduct and hyperactive disturbances are substantially more prevalent in males, are at higher risk to suffer a traumatic injury (Rutter, Chadwick, & Schachar,

1983). This is especially the case for children who suffer mild brain injuries (Brown, Chadwick, Shaffer, Ruter, & Traub, 1981; Chadwick Rutter, Brown, Shaffer, & Traub, 1981; Rutter *et al.*, 1980). In addition, emotional disturbances in the mother (Brown & Davidson, 1978; Hjern & Nylandor, 1962) and parental instability (Klonoff, 1971; Rutter *et al.*, 1983) are factors associated with an increased risk for traumatic head injury in children.

The failure of most research studies to ascertain the pretraumatic status of the child has led to a rather substantial literature of dubious validity regarding the consequences of craniocerebral trauma. With respect to clinical evaluation, the fact that certain children are at elevated risk to suffer trauma underlines the need to obtain as much information as possible about the child's premorbid status and home environmental context.

In summary, craniocerebral trauma is a common occurrence in childhood and, indeed, is the leading cause of death in children. It is not a randomly distributed event. Children with behavioral disturbance and those who have a disturbed home life due to parental conflict or psychopathology are at heightened risk to suffer a head trauma. Males greatly outnumber females. Also, the cause of the trauma changes with age. Moreover, the effects of the trauma are not constant. For example, Jennett (1972), controlling for severity of injury and duration of coma, found that the mortality rate from brain trauma is greater in children under 5 years of age than in individuals between 5 to 20 years of age. In nonfatal injuries, children under 5 years of age are also more likely to suffer posttraumatic seizures than older children. In addition, a less severe brain injury is more likely to produce a posttraumatic seizure disorder in younger than in older children (Jennett, 1975). Thus, given the diversity of factors involved, general conclusions about the consequences of traumatic brain injury in children may be misleading. At the present level of understanding, it may be more useful to simply explicate the factors that are known to influence outcome from trauma. To this end, the following discussion reviews the neurological and psychological literature on the types,effects, and sequelae of craniocerebral trauma.

DESCRIPTION

TYPES OF CRANIOCEREBRAL TRAUMA

Closed Head Injury. There are two basic types of traumatic injury to the brain, each producing different neurological and psychological sequelae. The first and most common type of trauma involves a closed head injury. It usually occurs after either sudden acceleration or deceleration of the head as it strikes a solid surface, thereby causing a crushing impact to the skull.

The most severe brain injuries usually happen when the head suddenly stops moving upon impact with some object. This event produces two kinds of mechanical forces: *contact* and *inertia*. Contact on impact results in both horizontal and rotational movement of the brain within the skull. The effects of contact are such that the brain is injured more or less at the site of the impact of the skull and, depending on the force and vector of the insult, at a contrecoup site that usually is linearly opposite to the primary contact site. The forces of inertia produce a gradient of stress that causes brain tissue destruction and vascular hemorrhaging. Sheering of the cerebrum, in which parts of the cortex are rubbed against sharp or rough inner bony surfaces of the skull in places such as the orbital plate, falx cerebri, and sphenoid wing, as well as tension in the brain causes tissue to tear apart. Moreover, sudden compression of the brain mass also occurs and may synergistically interact with the effects of the other forces in a closed head injury to produce neurological sequelae of varying types and severity.

In sudden acceleration-deceleration, the dissipation of pressure typically moves in a downward direction, thereby affecting the brainstem and causing a disruption of the reticular activating system. In mild cases of trauma, this may be subjectively experienced as "seeing stars," whereas, in severe trauma, irreversible coma and even death may ensue. It is important to note that although sudden acceleration-deceleration often culminates in impact of the head against another object, the sudden change in momentum itself may also be sufficient to induce neuropathological changes (Boll, 1983). Whether sudden acceleration-deceleration by itself can produce lasting cognitive or emotional disturbance is, as yet, still unknown.

The neurological pathology incurred from a closed head injury is generally diffuse. The corpus callosum, temporal cortex, and midbrain tegmentum are, however, especially vulnerable to injury, primarily because the location of these structures in the cranial cavity renders them liable for sheering or disruption from mechanical forces (Mealey, 1968).

In addition to brain tissue damage, craniocerebral trauma often results in cerebrovascular disturbances. After even relatively slight brain injury, stretching and hemorrhaging of capillaries can take place. Traumatic aneurysms and damage to the internal carotid artery at the locus of its entry into the base of the skull may occur that, if severe enough, can have fatal consequences.

Skull fracture is common in cases of severe impact. Under such circumstances, the skin surrounding the skull often remains intact even though the skull is depressed or perforated. An inbending at the impact point and outbending in the surrounding area is frequently observed after a high velocity impact. This is commonly accompanied by brain contusion and laceration of the meninges.

Penetrating Head Injury. The second type of brain trauma occurs upon penetration of the skull, exposing the meninges, and potentially causing cortical and subcortical injury. The most common cause of this type of injury is from a bullet wound, although under extraordinary circumstances the impact of a sharp object against the skull (e.g., a knife) can produce a penetrating brain injury.

The immediate and long-term consequences of a penetrating injury are typically less severe than in a closed head injury. Despite the higher risk of infection and focalized intracranial hematoma in penetrating wounds (Miller & Jennett, 1968), there is more generalized disruption of brain and vascular functioning in closed head injuries (Dugger, 1964). Also, the risk for posttraumatic seizures is greater in a closed compared to a penetrating head injury (Black, Shepard, & Walker, 1975; Jennett, 1975).

NEUROLOGICAL SEQUELAE OF TRAUMATIC BRAIN DAMAGE

Penetrating and closed injuries do not, as a rule, result in discrete pathological changes. Rather, as Figure 1 depicts, there is typically a disruption of biochemical and physiological homeostasis that may even be a more important determinant of clinical course and prognosis than the direct effects of the brain trauma. However, the structural damage to the cerebrum following closed head injury is frequently quite extensive, encompassing not only the sites of impact from the effects of the coup and contrecoup, but additionally may include injury resulting from brain rotation, tension, and compression in regions that are remote from the trajectory of the impacting force. The extent of morphological alteration resulting from a penetrating object is, in contrast, more circumscribed and typically is confined to the path of object entry into the brain.

A point to be emphasized is that simple cause-and-effect relationships are difficult to delineate, if at all even possible, in traumatic brain lesions. Referring again to Figure 1, it can be seen that trauma not only produces structural damage to the cerebrum and brain stem but also impairs the organism's capacity to fulfill the brain's metabolic needs and disrupts hemodynamic homeostatis as well as neurophysiological

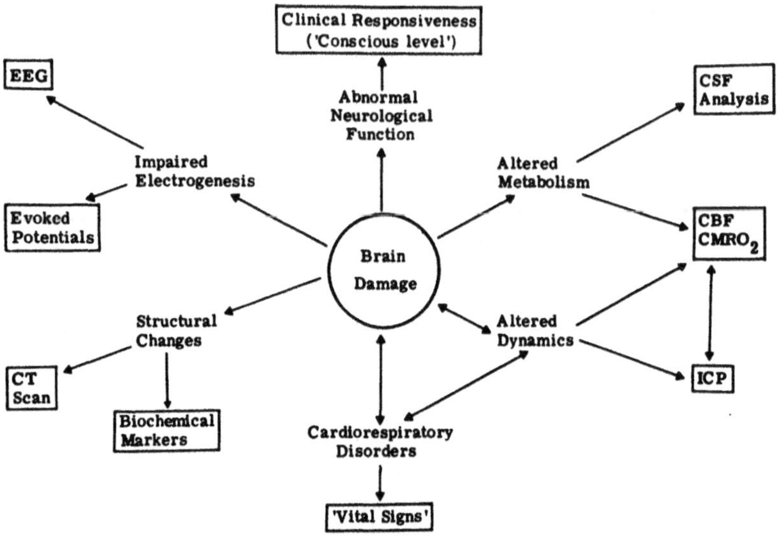

FIGURE 1. Pathology associated with craniocerebral trauma. From *Management of Head Injuries* by B. Jennett and G. Teasdale, 1983; Philadelphia: Davis, Copyright 1983 by Davis. Reprinted by permission.

functioning. These diverse manifestations are ultimately reflected in cognitive and emotional disturbances. The psychological disturbances, therefore, cannot be attributed to any one specific factor but instead represent the cumulative effects of the neurological injury. Next are described the most commonly found consequences of craniocerebral trauma that can influence psychological functioning.

Extradural Hemorrhage. The incidence of extradural hemorrhage is estimated to be between 1% to 3% across all age groups (Herzberger, Harwood-Hash, & Hadson, 1964). Extradural hemorrhaging is uncommon, however, in children under 2 years of age. Where the trauma has fatal consequences, extradural hemorrhaging is a factor in about 20% of the cases (Mealey, 1968; Milhorat, 1978).

An extradural hemorrhage most frequently occurs if the impact site is on the lateral aspect of the head. At the location of impact, the skull is depressed, thereby causing the dura to be stripped from the inner surface of the cranium as the impact point of the skull rebounds. The inbending and subsequent rebounding of the skull also causes the thin-walled interposed blood vessels to tear, resulting in bleeding in the extradural space. In infants, because the skull is still resilient, hemorrhaging may occur without a concomitant skull fracture.

Hematoma. Hematomas (blood clots) are usually unilateral. The size of the hematoma is dependent on a number of factors, of which the duration of hemorrhaging associated with either arterial or venous spillage is probably the most important. The most common hemorrhage is consequential to a laceration of the middle meningeal artery or to one of its branches.

Death generally occurs without emergency surgical intervention. Even with successful surgical intervention, the postsurgery prognosis is guarded. Neurological disturbances, including pseudobulbar palsy, spasticity, hemiplegia, hemianopia, and even cortical blindness may remain and comprise permanent features of the child's disability. Convulsions of a focalized nature are also common, typically beginning on the side of the face contralateral to the lesion and eventually encompassing the arms and legs.

The child may appear normal for a period of time, ranging from a few minutes to a few days following the trauma. Then, in reaction to cerebral compression, rapid deterioration occurs. The symptom picture includes lethargy, vomiting, irritability, and headaches. Ultimately the child lapses into a coma. At this stage, even if biological survival can be effected through emergency medical-surgical intervention, a permanent vegetative state may still result (Milhorat, 1978).

Intradural Hemorrhage. Bleeding underneath the dura, resulting from rupture of the thin-walled veins extending from the cortex to the dural sinuses, is a common sequel of brain trauma. Approximately 80% of subdural hematomas occur in infancy (Herzberger *et al.*, 1964). At this stage of central nervous system (CNS) maturation, the veins are particularly fragile and, unlike adults, are not supported by Pacchionian granulations. Thus, even a rather mild head injury can produce hemorrhaging and subsequent hematoma. Not surprisingly, therefore, birth events and early postnatal trauma may result in a subdural hematoma that may go undetected, and subsequently when revealed, its cause may be difficult to unequivocally document (Milhorat, 1978).

Approximately 50% of cases result in death. Among survivors, there is usually a bilateral distribution of hematomas, and in severe cases the hematomas may even envelop most of the two cerebral hemispheres. Seizures following recovery occur in 50% to 90% of cases (Jennett, 1975; Mealey, 1968).

Although trauma is a major cause of intradural hematoma, other causitive factors should also be considered, especially where a specific etiology cannot be implicated. Anemia, dysentery, and pneumonia are particularly suspect in the overall medical history. Malnourishment, often accompanied by physical abuse and poor parenting skills causing accidental head injury, also needs to be investigated as a causitive factor.

Without surgical intervention, softening of the cortex and subcortex underneath the hematoma occurs. Even with successful aspiration, or removal of the hematoma with craniotomy, the long-term prognosis is not favorable. Epilepsy, optic atrophy, and cerebral palsy are common permanent sequelae. About 70% of cases develop stuttering or become eneuretic; however, the extent to which these disturbances are due to direct neurological pathology or the child's emotional reaction to a chronic and severe disability is unknown (Milhorat, 1978). Not surprisingly, the presence of a subdural hematoma is associated with significant impairment on neuropsychological tests measuring cognition and psychomotor efficiency (Klove & Cleeland, 1972).

Traumatic Arachnoid Cysts. A severe head injury will occasionally result in the development of an encapsulated fluid collection in the pia-arachnoid. The mechanisms responsible for development of such a cyst are, however, not well understood. The cyst usually occurs directly underneath the impact point, and if not removed may cause porencephaly or brain atrophy. Frequently, the inner table of the skull erodes into which the cyst protrudes.

Clinically, localized and intense headaches are experienced. Depending on the location of the cyst, there may be hemiplegia or other focalized neurological symptoms. Presumably, cognitive deficits are manifest as well, although, as yet, no neuropsychological investigations have been conducted.

Subdural Hydroma. If the arachnoid membrane is ruptured, cerebrospinal fluid (CSF) can seep into the subarachnoid spaces. Because CSF cannot be readily absorbed, it remains on the cortical convexity beneath the dura, thereby deforming the ventricles and compressing the brain.

The clinical presentation is very similar to that found in subdural hematoma. Headaches, vomiting, and drowsiness are common. The specific effect of a subdural hydroma on cognitive functioning is not possible to ascertain because it invariably occurs in conjunction with other significant neurological sequelae; however, given the substantial cerebral changes caused by this condition, it is safe to conclude that its presence is at least an additive factor militating against psychological recovery.

In summary, craniocerebral trauma has multiple neurological effects. Not only is brain tissue destroyed as the result of the impact event and subsequent anoxia, but neurological functioning is further compromised by disruption of metabolic efficiency and hemodynamic homeostasis. Consequently, the posttraumatic psychological manifestations depend on the parameters of the trauma and the pattern and severity of neurological disturbance as well as the child's age and premorbid characteristics. The point to be underscored is that there is no simple or defined relationship between the site of impact on the skull and pattern of psychological disorder. Rather, the psychological presentation posttraumatically is the consequence of premorbid factors interacting with the cumulative idiosyncratic multisystem disruption of several biological systems.

COGNITIVE SEQUELAE OF CRANIOCEREBRAL TRAUMA

The cognitive effects of traumatic brain injury differ between children and adults. This is primarily due to the fact that children, up until at least midadolescence, are undergoing functional maturation of the brain and, hence, still acquiring cognitive skills. Thus, whereas the focus of measurement in traumatically injured adults is to determine the nature and extent of capacities lost or reduced, the examination in children must also be concerned with the degree to which the individual is additionally compromised in acquiring specific cognitive skills that were not yet established at the time of injury. For this reason, determination of the effects of traumatic brain injury on cognitive functioning can be most comprehensively understood within the context of the overall developmental process.

The following discussion reviews the literature pertinent to those factors that have been found to influence posttraumatic cognitive functioning in children.

Duration of Unconsciousness. Studies with primates, in which a loss of consciousness is induced for even a few seconds by sudden acceleration-deceleration, have revealed histopathological changes in the brainstem (Adams et al., 1981). In humans, a brief interval of unconsciousness, that is, less than 1 hour, often can cause transitory disturbances such as somnolence, hemiparesis, blindness, visual distortions (photopsia, gray coloring), irritability, vomiting, and neurological signs of brainstem disturbance (Kompf Neundorfer, Ekrest, & Wallesch, 1977). In one neuropsychological study of 9- to 13-year-old children who suffered a loss of consciousness that did not exceed 15 minutes, Gulbrandsen (1984) obtained test data evidence for persisting cognitive impairment 4 to 8 months after the trauma, even though this was not reflected either on academic performance or in the form of subjective complaints about cognitive capacity. Of additional interest is the fact that the deficits were most pronounced in the younger children and on the more complex types of cognitive tasks.

Permanent physical and cognitive impairments are typically observed if there is a prolonged period of unconsciousness (Stover & Zeiger, 1976), although it is noteworthy that full cognitive restitution has been reported in cases of prolonged coma (Flach & Malmros, 1972; Hjern & Nylandor, 1962). Also, it has been reported that the severity of posttraumatic cognitive deficits is correlated with the duration of coma (Brink, Garrett, Hale, Woo-Sam, & Nickel, 1970; Levin & Eisenberg, 1979; Winogron, Knights, & Bawden, 1984). Thus, although it is not surprising that prolonged unconsciousness is associated with neuropsychological impairment, it is noteworthy that even after relatively brief periods of unconsciousness, cognitive deficits are present. These manifest impairments are greater in younger compared to older children. (Gulbrandsen, 1984; Levin & Eisenberg, 1979; Winogron *et al.*, 1984). What is not clear from these studies is whether these deficits are permanent and the minimal duration of unconsciousness that is required to produce a lasting cognitive impairment.

Coma duration would, at first glance, appear to be an accurate and objective index of trauma severity. However, coma duration may be quite difficult to quantify. It is often unclear when consciousness is regained posttraumatically. Also, the child may not necessarily experience continuous unconsciousness from the moment of impact but rather may lapse into coma only after the onset of hemorrhaging. Thus, the measurement and factors responsible for coma are too variable to be usefully employed as a single index of trauma severity for predicting cognitive outcome.

Concussion. Concussion is defined as the disruption of neural functioning due to mechanical impact to the head. It is not known if a single concussion, without a loss of consciousness, can have lasting cognitive effects. Multiple concussions are known to produce permanent neurological impairment in athletes (e.g., boxers), but whether children, either through physical abuse or sports injury who experience multiple concussions, but otherwise are not rendered unconscious, are likewise cognitively compromised has not been researched.

Skull Fracture. Fracture of the skull is not predictive of posttraumatic cognitive outcome (Jennett, 1972). Secondary complications, however, from infection can exacerbate the overall neurological status of the child such that cognitive deficits will be manifest. Penetrating wounds and compound fractures that expose the middle ear or nasal sinuses pose the greatest risk for infection and subsequent cognitive impairment.

Posttraumatic Amnesia (PTA). Posttraumatic amnesia duration is the interval between the time of the head injury and the time the child can first sustain intellectual interaction with the environment. The advantage of employing PTA duration as an index of trauma severity over simply the duration of the coma is that uncertainty is eliminated regarding when continuity of consciousness is established. It is not always clear when consciousness is fully regained after coma, thus making it difficult to precisely ascertain the duration of unconsciousness. In contrast, the end point of PTA can be operationally measured as the time at which the child is spatially and temporally orientated such that new memories can be formed on a continuous basis. Furthermore, unlike coma duration that defines trauma severity according to state of consciousness, PTA defines severity in physical as well as psychological terms by including both duration of coma *and* anterograde amnesia in the measurement.

Posttraumatic amnesia duration has been found to be a very useful index for predicting long-term cognitive recovery (Rutter *et al.*, 1980). A shortcoming, however, resides in the difficulty of testing children, especially very young children, who may be unable to adequately respond to an interview-based evaluation of memory capacity and spatiotemporal orientation. Moreover, after attaining consciousness, many traumatically head-injured children exhibit such varied symptoms as irritability, lethargy, nausea, hypothermia, dizziness, and headaches. Mutism is also not uncommon, particularly if the injury resulted in damage to the basal ganglia (Levin *et al.*, 1983). Language impairments caused by the injury may further hamper testing the child during the acute posttraumatic period. These symptoms may persist long after consciousness has been regained. Thus, acquiring the child's cooperation may be difficult because motivation and, indeed, the capacity to participate in an examination of cognitive processes is likely to be less than optimal.

Strub and Black (1981) propose a classification of head injury severity based upon duration of PTA. Despite the previously mentioned measurement limitations and interindividual variability in recovery course, their classification schema nonetheless provides operationally useful guidelines for categorizing trauma severity. In their schema, a PTA of between 0 to 15 minutes classifies the head injury as slight, whereas a PTA of between 15 to 60 minutes is considered mild. Moderate trauma is associated with a duration of between 1 to 24 hours, whereas a severe injury has a PTA interval of between 1 to 7 days. Beyond 7 days PTA, the trauma is classified as very severe. Though somewhat arbitrary, this classification provides the clinician a framework for estimating severity of injury that has prognostic value. Chadwick, Rutter, Brown, Shaffer, and Traub (1981), for example, found no evidence for a persisting intellectual impairment if the PTA was less than 24 hours. Nor were intellectual sequelae reliably seen if the PTA duration ranged up to 7 days. On the other hand, persisting intellectual impairment was typically observed in children if the PTA period exceeded 7 days. Thus, a very severe injury, at least as indexed by PTA duration, is required to produce a lasting intellectual impairment.

Pathophysiological Complications. Advances in radiographic techniques and biochemical analysis potentially afford the opportunity to quantify pathophysiological changes that can predict the course and ultimate level of cognitive restitution. Brain oxygen metabolism and cerebral blood flow are two examples of biological processes that have been demonstrated in adults to correlate positively with cognitive capacity. As yet, attempts have not been made to determine if these and other biological variables can predict posttraumatic cognitive recovery in children. Indeed, very little effort has been expended to assess the extent to which features of the pathophysiological presentation are associated with head trauma outcome. Intracranial pressure during the acute posttraumatic period has, for example, not been found to be predictive of cognitive deficit (Winogron *et al.*, 1984). Blood pressure during the early posttraumatic period has, on the other hand, been observed to have some prognostic value on recovery (Overgaard *et al.*, 1973). The presence and extensiveness of cerebral infarction and ischemic lesions, duration and severity of edema, arterial thrombosis and CSF acidity, and flow and absorption have not been investigated. With respect to these latter variables, it is particularly important to ascertain if the degree of CSF acidity, due to the accumulation of lactate from anoxic and damaged tissue, predicts the course and level of cognitive recovery (Cold, Enevaldern, & Malomoos, 1975). Without a multivariate research strategy, in which the additive and interactive effects of numerous pathophysiological variables can be simultaneously assessed for their contribution to posttraumatic cognitive status, the capacity to predict the course and level of cognitive restitution following craniocerebral trauma is bound to be very limited.

Threshold for Psychological Sequelae. The available findings indicate that a PTA duration of less than 24 hours does not usually result in permanent psychological impairment. Indeed, a PTA interval of between 2 to 7 days is generally also associated with a favorable prognosis (Chadwick, Rutter, Brown, Shaffer, & Traub, 1981). Beyond 7 days PTA duration, psychiatric and cognitive sequelae commonly persist, although even from such a severe injury, substantial cognitive recovery may take place. A PTA of 3 weeks produces lasting psychological deficit. The latter findings, based largely on the work of Rutter and his colleagues (Brown *et al.*, 1981; Chadwick, Rutter, Thompson & Shaffer, 1981; Chadwick, Rutter, Shaffer, Shroat, 1981; Rutter *et al.*, 1980). demonstrate rather unequivocally that a severe head injury, at least as indexed by PTA duration, is required for permanent psychological sequelae to be manifest. This conclusion must be tempered, however, by the fact that there are substantial individual differences in the pathophysiological manifestations of traumatic brain injury. Hence PTA duration as a threshold index for predicting outcome should be viewed as a general guideline and not applied to individual cases for making prognostic inferences.

Other investigators, employing coma duration as the index of trauma severity, have found that a more mild injury is associated with cognitive sequelae (Brink *et al.*, 1970; Gulbrandsen, 1984; Levin & Eisenberg, 1979; Winogron *et al.*, 1984). These studies, unlike those of Rutter and colleagues, did not employ a prospective paradigm and, hence, the extent to which the residual cognitive deficits were affected by premorbid status of the child cannot be determined. For instance, Mahoney *et al.* (1983) reported that 18% of their sample of trauma cases (n = 91) exhibited either language delays or signs of minimal brain dysfunction prior to trauma.

In a study of severely head-injured ten-year-old children, Brink *et al.* (1970) found that duration of coma was correlated with posttraumatic IQ score. A mean duration of 1.7 weeks coma was not associated with subseqent IQ deterioration. However, intellectual decrements to the level of borderline IQ, mild mental retardation, and severe mental retardation were found where the average coma duration was 3, 8, and 11 weeks, respectively. Other investigators have found that coma duration of 7 days or longer is associated with permanent neurological and psychiatric impairment (Heiskaven & Kaste, 1974; Richardson, 1963). The disturbances most frequently reported included memory deficits, social maladjustment, and academic difficulties. Again, it is important to point out that there is substantial interindividual variability on outcome. Mahoney *et al.* (1983), found, for example, that of 14 subjects who had been in coma for 2 weeks, 9 had no persisting neurological sequelae.

Thus, although there is evidence that even relatively modest trauma can produce cognitive impairment, there is also indication that many children fully recover from severe injuries. Part of the ambiguity is due to the problem of employing single-index measures of severity without taking into consideration premorbid factors and individual variation in the pathophysiologicla disturbance. Moreover, the outcome criterion is another factor responsible for the discrepant findings among the various investigations. Neuropsychological test measures are very sensitive indicators of cerebral integrity and, hence, yield results that are at variance with results obtained from studies employing psychometric tests of intelligence. Consequently, the differences among the various investigations with respect to the measure of cognitive capacity also adds to the difficulty in defining the threshold of injury severity required to cause lasting cognitive impairment.

Long-Term Cognitive Effects. In a large-scale project examining the association between age at time of trauma and cognitive outcome, Klonoff, Low, and Clark (1977) longitudinally monitored the cognitive capacity of 131 children between the ages of 3 to 9 and 100 children between 9 to 16 who were hospitalized because of a head injury. By 5 years posttrauma, significant attrition in the sample had occurred, reducing the younger cohort to 75 subjects and the older group to 39 subjects. The younger and older subjects were comparable at the time of hospitalization with respect to demographic characteristics and pathophysiological presentation. The results of this study indicated that for both the younger and the older age groups, most of the cognitive recovery, as measured by a battery of intellectual and neuropsychological tests, took place within the first 2 posttrauma years. Improvements were noted, however, for up to 5 years after the injury for certain cognitive processes. After 5 years, the older subjects still exhibited deficits on 12% of tests in the neuropsychological battery compared to younger children who were impaired on only 3% of the tests in the battery. There was also a higher incidence of EEG abnormalities in older (16%) than younger (5%) subjects. In contrast, neurological symptoms did not discriminate the two age groups; 38% of the younger subjects compared to 31% of the older subjects had persisting symptoms after 5 years.

Three other findings from this investigation are noteworthy. First, there is much variability between children in the course and pattern of cognitive recovery. This fact needs to be borne in mind whenever interpreting mean scores of groups of subjects. Second, IQ scores do not parallel the performance scores on neuropsychological tests. Hence, it can be concluded that tests of intelligence and neuropsychological capacity tap different cognitive processes. Third, prediction of long-term cognitive outcome is very difficult. Employing multivariate statistical procedures that incorporated multiple measures of brain injury severity, initial Full Scale IQ, duration of unconsciousness, duration of PTA, EEG abnormality rating, mother's gestation period, child's age, and retrograde amnesia, it was found that only about 20% of the variance could be accounted for on neuropsychological test scores 5 years posttrauma.

Effects of Age on Cognitive Outcome. Levin and Eisenberg (1979) examined the effects of head injury in a group of 6- to 12-year-old children and 13- to 18-year-old adolescents. Only short-term outcome was assessed, this being at a median of 28 days posttrauma for the younger subjects and 22 days posttrauma for the older subjects. It was found that the greatest impairment occurred in the younger subjects. The most salient cognitive deficit was in memory storage and retrieval. Intellectual capacity was also adversely affected by a severe injury.

Although it has been generally found that the prognosis for cognitive recovery is better for younger than older children (Gulbrandsen, 1984; Levin & Eisenberg, 1979; Winogron *et al.*, 1984), the study by Klonoff *et al.* (1977) illustrates that this is not an invariant finding. Short- and long-term prognosis may interact with age at the time of injury. In this context, craniocerebral trauma has qualitatively different effects on children under 2 years of age than on older children (Black *et al.*, 1975), suggesting that there may be an interaction between the type and severity of cognitive deficit and level of nervous system maturation.

Specificity of Cognitive Impairment. Psychological processes are subserved by functionally specialized cortical regions and systems. In the broadest sense, this is indicated by the fact that the left and right cerebral hemispheres subserve overlapping but nonetheless different cognitive functions; the left (dominant) is primarily responsible for language-mediated cognition, whereas the right (nondominant) is specialized for visuospatial or nonsemantic cognition. Within each hemisphere, particular cortical regions also subserve specialized functions. For instance, the pars triangularis (Broca's region) in the left frontal region subserves expressive language ability, whereas Wernicke's area, adjacent to the transverse gyrus of Heschl in the left temporal lobe, subserves receptive language capacity. It is not possible here to review in detail the development of brain functional organization; suffice it to say, that depending on the location of a cerebral lesion, there usually occurs predictable cognitive manifestations, although it should be emphasized that there is no isomorphic cortical representation for the various cognitive processes. For a thorough discussion of brain–behavior relationships, the reader is referred to Walsh (1978), and, with specific reference to child development, to Spreen, Tupper, Risser, Tuokko, and Edgell (1984).

The specificity of association between type of cognitive impairment and cortical locus of traumatic injury has not been systematically explored. In one such study, Chadwick, Rutter, Shaffer, and Shroat (1981) examined 97 children under 12 years of age who, at least 2 years previously, suffered a compound depressed skull fracture. Brain damage was confirmed by the presence of a dural tear accompanied by cortical damage observed at the time of surgery. The children were all administered the WISC and a battery of neuropsychological tests. Surprisingly, age was not found to be related to the magnitude of cognitive impairment, perhaps because the WISC is a rather insensitive measure of cerebral integrity. Nor was length of dural tear related to intellectual capacity.

However, duration of unconsciousness, cerebral edema, posttraumatic epilepsy, and neurological abnormality all influenced the magnitude of intellectual impairment.

In the previously cited study, the greatest intellectual and learning impairments were evidenced in children who suffered diffuse brain injury compared to children who suffered a focal brain injury. With respect to the subgroup of children who suffered a focal injury, no differences in reading ability and WISC IQ measures were found between those who incurred a slight versus severe localized trauma. Thus,for focal brain injury, severity of trauma does not appear to be a major influencing factor on intellectual capacity. Of particular significance is the fact that no association between lesion lateralization and type or pattern of cognitive deficits was noted. Moreover, within each hemisphere, the site of injury was not associated with specific intellectual sequelae or reading retardation. Thus, although this study, as well as others by this group of investigators (Chadwick, Rutter, Brown, Shaffer, & Traub, 1981; Chadwick, Rutter, Shaffer, & Shroat, 1981), found a greater propensity for visuospatial than verbal deficits, no systematic association between type of cognitive deficit and anatomical site was found. Intellectual deficits following craniocerebral trauma were most likely to occur after either generalized brain damage or after a severe focal injury. In the case of focalized injury, lesion site did not play a prominent role in determining the types of deficits on intellectual testing. Whether the same conclusions can be drawn employing neuropsychological test measures that are more sensitive for deatecting focal cerebral pathology remains, however, to be determined.

Psychiatric Sequelae. Severe traumatic head injury often results in emotional or psychiatric disturbances. These disturbances have been found by Brown *et al.* (1981) to be the direct consequence of the brain injury. The psychiatric presentation is not the same for all brain-injured persons but rather can be quite diverse in terms of manifest symptoms: The most common features are anxiety, irritability, emotional lability, and general fatigue or apathy (Richardson, 1963). Psychiatric disturbance is most likely to occur in children who have persisting neurological disorder, although it is noteworthy that individuals without neurological abnormality have a psychiatric disturbance in almost 50% of cases (Brown *et al.*, 1981).

The cortex is not equipotential with respect to posttraumatic psychiatric sequelae. Shaffer, Chadwick, and Rutter (1975), in their study of 98 children with focal injuries, found that a lesion in either the left posterior or right frontal cortical region was more likely to be associated with emotional and behavioral disorders than a focal lesion to other cortical regions. Specific symptoms, however, such as inattention, aggressivity, hyperactivity, and antisocial behavior were unrelated to the site of injury. In an interesting study of 36 pairs of monozygotic twins, discordant for head injury, Dencker (1958) found a higher incidence of stubborness, negativism, temper outbursts, and cognitive rigidity in the head-injured subjects. No particular or unique pattern of psychopathological disruption was found in the head-injured group, however. Thus, controlling for whatever genetic predisposition that may have been present pretrauma, this study illustrates that a head injury during childhood increases the risk for psychiatric problems in adulthood. Moreover, the head-injured subject often did not attain as high a level of social status as the unaffected twin in adulthood.

The quality of the child's social environment also influences the likelihood of psychiatric symptoms emerging after craniocerebral trauma. Children suffering a unilateral compound depressed fracture are at increased risk for a psychiatric disturbance if the parents are separated or divorced, had psychiatric problems themselves, or if there are four or more siblings in the same household (Brown *et al.*, 1981; Shaffer *et al.*, 1975). Parents who react to the child's head injury by either reducing discipline or becoming overprotective also increase the child's risk for developing a psychiatric disturbance (Brown, 1982).

Thus, severe craniocerbral trauma augments the risk for a psychiatric disturbance in children. These manifestations do not comprise one or more specific psychiatric diagnoses but rather are reflected as an admixture of psychiatric symptoms. These disturbances appear to be the result of the direct effects of the trauma. However, environmental factors, particularly home stability, parental psychiatric adjustment, and parental reaction to the child's injury appear to also significantly influence the likelihood of a psychiatric disturbance emerging posttraumatically. In addition, a preinjury behavioral disorder, even if of a rather trivial nature, increases the risk for a psychiatric disorder after trauma (Brown *et al.*, 1981; Harrington & Letemendia, 1958). Finally, somatic problems such as migraines, hemiparesis, and seizures may also contribute to the emergence of psychiatric disturbances. Therefore, one must be cognizant of the multifactorial etiology of the psychiatric and behavioral disturbances in the traumatically brain-injured child.

PSYCHOLOGICAL ASSESSMENT

Severe head injury, as the previous discussion illustrated, is often associated with persisting cognitive and psychiatric sequelae. In evaluating the head-injured child, it is critical that the clinician recognize the child's changing clinical condition. Because recovery progresses for several years after the trauma, it is not possible to determine what the ultimate level of restitution will be upon testing the child on only a single occasion. Also, performance on cognitive tests is more variable in the brain-injured child. Behavioral and emotional lability as well as motivational problems, such as lethargy and apathy, particularly during the acute posttraumatic period, may produce test results that do not validly reflect the child's optimal level of functioning. Consequently, it is necessary that serial evaluations be conducted in order to monitor the recovery process. With respect to cognitive processes, this entails comparing current performance with expected levels of performance of normal children during psychological development. To restate this point in a different form, it is important to determine if the injury has produced a constant *magnitude* of deficit but otherwise did not affect the *rate* of cognitive development thereafter. By performing serial evaluations, using cognitive tests that either have equivalent forms or yield results that are not affected by practice, it is possible to ascertain the consequences of the trauma in the context of developmental maturation: that is, whether the manifest impairments relate only to the level of functioning or also result in a reduced rate of acquisition of cognitive processes.

Bearing the preceding points in mind, a comprehensive psychological assessment must address three broad spheres of functioning: These are the cognitive, behavioral, and emotional status of the child. The following discussion reviews the various test measures available for performing each of these types of evaluations.

NEUROPSYCHOLOGICAL ASSESSMENT

Because of the diversity of cognitive processes required for educational and vocational success, it is essential that an assessment strategy be adopted that comprehensively examines intelligence, language, memory, attention, sensation, motor efficiency, visuospatial integration, and psychomotor integration. Traumatic brain injuries have been frequently found to result in impairments in these cognitive processes, although the particular presentation varies from child to child (Brink *et al.*, 1970; Chadwick, Rutter, Brown, Shaffer, & Traub, 1981; Gulbrandsen, 1984; Klonoff *et al.*, 1977; Levin & Eisenberg, 1979; Levin, Eisenberg, Wigg, & Kohayashi, 1982; Winogron *et al.*, 1984). Given the multidimensional nature of cognitive functioning, it should be evident that single-measure evaluations of "organicity" using the Bender-Gestalt or, for that matter, any other screening instrument, are inadequate. The objective of a neuropsychological assessment is to profile the child's cognitive strengths and weaknesses following trauma such that rehabilitation efforts can be targeted to the processes most in need of remediation for educational and occupational adjustment.

In conducting a neuropsychological evaluation, at least two different strategies can be employed. One assessment strategy is to administer a commercially available standardized battery that examines a broad range of cognitive processes. Two such test batteries applicable for children are the Reitan-Indiana Neuropsychological Battery and the children's version of the Luria-Nebraska battery. Though substantially different in theoretical framework and testing format, these two batteries essentially tap the same cognitive processes. The Luria-Nebraska battery takes less time, however, to administer. On the other hand, the Reitan-Indiana battery, having been in use much longer, has perhaps greater proven validity. Both of these neuropsychological batteries assess a broad spectrum of cognitive capacities, which can assist in lesion lateralization and localization, although this may not be of much relevance for head trauma. Even what is more important than lesion localization is the fact that these two instruments can provide information about the level of cognitive functioning across diverse processes known to be integral for successful educational and vocational adjustment.

The second type of assessment strategy involves compositing a test battery from the diverse assortment of neuropsychological tests presently available that is suited to the particular needs and objectives of the clinician. This may involve utilizing individual test measures deemed to be of particular importance (e.g., tests of memory, psychomotor efficiency, etc.); specialized modality-specific batteries (e.g., Bruninks Test of Motor Proficiency); or tests that provide neuropsychological information that is relevant to functioning in particular situations (e.g., Detroit Tests of Learning Aptitude).

Table 1 depicts the areas of cognitive functioning and lists the neuropsychological tests that can be used in a comprehensive assessment of brain-injured children. The use of any particular test depends more on the preferences of the clinician than on the objective properties of the specific test measure because within each category of function the various tests share a significant amount of variance. Preference should, however, be given to tests that are brief, inasmuch as the child's capacity and motivation to participate in a long testing session may be compromised by the brain injury. Also, tests that are readily quantified and yield age-corrected scores are recommended because they allow for objective monitoring of cognitive recovery with reference to chronological expectations. Finally, tests that have a wide range of difficulty are preferred because they are most sensitive to detecting performance

TABLE 1. DIMENSIONS OF COGNITIVE FUNCTIONING AND SELECTED MEASURES APPLICABLE FOR ASSESSING THE TRAUMATICALLY BRAIN-INJURED CHILD[a]

General Level of Performance
Symbol Digit Modalities Test
Trail Making Test
Stroop Color-Word Test
Ravens Progressive Matrices
Abstracting Ability
WISC-R Similarities Subtest
Goldstein-Scheerer Object Sorting Test
Category Test from Halstead Reitan Battery
Proverbs Tests
Wisconsin Card Sorting Test
Sensory and Perceptual Capacity
Schrier Visual Screening Test
Rhythms Test from Halstead Reitan Battery
Speech Sounds Perception Test from Halstead Reitan Battery
Hooper Visual Organization Test
WISC-R Maze Test
Developmental Test of Visual Perception (Frostig)
Developmental Test of Visuomotor Integration (Beery)
Tactual Performance Test
Memory
McCarthy Mental Maturity Scale Memory Subtest
Stanford-Binet Memory Test
Detroit Test of Learning Aptitude Attention and Memory Tests
Language
Token Test
Illinois Test of Psycholinguistic Ability
Halstead-Wepman Aphasia Screening Test
Psychomotor
Purdue Pegboard
Dynanometer
Grooved Pegboard
Finger Tapping Test
Bruninks-Oseretsky Test
Visuospatial and Constructional Capacity
Bender-Gestalt
WISC-R Block Design and Object Assembly Tests
Rey-Ostereith Complex Figure Test
Minnesota-Percepto-Diagnostic Test

[a]Detailed descriptions of these tests can be found in various sources, including Buros's *Mental Measurements Yearbook* (8th ed.), Highland Park, NJ, Gryphon Press, 1978, and M. Lezak, *Neuropsychological Assessment* (2nd. ed.), New York: Oxford University Press, 1983.

variability, and, by beginning with items that are not very demanding, they can capture the child's interest and motivation.

EMOTION AND BEHAVIORAL ASSESSMENT

As noted previously, craniocerebral trauma often produces emotional and behavioral disturbances. Approximately 28% of children admitted to hospital for treatment of a head injury exhibit significant psychiatric disturbance 1 year posttrauma (Black, Jeffries, Blumer, Wellner, & Walker, 1969). The prevalence of these sequelae illustrate that they cannot be ignored in conducting a psychological examination. The presence and severity of such disturbances can be assessed from two different perspectives. First, it can be determined if emotional or behavioral disruption is sufficiently disturbed so as to qualify the child for a psychiatric diagnosis. Employing a structured interview such as the Diagnostic Interview Schedule for Children (DISC) (Costello, Edelbrock, Dulcan, Kalas, & Klavic, 1984), it is possible to obtain the information needed to make a psychiatric diagnosis that meets DSM-III criteria. A particular advantage of the DISC is that it also obtains lifetime history data for certain psychiatric disorders; hence, it is possible to separate, albeit retrospectively, the psychiatric effects of the injury from a disturbance that may have antedated the trauma.

A second approach entails employing a multivariate assessment strategy. It is especially useful if the manifest impairments are not severe enough to warrant a diagnosis. In these circumstances, information is accrued in the form of severity ratings across a number of emotional and behavioral dimensions. An informant, usually a parent or teacher, is administered the rating scale in order to document psychopathology in the home and school environments. The most comprehensive of the rating scales is the Child Behavior Checklist (Achenbach & Edelbrock, 1983). It assesses current functioning across a variety of dimensions of emotional, social, and behavioral adjustments. The scales are (a) Schizoid/Anxious, (b) Depressed, (c) Uncommunicative, (d) Obsessive-Compulsive, (e) Somatic Complaints, (f) Social Withdrawal, (g) Hyperactive, (h) Aggressive, (i) Delinquent, (j) Internalizing, and (k) Externalizing. In addition, the checklist yields three types of competency scores: activities, social, and school. Furthermore, the Child Behavior Checklist affords the opportunity to identify key problem behaviors or symptoms that may have emerged following a head trauma. The relative brevity of this instrument, combined with the fact that it assesses areas of psychosocial and emotional functioning that are commonly affected by a head injury, recommends its use as a major component of the overall psychological evaluation as well as for monitoring the recovery course of the traumatically brain-injured child.

CASE STUDIES

G. B., an 11-year-old boy, was kneeling in the on-deck circle during a little league baseball game when the bat flew out of the grasp of the hitter at the plate. The bat hit G. B. on the side of the head, rendering him unconscious. Within 3 or 4 minutes, consciousness was regained, at which time he was taken to a local hospital emergency room.

A clinical neurological examination was performed and skull X rays obtained. No evidence for either neurological disturbance or fracture was found. The boy was subsequently sent home with his parents with the admonition that any physical complaints reported by the child, such as headaches, dizziness, or weakness, or if any changes in mood or behavior were observed, he should be returned immediately for further medical evaluation.

The preceding case exemplifies the most common type of mild head injury. This is usually manifest as a brief period of unconsciousness, and there are no neurological sequelae.

D. H., an 8-year-old boy, was engaging in unsupervised play. Pretending to be a parachutist, he leaped off the roof of a garage holding an open umbrella. Upon hitting the pavement below, he was rendered unconscious where he remained for an undetermined period of time. Upon being discovered by a neighbor he was carried home from where an ambulance was summoned. Examination by the paramedic team revealed intact vital signs, and he was transported to the nearest trauma center.

Almost simultaneous to arrival at the hospital, D. H. began to regain consciousness. Although not possible to specify precisely, he was estimated to have been unconscious for about 1 hour. Skull X rays did not reveal evidence for a fracture. Neurological testing, conducted within 2 hours after the injury, revealed a clear sensorium, normal reflexes, and no difficulties communicating. Apart from an injury to his ankle, no other sequelae from the trauma were evident. However, as a precautionary measure, the parents were advised to hospitalize the child overnight, which they readily agreed to do.

Within about 6 hours, at about 7:00 P.M., the child began to complain of headaches. Behaviorally, he appeared hypoactive and disinterested in his environment. A deterioration in clinical status apparently was occurring, resulting in emergency preparation for neurosurgery based on the conclusion that hemorrhaging was taking place.

By the time D. H. was prepared for surgery, there was a substantial increase in intracranial pressure; this was recorded as high as 50 mmHg. Aspiration of the hemorrhaging blood and cauterization of the responsible vein were successfully accomplished. Postoperative recovery was uneventful.

As a result of declining academic performance, D. H. was referred for testing to the school psychologist approximately 6 months after the injury. On the WISC, a Verbal IQ of 101 was obtained, but the Performance IQ was only 78. The magnitude of discrepancy between the VIQ-PIQ scores suggested, along with findings from the Bender-Gestalt Test, that there was significant cerebral dysfunction.

At this juncture, D. H. was referred for comprehensive neuropsychological testing to be conducted at the university medical center. The evaluation, conducted about 7 1/2 months postinjury, consisted of the Reitan-Indiana Neuropsychological Battery and included tests of abstracting, praxis, language skill, motor speed and coordination, and visuospatial abilities. Results of the assessment pointed to impaired motor control, inattentiveness, and impaired conceptual abilities. Communication capacities were not impaired. Behavioral ratings by the mother, employing the Child Behavior Checklist, indicated a tendency toward hyperactivity, anxiety, and social withdrawal. Repeat testing, employing the same battery 6 months later, did not reveal any significant changes.

Although it is unknown if there was any subsequent improvement in cognitive performance, the preceding case study aptly illustrates several points. First, it appears that the complications developing from the trauma were very severe, indeed life threatening, and substantially contributed to the overall manifest impairments. Second, as a screening device, the WISC was sensitive enough in this case to implicate disrupted cerebral functioning, which in conformity with research findings, was featured by inferior Performance IQ relative to Verbal IQ. And third, the pattern of cognitive deficits pointed to a generalized cerebral impairment rather than implicated a focal lesion. The consequences of a localized lesion are described in the following case study.

While playing near her home, K. L. E. was accidently shot in the head by her twin brother, who was shooting at squirrels. The bullet entered the skull on the right side and lodged in her brain. Radiological examination revealed a penetrating wound in the area of the right anterior frontal region of the cerebrum.

At the time of injury, K. L. E. was a fifth-grade student performing near the top of her class. There were no behavioral or emotional problems prior to the injury. Serial neuropsychological examinations were conducted; the first was at 6 months postinjury and the next two at yearly intervals thereafter.

The results of testing revealed mild disturbances in intellectual and cognitive functioning. Impairments in short-term memory, visuospatial capacity, and attention were observed. Her affect, however, was characterized as labile and with episodic aggressive outbursts and impulsive behavior. Disruption of sleep patterns had also been a persistent posttraumatic sequela.

Upon testing again 3 years after the injury, some improvement was noted in the previously mentioned congitive capacities. However, academic performance was still not at the same level as it was preinjury. Subsequent informal follow-up several years later revealed that she was able to be accepted into a university. Although her academic performance never attained the level expected on the basis of her preaccident performance, she was nonetheless managing quite well. Persisting difficulties appeared to be present in emotional regulation and impulsivity, which according to her older sister, seemed to be a factor in her unstable social and heterosexual relationships.

The preceding case summary illustrates two important points. First, the cognitive impairments were circumscribed to those capacities that are known to be subserved by the anterior/frontal cortex. And second, the episodic aggression, emotionality, impulsivity, and sleep dysregulations indicate disruption as well of limbic mechanisms as the result of the penetrating bullet wound. The anterior frontal and orbital regions of the cerebrum function as the association area of the limbic system, and together are integrally involved in cognition, emotion, and motivation. It is noteworthy in this case that disturbances were noted in each of these aspects of psychological functioning.

E. T., a 12-year-old boy, was admitted to the emergency room presenting a broken arm and a number of burns and bruises around the upper body. Examination of the child by the attending physician led him to suspect a history of child abuse. Although cooperative, E. T. was extraordinarily quiet and offered a sullen expression.

A social worker summoned to the emergency room interviewed the mother who described a chaotic home environment. Her common-law husband was described as abusive to her and her children, particularly while he was under the influence of alcohol or other drugs. E. T. was a particular target of his aggression. He was described as a very active boy with intense moods, defiance to authority, and difficult to manage. According to his mother, E. T. did not get along with her husband, where even in the best of times, it was a relationship characterized by mutual dislike.

The child was admitted to the hospital for treatment of his injuries. Legal authorities were notified, and discussions were implemented to decide how to best protect the welfare of the child.

On the second day after admission to the hospital, a psychological evaluation was performed. The results indicated that E. T. was an exceptionally bright young boy, having obtained a WISC RIQ of 121. His Performance IQ was, however, very inferior to his Verbal IQ, suggesting that despite his superior intellectual capacities, he still might have neurological disturbance. Rather marked impairments were noted on the Block Design and Object Assembly subtests. On both of these WISC subtests, he obtained scaled scores of 81. Neuropsychological testing revealed deficits as well on the trail-making test, target test, and tactual performance test. The CT scan revealed evidence for multiple small hematomas. Upon discharge from the hospital, E. T. was placed in a foster home.

This case study reveals a number of points relevant to head trauma. First, although multiple lesions and neuropsychological deficits were observed, it is not possible to unequivocally implicate the child abuse as the cause of the hematomas. Perinatal injuries, for example, could have been the primary etiological factor. Second, the child's behavioral disposition and environmental circumstance were, in all probability, risk factors for incurring head trauma. Third, even though the hematomas were bilaterally distributed, the impairments were most marked on tests of perceptual and spatial capacity. Thus it is not possible to formulate definitive conclusions about the lateralization of a lesion solely from neuropsychological tests.

In summary, the preceding four case studies, drawn from the files of the authors, illustrate the range and type of manifestations that can result from traumatic brain injury. The number of potential etiological factors is limitless. However, more important than the cause, is an understanding of the nature and severity of the neurological disruption. These factors, combined with an understanding of the psychosocial context, enable comprehension of the consequences of craniocerebral trauma so as to implement targeted rehabilitation strategies that are specific to the child's needs.

SUMMARY

Craniocerebral trauma in children has multiple causes and consequences. The complexity and manifold number of factors involved do not warrant simple or general conclusions about the effects of trauma on neurological or psychological functioning. Although severe injury can produce lasting sequelae, there is also indication that, for some children, even relatively mild injury may permanently impair psychological functioning.

This chapter discussed the variables that need to be considered in evaluating the traumatically head-injured child. Although a number of variables have been identified that are known to affect prognosis, it remains to be determined how they interact to affect the course of recovery. From a clinical standpoint, extreme caution must be exercised in drawing conclusions about the individual case because outcome is influenced by the child's premorbid characteristics, home life, and particular pathophysiological manifestations of the trauma. Given the still-primitive state of knowledge, diagnosis and intervention must therefore be based on the parameters associated with the individual case and guided by the acumen and skill of the clinician.

REFERENCES

Achenbach, T., & Edelbrock, C. (1983). *Manual for the Child Behavior Checklist*. Burlington, VT: University of Vermont, Department of Psychiatry.

Annegers, J., Grabow, J., Kurland, L., & Laws, E. (1980). The incidence, causes, and secular trends of head trauma in Olmstead County, Minnesota, 1935–1974. *Neurology, 30*, 912–919.

Black, P., Jeffries, J., Blumer, D., Wellner, A., & Walker,A. (1969). The post-traumatic syndrome in children: Characteristics and incidence. In A. Walker, W. Caveness, & M. Critchley (Eds.), *The late effects of head injury* (pp. 679–688). Springfield, IL: Charles C Thomas.

Black, P., Shepard, R., & Walker, E. (1975). Outcome of head trauma: Age and post-traumatic seizures. In CIBA Foundation Symposium 34, *Outcome of severe damage to the central nervous system* (pp. 215–219). New York: Elsevier.

Boll, T. (1983). Minor head injury in children—out of sight but not out of mind. *Journal of Clinical Child Psychology, 12*, 74–80.

Brink, J., Garrett, A., Hale, W., Woo-Sam, J., & Nickel, V. (1970). Recovery of motor and intellectual function in children sustaining severe injuries. *Developmental Medicine and Child Neurology, 22*, 565–571.

Brown, G. (1982). Unpublished data on head injury cited in M. Rutter, O. Chadwick & D. Shaffer (Eds.), *Developmental neuropsychiatry*. New York: Guilford, 1983.

Brown, G., & Davidson, S. (1978). Social class, psychiatric disorder of mother, and accidents to children. *Lancet, 1*, 378–381.

Brown, G., Chadwick, O., Shaffer, D., Rutter, M., & Traub, M. (1981). A prospective study of children with head injuries: III. Psychiatric sequelae. *Psychological Medicine, 11*, 63–78.

Buros, O. K. (1978). Mental measurements yearbook (8th ed.). Highland Park, NJ: Gryphon Press.

Butler, N., & Bonham, D. (1963). *Perinatal mortality*. Edinburgh: Livingstone.

Chadwick, O., Rutter, M., Brown, G., Shaffer, D., & Traub, M. (1981). A prospective study of children with head injuries: II. Cognitive sequelae. *Psychological Medicine, 11*, 49–61.

Chadwick, O., Rutter, M., Thompson, J., & Shaffer, D. (1981). Intellectual performance and reading skills after localized head injury in childhood. *Journal of Child Psychiatry and Psychology, 22,* 117–139.

Chadwick, O., Rutter, M., Shaffer, D., & Shroat, P. (1981). A prospective study of children with head injuries: IV. Specific cognitive deficits. *Journal of Clinical Neuropsychology, 3,* 101–120.

Cold, G., Enevaldern, E., & Malmros, R. (1975). Ventricular fluid lactate, pyruvate, bicarbonate and pH in unconscious brain-injured patients subjected to controlled ventilation. *Acta Neurologica Scandinavica, 52,* 187–195.

Costello, A., Edelbrock, C., Dulcan, M., Kalas, R., & Klavic, S. (1984). *The NIMH Diagnostic Interview Schedule for Children (DISC).* Unpublished manuscript, Western Psychiatric Institute and Clinic, University of Pittsburgh, Pittsburgh.

Dencker, S. (1958). Closed head injury in monozygotic twins: II. Intrapair variation in psychiatric and social variables. *Acta Psychiatrica et Neurologica*(Suppl. No. 122).

Dugger, G. (1964). Head injuries. In T. Farmer (Ed.), *Pediatric neurology* (393–442). New York: Harper & Row.

Flach, J., & Malmros, R. (1972). A long-term follow-up study of children with severe head injury. *Scandinavian Journal of Rehabilitation Medicine, 4,* 9–15.

Gratz, R. (1979). Accidental injury in childhood: A literature review on pediatric trauma. *Journal of Trauma, 19,* 551–555.

Gulbrandsen, G. (1984). Neuropsychological sequelae of light head injuries in older children 6 months after trauma. *Journal of Clinical Neuropsychology, 6,* 257–268.

Harrington, J., & Letemendia, F. (1958). Persistent psychiatric disorders after head injuries in children. *Journal of Mental Science, 104,* 1205–1218.

Heiskanen, O., & Kaste, M. (1974). Late prognosis of severe brain injury in children. *Developmental Medicine and Child Neurology, 16,* 11–14.

Herzberger, E., Harwood-Hash, D., & Hadson, A. (1964). Head injuries in children: A survey of 4465 consecutive cases at the Hospital for Sick Children, Toronto, Canada. *Clinical Neurosurgery, 11,* 46–65.

Hjern, B., & Nylandor, I. (1962). Late prognosis of severe head injuries in children. *Archives of Diseases of Children, 37,* 113–116.

Jennett, B. (1972). Head injuries in children. *Developmental Medicine and Child Neurology, 14,* 137–146.

Jennett, B. (1975). Late effects of head injury. In M. Kirchley, J. O'Leary, & B. Jennett (Eds.), *Scientific foundation of neurology* (pp. 441–451). London: Heinemann.

Jennett, B., & Teasdale, G. (1983). *Management of head injuries.* Philadelphia: Davis.

Klonoff, H. (1971). Head injuries in children: Predisposing factors, accident conditions, and sequelae. *American Journal of Public Health, 61,* 2405–2417.

Klonoff, H., Low, M., & Clark, C. (1977). Head injuries in children: A prospective five-year follow-up. *Journal of Neurology, Neurosurgery, and Psychiatry, 40,* 1211–1219.

Klove, H., & Cleeland, C. (1972). Relationship of neuropsychological impairment to other indices of severity of head injury. *Scandinavian Journal of Rehabilitation Medicine, 4,* 55–60.

Kompf, D., Neundorfer, B., Ekrest, W., & Wallesch, C. (1977). Transitory impairment of vision after light head trauma in childhood. *Neuropediatric, 8,* 354–359.

Levin, H., & Eisenberg, H. (1979). Neuropsychological outcome of closed head injury in children and adolescents. *Child's Brain, 5,* 281–292.

Levin, H., Eisenberg, H., Wigg, N., & Kohayashi, K. (1982). Memory and intellectual ability after head injury in children and adolescents. *Neurosurgery, 11,* 668–673.

Levin, H., Madison, C., Bailey, C., Meyer, C., Eisenberg, H., & Guinto, F. (1983). Mutism after closed head injury. *Archives of Neurology, 40,* 601–606.

Lezak, M. (1983). *Neuropsychological assesment* (2nd ed.). New York: Oxford University Press.

Mahoney, W., D'Souza, B., Haller, A., Rogers, M., Epstein, M., & Fireman, J. (1983). Long-term outcome of children with severe head trauma and prolonged coma. *Pediatrics, 71,* 756–762.

McHenry, T., Girdany, B., & Elmer, E. (1963). Unsuspected trauma with multiple skeletal injuries during infancy and childhood. *Pediatrics, 31,* 903–908.

Mealey, J. (1968). *Pediatric head injuries.* Springfield, IL: Charles C Thomas.

Melchior, J. (1961). The incidence of head injuries in children. *Acta Paediatrica, 50,* 47.

Milhorat, T. (1978). *Pediatric neurosurgery.* Philadelphia: Davis.

Miller, J., & Jennett, W. (1968). Complications of depressed skull fracture. *Lancet, 2,* 991–995.

Overgaard, J., Christensen, S., Hvid-Hansen, O., Haase, J., Lund, A., Hein, O., Pedersen, K., & Tweed, W. (1973). Prognosis of head injury based on early clinical examination. *Lancet, 2,* 631–635.

Raphaely, R. C., Swedlow, D. B., Downes, J. J., & Bruce, D. A. (1980). Management of severe pediatric head trauma. *Pediatric Clinics of North America, 27,* 715–727.

Richardson, F. (1963). Some effects of severe head injury: Follow-up study of children and adolescents after protracted coma. *Developmental Medicine and Child Neurology, 5,* 471–482.

Rutter, M., Chadwick, O., Shaffer, D., & Brown, G. (1980). A prospective study of children with head injuries: 1. Design and methods. *Psychological Medicine, 10,* 633–645.

Rutter, M., Chadwick, O., & Schachar, R. (1983). Hyperactivity and minimal brain dysfunction: Epidemiological perspectives on questions of cause and classification. In R. Tarter (Ed.), *The child at psychiatric risk* (pp. 88–107). New York: Oxford University Press.

Shaffer, D., Chadwick, O., & Rutter, M. (1975). Psychiatric outcome of localized head injury in children. In CIBA Foundation Symposium, *Outcome of severe damage to the central nervous system* (pp. 191–213). New York: Elsevier.

Spreen, O., Tupper, D., Risser, A., Tuokko, H., & Edgell, D. (1984). *Human developmental neuropsychology.* New York: Oxford University Press.

Stover, S., & Zeiger, H. (1976). Head injury in children and teenagers: Functional recovery correlated with the duration of coma. *Archives of Physical Medicine and Rehabilitation, 57,* 201–205.

Strub, R., & Black, F. (1981). *Organic brain syndromes. An introduction to neurobehavioral disorders.* Philadelphia: F. A. Davis.

Tarter, R., Hegedus, A., Goldstein, G., Shelly, C., & Alterman, A. (1984). Adolescent sons of alcoholics: Neuropsychological and personality characteristics. *Alcoholism: Clinical and Experimental Research, 8,* 216–222.

Walsh, K. (1978). *Neuropsychology: A clinical approach.* New York: Churchill Livingstone.

Winogron, H., Knights, R., & Bawden, H. (1984). Neuropsychological deficits following head injury in children. *Journal of Clinical Neuropsychology, 6,* 269–286.

Index

ABS-Public School Version, 192
Adolescent Emotional Factors Inventory (AEFI), 137
American Association on Mental Deficiency Adaptive Behavior Scale (ABS), 192
Anxiety Scale for the Blind (ASB), 136
Attention Deficit Disorders, 214–217, 224–237
  associated problems, 216–217
  diagnostic criteria, 215
  with hyperactivity, 216
    behavioral observations, 230–232
    evaluation interviews, 228, 230
    peer sociometric ratings, 232–233
  measures of assessment, 234–237
    Continuous Performance Tests (CPT), 235–236
    Matching Familiar Figures Test (MFF), 236
    Paired Associate Learning (PAL), 236
Auditory Projective Test, 137
Autism, 155–177
  behavioral assessment, 170–172
  case description, 172–174
  description, 156–162
    history, 160–162
    inappropriate affect, 160
    ritualistic behavior, 158
    self-injurious behavior, 159–160
    self-stimulation, 159
    sensory deficit, 159
    social behavior, 157
    speech and language, 157–158
Autism (*Cont.*)
  diagnostic criteria, 162–164
  differential diagnosis, 164–166
  evaluations, 166–169
    Autism Screening Instrument for Educational Planning (ASIEP), 169
    Behavior Observation Scale for Autism, 169
    Behavior Rating Instrument for Autistic and Atypical Children (BRIACC), 168, 169
    Childhood Autism Rating Scale, 169
    Rimland's Diagnostic Checklist for Behavior-Disturbed Children, 168
Autism Screening Instrument for Educational Planning (ASIEP), 169

Balthazar Scales of Adaptive Behavior, 192
Bas-Relief Test, 138
Bayley Scales of Infant Development (BSID), 186–205
Behavior Observation Scale for Autism, 169
Behavioral Rating Instrument for Autistic and Atypical Children (BRIACC), 168–169
Behavioral Analysis History Questionnaire, 24
Bender Visual-Motor Gestalt Test, 101–102
Bernreuter Personality Inventory (BPI), 135
Blind Learning Aptitude Test (BLAT), 127, 189

Brazelton Neonatal Behavioral Assessment Scale—Revised (BNBAS-R), 203
Brigance Diagnostic Inventory of Basic Skills (BDIBS), 195
Brigance Diagnostic Inventory of Early Development, 199
Brigance Diagnostic Inventory of Essential Skills (BDIES), 195
Bruininks-Oseretsky Test of Motor Proficiency (BOTMP), 196

California Psychological Inventory (CPI), 135–136
Career Assessment Inventory, 58
Carolina Record of Individual Behavior (CRIB), 203, 205
Child Behavior Checklist (CBCL), 135, 192, 226, 319
Childhood Autism Rating Scale, 169
Clinical Evaluation of Language Functions (CELF), 190
Conners Abbreviated Parent-Teacher Questionnaire (CAPTQ), 224
Conners Behavioral Checklist, 76
Conners Parent Rating Scale (CPRS), 224
Conners Teacher Rating Scale (CTRS), 224
Continuous Performance Tests (CPT), 235–236
Cooperative School and College Ability Tests, 128
Craniocerebral trauma in children, 229–326
  case description, 320–323
  cognitive sequelae, 307–315
    aging effects, 312–313
    concussion, 308
    long-term effects, 312
    pathophysiological complications, 310
    posttraumatic amnesia (PTA), 309–310
    psychological threshold, 310–312
    skull fracture, 308
    specificity of impairment, 313–314
    unconsciousness, duration of, 307–308
  neurological sequelae, 303–307
    extradural hemorrhage, 304
    hematoma, 305
Craniocerebral trauma in children (*Cont.*)
  neurological sequelae (*Cont.*)
    intradural hemorrhage, 305
    subdural hydroma, 306–307
    traumatic arachnoid cysts, 306
  psychiatric sequelae, 314–315
  psychological assessment, 315–320
    Child Behavior Checklist, 319
    Diagnostic Interview Schedule for Children (DISC), 319
    emotion/behavioral, 319–320
    Luria-Nebraska battery (children's version), 317
    neuropsychological, 316–319
    Reitan-Indiana Neuropsychological Battery, 317
  types, 301–303
    closed head injury, 301–303
    penetrating head injury, 303
Crawford Small Parts Dexterity Test, 129

Davids Rating Scale for Hyperkinesis, 227
Denver Scale of Communication Function, 101
Developmental Profile (DP), 191
Developmental Programming for Infants and Young Children, 198
Developmental retardation, 179–212
  assessment, 184–196
    adaptive and socioemotional, 190–193
    cognitive, 186–187
    communication, 189–190
    learning skills, 193–195
    neuromotor, 196–197
    norm-based, 185–186
    specific achievement measures, 195–196
    specialized cognitive measures, 187–189
  case description, 204–209
  criterion-based assessment
    developmental curriculum measures, 198–199
      Brigance Diagnostic Inventory of Early Development, 199
      Developmental Planning for Infants and Young Children, 198
      Early Intervention Developmental Profile (EIDP), 198, 205

Developmental retardation (*Cont.*)
criterion-based assessment (*Cont.*)
develop. curriculum measures (*Cont.*)
Learning Accomplishment Profile (LAP), 198
Oregon Project Curriculum for Visually Impaired and Blind Preschool Children, 199
Preschool Developmental Profile, 198
Programmed Environments Curriculum (PEC), 199
Uniformed Performance Assessment System (UPAS), 199, 205
skill mastery evaluation, 197–198
specialized curriculum measures, 199
diagnosis and assessment, 185–197
ABS-Public School Version, 192
American Association on Mental Deficiency Adaptive Behavior Scale (ABS), 192
Balthazar Scales of Adaptive Behavior, 192
Bayley Scales of Infant Development (BSID), 186
Blind Learning Aptitude Test (BLAT), 189
Brigance Diagnostic Inventory of Basic Skills (BDIBS), 195
Brigance Diagnostic Inventory of Essential Skills (BDIES), 195
Bruininks-Oseretsky Test of Motor Proficiency (BOTMP), 196
Child Behavior Checklist (CBCL), 192
Clinical Evaluation of Language Functions (CELF), 190
Developmental Profile (DP), 191
Developmental Test of Visual-Motor Integration (DTVMI), 196
Gesell Developmental Schedules (GDS), 186
HICOMP Preschool Curriculum, 198
Hiskey-Nebraska Test of Learning Aptitude (HNTLA), 189
Leiter International Performance Scale (LIPS), 188
KeyMath Diagnostic Arithmetic Test, 195
Preschool Behavior Questionnaire (PBQ), 192

Developmental retardation (*Cont.*)
diagnosis and assessment (*Cont.*)
Peabody Development Motor Scales (PDMS), 196
Peabody Individual Achievement Test (PIAT), 193
Peabody Picture Vocabulary Test—Revised (PPVT-R), 190
Pictorial Test of Intelligence (PTI), 188
Revised Behavior Problem Checklist (BPC), 192
TMR (Trainable Mentally Retarded) School Competency Scales, 192
Vineland Adaptive Behavior Scales (VABS), 191
Vineland Social Maturity Scale, 191
Wide Range Achievement Test—Revised (WRAT-R), 193
Wisconsin Behavior Rating Scale, 192
Woodcock-Johnson Psychoeducational Battery (WJPEB), 194
Woodcock Reading Mastery Tests (WRMT), 195
diagnosis versus assessment, 179–181
genotype, 180
phenotype, 180
Stanford-Binet Intelligence Scale (SBIS), 183–187
Wechsler Intelligence Scale for Children—Revised (WISC-R), 183, 187
See also diagnosis and assessment
diagnostic-prescriptive, 183
diagnostic strategies, 181–183
mental retardation, definition of, 181–182
testing instruments, 183
evaluation strategies, 183–185
assessment, 184–185
hearing-impaired or deaf children (Hiskey-Nebraska Test of Learning Aptitude, HNTLA), 189
neuropsychological assessment, 199–202
diagnostic-prescriptive model, 202
interactive analysis, 202
process analysis, 200–202
Brazelton Neonatal Behavioral Assessment Scale—Revised (BNBAS-R), 203
Fuerstein approach, 202

Developmental retardation (*Cont.*)
neuropsychological assessment (*Cont.*)
process analysis (*Cont.*)
General Cognitive Index (GCI), 201
Kaufmann Assessment Battery for Children (KABC), 200
Luria-Nebraska Neuropsychological Battery for Children (LNNBC), 200
Matching Familiar Figures Test (MFFT), 202
McCarthy Scales of Children's Abilities (MSCA), 201
process evaluation, 199–200
Developmental Test of Visual-Motor Integration (DTVMI), 196
Diagnostic Interview Schedule for Children (DISC), 319
Diagnostic Reading Tests, 128
Draw-A-Person Test, 101–102

Early Intervention Developmental Profile (EIDP), 198, 205
Emotional Factors Inventory (EFI), 137
Evaluation of intelligence, achievement, aptitude, and interest, 41–67
aptitude, 42
current issues in assessment, 58–62
intelligence tests, 58–60
stability of IQs, 60–62
future directions, 62–63
computer technology, 62–63
neuropsychology, 62
history, 43–58
achievement tests, uses of, 54–57
development of interest measures, 46
Strong Vocational Interest Blank (SVIB), 46–48
intelligence tests, development of, 43–46
intelligence tests, uses of, 48–54
Wechsler Intelligence Scale for Children—Revised (WISC-R), 51
interest measures, development of, 46
item development, 46–48
measuring interests, 57–58
Career Assessment Inventory, 58
Strong-Campbell Interest Inventory, 57

General Cognitive Index (GCI), 201
Gesell Developmental Schedules (GDS), 186
Gray Oral Reading Check Tests, 128

Halstead-Reitan Neuropsychological Test Battery, 74
Haptic Intelligence Scale for the Adult Blind (HIS), 126
Hearing impairment, 93–114
case description, 108–109
description, 94–95
evaluations, considerations for, 96–98
evaluations, strategies for, 98–103
case history, 102–103
interview, 103
medical examinations, 103
observation, 103
simulated work setting, 102
tests, 99–102
See also individual test
history and development, 95–96
research findings, 103–107
HICOMP Preschool Curriculum, 198
Hiskey-Nebraska Test of Learning Aptitude (HNTLA), 28
Home Observation for Measurement of the Environment (HOME), 203
Home Situations Questionnaire (HSQ), 227
Hyperactivity, 216–217
medical evaluation, 233–234
Hyperactivity/attention deficit disorders/learning disabilities, 216–260
case description, 244–248
history and development, 221–223
minimal brain dysfunction (MBD), 222
strategies for evaluation, 223–244
Child Behavior Checklist (CBCL), 226
Conners Abbreviated Parent-Teacher Questionnaire (CAPTQ), 224
Conners Parent Rating Scale (CPRS), 224
Conners Teacher Rating Scale (CTRS), 224
Davids Rating Scale for Hyperkinesis, 227
Home Situations Questionnaire (HSQ), 227

Hyperactivity/attention (*Cont.*)
strategies for evaluation (*Cont.*)
Hyperkinesis Index, 224
Personality Inventory for Children (PIC), 227
Revised Behavior Problem Checklist (RBPC), 227
Werry-Weiss-Peters Activity Scale, 227
See also individual classification
Hyperkinesis Index, 224

Illinois Test of Psycholinguistic Abilities (ITPA), 101
Interim Hayes-Binet Intelligence Tests, 123–124
Iowa Tests of Basic Skills, 129

Kaufman Assessment Battery for Children (K-ABC), 200, 238
Kaufman Test of Educational Achievement (K-TEA), 240
KeyMath Diagnostic Arithmetic Test, 195
Kohs Block Design Test, 127
Kuder Preference Record, 130

Learning Accomplishment Profile (LAP), 198
Learning disabilities, 218, 238–244
achievement/intelligence tests, 238–241
Kaufman Assessment Battery for Children (K-ABC), 238
Kaufman Test of Educational Achievement (K-TEA), 240
McCarthy Scales of Children's Abilities, 238
Peabody Individual Achievement Tests (PIAT), 241
Wechsler Intelligence Scale for Children—Revised (WISC-R), 238
Wechsler Preschool and Primary Scale of Intelligence (WPPSI), 239
Wide Range Achievement Test (WRAT), 241
Wide Range Achievement Test—Revised (WRAT-R), 241
neuropsychological assessment, 243, 244
similarities with ADD, 220–221
Leiter International Performance Scale (LIPS), 28, 188
Luria-Nebraska Neuropsychological Battery for Children (LNNBC), 75, 200, 317

Matching Familiar Figures Test (MFFT), 202, 236
Matson Evaluation of Social Skills with Youngsters (MESSY), 133
Maxfield-Buchholz Scale of Social Maturity for Pre-School Blind Children, 131–132
McCarthy Scales of Children's Abilities (MSCA), 201, 238
Mental retardation
definition of, 181–182
See also Developmental retardation
Mental Status Interview, 24
Metropolitan Achievement Tests, 128
Minnesota Multiphasic Personality Inventory (MMPI), 25, 135–136
Minnesota Rate of Manipulation Test, 129
Myers-Ruch High School Progress Test, 128

Neuropsychological assessment, 68–69
approaches to, 73–77
Conners Behavioral Checklist, 76
Halstead-Reitan Neuropsychological Test Battery, 74
Luria-Nebraska Neuropsychological Battery, 75
assessment model, 79–83
future directions, 83–85
Scales for the Assessment of Language Samples (SALS), 83–84
history and development, 70–73
issues in child assessment, 77–79

Oregon Project Curriculum for Visually Impaired and Blind Preschool Children, 199
Overbrook Social Competency Scale, 132

Paired-associate learning (PAL) task, 236
Peabody Developmental Motor Scales (PDMS), 197
Peabody Individual Achievement Test (PIAT), 193, 241

Peabody Picture Vocabulary Test—Revised (PPVT-R), 190
Pennsylvania Bi-Manual Worksample, 129
Perceptions of Developmental Skills, 203
Performance Scale for the Adult Blind (PSAB), 126
Perkins-Binet, 123
Personality Inventory for Children (PIC), 227
Physical and developmental disabilities
  issues in assessment, 8–11
    bias in assessment, 10–11
    inappropriate use of test, 10
    qualifications of personnel, 9–10
    technical adequacy, 8–9
  an overview of, 3–15
  purposes of assessment, 6–8
  upsurge in interest, 3–6
Pictorial Test of Intelligence (PTI), 188
Preschool Attainment Record, 22
Preschool Behavior Questionnaire (PBQ), 192
Preschool Developmental Profile, 198
Programmed Environments Curriculum (PEC), 199
Psychological evaluation, 19–39
  background information, 20
  characteristics of the psychologist, 29–32
  decision making, 32–34
Psychological interview, 20–24
  Behavioral Analysis History Questionnaire, 24
  Mental Status Interview, 24
  Preschool Attainment Record, 22
  Vineland Social Maturity Scale, 22
Psychological testing, 24–29
  Hiskey-Nebraska Test of Learning Aptitude, 28
  Leiter International Performance Scale, 28
  Minnesota Multiphasic Personality Inventory (MMPI), 25
  Rorschach test, 25
  Sixteen Personality Factor Questionnaire (PF), 25
  Stanford-Binet Intelligence Scale, 25, 27
  Thematic Apperception Test, 25
  Wechsler Adult Intelligence Scale (WAIS), 27
Psychological testing (*Cont.*)
  Wechsler Intelligence Scale for Children (WISC), 25, 26, 28

Raven's Progressive Matrices, 127
Reitan-Indiana Neuropsychological Battery, 317
Revised Behavior Problem Checklist (RBPC), 192, 226
Rimland's Diagnostic Checklist for Behavior-Disturbed Children, 168
Rorschach test, 25, 138
Rotter Incomplete Sentences Blank, 137

Scales for the Assessment of Language Samples (SALS), 83–84
Sequential Tests of Educational Progress, 128–129
Shane-Bashir matrix, 286–287, 288
Singer Vocational Evaluation System, 102
Sixteen Personality Factor Questionnaire (PF), 25
Speech and language disorders, 261–298
  assessment levels, 271–272
  classification, 276–277
  communication
    development/components, 264–270
    nonlinguistic acquisition, 265–266
    nonlinguistic aspects, 264–267
    nonlinguistic skills and assessment, 266–267, 293–298
    prelinguistic aspects, 267–270
  communication assessment, 265, 270–289
    language dimensions, 271
    speech production, 270–271
  communication evaluation, 262–263
  definition of, 261–262
  diagnostic assessment, 275–276
  format description, 263–264
  interdisciplinary evaluation, 263
  language assessment, 283–285
  language disorders, evaluation of, 282–283
  nonvocal communication, alternative and augmentative systems of, 285
  prescreening, 272
  programming, assessment for, 276
  screening, 272–273
    protocol examples, 273–274
  Shane-Bashir matrix, 286–287, 288

Speech and language disorders (*Cont.*)
speech production disorders, assessment of, 278–282
articulation, 278–279
disfluency, 280–281
phonation/resonance, 279–280
prosody, 281–282
Stanford Achievement Tests, 128–129
Stanford Achievement Tests, Special Edition for Hearing Impaired Students (SAT-HI), 100
Stanford-Binet Intelligence Scale (SBIS), 25, 27, 183, 187
Strong-Campbell Interest Inventory, 57, 61
Strong Vocational Interest Blank (SVIB), 26–28, 61, 130

Taylor Manifest Anxiety Scale (TMAS), 136, 137
Teare Sentence Completion Test, 137–138
Thematic Apperception Test (TAT), 25, 137
TMR (Trainable Mentally Retarded) School Competency Scales, 192

Uniform Performance Assessment System (UPAS), 199, 205

Valpar Component Work Sample Series, 102
Vineland Adaptive Behavior Scales (VABS), 191
Vineland Social Maturity Scale, 22, 131, 191
Visual impairment, 115–153
assessments, development of, 119–121
considerations and issues, 139–146
administering of tests, 142–145
development, 140–142
examiner, 139
referrals, 139–140
vision, 140
description, 118–119
evaluations, strategies for, 121–139
Adolescent Emotional Factors Inventory (AEFI), 137
Anxiety Scale for the Blind (ASB), 136
Auditory Projective Test, 137
Bas-Relief Test, 138

Visual impairment (*Cont.*)
evaluations (*Cont.*)
Bernreuter Personality Inventory (BPI), 135
Blind Learning Aptitude Test, 127
California Psychological Inventory (CPI), 135–136
Child Behavior Checklist, 135
Cooperative School and College Ability Tests, 128
Crawford Small Parts Dexterity Test, 129
Diagnostic Reading Tests, 128
educational/vocational assessment, 128–131
emotional and behavioral assessment, 135–139
Emotional Factors Inventory (EFI), 137
Gray Oral Reading Check Tests, 128
Haptic Intelligence Scale for the Adult Blind (HIS), 126
intellectual assessment, 121–128
Interim Hayes-Binet Intelligence Tests, 123–134
Iowa Tests of Basic Skills, 129
Kohs Block Design Test, 127
Kuder Preference Record, 130
Matson Evaluation of Social Skills with Youngsters (MESSY), 133
Maxfield-Buchholz Scale of Social Maturity for Pre-School Blind Children, 131–132
Metropolitan Achievement Tests, 128
Minnesota Multiphasic Personality Inventory (MMPI), 135–136
Minnesota Rate of Manipulation Test, 129
Myers-Ruch High School Progress Test, 128
Overbrook Social Competency Scale, 132
Pennsylvania Bi-Manual Worksample, 129
Performance Scale for the Adult Blind (PSAB), 126
Perkins-Binet, 123
Raven's Progressive Matrices, 127
Rorschach test, 138
Rotter Incomplete Sentences Blank, 137

Visual impairment (*Cont.*)
evaluations (*Cont.*)
Sequential Tests of Education Progress, 128–129
social and living skills assessment, 131–135
Stanford Achievement Tests, 128–129
Strong-Campbell Vocational Interest Blank, 130
Taylor Manifest Anxiety Scale (TMAS), 136–137
Teare Sentence Completion Test, 137–138
Thematic Apperception Test (TAT), 137
Vineland Social Maturity Scale, 131
Wechsler Adult Intelligence Scale (WAIS), 124–126
Wechsler Adult Intelligence Scale—Revised (WAIS-R), 124
Wechsler Intelligence Scale for Children (WISC), 124–125
Wechsler Intelligence Scale for Children—Revised (WISC-R), 123
Wechsler Preschool and Primary Scale of Intelligence (WPPSI), 124
Wide Range Achievement Test, 128
Visual impairment (*Cont.*)
evauations (*Cont.*)
Youth Self-Report Form (YSRF), 135
historical aspects of, 115–117

Wechsler Adult Intelligence Scale (WAIS), 27, 124–126
Wechsler Adult Intelligence Scale—Revised (WAIS-R), 99, 124
Wechsler Intelligence Scale for Children (WISC), 25–26, 28, 124–125, 238
Wechsler Intelligence Scale for Children—Revised (WISC-R), 51, 99, 123–124, 183, 187
Wechsler Preschool and Primary Scale of Intelligence (WPPSI), 124, 239
Werry-Weiss-Peters Activity Scale, 227
Wide Range Achievement Test (WRAT), 100, 128, 241
Wide Range Achievement Test—Revised (WRAT-R), 193, 241
Wisconsin Behavior Rating Scale, 192
Woodcock-Johnson Psychoeducational Battery (WJPEB), 194
Woodcock Reading Mastery Tests (WRMT), 195

Youth Self-Report Form (YSRF), 135

GPSR Compliance

The European Union's (EU) General Product Safety Regulation (GPSR) is a set of rules that requires consumer products to be safe and our obligations to ensure this.

If you have any concerns about our products, you can contact us on ProductSafety@springernature.com

In case Publisher is established outside the EU, the EU authorized representative is:

Springer Nature Customer Service Center GmbH
Europaplatz 3
69115 Heidelberg, Germany

Batch number: 10761599

Printed by Printforce, the Netherlands